THE REBEL OF
RANGOON

THE REBEL OF
RANGOON

A TALE OF DEFIANCE AND DELIVERANCE IN BURMA

DELPHINE SCHRANK

NATION
BOOKS

Published by Nation Books,
A Member of the Perseus Books Group

116 East 16th Street, 8th Floor
New York, NY 10003

Nation Books is a co-publishing venture of
the Nation Institute and the Perseus Books Group

Books published by Nation Books are available at special
discounts for bulk purchases in the United States by corporations,
institutions, and other organizations. For more information,
please contact the Special Markets Department at the Perseus Books Group,
2300 Chestnut Street, Suite 200, Philadelphia, PA 19103, or call (800) 810–4145, ext. 5000,
or e-mail special.markets@perseusbooks.com.

Designed by Cynthia Young

Library of Congress Cataloging-in-Publication Data
Schrank, Delphine.
The rebel of Rangoon : a tale of defiance and deliverance in Burma / Delphine
Schrank.
pages cm
Includes bibliographical references.
ISBN 978-1-56858-498-0 (hardback)—ISBN 978-1-56858-485-0 (e-book)
1. Nway. 2. Political activists—Burma—Biography. 3. National League for
Democracy (Burma)—Biography. 4. Burma—Politics and government—1988–
5. Dissenters—Burma—Biography. 6. Aung San Suu Kyi—Friends and associates.
7. Democracy—Burma—History—21st century. 8. Rangoon (Burma)—
Biography. I. Title.
DS530.68.N85 2015
959.105'3092—dc23
[B]
2015016472

ISBN: 978-1-56858-508-6 (international edition)

10 9 8 7 6 5 4 3 2 1

For my friends in Burma
and all they've taught
me about being alive

CONTENTS

PREFACE

The mass and majesty of this world, all
That carries weight and always weighs the same
Lay in the hands of others; they were small
And could not hope for help and no help came:
What their foes like to do was done, their shame
Was all the worst could wish; they lost their pride
And died as men before their bodies died.

—W. H. AUDEN, "THE SHIELD OF ACHILLES"

HIS EYES, FIRST.

Clear and narrow set, they looked to history, to the future, and across his country, ethereal and spiritually gorgeous. People called it the "Golden Land." But in his time—in our time too—it sprawled still in darkness.

The story that follows is primarily viewed through his eyes to tell of his people's struggle against five decades of authoritarian rule. Those eyes, that perspective, belong not to a king nor to a distant scholar. He was a young man when I met him, an ordinary citizen with extraordinary ambition, an impulsive daredevil who became a seasoned political strategist. He is not alone in this story. He is not alone in his struggle. In these pages, I call him "Nway."

But it is his life, and those of dozens of his peers, that opened for me a distant world: a community of ordinary citizens, people who knew themselves to be poor players with little time to strut and fret, even as they each took up their baton in a long and wearying effort, and insinuated themselves into that age-old tale of the little slingshot-wielder against the weaponized machinery of an all-powerful, ruthless state.

A people's decades-long struggle for democracy across generations and borders is not a catalogue of successive glories. Nor is it a tale of constant carnage and boisterous revolution. It is a story of dedication and endurance, of a solitary man or woman stumbling out of the masses, tiptoeing even, trying a first step, then another, and trudging forward, onward, making new tracks on shifting ground toward a future misted in uncertainty. It is the story of the grunt in the trench, dispelling his fear with quips, cold and hungry, and refusing to desert—and the months- or years-long stretches of boredom and apparent inactivity between brief, world-changing firestorms. It is a story, sometimes, of failure, of battles lost and lost again, and the lessons drawn from them, with which to evolve and grow and refill ever-decimated ranks across the relentless sweep of time.

Foremost, it is a mindset: of daring to stand up against prescribed ritual; to call the lie of a totalitarian or post-totalitarian system; to begin with one's thoughts, at the level of consciousness, to simply say no.

Vaclav Havel wrote about that mindset in his 1978 essay, *The Power of the Powerless*. Aung San Suu Kyi, the 1991 Nobel Peace Prize laureate, wrote about it too, and talked about it, and preached it in her every word and action since she emerged in 1988 as the leader of the movement in which Nway would find his life's vocation a decade later.

Of Burma, Myanmar—a country whose very choice of name since 1989 bespeaks one's political sympathies—this book is not an exhaustive history. Nor is it a chronological blow-by-blow of its democracy movement. As far as possible, I have also tried to do away with the filter of a stranger, of a foreign journalist—of me—encountering with awe the mystique of a tropical dictatorship wrapped in the scent of green papaya. My endeavor is to look outward, with their eyes, through their hearts, from their weeds—and so begin to capture what they hoped, what they felt, what they tried.

What I have depicted is fragmentary, and fractured in the telling, because the actions of its protagonists are fragmentary. How they operate, and when, is of necessity under conditions of mistrust and miscommunication, in a half-light of information and misinformation. At times they are as trapped as their countrymen within the constraints and distortions of authoritarian rule. How also does a culture and a climate, the texture of the land, the structure of its cities, shape those same mindsets? In the day-to-day choices that people make, how does historical memory converge with personal dreams and setbacks, and the attempt to *just get on with it*, without any of that mattering? Why do they choose to do what they do? Do they have a choice?

Within fragments are entire worlds. Each scene might contain a microcosm of the larger whole, of their challenges, of their society.

As I write this in January 2015, the extreme repression of successive military rulers since 1962 has yielded to the greater flexibility of a quasi-civilian government. Political and economic reforms began, in late 2011 and early 2012, to loosen the state's controls. Political prisoners were released. Censorship was eased. Western countries began to ease sanctions on the country, its industries, its junta, and its business associates. The sanctions had been imposed in waves since nationwide elections on May 27, 1990, when the then-junta ignored the resounding victory of Aung San Suu Kyi's pro-democracy party, the National League for Democracy, or NLD. Full diplomatic relations with the United States, revoked since then, have been restored. Burma has been welcomed back to the fold of acceptable nations. Businesses are rushing in.

But Burma is not yet a democracy. The traumas of past decades have still to play out. Demagogues have directed mobs, in the name of Buddhism and the Buddhist cultural identity of the country, in vicious attacks against its Muslim minorities. Civil war with other avowedly distinct ethnic groups around the border is unresolved. People are hungry, fleeing their villages, trapped in camps, and hated.

And yet, undoubtedly, the terms of the struggle for freedom and human rights have changed. The reasons for this, for the slow cracking apart of Burma from an oppressive, inward-twisted gaze, are many, and converging. They include grave anxieties about the unfettered influence of China, Burma's hulking northern neighbor; the pride of a country that lost its economic significance in the region; the unlikely consequences that flowed from a new parliamentary system that was set up in early 2011; the resignation of the strongman Senior General Than Shwe, and the role of his reformist successor, a former brigadier general, now President Thein Sein, who took off his uniform and dared to begin to change.

I submit, in these pages, that there is another reason too.

Descriptions of freedom struggles conventionally highlight a charismatic leader who descends from near-Olympian heights to corral and rally a victimized mass of amorphous (but resilient!) fellow citizens. If that person doesn't guide his people toward deliverance exactly, he alone shakes awake their spirit of resistance. Aung San Suu Kyi, in such a telling, rightly joins a long line of greats that includes Mahatma Gandhi, Martin Luther King Jr., Vaclav Havel, and Nelson Mandela. If others there be in these ongoing stories of emancipation, they are depicted often as little more than sidekicks, passive "survivors of authoritarian rule."

But Aung San Suu Kyi, kept under house arrest for fifteen years since 1989, has above all been the torchbearer of her people's hope. She assumed that role when she burst onto the Burmese political landscape in 1988, almost by accident, in the midst of a massive nationwide uprising against the quarter-century misrule of a general named Ne Win. To assume she has stood alone, to extract her from the larger story of the dissidents and the deeper history around her, diminishes not only her achievements but the sheer human intelligence and the vitality of the culture in which she roots her ideas and legitimacy.

It is those dissidents who are here featured. Some of them came to be known to their countrymen. Most remained anonymous. Together they formed part of a diffuse and ragged multigenerational movement, an oft-dismissed band of hard-bitten oddballs and dreamers, suspected double agents, and supposed incompetents whose quixotic posturing was so relentless, and ultimately significant, that it begins to explain how and why a military junta at the height of its powers suddenly and dramatically began in 2011 to crack apart a smidgen of political space. It begins to explain how and why a country locked away as a pariah for decades emerged anew onto the global stage, at the heart of the world's fastest growing economic region, and at the center of not one but two intensifying geopolitical standoffs: India and China, and China and the United States.

Across the years, they would not die, would not break under the beatings and harassments and exiles, under the lies and the divide-and-conquer rule of a senior general schooled in psychological warfare. They endured and fought back across constant brutality and half a dozen failed uprisings. They regenerated from regularly demolished ranks, turned violent, turned peaceful, doubted themselves, educated themselves, dissipated, fragmented, forded the fragmentation, recruited, forged alliances, and appropriated the international legal framework to push for global action. Among social movements and what some like to call global civil society, they became an international model of creative resistance.

Because of their intentional invisibility and the difficulties imposed on foreigners who might have tried to access them, their maneuverings, however dramatic and resonant, remained wholly underreported. But, by the junta they opposed, they could never be ignored.

ॐ

IN 2009, WHEN THIS BOOK OPENS, Burma sat among the world's charity cases, competing for bottom global rankings on development, health care, and the most basic civil and political freedoms. No other authoritarian system, barring North Korea's, had for so long maintained its grip on every aspect of power, from the economy to education, to the hierarchy of the hallowed Buddhist monastic community.

In the border areas, sites of ongoing civil war or fragile ceasefires, civilian life came cheap. Though prohibitions on information rendered all official data opaque and statistics whimsical, evidence piled up of indiscriminate killings, forced displacements, forced labor, systematic rape, press-ganging, torture, and arbitrary detentions.

The education system had been deliberately wrecked to undercut a tradition of anti-government organizing among students. Identity registration and declarations of ethnic and religious appurtenance were a prerequisite for travel, work, or play. The usual societal dynamics of authoritarianism prevailed: fear, self-censorship, serial mistrust. You never knew who might be watching. You never knew when the knock in the night might come.

It didn't have to be that way.

Burma sprawls like a great kite as a flat river valley ringed by rugged highlands that border five countries, with a vast, southern mouth to the Indian Ocean. One day, indubitably, it was to be the continent's strategic crossroads. Under British colonial rule, Rangoon, its capital, had already become a cosmopolitan hub. Intricate waterways and the mighty Irrawaddy River favored commerce and communication. By the 1930s, the fertile soils of the southern half of the country and the Irrawaddy Delta had transformed Burma from an isolated tropical exoticism into the rice bowl of the world. The Second World War wrought havoc on the economy, but Burma remained an exporter of rice, and oil, too—a rarity among developing nations. Prosperity beckoned beyond in an abundance of natural resources: jade and fabled "pigeon-blood" rubies; petroleum; natural gas; silver; gold; tin; and fine hardwoods, including seventy percent of the world's teak.

At independence in 1948, and in a decade of parliamentary democracy, Burma had been the shining promise of Southeast Asia. Its education system encouraged unparalleled social mobility and the advancement of a rich literary tradition. Its universities attracted Asia's best and brightest. Its class of trained urban professionals had absorbed the legal legacy of the British parliamentary system with little loss to national idiosyncrasy. The values of Theravada Buddhism, the religion of about eighty-nine percent of the people, and the central role in daily life accorded to its monkhood, the *sangha*, provided

justification for individual agency and a moral compass in even the most remote
rural communities.

But the fledgling democracy that emerged at the astrologically auspicious
hour of 4:20 a.m., January 4, 1948, was seeded with challenges. Within hours
of independence, armed uprisings broke out from communists and minority
groups in the hinterlands that framed the great river valley in a horseshoe. They
seized on the new government's institutional fragility to press for degrees of autonomy, distrustful of the Buddhist, Burman ethnic majority who had for centuries dominated or attempted to dominate them from kingdoms in the central
plain. Flattened already by brutal fighting between Japan and the Allies during
the Second World War, the country became a proxy theater of conflict for
China's civil war, a base for the anti-Communist Kuomintang.

Hope for leadership that might have transcended those divides, or at least
neutralized the bitter political factionalism of the next few years, had died with
Aung San, a widely revered young nationalist who founded his nation's military
with help from the Japanese to kick out the British; turned it instead against
the Japanese; and forged an agreement for a future federal union of Burma
with much of the leadership of the restive ethnic minorities. He had the undis-
puted loyalty of the rank-and-file and the trust of the minorities. The head of
the soon-to-breakaway moderate faction of the Communist Party of Burma was
his brother-in-law. But on the morning of July 19, 1947, months shy of the independence from Britain that he had worked almost singlehandedly to secure,
Aung San was shot dead. Down with him in a rain of semiautomatic gunfire
went eight of the country's most competent future leaders, all members of his
elective proto-cabinet.

By 1958, the government led by Prime Minister U Nu declared itself overwhelmed by the countrywide violence and internecine political bickering. He
turned over the reins of power to an Army caretaker government, under General
Ne Win. Elections in 1960 returned the country to Nu and civilian rule. In 1962,
on the pretext of impending secession by the Shan and other minority groups,
General Ne Win seized power again, this time in a coup. His "Revolutionary
Council" vested him with full powers, under which he promptly asserted the
mastery of the Buddhist Burmans, indefinitely suspended the 1947 constitution,
and installed one-party rule under a new Burma Socialist Program Party, the
BSPP. He also dynamited the Rangoon University Student Union; attacked
opponents; imposed censorship; and sealed off the country from all foreign
relations.

Under a hodgepodge of Buddhism and socialism that he called the "Burmese Way to Socialism," he nationalized foreign and domestic businesses and the news media, rewrote the school curriculum, and the country began its long downward spiral to the humiliation of a 1987 United Nations designation as a "Least Developed Country." That year, a demonetization of small currency bills overnight wiped out about eighty percent of the people's savings. Whether the measure was a caprice of numerically motivated economic paranoia—the new notes were in denominations that reflected Ne Win's famous preference for the number 9—or whether it was a poorly executed attempt to undercut the black market, it struck home as the culmination of his twenty-six-year misrule.

What happened next was a story of national combustion—of a teashop brawl that broadened over several months to become a revolution, followed by a quick and bloody counterrevolution. One military regime fell, soon to be replaced by another, still more insidious and repressive.

What happened also was the birth of a democracy movement.

Spearheaded by a band of increasingly strategic university students, the uprising of 1988 spread to every sector of society and to towns and cities across the country. Sparked in March, it had succeeded by July in forcing the resignation of General Ne Win. Another general took his place, dubbed the "Butcher of Rangoon" for his role weeks earlier in the deaths of almost three hundred students at the hands of riot police. The young leaders of the student union, the All Burma Federation of Student Unions, called for a nationwide strike.

On August 8, 1988, at least two million people poured into the streets.

Soldiers responded by firing into crowds, and beating or bayoneting protesters with impunity. But the crowds kept coming. The Butcher resigned, and his successor, Dr. Maung Maung, was a famous lawyer, a protégé of General Ne Win, who lifted martial law, released prominent dissidents from detention and called for BSPP leaders to consider a referendum on whether to scrap the one-party state. For many, Dr. Maung Maung was a puppet, acting at the behest of the old strongman, Ne Win. By the last week of August, all semblance of government had ground to a halt. Committees of citizens and monks assumed administration of towns and communities, newspapers proliferated, and the streets became communal stages for a twenty-four-hour carnival atmosphere.

On September 18, a new junta seized power, and re-imposed martial law as a self-dubbed "State Law and Order Restoration Council," or SLORC. Summary executions followed mass arrests. Plausible estimates placed the number of deaths between July and October in the mid-thousands.

In the heat of it all, the daughter of Aung San, the martyred independence hero, had coincidentally returned from her home in England to tend her ailing mother in Rangoon. The daughter, Aung San Suu Kyi, initially drew crowds because her delicate features bore striking resemblance to her father, whose portrait people had borne through the streets. She had his eyes, and, as it turned out, his charisma. Her speeches revealed a forcefulness and clarity of purpose that quickly established her as the voice of people's aspirations.

On August 26, she stood at the West Gate of ancient Shwedagon Pagoda, the country's most sacred Buddhist shrine, and introduced herself to an audience of hundreds of thousands. She had lost her father when she was two. She had been abroad since her teens, and had married a British scholar, a foreigner. "Some people have been saying . . . that I know nothing of Burmese politics. The trouble is that I know too much. My family knows best how complicated and tricky Burmese politics can be and how much my father had to suffer on this account." Over and over, to the people, she appealed for discipline and unity. They had, she said, made their message clear. Their demands were emphatic: an end to one-party rule and for free and fair elections to establish a multiparty system. She called for tolerance and forgiveness for the armed forces, whom she asked, in turn, to become a force in which the people could once again place their trust and reliance.

Recalling the project for the nation begun by her father, she defined the terms of the 1988 revolution as an extension of the same quest: for freedom and democracy. "I could not as my father's daughter remain indifferent to all that was going on," she said. "This national crisis could in fact be called the second struggle for independence." To Aung San Suu Kyi and her lakeside villa at 54 University Avenue gravitated prominent politicians, respected former military officers, urban professionals, communists, students, and sundry other thousands who still openly defied military rule. On September 24, 1988, they formed the National League for Democracy.

Within months, Aung San Suu Kyi, the NLD secretary general, was under house arrest and the NLD vice-chairman, former general Tin Oo, had been sentenced to hard labor. Still the NLD went on to sweep the surprisingly free and fair elections that the SLORC held on May 27, 1990. Apparently shocked at the extent of its unpopularity, the junta ignored the results. It threw the most dynamic leaders of the NLD and hundreds of other dissidents in jail, banned all other opposition parties except a few enfeebled ethnic versions, and systematically began suppressing all dissent.

University students fled the cities by the thousands to build a fighting force in the malarial border areas, forging expedient alliances with the tougher ethnic-minority armies. Devoid of resources, sickening in the jungle, they never stood a chance. Defeated in a final military offensive on their headquarters that they shared with ethnic Karen rebels, they frittered away into an alphabet soup of exile groups in India, China, or mainly into Thailand.

Across the next two decades, hundreds of prominent dissidents revolved in and out of detention, a number that had doubled with many facing multi-decade sentences since the short-lived "Saffron uprising" in 2007. At least one-fifth of them, at any time, were members of the NLD.

The SLORC never relinquished power. In 1989, it began tinkering with language. Burma was henceforth to be called "Myanmar," on a claim, later disputed by scholars, that the new appellation was more inclusive for a people that comprised not just the Burman but 135 ethnic groups. Rangoon became "Yangon," and other cities reverted to more traditional transliterations. Within five days, the United Nations accepted the changes and the world followed suit. A few holdouts—the United States, Britain, and other countries of the West—aligned with democracy activists who refused to recognize the SLORC's usurpation of power. They preferred "Burma." They preferred "Rangoon." In 1997, in a bid to join ASEAN, the Association of Southeast Asian Nations, the SLORC took advice from a Washington–based public relations firm, and, along with a reshuffling of officers, changed its name to the less farcically unpalatable State Peace and Development Council, the SPDC.

Nearly bankrupt when it first seized power, the SPDC fattened in the next two decades off sales of gas, oil, timber, and precious gems, and contracts to a slew of heatedly competing Asian companies for the construction of deep-sea ports, pipelines, and hydropower projects. Under a new Number 1, a pug-faced senior general called Than Shwe who slithered discreetly up the chain of command to head the junta since 1992, it stocked the receipts in private offshore bank accounts. The rest it poured into the military arsenal and giant vanity projects, including a new capital built from scratch in the searing central scrublands, 250 miles due north from Rangoon. They called it Naypyidaw, "Abode of the Kings."

Though the junta had partially liberalized the economy after 1988, its eleven generals and all ranking officers of the Tatmadaw, the Armed Forces, continued to wield outsized personal power and influence, in large part through the awarding of contracts and licenses and a symbiotic relationship with a narrow sliver of tycoons, including a handful who made their fortune in the drug trade around the Golden Triangle, a mountainous plot shared with Laos and Thailand, whose opium poppy crop ensures that Burma remains the world's second largest supplier of opium and heroin, after Afghanistan. What social welfare infrastructure had been maintained under the BSPP was slashed in a new, ruthless brand of state capitalism. Defense swallowed more than forty percent of total state expenditure. Within fifteen years, the army had more than doubled in size, to about four hundred thousand troops. The poorest citizens, if they weren't press-ganged, were lured to its ranks for its separate world of schools, housing, health care, and commodities. Once modeled on West Point, the Defense Services Academy, the elite officer-training school, taught a new, fear-based, more xenophobic curriculum.

The junta failed to respond with any measure of efficiency to social emergencies such as the rapid spread of AIDS or heroin addiction. Living standards among farmers plummeted as state procurement of rice and other staples kept prices artificially low, a blowback from attempts to appease city dwellers with cheap necessities so as to prevent another urban uprising inspired yet again by food shortages and inflation.

On August 15, 2007, the junta compounded the general economic distress with sudden, radical price hikes on gasoline, diesel fuel, and compressed natural gas. Everyone felt the hit, including members of the revered Buddhist monkhood, the *sangha*, who depended on lay civilians for patronage and daily donations into their alms bowls.

Small, isolated protests from civilians and monks broke out in towns and cities. Most were rapidly snuffed out. A report spread about violence from state officials against monks in the northern town of Pakokku on September 5. The perceived sacrilege begat outrage, which begat a shadowy new monk alliance, which begat an ultimatum to the junta, calling for an apology. The deadline passed. The junta failed to answer.

Tens of thousands of monks poured into the streets. For the color of their robes, observers dubbed the moment the Saffron uprising. They managed a week of steadily swelling marches, joined by growing numbers of civilians, before security forces brutally charged in.

Within eight months, on the night of May 2–3, 2008, Tropical Cyclone Nargis made landfall. It tore through the flatlands of the Irrawaddy Delta and across Rangoon with a force more deadly than any natural disaster since the Asian tsunami of 2004. The toll of dead and missing mounted to at least 138,000, with credible estimates of another 2.4 million left without shelter, food, water, or prospect of recovering their livelihoods.

As international humanitarian agencies fought to get inside, the military junta downplayed the damage and dragged its feet. Visas were refused, permits to travel within the country jammed in a bureaucratic bottleneck, and American, British, and French naval vessels hovered off the Burmese coast, bracing for a green light that would never come to chopper in first-tier emergency supplies.

⁓

IT WAS ABOUT THEN THAT MY EDITORS at the *Washington Post* gave me my marching orders: "Get in, get the story, and get out."

Authorities were picking off foreign reporters like flies. A BBC journalist had been frog-marched from passport control back onto a plane, and officials turned fast on a Korean photojournalist who gave herself away by snapping photos at the closely watched NLD party headquarters. The back page of *The New Light of Myanmar*, the state mouthpiece, warned helpfully of "Skyful Liars Attempting to Destroy Nation." It elaborated: "BBC lying, VOA deceiving, RFA setting up hostilities: Beware! Don't be bought by those ill-wishers." The handful that made it in wrote of reaching the delta as stowaways in trucks and boats, smuggled under bags of rice.

Like most foreign journalists, I lied on my visa application about my occupation and work history and went in under the guise of tourism. Should I bring in the satellite phone? How would I conceal my notebooks? Would I find myself a fixer? I was a rookie and I was terrified—of getting caught off the audible pounding of my heart in the queue to immigration; of x-rays poised to catch the curious bulges in my socks and underwear where I had, with thanks to the *Post*, tucked a drug lord's stash of crisp hundred-dollar bills; of not reaching the storm survivors trapped behind government checkpoints; and, especially, of not making heads or tails of a country that days before I could barely place on the map.

The "Burma-heads" in Bangkok offered counsel: *Steer clear of people too enthused to speak to a foreigner; they are government agents.* This was confusing. Burmese as a rule chuckled and blushed or shut up like clams when questioned about matters of politics, especially by lumbering, fresh-off-plane Westerners. Barring the dubious enthusiasm of a "Mr. Zee" at the airport and his well-thumbed album of foreigners whom he claimed to have run to the delta, the few people who dived in with anti-government rants or offered themselves as guides were welcome relief. Any outside advice slipped fast.

My lone local contact, a wily doctor, whisked me around Rangoon in a wheezing contraption of a native variety of vehicular dilapidation commonly identified by windows that require you to roll them down with pliers; car supply was sufficiently restricted that black market imports, such as the standard twenty-year-old Toyota Camry, sold at the time for about $25,000. I met jewelers, journalists, lawyers, government servants, housewives, actors, militant monks—ordinary folk, in sum, who became friends the way I quickly learned to make friends in Burma— bonds of trust sealed in seconds on an exchange of glances.

I grew more reckless, gleaning contacts off diplomats, seeking out the kinds of people who would be watched. Like the Burmese, I learned to see the holes in the system, to tell a half-truth, to blink and smile and speak in metaphors. To my editor in Washington, and sources in Burma, I emailed cryptic messages under an absurd pseudonym. And when I emerged, I wrote about storm survivors' efforts to rebuild; the effects of general economic collapse; the political rite of passage that was prison; a rising generation of activists; and the emergence of a citizen movement fueled on quiet rage.

With a knowing half-smile from a savvy employee at a derelict Rangoon tourist agency, I had ducked past four army checkpoints to reach the storm-ravaged delta, handing to each a copy of a permission slip—complete with mug shot and passport number, and a promise not to engage in politics—which my tourist agency accomplice had secured from the Ministry of Tourism with a bribe of four hundred dollars. I went as a "private donor," sharing space in a hired van with twenty boxes of instant noodles, five of candles, and five of soap that we distributed at wrecked villages along the way. We hired a fisherman's vessel and headed four hours downriver, stopping finally at the site of a village that looked like it had been blitzed, a cratered landscape of muddy pools, debris, and the bones of water buffaloes. No one had found it yet. It had been built in a former mangrove reserve, not far from a hidden naval base. It wasn't meant to have existed. One bamboo stick at a time, plank by smashed plank, its inhabitants were attempting to piece their lives back together. On the night of the storm, 660 people of a former population of 943 had disappeared.

The storm was the worst natural catastrophe to hit Burma in modern times. Its ferocity was briefly matched by the response of the population as they tuned into illicit shortwave radio broadcasts and heard how their government first denied the extent of the damage, then blocked foreign aid from reaching survivors. So they took it upon themselves. I watched them gather at dawn and by night across the tree-clogged intersections of Rangoon—monks, bands of friends, actors, doctors, housewives, colleagues, whole neighborhoods. For days at a time they shuttered their shops and clinics, hired trucks and boats, and threw together bags of rice, blankets, candles, soap, and cooking oil. They negotiated and fought their way through checkpoints and army convoys, surrendering goods when ordered, clinging to the rest, and rattling for hours down the lone broken road to the delta or navigating a maze of tide-locked rivulets to find survivors in dozens of forsaken towns and villages. They returned with tales of official confiscations and neglect, of bloated bodies floating in the bracken rice paddies, of frail men and women evicted from refuges to nonexistent homes, of government rice handouts fit only for pigs.

The trauma from the crackdown on the "Saffron" uprising had lingered. But social activism, long thought leveled under laws that forbade assembly or associations of more than five, offered a subtle new way to push at the confines of the state. In the months that followed, I watched many of those small groups become unofficial nonprofits. They operated under the radar, treading a delicate line between humanitarian aid and politics. I met also with members of loose, lateral networks that had long lain dormant under the cover of pagoda-cleaning activities, book clubs, and funeral dispatchers. I noticed a pattern of activists connecting and coordinating, even from hiding.

So much for my marching orders. It was often said, outside the country and within, that all underground movement had been suppressed and dissolved. Instead I had discovered a spirit, a burning impulse for freedom, and a lexicon of gallows humor. Over the next few years, I returned and returned, still hiding my notebooks, watching and learning, and building on relationships of fragile trust. With Aung San Suu Kyi at the helm, even as authorities held her incommunicado, Burmese were grasping at threads of a sui generis rebellious politics. Something in that mindset compelled me to dig deeper.

The Rebel of Rangoon is the fruit of that inquiry.

⚬⚬⚬

DATES, PLACES, AND ALL THE FACTS and factoids contained herein are, to the best of my ability, correct. But I have made free use of names. Partly this is to help shield identities, partly this is to overcome the distance caused by Burmese names that are to Western readers often impenetrable and difficult to pronounce. (Burmese have no first and last names. These correspond instead to the day of the week on which they were born combined with virtuous attributes that parents hope to encourage in them.)

Activists, if they are not currently public figures, are often referred to by pseudonyms or aliases that they employ amongst themselves to protect against eavesdroppers and spies. Those that are email handles have been slightly altered. For the code name of one activist whose activities under it remain sensitive, I used a synonym. My only other invention is "Nway," though it derives from a transliterated syllable in one of the pseudonyms that he regularly employed.

Or I call them, as they address others, by kin terms that double, in Burmese society, as honorifics. In this instance, they also conjure the palpable sense of a dissident movement as a family, with all the attendant dysfunction and emotional baggage this might suggest. There are for instance, the *Big Brothers*, the former student leaders of the 1988 uprising; *Auntie* for Aung San Suu Kyi; several *Uncles*; and two *Grandpas*.

I employ "Burma," and "Rangoon," in lieu of "Myanmar" and "Yangon." This is a choice—and I take it in stride. Scholars prefer to employ the usage of the junta since 1989 as a way of distinguishing between the separate historical periods and governments. I follow the usage of the newspaper that first sent me, which in turn followed the usage of the US State Department. Likewise, this is a story told from the vantage point of people who have for the most part resisted that name change, and I here follow their lead.

A word more. Struggles for freedom are often euphemisms for tactics of blood and ideologies of hate. None of the men and women in these pages are fanatics. Murder and hate are their antithesis. They chose a struggle of nonviolence, of returning justice and rights to people according to the highest international standards. For them, the means justify the ends.

To describe the underground is also to shine a light on its dirt. Their family affairs are theirs alone. But to reveal aspects of their less-pristine actions is to more honestly render the weight of the constraints under which they have been forced to maneuver. Among their greatest sorrows are the wounds they have inflicted upon each other.

Nway's story forms the backbone, a dissident's life as a mirror to the transformational currents of his country and his movement. Like those of his friends and community, his was no more or less valid and tragic than the dozens more I was privileged to hear. Each person here depicted would be the first to point this out. I chose them because they were at the center of the movement, working within or alongside the National League for Democracy. I had yet to read that story. And so I felt it was my job to write it.

Part I depicts a few months of disconsolation and defiance, almost of a spinning in place. Part II yields to historical movement, and each chapter accordingly moves forward a year. Central to this tale is Nway's often-fraught and ever-deepening partnership with his one-time rival "Nigel." Their growing friendship, intertwined with the unfolding lives of the newbies and drifters around them or the wizened dissidents anguishing over alternatives, plays against a backdrop of swiftly moving national events toward the most significant battle the movement faced in generations—a race against the elections of November 2010, the country's first elections in twenty years that threatened to consolidate and entrench fifty years of military rule—and then all that followed.

Into Nway's life, I became for weeks at a time a fly on the wall, as far as was possible for an underground foreign journalist tracking a wanted man in a police state. I also spent hundreds of hours across four years in the company of the individuals who are here depicted. My reporting for this book is documented in sixty-three notebooks and in hundreds of hours of digital audio and video recordings. Where I was not present to witness a scene, I have relied on repeat interviews and, wherever possible, supplemented and cross-verified my reporting with information shared by others, and relevant news articles, reports, and books.

Until 2012, foreign reporters, like foreign human-rights activists and anyone suspected of "doing politics," were not allowed in the country. Like most visiting journalists, I wrote without a byline. I pinballed between tourist sites after sensitive interviews, avoided the same drivers, frequently changed hotels, and one time, suspecting I had intelligence on my tail, headed a few days up-country. Conversing by phone or email—likely monitored on one or both ends—was an exercise in meaningful circumlocution. Flying out each time involved a delicate chaos in my hotel room as I scrambled to hide notebooks and business cards, or scribbled over phone numbers and dispersed addresses across my luggage, ripping up anything unnecessary, and stuffing the rest into socks and sleeves and pockets. Until 2012, there were places I could not go and people I could not see. Official data and official interviews were impossible to come by without sacrificing the chance to work among the people who had given me access.

For all that, to my sources, I never needed to misrepresent myself. But my presence as a foreigner inevitably sometimes changed events and scenes. When I appear in the book, it is in the third person, and I try to show myself as they saw me. All I risked, in truth, was instant deportation and blacklisting from future visas; I always had the option of flying home, to safety. Far more troubling, and likely, were prospects of unwittingly leaving a trace, and the consequential tracking down and harassment of the people who had helped me every day, for hours, without a second's hesitation.

It is a great relief to relate what follows without as justified a fear of repercussions—although the chances of this continue to exist. The old laws with which the government systematically repressed dissent are still on the books. Most important, the individuals described in these pages knew of and condoned my purpose. When I wavered, worrying that I might in any way put them in jeopardy, they encouraged me, repeatedly, to tell all. It was a great risk to open their lives to me. To salute their courage now, though courage it was, feels like condescension, as if my work were of greater significance than all the other risks they undertook in their everyday lives. For all the hours and effort they spent patiently educating a foreigner about their land and their history, spelling out names that eluded me again and again, confessing their dreams and secrets, I have undying gratitude. But as with all things, they were just doing what they felt they had to do.

And so, to their eyes.

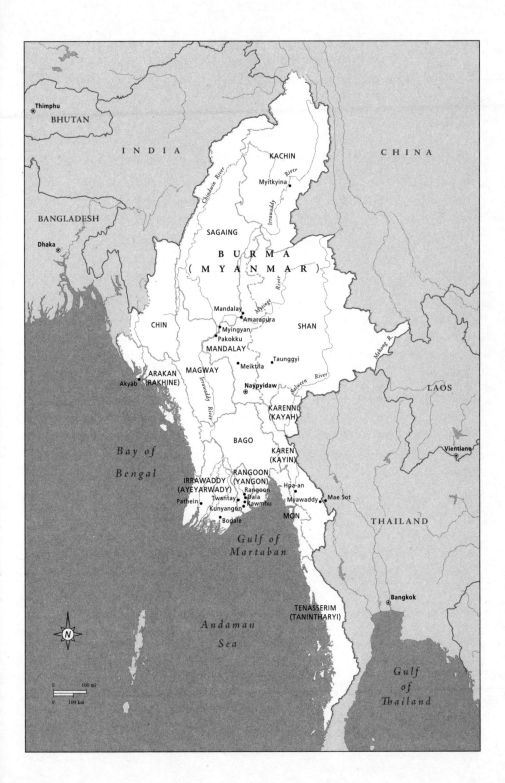

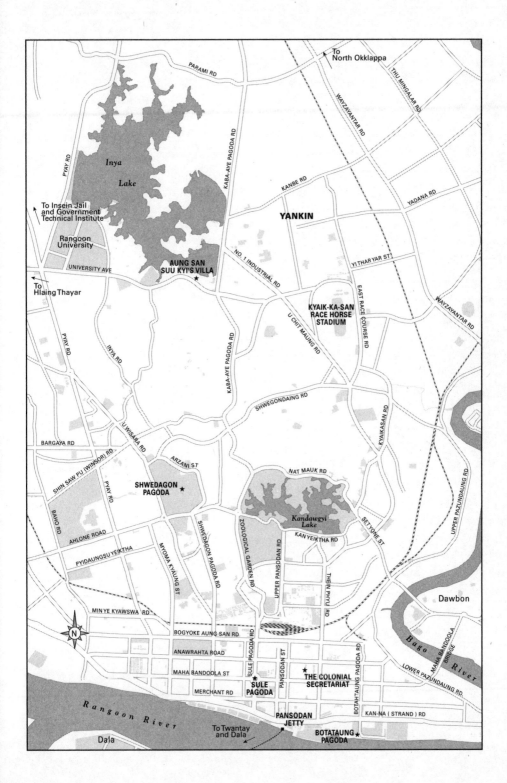

PART I

1

NWAY

ON THE EVENING HE DISCOVERED he was a target of the Dogs, Nway played a joke.

First, though, he walked. That is to say, with dusk descending on Rangoon, an intelligence agent closing in on his tail, and the terror of impending arrest exploding in his solar plexus, he did the exact opposite of what a young man might who is febrile and fleet-footed with a jungle-tough aptitude for survival. Steps ahead of his tracker, who was older and driven by something less potent than raw nerve or existential necessity, Nway swallowed hard, squared his shoulders—and slackened his pace.

Away from the Office. Hard left along a sidewalk that dipped and dead-ended into child-sized sumps and the raveled roots of centenarian tamarinds. Down an alley that snaked past penny-a-bowl, tarpaulin-tented teashops and slipshod, teakwood shacks: the sorry innards of a city of four or maybe five million—no one really knew—that tolerated slum-rot at its center because few besides the officer corps had it much better.

The Dog might have access to a motorcycle—in Rangoon, only intelligence agents were allowed them—and catch him within seconds. Defiant of that possibility, Nway headed fast but tempered for the nearest crowd, for life, or, as luck would have it, a public bus, just pulling into the gutter. He shoved his sliver of a form into the flatbed rear. Bodies pressed in tight. The female passengers, typically, could scarcely hope to spare their modesty. He knew as a rule that they hated the carnal innuendo, the liberties in packed places that men

3

could take, rubbing up against their hips. Early in life, he'd made it a point of principle to protect the honor, or at least the basic comforts, of the girls around him. Even now, on reflex, the thought occurred to him that it wasn't right to add to their unease.

The man climbed aboard beside him.

Nway was flummoxed, briefly. Then it came: the intuitive knowing, the glimmer of a limpid certainty that he was learning fast to sense in the midst of crises.

He fished about inside his pocket, leaned in toward the conductor, and pressed into his palm sufficient fare for two.

He wouldn't have thought to call the payment of his tracker's fare a bribe, exactly. He meant it more as an act of loving-kindness, an inspired deployment of a tested tactic that he had sourced almost unwittingly in the Buddhist morality that infused his countrymen's efforts to free themselves of authoritarian rule. Most often it manifested as a goading of young men and women into his circle of political influence with steady accretions of small considerations: cigarettes to bum; cups of tea purchased; tunes from favorite bands painstakingly downloaded through proxies from terminally sick connections in late-night Internet cafés, then transferred onto MP3s. A government agent on the job was as underpaid as the rest of them. He would be pleased to pocket his unused change.

The man was suitably disarmed.

"Ah," he said. "You know who I am? So—we can cooperate."

It was a dumb line.

Of course Nway knew him for an intelligence agent. He had emerged when Nway left the Office from the hut directly over the road. For all its plastering in sunny yellow ads for ready-mixed tea powder, it served no other purpose than to shelter Special Branch police investigators. They dressed in plain clothes—a simple *longyi*, a sarong; a baseball cap; sometimes a pair of aviators—but scarcely bothered beyond to hide their cameras or motorcycles or notepads, eternally watching.

The agent's line, moreover, was an obvious opening, an invitation for a longer conversation, which, after a bit of shifty give-and-take—a threat, a confession, some inevitable soul-searching, and a salting with promises of material relief and assurances of lifelong status—might yield another defection to the state. In the parlance of the military junta, that translated roughly to joining the "defenders of national unity" against "internal and external destructive elements," a vague, nefarious crew who might include "foreign destructionists," "those relying on external elements, acting as stooges, holding negative views," or types like Nway: half-assed, misty-eyed youth from the refuse of a ragtag political party led by that foreigner's whore.

Nway didn't bite.

"Where are you from?" he asked the man.

"Special Branch."

"Do you get fees for this?"

"Yes," he said. He paused. "I'm just doing my job."

"And I'm doing mine," Nway shot back.

No, he corrected himself. *Don't give him that opening.*

Barely out of his twenties, Nway had spent eleven years on the frontlines of dissidence, much of it working in the Office for that ragtag political party. Still he could have trouble taming his passions. How often had he combusted, ready to lose big for a quick win on some matter of conviction? On a surge of emotion, he'd quit medical school; turned down a certificate from the British Council; even, six months earlier, resigned from the Office. It had meant the end of the world as he knew it, the need to reconceptualize everything he had worked for, long after he had understood like a light switched on inside that politics, and the fight for democracy, were to be his life.

None of his recruits would have described him as methodical, not in the way that they talked of Nigel, his sometime associate. Neither had Nway his best friend Arthur's patience with a thought, evidenced in its slow molding, flickers of it in the creasing around his eyes and mouth, before it emerged fully formed, weighted with insight. If Nway's tempo had long riffed off theirs as the more skittish, the more improvisational and sly, he also had a rare talent when others froze up or panicked. In those moments, his capacity for leadership—or at any rate, for managing the complex maneuvers of a group needing to think fast and flee faster—flared like a beacon in the night.

The bus lurched and racketed down roads cracked and potholed and shining still from the day's last rainstorm. The man was middle-aged. Doubtless he was married, with two or three children, and living in some peeling government barracks that Nway could guess had the merit of both storm-safe walls—not the bamboo-and-thatch of a hut sinking into sewage—and sufficient sense of segregation from the wider civilian population to facilitate perceptions that they were the enemy.

Nway didn't look. Didn't ask. He might have unnerved the man with the audacity of one of his twelve-o'clock stare-downs. Better to angle away his chin. Dark-skinned and lithe, he had a preference for an anarchic mane that conveniently flopped across the fine-boned symmetry of his face. But it couldn't hide the peculiar intensity of his almond gaze, nor his tendency to blaze it straight into an interlocutor's eyes, heedless of the local preference for sidelong half-glances.

As for curiosity, too often it killed the cat. Conversation at this juncture across the state-civilian divide would invite nothing but trouble, even for a young dissident with a penchant for verbal provocation and deviant persuasive ability. Best to stay mute and know less, or so they'd all been taught. Which was something of the core national problem and Nway knew it viscerally. But he knew as well, and was learning fast, to pick his battles.

Perhaps the agent's job was indeed just a job, the bureaucratic transaction of some mid-level functionary. Perhaps it was an order followed, not because the man lacked morality or courage, but because both withered before the shame of failing his direct superiors. Perhaps that tangible, immediate shame outweighed the more diffuse but greater shame of somehow failing his society in the construction of some abstract future that he had no reason to believe would ever come. Perhaps he was a minefield of competing shames: hated his work, and himself still more, for doing what his cousins and aunts, his brothers and unborn children might one day revile him for and every time he caught his reflection in some cracked window-pane, he wondered; wondered if there weren't, after all, some other way than spying on his fellow citizens and hunting them down to feed the detention system as if it were a python starved for its own offspring.

Perhaps, far more likely, he didn't think at all. Or automatically enough that he had never questioned the junta's propaganda, the triumvirate of slogans relentlessly repeated about national unity and stability, about progress toward economic development and "discipline-flourishing democracy," about the blood and sweat of the Tatmadaw, the armed forces, serving no purpose less patriotic than to hold together the Union, mother and father of it both, joining forces with the people to eradicate all saboteurs. Perhaps—

"Where are you going?" the man asked.

Nway was going, he decided then and there, to the newsroom of a magazine where he had lately found a scrap of work translating foreign news clippings, less because he had any interest in exploring how to slip allegory past the censors and into print, in the way of many of the country's journalists. Nor did he want the salary, though he needed every last crumpled *kyat*. One among the dozens of private journals of recent years that sidewalk purchasers

scoured for veiled filaments of anti-authoritarian ideas between the latest
football scores and horoscopes, the magazine provided him cover for regular
interaction with its editor. This was a transient opportunity, to be seized with
the urgency of the rice farmer planting his crop in a race against the June
rains. The editor was a senior politician fresh off a six-week detention, three
years after a fifteen-year incarceration, and as likely to see again the inside
of another jail cell as the next monsoon. In fact, Nway told himself, tracking
down his editor was exactly the excuse he would use to explain his reasons for
loitering at the Office.

The Office was his code for the headquarters of the National League for
Democracy, or NLD—full name and acronym to be deployed openly only with
strategic intent. Technically, the NLD was legal, the country's lone institutional
holdout for democracy. In practice, to speak its name aloud was to invite suspicion that one had political ideas; and to have political ideas was to be dangerous.

Right now, Nway could say to his tracker, if it came to that, that he had sim-
ply been relaying news to his boss. Was it any fault of his if that editor, Uncle
Ohn Kyaing—*Uncle* was a token honorific—happened to double as a known
NLD executive?

Leaping off the bus, he bolted into the newsroom and stayed as long as he
could fake a purpose that could be construed as professional. The intelligence
agent would inevitably drift away, from boredom mainly—evening's worth
of fear-mongering starkly accomplished, and not enough wage to warrant extra effort. Nway wasn't important, a messenger at most. It was a lie he liked to
tell himself, and not because he might have actually thought himself more vital
to either the NLD or the wider movement for democracy that it represented.
To subvert his own sense of self-importance, to never set much store by it—if
he thought about it, which he didn't much—was a homegrown form of modesty that doubled as self-protection. In his native Twantay, a river ferry and
a motorcycle ride away, he might have already forged a reputation. But here
in the nerve center of his country's history, in downtown Rangoon among the
many mildewed haunts of greater men and women, he was, he insisted often,
"nothing." That he might, as such, be worthy of a genuine investment of state-
sanctioned time seemed scarcely conceivable.

It was daft, though. First time he had had shown up at the Office in over six
months and—boom!—out shot a Dog, chasing him down the road until he was
scared so silly he was now cowering like a turtle in the shell of a building, with
scarcely half a pack of cigarettes for solace.

Truth be told, he had never yet found a decent enough reason to risk a return to NLD headquarters, a thrice-raided, three-story shack near the Shwedagon Pagoda with moldering walls and dust-caked wooden cabinets. Its members were fond of calling it "the cowshed," resigned to the irony that it stood in all its lamentable glory as the final outpost for the democratically mandated ruling party—a political alliance that in the last countrywide elections, on May 27, 1990, had won eighty-two percent of the seats for a parliament that had never been allowed to sit.

That election had been their only chance in fifty years for a return to democracy by the ballot. It had been held under the auspices of the junta that had seized power on September 18, 1988, as a self-proclaimed State Law and Order Council, the SLORC. Its brutal reassertion of "law and order" had included firing indiscriminately into crowds of tens of thousands who had persisted, since the bloodily suppressed nationwide uprising of August 8 of that year, with near-daily marches, sit-ins, and hunger strikes, waving the national flag, or the Buddhist flag, or the flag of the old, colonial-era Student Union.

The SLORC had taken over from President Maung Maung, who had taken over a month earlier from General Sein Lwin, "the Butcher of Rangoon," who had taken over a month earlier still from General Ne Win, the strongman who had wielded sole authority since 1962, turned the country from a parliamentary democracy into a single-party state, and steadily steered it into ruin. He had resigned in July as chairman of the Burma Socialist Program Party, unable to ignore the nationwide furor that had surged since lethal attacks on university student demonstrators in March. But he couldn't resist a parting threat in his final speech that "when the army shoots, it shoots to hit." First the "Butcher" and then the SLORC had made sure to fulfill his bidding.

Pledging to carry out elections promised in the twenty-nine-day presidency of Dr. Maung Maung amid the millions-strong protests of August, the SLORC had suggested nothing less than a return to multiparty rule. It had been a fair fight to the polls, discounting the prior imposition of martial law and the fact that key NLD party executives had already been incarcerated: the NLD Vice Chairman, Tin Oo, had been sent to hard labor and the party secretary general, Aung San Suu Kyi, to house arrest. Still, the military-backed party had lost everywhere, even in districts heavy with its members. The vote count had even been published in the national gazette. Taken thoroughly aback at the extent of its rout, the SLORC ignored the results. A month later it issued an edict declaring that the vote had served no other purpose than to elect representatives to a constitution-drafting committee. When winning candidates objected, most of them from the NLD, the SLORC threw them in jail.

It had all been downhill from there.

Eighteen years later—or, the previous October—Nway had led a mass walkout of NLD youth members in a bad stink over the sclerotic leadership of the party by its caretaker chairmen. They were three former army officers in their eighties and nineties who, it was felt, would have offered better service to the country spending their silver years wheezing into a mango orchard. The party's most dynamic leaders—if they weren't still scattered among prisons on the far fringes of the country, under house arrest, in exile, harassed into retirement, or dead—lived furtive lives: landlines tapped, movements tracked, knocks on doors for spot interrogations predictable, if unpredictably scheduled. Had they only been allowed to meet or plan, the party's spirit might even have survived the long, wasteland years without the leader whom the world beyond knew as the 1991 Nobel Peace Prize laureate, Aung San Suu Kyi. At home, her name banished from the press, people called her simply the Lady. Nway and most of his peers preferred *Auntie*.

Few were fooled that the junta's benign acceptance of party chair Uncle Aung Shwe and his deputy, Joint Secretary U Lwin, was anything less than a deliberate blow, as if they were stuffing some dead animal for showcasing. In the absence of adversarial opinion, and with Auntie incommunicado since 2003, when she began her third term of house arrest, Aung Shwe had spent a half-decade putting the party on ice, forbidding public political actions and preventing contact with other dissident groups. Perhaps he was merely trying to salvage its amputated corpse, keeping it on life support until—some fresh moment.

But he had refused, even after multiple attempts at persuasion by other party elders, to let anyone from the NLD march in the name of the party in the street protests of August and September 2007—the "Saffron uprising"—the people's first collective cry against military rule since 1988. The monks had eventually taken up the baton, thousands of them pouring red down the boulevards, bald of pate and often bare of foot. But they'd had no strategy. No endgame. No political plan. Nway was sure of it: Aung Shwe's passivity had cost them the revolution.

"How we feel, you know?" Nway would say, grasping for words, devoid for once of his quick wit. "This is the leading-role party. You know? I don't know how to express my heart. You know we did it"—*it* being the civilian activists' initial response to the junta's radical price hikes on fuel in mid-August 2007; the backroom encouragement of the monks; the strategic infiltration into civilian crowds to incite them into generalized defiance "very secretly, very carefully, and we give a lot of time, and then we have to hide."

In its heyday, the NLD had claimed a membership of two million. That was about one-twentieth of the population. But those had been only the officially registered, complete with names, national registration numbers, photographs, and addresses on laminated cards, and they had signed up during the difficult months after the SLORC seized power. Thereafter, the generals shuffled through different portfolios and, in 1997, the SLORC changed its name to the State Peace and Development Council, the SPDC. But its stranglehold on nationwide dissent persisted. Throughout the two decades after 1990, there could be no public polls, no verifiable means of tracking the ebb and flow of support from the silent majority. It was enough that crowds amassed to see Auntie and her deputies whenever they'd roamed free. Greater proof still of the NLD's ongoing significance was a multi-fronted campaign to smear or smash it into irrelevance.

Through it all, as members hemorrhaged for real or in fictive government news clippings, and as the NLD's bold, red sign rusted on more than two hundred forcibly shuttered party chapters in homes and huts nationwide, the "cowshed" on West Shwegondaing Road had endured as a stubborn barnacle, a hole-in-wall poke in the eye at the junta's Ozymandian assertions of legitimacy.

In 2008, in a twist as typical of the historical vicissitudes of politics in Burma as it was maiming to the party, the youngest NLD members had skipped the more gentle irreverence to an elder that would have come of speaking their frustrations aloud and instead gone straight for mutiny. Just over a year after the Saffron uprising, it took a final trivial decision by Aung Shwe, a single youth meeting, and 109 young men and women resigned, which was all the more damning because it had taken the NLD two decades and wave upon wave of arrests, to build anew a youth wing worthy of the fight.

Few outside had any inkling that the walkout was no surrender—not, that is, a clean exit from opposition to the junta. A US embassy cable had informed Washington on October 17, 2008, that it would "watch closely to see if the youths' resignation was a one-off event or the beginning of broader divisions within the party," a rare, visible display of recent discontent within a movement that had a long history of splintering on personal disagreements. It had only been a few days since a first party gathering in over a decade, and another

Rangoon-to-Washington cable on April 29, 2009 noted anew the sense of impending internal crisis: thirty NLD members, including fifteen who had been elected in the neglected vote of 1990, had just submitted a letter calling directly for the chairman's resignation.

It was small-fry stuff, relatively. But in a universe of political dissidence that was forced of necessity to hide its inner mechanics, Nway's walkout spoke of a growing dissatisfaction with the stagnant policies of old. It echoed the sentiments of a population that was increasingly impatient with the party's fossilized fixation on the 1990 elections, by now so ancient that a new generation had been born and come of age recalling them not at all.

The fact of the matter was that the youths' walkout had offered an opportunity to vanish, to dive underground into a semi-clandestine space of nonviolent revolutionary activity inhabited by shifting configurations of at least a half-dozen groups with varying degrees of strategic sophistication, institutional memory, and transnational resourcing. Henceforth Nway and his crew would avoid the hornet's nest of the Office, which was swarming always with informers and out of touch, in any case, with the granular grievances of the people from the towns and farmer hamlets that they claimed to represent, even now, nineteen years after an election victory that they had never been allowed to assert. Democracy in government was their particular pipedream. But democracy of poverty: that kind sprouted among the leprous crawl of Rangoon's backstreets, metastasized into slums, and fanned out in a filigree of farmer hamlets among the paddies and parched flatland to the southern barricade of the sea, and north-east-westwards to a pincer of wild peaks that bordered Bangladesh, India, China, Laos, and Thailand. The idea of it, poverty's willful embrace of whomever, when Nway considered it, was funny; dark, though, in the way of much of his humor, because the jokes, like now, were mostly on them.

But today, Nway had his reasons for making it back to the Office. He had meant it to round up straggler activists for a vigil outside the gates of Insein Prison. It wouldn't have been the most explosive of protests; he'd have been lucky to muster a half-dozen. Grandpa—Win Tin, the NLD's longtime strategist—would stand among them, lion-maned and wearing his trademark prison blues, which he had refused to take off since he'd been released from the selfsame jail where he had sat out the previous nineteen years. Give or take the likelihood that the old firebrand would offer some colorful quote to a journalist reaching him from exile through Nway's preciously guarded cell phone, or a decent photograph of the crowd uploaded to the outside world, they could rest assured that the news would find its way back into Burma. Just so, they would register their solidarity with Auntie.

Auntie: uncontested in leadership, irredeemably fearless, and that day on trial in Insein Prison. She was charged with breaking the terms of her house arrest after an American tourist had on May 3 swum across the vast, algae-lurid lake to her villa, and taken shelter for the night. The trial, a closed-door affair with sporadic invitations for foreign diplomats, had all the markings of the usual perversions of the legal system. But this one had a coincidental brilliance: Auntie's third term of house arrest had been set to expire on May 27, within days of the tourist's intrusion. The bet in the backrooms of teashops or in private kitchens wasn't on whether they would spare her a fresh sentencing. It was on how long they would give her for her newest term.

From the newsroom that was serving as his refuge, Nway emerged into the darkening street, a copy of the latest edition of the magazine tucked under his arm. Noodle soups splashed out of bowls and samosas danced in woks of oil at makeshift restaurants that spilled across the sidewalks, crowded thick with evening diners. Generators spluttered to life, wires vibrating to halogens strung off the banyans and the coconuts, because in 2009, in this city of nearly five million, in a country rich in natural gas and offshore oil, with rivers churning with hydropower potential, there was still no steadfast state supply of electricity.

Leavened by thoughts of organizing tomorrow's vigil for Auntie—he was fast learning how naturally it came to him to connect a web of activists, from senior Uncles to some new punk he'd recruited out of a beer haunt in Chinatown and thence on, via Gchat, to some pseudonymous ex-revolutionary in the outside world—drifting, in sum, into the reverie of his emerging art, he headed straight into the man with the unbecoming plain clothes and the still less becoming expression who had loitered in the street.

Waiting for him.

Gut-punched, Nway bounded toward another bus, leapt off, flung himself aboard a third. The agent, at each increment, stayed close.

There was no way out. Apparently Nway was, after all, a catch worthy of a pursuit.

He struck up a conversation.

"Look," he said, unfolding the magazine, "here are my articles." *You see?* he meant to say. *I'm not a politician, just an honest type like you trying to earn a wage. Not my fault my boss works at the National League for Democracy.*

"You NLD types," said the intelligence agent, with something that might have suggested respect. "You are very educated."

That was undeniable. The executives of the National League for Democracy had been lawyers and doctors, geologists and civil servants: the cream of Burma's urban intelligentsia, sufficiently fed up with the quarter-century free-fall under General Ne Win of their country's destiny that they had packed in their jobs, their social ecosystems, their prospects of quiet lives watching their children grow, for the poisonous rewards of self-sacrifice, prison, torture, and some amorphous dream of a future that they would never live to see, at least not before their next incarnations.

But he kept his insolence in check.

꙳

A BUS WAS HARDLY A NOVEL setting for a nose-to-nose confrontation between an agent and an activist. It wasn't even Nway's first.

That had come in 1998, just over eleven years earlier, on his virginal trip to the NLD. The day he'd picked had been as good as any—better, even, for those about to brave the passage into politics, because he chose an anniversary. It was Revolutionary Day, which recalled March 27, 1945, when General Aung San's Burma Independence Army rose up against the Japanese, who had promised to help free Burma from British rule, only to install an occupation more brutal.

The junta had taken to remembering the moment as Armed Forces Day. Back then, before it relocated the capital to Naypyidaw, March 27 had been an annual occasion for a downtown military parade, a self-congratulatory, chest-thumping show for the exclusionary viewing of those who either wore a uniform or boasted membership in the Union Solidarity and Development Association, the USDA, the junta's twenty-six-million-strong social apparatus.

"Only when the Tatmadaw is strong will the nation be strong," Senior General Than Shwe, the junta chairman, and army commander-in-chief, had said that year in his speech, citing a favorite slogan that featured in towns and cities on giant red billboards.

He'd done away with the usual rhetoric about "crushing and annihilating" destructive elements. Instead, he'd suggested "talks" with "parties or organizations" as necessary for "future unity." Observers read into the soupçon of novelty an olive branch intended for the NLD. It hadn't amounted to much. Aung

San Suu Kyi would have to wait another six years until the junta would engage her in substantive talks, and those had quickly broken down when Than Shwe, No. 1, thwarted the deal she had almost struck with his deputies.

Uptown at NLD headquarters on Shwegondaing Road or, that year, at Auntie's lakeside residence at 54 University Avenue, people would gather for staid affairs of solemn monumentalism. Analysts would later mark such occasions as the party's most visible sign of life: the party of the masses, not even an opposition so much as the government-in-waiting, reduced to commemorating anniversaries.

At least it meant a procession of speeches and a gathering of hundreds. Nway could melt in, unnoticed. If he choked, he could slip out and vanish. He had no cause as yet to doubt the service he would henceforth shoulder, but preemptive caution, like subtlety and subterfuge, were the natural due of minds inspired from birth to cheat a system they chafed at being trapped inside.

Authorities always matched the outpouring of activists and supporters with a battery of cameras, barbed-wire barricades on either end of the road, and soldiers and riot police deployed by the truckloads. To pass through the checkpoints required handing over details of one's identity: name, national registration number, address. It proved to be an entry into politics as lacking in anonymity as it was likely irreversible.

Afterward, he had been followed. Like today, an agent had climbed aboard his homebound bus. Scarcely out of his teens, Nway had seized up. He had been unable to master the nervousness churning in his gut. There had been other scares, long before and too many to count since. They had been greater, more tragic, the shocks and heartaches of daily life, the slow boring into the psyche of a state of perpetual siege. But none of them had the searing intensity of that first experience. It had marked him like a first kiss, a first love: an agent tracking him as politician, on his first, tremulous day as politician.

And of course it had turned out to be a trick of the mind. The man had about as much interest in him as in a discarded fruit peel. He had slipped out at the next junction. He had, Nway realized, merely been changing shift.

Years later, Nway could smile about it and forgive himself his temporary rigor mortis. "We didn't have to be arrested," he would say. "But psychologically, we have been very tired."

But luck of that kind didn't strike twice.

༄

THERE WAS LITTLE QUESTION ABOUT where next to head.

Another in his situation might have opted for the distant suburbs: perhaps to
Arthur, his best friend, in Hlaing Thayar, far to the northeast. With its tumble-
down shacks crammed around textile and soap factories and car-part shops, the
slum had stretched on and on as nothing more than muddy field when Arthur's
entire neighborhood had been trucked there on three days' notice in the martial
reconfigurations after the military coup of 1988. Or he might have headed north,
to his friend Nigel's parents in North Okklappa, another warren of straw-and-
thatch huts on trash-strewn alleyways that a still-earlier incarnation of military
rule had forced into existence on a similar whim of slapdash urban redesign.

He had a safe house, a room nine flights up a crooked stairwell whose entry barely cracked apart the space between a *biryani* restaurant and a newsstand
down Maha Bandoola Road. Its only signs of habitation, beyond the inevitable
thicket of cobwebs, were a litter of plastic bottles, several of them brimming
with cigarette ash, and a stack of rattan mats neatly folded against a window that
faced eastward onto the rusty roofscape of downtown boulevards around ancient Sule Pagoda. He called it *Nandau*—the Palace. And so it was code-named
with no less juicy irony among the activists of his network.

It had already proven its use because having a spy on one's tail was hardly
the only emergency to require asylum. More typical had been the particular
predicament that had befallen Nobleyan and Doe Doe, and whomever else he
might yet recruit. One after the other, at separate spots on the map, Nobleyan
and Doe Doe had faced parents who had discovered that their respective son
and daughter had all this time been skipping job-university-the-safe-confines-
of-corrupted-convention for political work. For which bit of news, the son and
daughter had been promptly cast out of homes and cut off from all income. Not
every young activist had the blessing of Nway's own rebellious parentage.

But to go to the Palace now, in plain view, was as good as leading an ox
to the trough. To do so would present the agent with a stark violation of the
law requiring that each citizen register nightly sleeping arrangements with local Peace and Development Council authorities, a readymade technicality for
instant arrest.

As for other acquaintances, the kind who might with the briefest exchange have let him hide inside their homes until his tracker lost momentum,
of those he had plenty. Iconic or unsung, they were scattered throughout the
city's sprawl. Tentacles of friendship crisscrossed the country to some he had
first contacted through trusted friends, or trusted friends of trusted friends,

people he had never yet met in the flesh and knew only as "Brilliant.nation@," "wewill_win2007@," "RuskinJ@," or "Williamhazlitt@." The e-mail handles and pseudonyms of his rolodex conjured dozens of utopias and a feast of obscure Victorian luminaries whose fustier tomes were among the rare tonics for the mind to still have the privilege of Burma's bookshelves.

But authorities had their networks, too. If township chiefs or local bloc officials decided on a tip or random fits of sudden bureaucratic zeal to spot-check a neighborhood for unregistered guests, Arthur, Nigel, their siblings, parents, and who knew how many casual dinner drop-ins risked two weeks each in a detention center, plus the usual hassles of extortion. On no account could he put them all in jeopardy.

Home, then. Though it was hardly a less-risky proposition.

They knew him by the hundreds, from Dala just over the river and all along the narrow canal road to Twantay. They knew him for the vocation he had chosen, that this sometime scuttling away in a chase with no obvious motive, no sense of an ending, and no measure at all of its relative gravity was part and parcel of an active political life.

If the responsibility for his actions and their consequences rested squarely on his own shoulders, he was first and foremost a native son of Twantay. Proximity to dozens of recognizable faces on whom he might call for an eleventh-hour favor might somehow, against the odds, yield a plan. It was a gamble, but a solid one: a town would protect its own, particularly if the situation in question had the rank smell of an attack by the state. That most people kowtowed most days to their most evident fears didn't mean they wouldn't rise up, come the time. On that assumption, vindicated by half a dozen protests and scores more flare-ups too tiny to even register beyond a particular block history, hinged the entire methodology of nonviolent revolutionary action.

But local authorities knew him, too. One move too brash, too sudden, across some inevitable tripwire, and dozens of informers and police up and down the food chain of local powers-that-be could step across his path.

If it came to that, he would find a way out. He always had.

This niggling sense, though, that the agent would drop away by nightfall—

Until then, at least, he could hold to his story: that he had, last October, resigned from politics, truthfully and publicly. Lies that skirted as close as possible to the truth offered the strongest alibis under duress, under the kinds of round-the-clock, four-day interrogations that would follow any trip to a detention center.

Forty minutes later, after a roundabout bus journey along roads crusted in the life of the street, corner betel-leaf stalls, fried-dough vendors, and thick crowds of men and women gliding by in their *longyis* on a gentle passage from workday to evening, he tumbled out where he would at about this time on any other night: the jetty.

It stretched out in a jut of dust and coconut trees on the far side of Strand Road, a boulevard punctuated with sporadic bursts of trishaw drivers pedaling past cracked and moldering colonial façades that had barely resisted a half-century of tropical damp and the consummate government neglect that had been Rangoon's personal tragedy. Commuters poured over the fine veins of former train tracks that functioned chiefly, at this hour, as trash receptacle for the smashed produce and offal innards left by the day's market hawkers. A makeshift television viewing station had gathered its first customers for the evening's football match. Ahead rose the boathouse, the hulking shadows of a few ferries, and, to the left, down a muddy ramp, a dozen or so skiffs.

He joined the masses in the boathouse, found a spare patch of pew, plopped down, sprang up, lit a cigarette, sucked in hard, and blew a cloud of smoke toward the window.

Beyond lay the river: as likely to carve a pathway to his freedom as a great wall cutting him off from the ease of a quick into-the-city escape. On the other bank, Dala barely twinkled, mangy and uneven, scarcely fighting back the jungle.

He didn't have to turn around to know. Watching him, pacing, working a cell phone, the agent slithered among the commuters waiting for the next ferry. Were he to follow Nway over the river, there would be no stopping him. Nway would have trouble relying on backstreets and safe houses, or anonymity in a crowd. He would have to come up with a plan.

He lit another cigarette.

It was rush hour for workers and day laborers heading back from the city. Even through his racing thoughts, through the echoing din in the boathouse, he couldn't help but pick up a conversation between two nearby young men.

"Listen, you go ahead and have a drink and wait for me. I'm going to meet my girlfriend. Then I'll come back."

"No, no, no. Don't cheat me. What if you don't come back? I'll have a problem. I'll go with you to your girlfriend."

"No, you can't! Just wait for me in Dala."

"I don't believe you. What if you don't come back?"

"I promise you! I'll come back, but first I have to go meet my girlfriend."

"Yeah, and I'll join you."

"You can't! Just wait!"

The beauty of it was that Nway recognized them. They were just familiar enough that they might have nodded in greeting if they passed each other in downtown Rangoon.

"Hey, what's going on?" he stepped in.

The first had declared the day his birthday and wanted his friend to buy him a celebratory beer at one of the makeshift dens under tarpaulins that passed for a bar in the rat-hole transience of Dala. The second—it wasn't entirely clear. It seemed he had a girlfriend and the prospect of visiting her first would lure him away—briefly only, he insisted—from the other young man who insisted on a companion, or someone to pay for his liquor, or at any rate who had about as much faith that the first fellow would return from his lovers' tryst as he might of a spirit lord, a *nat*, landing at that moment on his head.

"So," Nway offered, "how about I sit and have a drink with you, my friend, and we wait together until you come back from your girlfriend?"

When it suited, Nway had the ability to charm on sight. But it was a deceptive asset, as likely to induce charges from less impressionable acquaintances, and Nigel among them, of "manipulation." More helpful now was Nway's veneer of steadfastness, premised at minimum on the vague knowledge that his new companions might have that he was a scion of Twantay town's nurse, and afforded the luxury of a half-decent education. It meant he was a rough-and-tumble sort who knew how to have a good time but was not about to run off with your satchel's worth. You only had to glance at him to ascertain that he wasn't the town bum, and nobody's fool: a renegade in a rich delinquent's guise, with canvas pants and a T-shirt advertising a rock band that flew in the face of the preferred tradition of the *longyi* and a pressed shirt.

"Now we have a solution. So go on, be at peace, go find your girlfriend," he said, with the patrician ease of those more accustomed to giving than taking direction.

They might even know him for the activist he was, which meant he would be cast, depending on their sympathies, as somewhere between brave and crackpot. But if he could devote himself to the crazed struggle that most were too wary to touch, he could probably be depended on for an hour or two to man his post at a drinking station.

And just like that, with another of the small gestures that had become the foundation of his emerging and largely improvisational philosophy of politics-in-action, he bought himself some time. Authorities would never think to arrest him in a busy beer den. It was one of the stranger perversions within the larger perversions of the system that there seemed something almost unseemly about arresting an ordinary citizen in the midst of a crowd. Agents preferred discretion: the tempered knock on the door, the sharp tap on the shoulder.

Come with us, they'd say. *We have a few questions. Just a few. It won't be long.*
Most often they chose the night.

The problem Nway faced now was whether to abandon Rangoon's vast urban embrace and instead pit his dependence on hometown loyalties against the zealotry of small-town satraps. It had always been easier to control the towns and villages. Their self-importance had a way of upping their game.

But escape was turning out to require conspirators. Like intuition, it was primed on preparation: on experience and knowledge accumulated and rarified into a lightning bolt of pure sense, freed from the tick-tock of conscious reasoning. Nway's capacity for escape, rather like his intuition, had been a lifetime rarifying. He didn't know it, but when his time had come and the terror had seized him, and he fled the Office, leapt aboard that first departing bus, and then another and then a third, then melted into the crowds beside the jetty and waited, muscles primed, watching out of his peripheral vision for every move from the man on his tail—at that point Nway's sense of how he might vanish took form not as premeditated strategy but on happenstance that was actually nothing of the kind.

⚜

SO IT WAS THAT NWAY ENDED UP in a bar in Dala drinking one beer after the next with a casual acquaintance who, in another feat of inspiration meeting opportunity, turned into a second, and then a fourth, and then an entire table full of casual acquaintances who rallied less for the pit-stop drink than a unique occasion to out-sit the state.

The way it worked out was this:

Most nights, as he crossed the great yellow-brown span of the river and watched the toothy roofscape of Rangoon recede into a splotch that he could cover with his thumb, Nway would allow himself to dream. His country, the vast contradiction of his nation, had long thrived as a democracy; Aung San Suu Kyi, the Lady, Auntie, had never faced house arrest; and he was a businessman returning home to Twantay after a hard day's meetings in the city.

For a moment, as the skiff would skip across the ripples or bump over the wake of a cargo vessel heavy with logs or rice, he allowed himself to pretend he was not a politician. For a moment, he too, like his country, like Auntie, was free: free not in the mental realm, not, that is, with a meditator's enlightened detachment from the vicissitudes of thought and emotion, but free in the sense of a young man unburdened by an impossible cause. For a moment, carried there on the ripples of a river that emptied into the Gulf of Martaban then the Andaman Sea, then the Indian Ocean and the world beyond, he could float away, drift almost, untethered from the weight of it all.

The dream every night died stillborn in the mud of the riverbank at Dala. He left it like his cigarette butts, without another thought, in the hull of the flaking skiff that he had hired minutes before for a balled-up five-hundred *kyat* on the Rangoon jetty. The commute was scarcely long enough besides, even if he had ever thought to indulge the details of the fantasy: whom he worked for, the nature of his business, the texture of the modern opulence that might await him in Twantay instead of the impoverished reality. Didn't think of it again until perhaps the next evening rolled around and he had spent another day in his Open University classes at the British Embassy's cultural wing, with its air conditioning, its functional if scarcely continuous lighting, and plumbing that meant water not in troughs and wells, but out of faucets.

Tonight, however, there had been no dreaming, just as there had been no skiff. Against all the odds, the shaky certainty that he was nothing, a mosquito, an anonymous message boy, the agent would not cease and desist. Tonight, together with the young man who wanted a drink to celebrate his birthday, Nway boarded the ferry. He hated the ferry normally, hadn't the temperament for the slow shuffle over the gangway, the advance to the boat and off again on the other bank, behind women easing their way forward arm-in-arm, bags of textiles on their heads, men with jerry-cans, with boxes of Mandalay Rum, with everyone advancing at the lackadaisical, unruffled rhythm of lives that, for all the impermanence of everything, the cycle of *samsara*, promised interminable constancy until their very ends. Not when he could leap down from the gangway, skip among the mud and rocks where the skiffs washed up, fly up the stairs two or three at a time and alight in front of all of them, the first to hire a motorcycle-taxi from the waiting throng.

But patience tonight might prove the surest path to freedom.

Time, in fact, had always been the one element on which the democracy movement could gainfully depend. Dissent, unlike the military, barred none from entry, without prejudice to creed, skin color, or ethnic appurtenance. Most tiptoed to the threshold, or slipped over accidentally, tripping into politics from fractionally small disagreements with whatever ruling grated against the natural flow of their daily lives. A regime became its own worst enemy without ideology, without legitimacy, with prohibitions and small rules that politicized every aspect of society—permeating art, permeating agriculture and commerce, permeating the Buddhist monkhood that remained, for about eighty-nine percent of the population, the country's spiritual backbone. Thought itself, contaminated with censorship and self-censorship, mistrust and chronic fear, became a battleground. Each disagreement, however microscopic, became an act of resistance.

He headed toward a table in a den just over the unpaved parking lot, and ordered a first round. Limbs sprawled over a chair, his new friend declared himself thoroughly content.

"Actually, you might want to go home," Nway told him.

"What? Why?"

"You see that guy? He's Special Branch."

"What?"

"I'm being watched."

The friend blanched. The beer landed. He didn't drink. He didn't speak.

"Listen," Nway said, "don't worry. I'll take my responsibility."

Go, his eyes said. *I understand.*

The young man sat silent. At any moment, he could up and leave, innocent to any charge of complicity.

"Nway," he said at last. "You should have told me in advance."

He should have, it was true. But the moment for remorse had passed. The agent must have called his colleagues. Nway could pick out three, perhaps even four, hovering outside. One of them looked like he was scouting for a table in the drinking den.

"Hey," Nway said. "I have an idea. Let's make a joke."

It might have arisen from a native impishness. It might just as well have been inspired by wiser, well-loved folk—from Auntie, for starters, whose almost anthropological ability to see the absurdity of the system lent itself to a perpetual public gaiety, including fits of laughter that were often contagious.

There had also been the man who had wanted to give Nway the entire world. Nway tried not to think of him too often because some years before the man had disappeared and to recall him was to revive the entirety of the loss, the full measure of his family's buried anguish. But Nway often conjured the man with his jokes. He could have made a joke of every last, severed limb. When Nway shared them, if he shared them, he credited them sometimes to a fictive uncle. And both Auntie and the man who was not his fictive uncle, the twin pillars of influence, shared an infectious talent for pricking with humor the uncertain moment, the episodes of highest dread. On their wit, on the satire and dark quips of a pantheon of other heroes personal or national, Nway had watched the fear and bone-deep sadness deflate all round like a child's carnival balloon.

"Now we are under watch," Nway said. "Let's call every friend we can."

The young man smiled. Fun indeed, if a touch sadistic, to observe the selfsame shock explode with the force of a Water Festival projectile on each fresh bystander they managed to net. It wouldn't even be particularly difficult. From their perch on the rock-and-dust parking lot beside the jetty, a riverside slum's rough equivalent of a central piazza, they could pick out about as many casual acquaintants heading back to Twantay through Dala as dirt-smeared urchins returning from a day hawking sandalwood trinkets in the city.

"Hey!" they called out to the first pair they recognized ambling past. "Hi there!"

"How's it going?" one of them answered, waving, barely pausing. "We're going back!" It was the typical small talk of the wayfarer. Except:

"No, stay! Have a beer."

"You sure?"

"Yes! Join us!"

In they came, a couple of young commuters warding off nothing more pressing than the prospect of a possibly over-stewed curry, the endless twitter of the neighborhood gossips washing at the well, and the forty-minute bump to get there along the bad road back in the dead heat of the final days of summer.

"Before you sit—I have to tell you—we are under watch."

"What?

"Oh my god!"

They hovered momentarily, and sat. Once in on the joke, they joined the first two in netting another pair. And then, now six Twantay-bound young men—always men; the reputations of unmarried female friends could be felled in a single beer-den sighting—they caught a few more. Each time the warning from Nway landed as fannies dipped toward chairs. Each time, they did a double-take, froze in mid-descent, hopped back up, shouted an expletive, some passing expression of shock and horror. And each time, without fail, they sat. Building a fort around Nway. Impregnable. Fraternal. A collective thumbing of the nose at Special Branch police.

It warmed his heart, this show of solidarity. He didn't need to express it. He couldn't, had he even tried. One day, perhaps, they might all sit around with a bottle of whiskey under the mango tree near the clock tower in the center of Twantay and hand-wave the entire incident as so much shared nonsense. One day, when the struggle was over. One day, when he had returned to finish his medical degree, opened a rural clinical practice, and settled down with a pretty girl and a life of laughter and fresh crab curries perpetually bubbling over the charcoals. *One day*. The idea of it stabbed him with nostalgia for a future he knew more with every passing day could never be.

Arrest, for starters, was inevitable. He had skimmed past too often, with one too many turns of fortune's wheel that had felled so many friends and worthier comrades. The worst period had come early in his political life, a time of resurgent party activity with fresh attempts to rebuild the decimated ranks. Auntie would flit impromptu to each new local youth chapter in a constant cat-and-mouse with the spies who tailed her car. Arrests had come so frequently, with such relentless predictability after the opening ceremony for each chapter, that Nway began to conflate them with breakfast. "That is what we have for breakfast. That is our breakfast," he would say years later, because every morning, instead of a bowl of noodles soaking in fish stew from the corner teashop they would fill a thermos with strong green tea, turn on their shortwave radios, and tune in to the Burmese services of the BBC, or Voice of America, or Radio Free Asia, dependent on an exile in a faraway land for news from down the block. It was the surest way to hear the catalogue of yesterday's disappearances. And every morning, the catalogue included another recruit to a youth chapter, from their network, in their very neighborhood—gone in the night.

But not now. Not yet. There was simply too much to do.

"You know," he said, asked once to recall the most important moment of his political life, "for our struggle, every time is important. We must try for it in every second. The most important time is right now."

As for his young allies, they seemed every bit committed. Each one relaxed into his role, hamming up the noise and rowdiness, enjoying the ensemble performance.

At last came the straggler from the boathouse who had lingered in Rangoon to visit his girlfriend.

"Hey! I can't pay for all these people," he said.

"Don't worry, I'll get it," Nway offered, grinning. "Join us."

The young man duly pulled over a chair and squeezed into the party.

Nway watched him closely. There was twitchiness to him; when they dropped the bomb of their predicament on him, he'd jump ten feet in the air.

"You weren't really seeing your girlfriend, were you?" Nway leaned in, brow furrowed. "Come on. Where were you?"

The pranks, the jokes, the relaxed, childish antics into which Nway defaulted skidded always atop a state of nicotine-excited vigilance. A tremor half a block away, and he would jolt into dead seriousness. It was another legacy of authoritarianism, of a lifetime watching people he cared about all around disappear, that his muscles, his sense of self, were somehow always taut, tensed feline-like to spring. Something of that shift in him now was enough to uncork his acquaintance.

Out spilled the confession.

He hadn't been to see his girlfriend, the straggler said. There was no girlfriend. But there had been a marijuana dealer.

"Throw it away," Nway said. "Right now. Go. Go to the jetty and throw it in the river."

"No way!" It was good stuff, the young man challenged. Hard to come by. 'Specially in these parts. Very expensive; weeks'-worth of work for the purchase.

"Yes, but—that man over there. You see him? And that one? Do you want seven years too?"

The young man leapt up. Swore into the damp heat. Spun about, cursed, and cried. He spat onto the earth, a final, forlorn gesture of half-wit dignity, and shot out across the parking lot toward the black blur of the river. Laughter from the tarpaulin-tented beer den trailed behind him and shattered, like glass.

Darkness had fallen. The day's last ferry had returned to the other shore, creaking and hulking in a block of shadow at the foot of the city. Rangoon glowed now with the aura of a metropolis half-lit, half denied the light, resisting ever its own fearsome, inward-turned decay. It was as far removed from the modernity of Bangkok, a single hour's flight away, as a blot of ink from a blaze of blinding white. But it had once been great, and once the capital, and even now it burgeoned outward, a living palimpsest of the old and the less old. The generals could embalm national progress, abandon the country's metropolitan heart, tear up its history and try from scratch 250 miles north. With Naypyidaw, the new administrative capital since 2005 in the sterile central scrublands, they had built a clean vision of the future designed by their cronies and Chinese contractors, with mirror-windowed mansions, empty eight-lane highways and a ferocious soulnessness that seemed to prevent street life, human interaction, societal evolution at all.

But Rangoon, even forsaken, could never die.

Gazing at it from Dala, besides, the city seemed modernity incarnate. How easy to lose a man between its thickets of grand boulevards and twisting side alleys, the narrow back roads and alleyways lined in rotting stone-carved houses all hung with laundry; the dusty street-side refuges for the plastic-recyclers; the penny-a-copy photocopy suites tucked under tarpaulin. The sidewalks perpetually teemed with life, as if someone had turned the city inside out, by day with hawkers and peddlers staking out tiny patches, and by night with teashops and restaurants and people eking out a gust of air.

How easy in that organic chaos to spark some action, among hundreds of skinny locals chatting at makeshift corner teashops over their morning *mohingya* fish noodle soup or their evening teapot whiskey; or among the market throngs coming for their daily purchases from women whisking the flies off their offerings, their offal and gnarly vegetables, beside wooden warehouses eternally collapsing in a miasma of rotten smells.

How easy to fan them all into a collective combustion, a riotous repeat of the half-dozen street protests that across successive generations had failed and failed again to sink the regime.

But failure, Nway knew, was a relative measure.

꿍

AN OUTSIDER HAS THE ADVANTAGE HERE. Close observation over time, the sorting through of scenes from another person's life, the situation of that life within a wider movement and a larger time—together they yield themes of epic struggle that echo across the gulf of history and culture, back to Masada, into the French Maquis, and forward to the stones of Tahrir Square. *Courage, destiny*: big words that weigh too heavily, perhaps, on the back of a fragile and too-mortal frame. Yet out of the amorphous masses, we find our heroes, picking them from a field of dead, scattering the old bones into dust but letting one, the unknown, the not-yet-fallen soldier, rise and hover as a symbol, the better angel of our nature, reminding us that when you hit us, we will answer. In the scarred silences of curfew, under leaden skies of dictatorial new dawns, someone will steal out like a rat and disappear to fight. Someone—not you, not me, but him, that simple boy, no more unique, perhaps, than any of the rest—he'll hear the call. Rest easy then. Duck your chin into your chest and sell your wares unquestioning in the early morning markets. Pack your daughter's tiffin box with curry, fuel your battered car with rations.

Know that someone, however ordinary, carries with him all your hope.

2

NIGEL

JUNE 26, 2009, 8 P.M.

COME WITH US, they said. *We have a few questions. Just a few. It won't be long.*

They hadn't handcuffed or hooded him. That was a first. Neither him nor Kyaw Kyaw, sitting beside him, head hanging between his knees.

They had folded the pair into a car that was nondescript, typically beaten up, typically two decades old, typical in every way except for the lack of a license plate. In any case, it was night. Of course they would have waited until night. Rangoon at night was a world of shadows and intermittent visibility, harsh shapes carved from the halogens, sporadic stabs of halogens into the thick damp and nothing between but darkness, stray dogs, the sense of some spellbound quiescence.

He would have preferred to sign out of his Gmail account. He would have preferred to know he had killed the connection, that he had not just laid bare his plans, his politics, the full span of his contacts. He never said much in his emails. No one did. Exchanges were curt, transactional. But anyone suspicious could trawl for meaning. There were arrangements for meetings, suggestions of ideas, photos of half-built schools. There was *hi, I miss you* to blind-copied recipients with an attachment, refill.doc, that would turn out to be a press release. They might even have prior information on the identities of one or two of his inter-locutors. Of all his email handles, of all the decoys, thebrightnation@, left open on a monitor in an Internet café, had been his most sensitive.

So be it. Sometimes you just had to accept that it was going to be either the rock or the hard place. Far better that they take him away before they noticed the cloth bag tucked behind the computer at his feet. There was enough in there, more than enough, to land him seven, fifteen years—ah, who knew?

He was a dead man now, in any case. The thought hit him in the police car. It amazed him that he felt so certain: that he was dead, that he had nothing more to lose. They could do what they liked now. He relaxed a bit at the thought. It gave him a sense of freedom. Emancipation from fear: that was good. It would be helpful. It would keep him strong.

Self-awareness often surged in Nigel in just this way, flashes of insight in moments of acute necessity that taught him who he was, why he was there, what was to be his purpose. They came without premeditation, without prior claim to personal doctrine, or deep reflection, or a preternatural sense of a vocation that he had only really discovered by stumbling into it.

He lived, in that sense, in the present, just doing what he had to do. There was a karmic perfection therein, a sense that right action led to right consequence with no need to look backward. It meant he could be tranquil. That tranquility rested in turn on a bedrock of self-worth, which meant clarity about what felt right and what felt wrong, and the rarified sense that he was strong enough to act accordingly. Why that was exactly, he had never thought to question. All he knew was that he knew enough to teach everyone else.

"I never manipulate people," Nigel would say. "I just do what I say. I just say what I do. Like that. Among my friends. That's why they believe me. And our trust is stronger."

In retrospect, they must have been trailing him since the English class he had taught at the Office that morning. Afterward, he had taken the long bus ride back to check on his wife in their lean-to in Dawbon, a squatter-dense township just over Pazundaung Creek whose relative disregard for street-side sanitation bore all the markings of its origins as the city's former dumping grounds. Down an alley rimmed in stagnant water that couldn't entirely drown out the tropic weeds, Nigel and his wife lived as they always had, from one meal to the next, and they'd never much wanted for more than their shared dreams. But you couldn't eat dreams and you couldn't pay a doctor with them. Khine Sandar Win had been due for an appointment that day. Seven months pregnant now, and she was only getting thinner. She had always been lean, even at that first blinding glimpse of her as an apparition of flawless womanhood, sculpted into a silk *htamein*. But this latest whittling away was troubling, and he simply hadn't managed to dredge up enough for her checkup. For an instant, he'd had to admit that there might have been something in all those efforts to dissuade him from the marriage. Even on a good day, he couldn't fulfill the most basic duty that society required of a husband.

She didn't need consolation; wouldn't even want it. Her particular mettle was a lesson for many a brawnier man. The way she saw it, she had let him get her pregnant and for the offense, however blessed, he would have to shoulder twice the load to act on behalf of both of them. If she'd had his skills, the brief learning he'd acquired, she might have taught, too. Short of that, her contribution to the struggle required a different sort of engagement, but not the kind that her current condition permitted. Nor was their situation about to change soon. With her mother already at the market from first light, and Nigel's mother full with her own load between the Office and a slum at the other end of the city, it'd only be more difficult for Khine Sandar Win to find work with a newborn.

He had headed out at about 2:30 p.m. with a kiss, an empty stomach, and a determination to return with what money he could borrow from friends for the doctor, plus enough for food supplies to last them through the weekend. With the right ingredients, Khine Sandar Win made some mean fish cakes. Meantime, she needed all the meat and oil in what thin curry they had left. Nigel had long since grown accustomed to skipping breakfast and lunch without it much affecting the athletic sturdiness that set him apart from the matchstick figures all around.

But asking his students for money was another matter. As a rule, he rarely taught for pay. The whole point was to bypass an education system that sold its degrees and "cascade" whatever he'd learned back at the very people who needed it most—poor folk, people from the slums, boys and girls of the grassroots with as much aptitude and passion as anyone else, but without the language and context to give shape to their raw moral intuition. It was never hard to lure a quorum. He was effortlessly popular, to the point of luring the nephew of a local ward authority from the Union Solidarity and Development Association who had quietly expressed to his father how impressed he'd been with Nigel's leadership at a particularly hairy standoff between hundreds of protesting monks and security forces at the Shwedagon Pagoda. That was on September 26, 2007, the beginning of the crackdown on the Saffron uprising, and the USDA official had let slip that they were coming for Nigel next. That day, army troops and riot police began clubbing and tear-gassing protesters, raiding monasteries, and arresting monks and civilian suspects by the truckload. Nigel, thanks to the warning, made it out of the city minutes before the cars rolled up for him in his family's ward. It had been a humbling reminder that people's choices on either side of the state-civilian divide would always defy easy judgment.

His students came for the language practice. They stayed for the ideas— thoughts and provocations, subtle or frankly less so, on the real conditions of the country that he incorporated into exercises on vocabulary and grammar, along with small nudges to take all that onboard and begin, with it, to think. The best, the most open, responded as if they had been set aglow. From the ready talkers, you could always guess the sons and daughters of activists or like-minded folk who might have tasted open discussion at home. The rest didn't have to speak up much. He saw enough in a smile, a sudden widening of the eyes. Not everyone could forge overnight a confidence that flew in the face of an education system that taught only by rote, and of parents who, as a rule of thumb, thought it best to keep their children incurious. Timidity, besides, had its advantages. That regular at the corner table with the darting eyes and a stiffness that suggested he'd swallowed an umbrella might turn out to be an informer. He might, just as probably, be suffering a bad case of constipation.

But mistrust had the viral obstinacy of wild bamboo, impossible to cut back before it had sprouted elsewhere. Few could make it into their teen years without acquiring the skittishness of stalked prey. Part of the challenge was helping them find the sweet spot between paranoia and healthy self-protection.

Nigel was scarcely better educated and the quickest to admit that his fluency in English was, at most, a few pages of the *Oxford Learner's Dictionary* ahead of the next private tuition teacher. His schooling, until he had ventured beyond and seen how much he didn't know, had largely involved trying to make sense of the patterns and habits contained among North Okklappa's trash-strewn ditches and avenues of besieging poverty yielding into dump. A northern township populated by trishaw drivers and market hawkers, it had barely budged from the incipient state of general destitution in which the Military Caretaker Government of 1958 had wrested it into existence, forcibly relocating 74,647 people from a population of about twice that number who had been squatting in downtown Rangoon.

Born and raised in North Okkla until he married and moved to the southern township of Dawbon, Nigel had drawn from it, for all its puniness, a depth of field that would serve him well. He was a child of the urban slums, and he would never forget it, not into the months and years when, as now, he could count himself among the privileged. An NLD scholar at the British Council, the British Embassy's cultural wing, he had been a rare recipient of the kind of education that had allowed him to better diagnose and articulate his latent malaise. He could connect the daily injustices in his community and the lost promise of the post-independence parliamentary era to the language of universal human rights and to other countries' parallel struggles for freedom. It was the stuff of elder politicians' speeches, and of Auntie's. The more he had listened and learned, the more he knew there was to learn about the world. But everything would always come back to North Okkla, a microcosm of all that afflicted the human condition, everything in his country that was stalled and stuck.

His talent, he had discovered, was inspiration. He taught from personal example, with the casual warmth of a returning older brother who had briefly had the privilege of viewing the world from a higher perch. If he allowed in his classes a modicum of the deference traditionally accorded to the *saya*, the teacher, he also encouraged talking back, aiming for a rough-hewn classroom cacophony that would inculcate in his students nothing less substantial than the foundational idea of participatory democracy.

After his class, he had swallowed his misgivings and joined some of his students and a few friends for a drink, along with Kyaw Kyaw and his younger brother. Those two weren't rich, but they had jobs, if not the kind to talk about aloud. They'd be able to spare the money. He would pay them back. He didn't know how or when. It was enough that they knew him for his honesty. A plate of fried corn had landed, he had attacked it with unapologetic gusto and the whole table had drowned the day in tall tales and a round or three of cool Myanmar Beer. He'd scarcely registered whether the agents lingered. The tactic was just common enough that he had learned to concede to their presence much as he might to the repeat attack of a fly on his curry. Because: to wait all day for arrest—through morning, through the afternoon, and into evening—was to surrender. It was to let in the seep of poison, the belief that you could do nothing that was wholesome and true and important for your community. It was to throw up your hands in despair and give up, give in. For Nigel, relinquishing personal agency was as unnatural as tyranny.

Kyaw Kyaw and Nigel left the table early to head back to work, which meant to an Internet café. They settled in for the long slog of the dial-up, the power cuts, the zigzag around pages marked with a red bar, with ACCESS HAS BEEN DENIED, through proxy software that bounced their searches out of Dubai via Sydney, or perhaps tonight, depending on which of the proxies hadn't yet been hacked and shut, from Singapore via Malaysia. It was as good a time as any to catch a few winks, lulled by the heat trapped and vibrating between computers patched together from rejects that had slipped in from India, or China, or one or other member state of the Association of Southeast Asian Nations, ASEAN, whose businesses had found endless creative opportunities under the regional body's policy of "constructive engagement" with a government that the West had chosen to shun.

An hour passed, his cryptic email had slogged it through the HTML linkup before another blackout, and it was time to wrap up. Dawbon was far. He had to catch the last bus back or face the usual risks of an unregistered overnight stay. Kyaw Kyaw's brother wouldn't hesitate to offer shelter. Their friendship was intimate enough. But now that he had a handful of cash—

Then someone had tapped him sharply on the shoulder.

"Come with us," said the Special Branch agent. "We have a few questions."

There were two of them. Nigel recognized them instantly from the hut just over the road from the Office. They wanted Kyaw Kyaw too, sitting rapt at a nearby monitor.

Nigel didn't ask why they were arresting them. He didn't express surprise. He didn't resist. Resistance, in any case, was futile. If they wanted you, they came for you. What happened next was formulaic, a variation on a theme of four days. To be precise, it would be more in the vein of an endless day, seamless as a *longyi*; a day without sun, without moon, without sleep, without water, food, ability to lie flat, ability to do anything except take the beatings, the insults, hold the "airplane," the "motorcycle," perform the "*semigwa*" dance with its fine flicks of hip and wrist meant for the practiced body of a woman; whichever contortion or posture they chose from their catalogue of national favorites; and when you couldn't anymore, when your muscles gave out or your mind started to slip; when you'd soiled yourself, or the thirst had you begging for the outhouse so you could claw liquid from the urinal; when the threats began to land against your mother, your sick father, all your loved ones, and you couldn't tell anymore if you'd deviated even a hair from the script you'd stuck to that you might shield yourself against the machine-gun cycle of questions— then all that was left was to sell out, confess, name names.

He knew the routine.

The parade of punishments and degradations under interrogation had a multigenerational quality by now, passed from activist to activist, intelligence unit to intelligence unit. Didn't matter that, back in 2004, No. 1 had purged No. 3;

that down with him came crashing the entire military intelligence apparatus; and that all its surveillance functions had frittered apart into a half-dozen lesser departments that had supposedly never entirely recovered their vim. Didn't matter that the West had hit the country with wave upon wave of sanctions, squeezing ever harder at the junta's thinly veiled yearning for international legitimacy. Didn't matter that famous foreign nonprofits issued torture report after torture report. The International Committee of the Red Cross had come and gone. Political prisoners could read in their cells now. But the old interrogation styles had a way of sticking.

Three more SB agents waited in the car. He braced for them to return to the café. He had expected them to poke around their chairs, traffic with their monitors, at least order the café manager to hand over the data from their computers. With half a minute more, he might have kicked the cloth handle of his bag deeper under the desk, and cleared his search history, double-checked that he'd left no footprint, booted down. At least he couldn't reproach himself that last failing. Agents didn't do waiting. And the connection had been too slow. As if that wasn't handicapped enough by the cheap wiring, the indiscriminate failures of the power grid, the indifferent gnawing of a climate meant less for modern urban development than the putrefying circadian rhythms of primordial rainforest, it didn't take a genius to note the link between days-long Internet slowdowns and instances of suspected anti-government activity.

Sometimes they blacked out entire districts for no purpose more fathomable than the hell of it. You could see the value in it, though: quick and dirty, and limiting the need to train sufficient cyber spies to keep abreast of demand. It was never entirely clear how they were watching. Best merely to assume that somehow they were. There were so many ways. Every Internet café theoretically had a kit of mandatory surveillance devices. In the early days there had been keyboards that were said to record passwords; screenshots that flashed across desktops every five minutes; monitors positioned for easy over-the-shoulder viewing; and spy software to intercept transmitted data. Lately, the Directorate of Communication required monthly submissions of users' records, including date, time, screenshots, and a history of all URLs. The directives from the Ministry of Post and Telecommunication had shape-shifted and focused with the evolution of Internet penetration but their gist held: follow the rules, whatever they currently be, or face loss of license and punishment "according to the existing laws." Patrons, for their part, were duly warned with an old standby, a piece of copy paper stuck fading and limp on the wall of every café, perhaps under a box of fraying wires held together with a chopstick, reminding them that use of the Internet for political purposes was strictly forbidden. Nigel didn't like to put a manager at risk, but someone was always going to be on the wrong side of the law. At least he could claim the merit of his cause.

Poverty, as it had often been in his life, proved a wily ally. Access to either of the two state-controlled Internet service providers was kept so deliberately prohibitive that the vast majority of Internet users relied not on private accounts but instead on the cafés. The fee per hour was a relative pittance, though at two hundred *kyat*, or about thirty cents, it was still too much for the average slum kid. He could teach the basics of the Internet to whomever he wanted, help them pierce the information blockade or find dozens of new ways to counter the prohibitions on communication, but even his siblings couldn't afford the price of entry. No one except a few Western techno-utopians deluded themselves that the Web would ever be the vehicle for grassroots mobilization. Thus far, a country of bamboo-and-thatch huts with anywhere from fifty-four to sixty million people could claim about three hundred thousand sometime users. Which didn't mean for a second that the Internet hadn't opened a new front to be exploited to the full.

Meantime, it offered a rare growth industry. Surging business in the past few years created its own problems for officialdom. Bureaucratic disobedience tended to come of a piece with the sort of tech-savvy, entrepreneurial type who would be drawn to opening an Internet café. To eke out a profit meant he or she would have to offer patrons a proxy to bypass the censors. It was the only way to reach Gmail, or Gtalk, or any of the free search engines. Since the numbers of Internet cafés in the cities had exploded, compliance had proved increasingly tricky to monitor. And so the spy services had of late resorted to simply delivering lists of suspect clients.

It was just possible that Nigel had been among them.

He was careful to pick his cafés according to the general proclivities of their managers. This neighborhood had been less familiar to him, and he'd trusted Kyaw Kyaw with the choice. But it was always a gamble. Sometimes you just had to shrug and let it go. There would always be informers among them, always the mysterious bomb attack somewhere in the country and the attendant roundup of convenient suspects. If you looked too hard for every trap, you'd suffer paralysis. Besides, to that last drill—an explosion at a USDA office in June 2008 that had within weeks triggered a brief exodus of activists from

Rangoon—he owed the miracle of three days' privacy in a guesthouse with the infatuation who subsequently became his wife.

Nway would probably have known where to go. It was foul that they had recently fallen out. He had a nose for sniffing apart the sympathetic from the purely mercenary, a particular affinity for cultivating friendships among the richer folk in the city. That was part of what had grated, and part of what made Nway such a creative complement. Nigel had the more common touch. Nway, to Nigel, was the consummate businessman, always hoarding the gadgets, the fanciest cell phone, a sudden flourishing of blocks of cash with the offhand insouciance of someone who'd never been lacking it but knew too well how easily it purchased obeisance.

And because of it, or perceptions of such, the pair hadn't talked in weeks. It was something they couldn't or hadn't really hashed out openly—a longstanding friction of character and methods that a clandestine trip to Mae Sot, Thailand, four months earlier, had thrown into stark relief.

The last time they'd seen each other, Nigel had gone out of his way to invite Nway and two other young activists to meet with an American reporter. He'd picked a vast, empty restaurant on Kandawgyi Lake where the only sounds were the cawing of crows, and the rain, lobbing grenades at the tranquil green expanse. Even the waiters seemed too lethargic to bother eavesdropping. Nway had predictably blown in forty minutes late, predictably taken calls every few minutes to his cell phone, and predictably still managed to usurp the conversation with pithy answers to every question, before finally walking out with the reporter. Nigel and the others said nothing and simply vanished, as much from natural self-effacement as intentional secrecy.

But if the Dogs had walked in on him too, even Nway in all his cunning wouldn't have had time to shut down his computer connection. He always had five Gchat conversations going at once, as many pseudonyms, and Gmail accounts to such a number that he'd forgotten half their usernames. Undoubtedly he'd have had the genius, though, to reach down and just yank the plug. Which, come to think of it, is exactly what Nigel should have done.

And yet, the agents never bothered to linger in the Internet café. It meant they were half-hearted, or not particularly well briefed, or that they were low enough in rank and education that they had as little clue about the many uses of the Internet as the average street bum. It could mean several things, but most of all it meant they didn't have much on him.

Nor, apparently, on Kyaw Kyaw, which was surprising. Nigel would have assumed this was Kyaw Kyaw's crime: some slip-up, some trail of grains to his job as an underground reporter for the Democratic Voice of Burma. Someone else under duress could have talked. DVB reporters these days had it almost worse than politicians, with their equipment needs and mass data transmissions.

And there had been so much to record, so many events to upload and blast out of the country: the uprising of 2007, of course—whatever they could do to position their handhelds to catch the monks chanting in a great, saffron-robed hemorrhage down the streets or squatting in prayer in front of the barricades, and the soldiers with pointed rifles—and then the violence that had snuffed it all out. Barely eight months later, there had been the lethal devastation from Tropical Cyclone Nargis and, within days, the referendum on a new constitution. And there had been all the anniversaries and abuses small and vast to document since.

Kway Kway had been working on something, some footage that lured him out of the city for days at a time. He carried a camera. He had too much money. To his chest he might as well have pinned a sign that read *suspicious package*.

The police car bumped forward.

Nigel didn't know where they were going. He didn't know why. His body tensed. His heart was beating too loud. No one said a word. In the silence, he ran through what he would say. What to hold back.

What did Kyaw Kyaw know? Less than his brother. The contents of Nigel's email. Yes. Minutes earlier, they had shared a computer monitor. They were sending a joint note to a DVB editor. And Kyaw Kyaw knew something about—

No. No sense in dwelling on that.

The car pitched.

If only he could catch his friend's eye. If he could just exchange a gesture of solidarity.

Suddenly he felt that snowfall of calm, that sense of his own death. Something unknotted in his stomach.

He wondered. It wasn't that he felt no more responsibility. He felt it toward his students. He felt it toward his country. He felt it down to his bones. He felt it sharpest of all toward his wife, his tough-as-ox-hide, scrappy warrior of a wife.

She'd know soon enough. The rounds of phone calls would signal the suspicion within minutes. Kway Kway wouldn't pick up, so someone would call Thu Rein, his brother. Thu Rein would say: *No, no. Kway Kway's not back from the café*. Another call minutes later, checking in on Nigel, would register the same.

It would trigger the round robin until midnight or later, depending on the relative degree of that night's risk, in an improvised buddy system, unofficial and limited to circles of activist friends. Where contacts overlapped, word spread fast, faster, if they were alert enough, than the next hit by the Dogs on one or other of their houses.

Then it was a race against the formula: four days for all of them to disperse, which was about the time the Dogs factored to break an average catch. No one wanted to think about it, preparing mentally for interrogation. But no one, not even the toughest, could predict whether or not he'd snap.

Another pothole. He recoiled. It was an automatic reflex. Not his mind. *Not his mind.*

Only a week earlier, a rumor had trickled through the cell phone circular that Nigel had been arrested on his commute back. He hadn't given it much thought. Now it struck him as sinister—a plant from a possible informer in their midst to check what he would do, whom he would see, and where he might go next.

The dark shapes of the city blended into a blur outside the car window.

However this arrest had come about, on a charge fictive or real, he had somehow, through some turn of events, brought it upon himself. To him fell the responsibility for his choices. On him fell the physical penalty. No matter what would follow, he would not talk, or compromise another soul.

The car was swerving north, northwest. But to where? Toward Insein Prison? Some dank hole down a side-alley?

They had every prerogative to break his ribs and dispatch him for decades to some pestilential cell, too far for his wife to afford the travel for the trimonthly, quarter-hour visit. They could as easily spare themselves the trouble, just kill him, and cremate his body, to dissipate all evidence of injury. It wouldn't exactly be the first time, not for someone as insignificant. In previous months alone, three of Khine Sandar Win's friends had died in custody. They had been picked up with her during Saffron, carted to the race horse stadium that they'd turned for the occasion into a mass detention center, and two of them had died in the interrogation, just feet from where they were electrocuting her. The third, she'd heard, had been lost within weeks to a malarial forced labor camp, hacking at rocks or heaving military equipment on nothing but rotten rice, regular boot-beatings, and mouthfuls of scorching air. And come to think of it, there was that whisper, too, of Nway's father—

But to ponder all that was to pine for conditions over which Nigel no longer had any control. It was to lapse into a tangle of sentiment, into terror, despair, false hope. There was no consolation in the acceptance of his end, no pretense of an outcome that was anything but bleak. Death—self-inflicted—was the way of the vanishing self. This ego, with its delusions of an exterior life, its attachments, its needs—to be fed, to be clothed, to be loved, washed, made to feel it had some purpose—all gone. What endured was pure consciousness, the essence of being in flux between space and time, between lives, the flicker that becomes again, endlessly reshaped, born into another form, another existence, until or unless it attained the blissful release of *nibbana*.

Never had the teachings of the Buddha been more apt, more deftly articulated to cope with the bludgeoning of daily life. Nigel, at the moment of his arrest, drew from the deep learning of his land, mentally shot himself in the heart, and it rendered him—invincible.

⋙⋘

I AM A POLITICIAN. But I'm a dead man. How can he kill me? I'm a dead man. He can't kill me.

He sat bolt upright on a chair.

"What do you do for a living?"

I am not afraid. I believe what I am doing.

The room was spare. Just big enough to cram in nine.

I'm a dead man. He can't kill me.

He fixed his eyes on a single man.

"Why did you learn English?"

They didn't have anything on him. All they had were scraps.

"Why have you learned English?"

I believe what I am doing is right.

There were eight of them. Four sat in a line straight in front of him, shooting out questions. One had three stars on the shoulder of his uniform.

"What do you do for a living?"

Someone ducked behind him and hit him on the back of his head. Another slapped him across the eyes.

And so it would begin. He had to stop it now. Had to find another way.

He kept his gaze on that single man. Directed his answers only at him. He felt calm, lucid, terrifically strong. His senses seemed sharpened somehow, attuned to the creak of doors beyond the room, to the beating of wings among the flies that circled the bare bulb above.

"What do your parents do for a living?"

They didn't like his answers. They were growing impatient. Another slap.

The man whose gaze Nigel held had three stars on the shoulder of his uniform. It marked him as the ranking officer. He didn't need to hit, didn't want to touch. More power in the attitude of distance. Nigel could see it in his eyes.

"Why did you learn English? Where did you learn English?"

"Please tell them not to hit me," Nigel said to the three-star. "If they hit me I will say nothing."

There was no venom in his voice, nor any pleading. He conveyed no hint of emotion beyond the tacit respect of a man to his peer.

"If they do like that, I won't say anything. I've never done anything wrong. I am a teacher. I take the responsibility for my community on my shoulders. You know, that's not my job. That's the job of the state, of authorities. Of you."

He sensed a pause, caught an exchange of glances. They seemed—shockingly—shocked.

There must have been something exasperatingly winning in his argument. In theory, not a single one of them could deny it. The generals had always felt a need to pay lip service to democracy, which meant, in practice, servicing the people in whose name they thereby claimed to rule. At every turn since 1962, and then again since 1988, they had twisted arguments and distorted facts, reneged on promises and stolen from the land. But never had they claimed to be anything other than caretakers steering the nation toward their oft-stated goal of "discipline-flourishing democracy." Each political milestone since had been justified accordingly: the elections of 1990; the lapsing of its results in the name of convening a convention to write a new constitution; the "seven year roadmap to disciplined-democracy" that had, with no coincidence, been announced within three months of a deadly state-sponsored ambush on Auntie's convoy at Depayin in 2003; even the seizure of power itself in 1988 by the SLORC, the State Law and Order Restoration Council, so named for the purpose of supposedly stabilizing the country before returning it to parliamentary democracy. It had all been a sham, empty of meaning, contradicted in the details and the practice, and any fool could see.

But since the previous year it was possible to argue, and with some force, that if the junta wanted to be held to its words, at least enough to one day chair ASEAN, the time had never been more apt. A new constitution had been accepted in the rigged referendum of May 2008. All official talk was directed now at the elections to be held some time in 2010, the first in twenty years. The constitution would then enter into force, and along with it, a new bicameral legislature, fourteen regional parliaments, and a theoretical separation of executive, legislative, and judiciary. The junta, the SPDC, would yield in uniform, if not in actual personnel, into a de facto civilian-led administration. Or so went the plan.

Not in his most delusional fantasies, however, could Nigel presume that he was the first to throw their rhetoric back at them. Even from closed prison trials, word escaped of fiery parting thoughts, or of silences as eloquent. The Big Brothers, the 1988 student leaders, were famous for them. About half a year earlier, charged with twenty-two offenses for triggering the 2007 Saffron uprising, a handful of them had simply turned their backs on the prison judge who had finally deigned to try them after about a year each in custody. In or out of interrogation, Ko Ko Gyi, their great strategist, had a fondness for pointing out that all police stations carried a sign out front that read, "May I help you?" Grandpa—U Win Tin—had once put it best: you couldn't easily break the type drawn to this business of opposition or to the conviction that defending human dignity and freedom was somehow worth the sacrifice of a conventional life. Almost every political detainee—at least those who hadn't admitted defeat, broken outright, died, or slipped into insanity—had his or her story of defiance, a private moment of resolve that shone through the darkness of solitary, secret face-offs with the "law." Khine Sandar Win had spat her curses hours before they'd set her free from Insein Prison, entirely not giving a rat's ass if she was blowing her best chance at early amnesty for the sake of a final, futile show of righteous pissiness. No, she had cried to the prison warden on the dawn of her impending release, after he had warned her to shut her mouth thereafter about conditions inside, and shut it too about herself. For the ticket through Insein's red gate and back into the broken world beyond, she would *never* compromise nor sign any form that would force her to renounce all political work. "You can only arrest me," she had shouted. "You cannot lock my mouth. You cannot Insein my mouth."

"WHERE did you learn English?"

Nigel proceeded, repeated what he knew that they already knew.

He taught English classes, yes. He learned, he told them, and then told them again, from the private tuition classes of the renowned U Win Naing. Yes, the one who taught at Lhedan Junction. Nigel had secured his place with a scholarship. How? Because he'd studied hard for his exams.

It wasn't false, exactly. It just barely cracked the surface. He had always been so careful.

To teach was a moral responsibility, he added, invoking religious sentiment. They had no business preventing him. If people worried all day about arrest, then nothing good would come to them, nothing good to the community, nothing good to anyone. If, as they said, they wanted democracy, it meant they had to allow participation in politics. They had to allow incentives for participating. "You say you are leading the country to democracy but you are banning people from politics."

There was no more hitting. Apparently they were allowing him his soapbox. Hours passed and blurred and blended.

Name parents' name what do you do what do they do where did you learn English why have you learned English?

The script of questions circled round and round, like the mechanical figurines in a pagoda's glass display sliding along the wooden tracks in robotic repetition of the *Jataka*, fables from the lives of the Buddha.

He should have felt his eyelids gum together. If he sensed himself falling asleep, he jolted back to life. He'd done this before, many times, many nights. For as far back as he could remember, he'd had a catlike ability to control his sleep, to pull near all-nighters for a week straight, snatch three or four hours in the early morning, and deal with the consequences later. How often had his mother scolded him for his habit of playing a guitar, shooting the breeze, too wired to lie down until the neighborhood rooster crowed? Was he aided by some bionic trait that he had honed in his glory days as a karate-do competitor, a bygone era of his life that had held real promise of a starry professional career, hinging on his combination of self-discipline and knife-edge precision of mind and body?

How many hours more? Interrogators rotated in and out, three, then four, then back to three. They didn't have anything on him. But they didn't need much. Evidence, in these instances, was a creature of invention. Then again, if Kyaw Kyaw were saying something—

"How do you feel about U Aung Shwe?"

Nigel snapped to attention. "I like him very much. He works hard. And he's very honest. His strategy is good."

"And Daw Aung San Suu Kyi? What do you think of her?"

"I like her too."

"And what about U Lwin?"

"He's also good. I support them all. Because the NLD is working for the country, for you too—the NLD is working for all of you."

The NLD is working for you.

He liked to imagine that his answers echoed inside them, that the possibility of another truth somehow scratched fine hairlines in the walls of misinformation, all those years denied the chance to think. Once an activist, always a teacher.

Their line of questioning was predictable. It was standard provocation about the NLD leadership, intended to test a detainee's degree of political fervor. Interrogators were always fond of asking opinions of U Aung Shwe and U Lwin, the ex-military officers and current party caretakers who were credited with freezing the party in time, issuing statement after impotent statement, and incensing hotheads of Nway's stripe who seemed to be bristling always for revolution.

It wasn't entirely provable that malice lay behind their ability to avoid arrest in lieu of the party's incarcerated dynamos, but Aung Shwe and Lwin were self-evidently the state's safe option. They had performed a decent enough job of scuttling the NLD's latent capacity for subterfuge, thus sparing the junta the more internationally condemnable dirty work of razing it entirely. Auntie, though, was another matter. Likely Nigel's interrogators enshrined her secretly in their hearts, and with as much ardor as the next citizen, if only because she was the daughter of everyone's hero, the founder of the Tatmadaw himself, General Aung San. But the threat that Auntie posed to the status quo was clear as a summer sky. People flocked to her by the tens of thousands. And it didn't take expert insight into the more byzantine intricacies of NLD factionalism, nor, with it, the knowledge that she had always dangerously drawn to her camp the civilians— artists and scientists, ex-commies and students—the same lynch mob, in sum, who had run riot over the country in 1988, tried again in 2007, and who would stop at nothing until the military had slunk definitively back to barracks.

So Nigel gave them a blanket standard, as irrefutable in its broad brushstrokes as the rest of his spin. The surprise was how often he could catch micro-flashes of shame surface on one or other of their faces. His suspicions, it turned out, had never been wide of the mark. They were simple folk, mired in greater misfortune, not because he didn't come from the same impoverished soup, but rather because they hadn't had his opportunities, much less the raw nerve to see the system for its lies and then to act accordingly.

Apparently they were sold on his neutrality, or his resolve, or merely his ability to reason with them until dawn. It was morning now. He'd made it through night one.

They tossed him into an adjoining room. Kyaw Kyaw had staggered in shortly afterward. Each of them had been handed a bowl of slop. Even for a slum kid who had no fear of live filth swimming in his curry, he couldn't bring himself to dignify the stuff with a single mouthful.

⟡

POLITICAL WORK HAD NEVER much tempted Nigel.

The emotion it used to conjure, in fact, had been resentment, which might have been his first indication that a passion for combating injustice had been an early constant. Politics brought nothing but trouble. Because of politics he had lived cramped together with eight siblings and their parents in a two-roomed hut on a muddy alleyway in North Okkla that was screwed tight on either end with informers and block authorities who spot-checked on their affairs almost as a sport. Because of politics, his family never knew if the cash would last beyond the next vat of rice. Because of politics, his parents were inevitably arrested, first one and then the other, for a month, and then for seven months, but the release dates were always mutable, and only clear in hindsight, and it had long since fallen to him to abandon the freedom of youth to shoulder the responsibility for his six younger siblings.

In another life, another place, Nigel would have been the kind of popular high-school success story who might have gone on to an athletic career, then an MBA and a job in finance. But the injustices that attended politics, the relentless, small-time participation of his parents in the big-time struggle for his country, had killed whatever professional aspirations had begun to take shape from the concentrated ambition of a sharpshooting teen. He had never lacked awareness of the greater good. But the only pathway toward a general contribution to his community, he had assumed, was through diligence and personal integrity.

If a thread connected the boy to the thirty-one-year-old activist he had become, he might have looked to the chronic desire to blaze his own trail. He had always been driven to excel. At every exam, he earned top marks, and as he clinched one victory after the next, he liked to challenge himself still more by advertising his impending successes to his schoolmates. There was nothing quite as focusing as the burn of shame that would come from losing face. Once, in the middle of an exam, his sister had dropped unconscious to the classroom floor. The students panicked. Nigel glanced up, took note, and dived back at his paper. He startled everyone with his indifference. He didn't care. He had nothing on that count to prove. She had, as usual, been playing up her histrionics as a decoy, when the fact of the matter was that she had preferred to giggle and gossip the previous days away with her friends instead of studying. Her only possible strategy had been to fake a fainting fit. Tough luck, tougher love.

Nigel was the kind of child on whom a parent pins great hope but few anxieties. In pregnancy, his mother had dreamed of her third-born swaddled in white, presented to her by a saintly man in a halo of white, a prophetic vision of a son for whom a destiny of karmic good deeds had been written in the stars. She named him Naing Ngan Lin, "Bright Country," which combined, in the traditional way, the letters of the alphabet that corresponded to the day of the week on which he was born with his virtues to come. *Nigel* was a pseudonym, adopted later in life to ease pronunciation among foreign friends.

But virtue could wait. Regular beatings from a grandmother did nothing to dissuade him from running off with her errand money, which he spent on a growing addiction for Japanese martial arts flicks. He'd been mesmerized by the coiled precision, the self-discipline required to master each gesture. His parents, laughing off his grandmother's old-school punishments for irreverence, decided instead to introduce him to a black-belt family friend.

His mother had in childhood been wealthy, the daughter of a skillful goldsmith, which had always proven a lucrative profession among a people who earned spiritual merit by applying fine gold-leaf to important shrines, and material security by banking their earnings in jewels and precious metal instead of paper. But General Ne Win's proto-socialist nationalizations had robbed her family of all inheritance. Then, in high school, she had fallen hard for her teacher. The teacher, honest and perpetually broke on account of it, fell hard in turn. The pair eloped, and three decades later they still exhibited all the mad, inopportune love on which their brood had been founded. Their politics had aligned too, and after 1988 and instances of ducking indiscriminate shelling from the armored boats patrolling the river into which North Okkla bled, the mother had dedicated herself to the NLD headquarters as one of the stalwart curry-makers of its Women's Committee. Nigel's father veered between free education to the children of the slum ward and work in the local NLD chapter.

The trouble was they had a growing family to feed. There was no pay in any of it, and even if they wanted to live a little more comfortably, the NLD label had a way of scaring off employers. It seemed so futile, all of it. Even as he thought he cared not a whit, preferring to spend his down time at the guitar or avenging a scrawnier brother, Nay Aung, in local street fights, or perfecting his karate-do, Nigel had always been dragged in and out of the homes of local

NLD folk, who might not always have had the most sophisticated theories but for whom a general animus toward authoritarianism was a given. They had sufficient flexibility on matters that might have turned a more traditional parental stomach and just enough jungle anarchy at home that when a younger sister at age fourteen declared herself a boy in all but anatomy and refused thereafter to wear a *htamein*, no one so much as batted an eyelid. Pixie-faced Suu Linn had always been feisty, at least as tough-minded as her brothers, and lesbianism had no relevance to her good heart. Still—if Nigel's parents had always distinguished themselves with a fondness for speaking aloud what others dared not say, and if there was no shame at all in living amongst the laborers of North Okklappa, not in a society in which the boundary between the classes had always been as slim as a biweekly helping of pork—they had unwittingly bequeathed to their lucid third a sense of dashed possibility.

With the universities closed after 1996, just as Nigel graduated high school, he had little inclination to notice that the reason for this latest academic shutdown was a series of straw-flame sit-ins and hit-and-run demonstrations from a clutch of students across Rangoon. It might have been dozens or hundreds, some from '88, a few from university, and snatches of them from down the block. Many were just schoolchildren. Their efforts lasted hours. There was no independent press to speak of, nor Internet to blast it out, even were anyone on the ground with cell phones and cameras to spread the news. Nigel, besides, had other plans.

What had begun as a hobby had quickly become another challenge. Nigel's karate-do *saya* found that the boy seemed to have eidetic recall. After a single viewing of a movie, he could mirror with remarkable precision the slow squats, coiled torsions, or surges of violent forearm flicks. With practice, he had internalized some forty positions. The teacher, bowing before the superior skills of the student, began to use Nigel as his personal encyclopedia, relying on him for the many attitudes of the more ritualistic, dance-like branch of the ancient Japanese martial art. As Nigel neared matriculation, his master pushed him toward selection by the Ministry of Fisheries to be groomed for a year as a middleweight, and it was one shining road from there to national competition and onto a Burmese title at the Southeast Asian Games.

Suu Linn, Nay Aung, and altogether half his siblings had inherited his father's heart-shaped face, fair and freckled with ginger hair, a coloring sufficiently rare that—insofar as ethnic labels had any morphological validity since the British Imperial administration had enforced them with a census—it suggested Burman mixed with some northern European ancestry. He shared with the rest his mother's relative heft, sable hair, and square jaw, a mien closer to the mountain folk of the hinterlands—the Karen, or even the Kachin. The look translated as cross eyes in a younger brother; in his older sister, as a smoky beauty; and in Nigel, as he matured, chiseled features and a solemnity about the gaze that conveyed an old soul's apprehension of history's uncertainties. A forelock of thick hair forever resisted his coconut-oiled parting and he carried himself with a confidence that defied his age and stood out against the more generalized self-effacing shuffle of other men in *longyis*. Together with a growing pile of sporting medals, the effect was an effortless ability to conjure the attentions of young women. Life was never a breeze exactly, but he was enjoying it mightily.

Along came 9/9/99. The number 9, beloved already of General Ne Win, had a special potency in numerology and the fourfold symmetry of the date held resonances to 8/8/88. Back then, the student leaders who had been fomenting sporadic protests since March had appealed through a lone source of dependable news, the BBC shortwave broadcast, for a national strike. The people heard. At 8:08 a.m. on the eighth day of the eighth month of 1988, the dock workers walked out. Within hours, in every major city, they were followed into the streets by at least a million workers, civil servants, students and schoolchildren, monks and housewives; even a battalion or three from the police and the air force. By nightfall, the streets were a bloodbath. For days, tens of thousands persisted with sit-ins and hunger strikes, or Molotov cocktails and slingshots, defying fire from Bren machine-gun carriers and snipers, and the accreting contamination among security forces of unfettered impunity.

For activists, many of them students who had fled into exile, the concordance of four numbers eleven years later seemed a fateful justification for a new "Day for Democracy" that would spark another national strike and this time lead to systemic, long-term change. For the junta of Senior General Than Shwe, that was bosh. Orders were dispatched, security forces were deployed to city intersections, and activists across the country were preemptively swept into detention. Into the prisons in 1999 went Nigel's parents. His mother had scarcely been let out before she fell into another pool of detained hundreds, arrested at the Rangoon Train Station on September 21, 2000, along with Auntie, who was sent back to house arrest for attempting a trip north to Mandalay.

His parents' NLD friends helped however they could. Their generosity, even as other neighbors shunned them, cracked apart something in his heart.

But it wasn't enough. With a younger brother, Nigel turned to selling pine cones for kindling by the side of the road. When that failed to generate enough, he followed a brother-in-law, a jade broker, to Mae Sot, a town just over the border in Thailand, hoping for employment in the sweatshops.

Eventually, he had found work in a factory that churned out T-shirts, besides others that specialized in trainers, mosquito nets, and whatever cheap textiles had been stitched together over the border at least since Western sanctions had largely shut down the industry in Burma. The sudden anonymity of migrant life had come as a shock. The job, though, came easily enough. He swiftly learned which pieces of cloth fit where. And draw, snip, sew, draw, snip, sew. Nigel's efficiency and evident spark drew the eyes of the factory manager who quickly saw a replacement for his less speedy supervisor. Within weeks he had the responsibility of several dozen underlings. Within days, he was fired. Shirts were disappearing. His underlings, underpaid and overworked, stole what they could. Rather than rat them out, he took the bullet.

He returned to a country reeling from inflation in double digits. The SPDC had increased fuel prices by nine hundred percent in October 2005. They had followed with a tenfold salary increase in April 2006 to civil servants, an attempt to counter the frustrations of their enforced mass relocation that year to the new capital, Naypyidaw. Government price controls were offset by years of economic mismanagement. Basic commodities prices were climbing ever higher and energy rations were never sufficient to keep alive people's generators without supplements from the steeper black market. The national electricity grid, unreliable at the best of times, offered at most one to three hours' supply a day to residents of Rangoon, and next to none elsewhere in the country. Meanwhile all the hydropower, natural gas, and oil that the population of a country could ever need was being funneled to China and Thailand for fat fees that people glimpsed, not in their failing healthcare, crumbling infrastructure, or deficient schools, but in the $50-million-worth of gifts and chandelier diamonds, and the lugubrious ostentation of the July 2006 wedding of No. 1's daughter. A video of the wedding went viral on the streets with the vigor of hardcore pornography.

People old enough to recall the periods of terrible scarcity—after the Second World War, at the height of the *dacoity*, or banditry, in the parliamentary era, or during the rice shortages that had followed Ne Win's nationalizations—complained that current times were ever worse. The general despair seemed vindicated, at least relative to the rest of the region, by whatever data on stunted growth, or maternal mortality, or dwindling years of schooling and other measures of human development could be reliably extracted. The United Nations Development Programme ranked Burma 129 out of 177 nations, landing it among the disaster zones of central and sub-Saharan Africa.

Throughout 2007, there were strikes in the factory zones; small one-off protests from human rights activists, or from the '88 Student Generation, the student union leaders who had spearheaded the protests of 1988. Scattered among prisons across the country throughout the next decade and a half, they had been released in spurts in 2004 and 2005, sent back to prison in 2006, and then, released once more, congealed anew as a tight fellowship.

In an attempt to re-enervate the wider population, and filling the void of the NLD's apparent inaction, they launched a series of civil disobedience campaigns that creatively circumvented the usual pattern of protest to crackdown. A "white" prayer campaign at Shwedagon Pagoda used the cover of religion to lure crowds of people every weekend wearing white in solidarity with political prisoners. Authorities could do nothing. But prison uniforms were thereafter changed from white to blue.

They followed with an Open Hearts campaign, launched on Independence Day, January 4, 2007. People were invited to write letters to No. 1, Senior General Than Shwe, pouring out whatever they wanted. So many responded, and with names and addresses and registration card numbers, even from remote parts of the country, that the campaign deadline had to be extended for a full month. They packed up all twenty thousand letters to send to the relevant authorities in Naypyidaw, and also to Senior General Than Shwe, Naypyidaw— exact address to be determined—and brought them to the Rangoon Post Office. The bundle never made it beyond Strand Road. The postal clerk on duty took one look at the package, shot another at the group as if they each had three heads, and stamped their offering with a black mark.

Oh well. At least they had amassed an irrefutable archive of people's grievances. They had also dangerously warmed up people's muscle to stand up for themselves.

Within months, on August 15, 2007, the junta bulldozed through the careful balancing act of people's daily lives. Overnight, it hiked the price of gasoline by sixty-seven percent, doubled that of diesel fuel, and quadrupled the cost of compressed natural gas.

Overnight, no one could afford to fill their fuel tanks, maintain their electric generators, pay their bus fares, or purchase basics for their meals in the local produce markets. Work ground to a halt. Public transport stalled. People were stuck, and sinking, and there was no one left to save them. Everyone was hit. Worst of all, they could no longer nourish their spirits. There was nothing left to donate to the monks who filed by each morning, reliant on collections in their alms bowls for their single noonday meals. Each morning, on each corner of the country, those moving filaments of maroon-swaddled monks, barefoot and smiling, renewed the Buddha's pledge to assuage hearts, and bring them peace of mind, no matter the travails of one's life. The sight of them was the one certainty in a cosmos of pitiless impermanence.

Protests broke out in half a dozen towns and cities, from monks and civilians both. The pinch was too deep, too widespread, and monks felt it with as much material as moral intensity. There were arrests, and outbursts of violence. A monk was lashed up and beaten. An alliance of monks called on the junta for an apology. The junta stayed mute. The monks responded by the tens of thousands, in the outpouring that came to be known as the Saffron uprising.

Nigel had always been struck by a proverb that seemed central to the conundrum of his society: *when the fire is bigger and bigger, no water can extinguish it. But when the water is stronger and stronger, it can put out any fire.* Never had that manifested more visibly than when he watched the city, from roads to rooftops, thronged with people. All along the boulevards from Shwedagon to Sule, laymen poured out to join the monks. Day after day, people linked hands, forming great human chains to protect the monks, moving forward, onward, through the rains of September, chanting the *metta sutta*, the ancient call of the Buddha for loving-kindness.

Each day as their numbers grew they took the measure of the silence from the junta for possibility. Perhaps this time the generals had been taken off guard. Perhaps this time they'd blinked. Perhaps this time something in their hearts would give. Any other action was inconceivable, a sacrilege against a faith to which the generals had always displayed the outward trappings of sincerest piety: photos of offerings in every shrine, commemorative plaques, a spree of new gold-and-jade pagodas mapping a fresh constellation across the country.

On the ninth day, trucks circulated with loudspeakers announcing a nighttime curfew and the enforcement of Order No. 2/88, the SLORC edict from September 18, 1988, that banned public gatherings of more than five. Soldiers and riot police deployed, arms akimbo, guns and shields at the ready. Barriers and barbed wire appeared across major roads and junctions. Among them were also the Masters of Force, the *Swann Arr Shin*, paramilitary thugs hired from the slums for a daily fee of about 2,000–2,500 *kyat*, or about $2.00–2.50, trained in the rudiments of organized brutality, then handed a bat, a lick of palm wine, and some untraceable order to more or less go nuts.

But the monks and the people kept gathering, kept pouring down the roads, wouldn't relent. Security forces threw tear canisters, smashed in skulls, and shot to kill. Monasteries were raided. At one point, in one spot, so many people were rounded up that they couldn't all fit onto the buses meant to cart them off to the Kyaik-ka-san Race Horse Stadium and the Government Technical Institute that had both been converted for the occasion into mass detention centers. Panic set in. People, predictably, began slinking back into self-protection.

It was about then that Nigel had flung himself into the breach. With two monks from his ward, he had hopped on a bus to reach an uptown meeting-point and found the roads toward it barricaded. Turning back, he had leapt onto a pedestal in the nearest pagoda downtown and cried until he was hoarse to who-ever would listen—students, mostly—to stand firm, to not give up, to have the courage to hold strong with the monks. There was nothing poetic in his phras-ing, no attempts at soaring rhetoric. It wasn't as if he'd ever read a speech in his life. Words spilled from his heart and he had talked on, unthinking, propelled by a rising tide of unbridled euphoria. In hindsight, the moment had crystallized a visceral sense of purpose. It had been his first, grand political gesture and he had never since turned back.

The lesson he drew at the time had been less personal. He had seen his coun-trymen by the tens of thousands march as one, willing to bare their faces to the cameras and videocams of the plainclothes officers among them. In their tears, in their cries and claps, in the solid, undeniable readiness to present themselves, come what may, they had for the first sustained instance since 1988 registered, as one people, their power. And there it was, for all to discern: simply a matter of mindsets. Gone was the general apathy he had always assumed among them. And when he spoke, he saw in the wonder of their expressions a yearning for guidance. To abandon their fear and stand up for what the vast majority of them at heart already knew, they needed the confidence to know they were not alone. It would always be thus: a need for leadership, a willingness to make a move if only someone—someone else—would take the first step.

Within days, the country had hunkered into spooked silence. Government agents began assiduously to match names to faces on photographs and to hunt down suspected ringleaders. People avoided each other's gazes. Monks were nowhere to be seen. Monasteries were shut and dark. The blood on their floorboards had yet to crust dry in the merciless monsoon damp. Nigel marched straight into NLD headquarters and signed up for membership.

༄

BY HIS SECOND MONTH IN A CELL, Nigel could shut his eyes and see the graffiti on the walls around him blazing into the backs of his eyelids.

Even in my dreams I won't say the truth.

He had been ticking off the days. It was mid-August, 2009, now. His wife would be close to term.

There had been no physical torture, no mental torture, not in any of the four nights they had hauled him back for a fresh round. No torture, if you didn't count the sleep deprivation, and he didn't much, because he'd managed to push through it without great effort. No torture, aside from the inedible food, some variation on prison *talapaw* curry, spiked with stones and leeches so that even pigs were said to turn their snouts up in disgust. No torture either, if you didn't consider indefinite detention on no charge without any prospect of an end date or the means to contact his wife, his family, anyone in the world beyond. Or the possibility of talking to a lawyer, say. Which he hadn't considered because what he knew of his rights to due process in pretrial detention was precisely nothing.

Nigel brooked no patience for self-pity. The rest had had it so much worse. The Lord Buddha knew why his experience had been such a cakewalk. He was cut from the cloth of those who had faith in people's basic decency: show a person your own and, as often as not, you'd shock his or hers back to the fore. Ward authorities and intelligence agents were no different, honest types often who hated their jobs and secretly respected his kind, particularly when they held strong. But he wasn't naïve enough to assume that they had spared him out of sudden saintliness.

In truth, the questions had scarcely dug, as if his interrogators didn't know where to look for more information besides his clipped half-truths, or didn't care enough to weasel it out. Their technique seemed sloppy. It wasn't exactly a secret that Special Branch police had never measured up since General Khin Nyunt's 2004 fall and, with him, the loss of hundreds of military intelligence officers whose training had once been patterned on the formidable Japanese Kempeitai. Perhaps SB agents selected their candidates for insults and rough handling much as the system picked off its criminals: arbitrarily, off the cuff, with a slapdash excess that was a bit like using a jackhammer to crack a nut.

Just as likely, they simply hadn't bothered. They knew he had been picked up by happenstance for the crime of frequenting, on one too many occasions, a young man who was proving ever more suspicious for carrying a video camera and for being able to afford the constant transport to haul it about and beyond town. At least Nigel had done well persuading them of his evenness, that he didn't need to go gangbusters on the evils of the system.

Also, he hadn't flinched. He could not allow himself to flinch. Too many friends had been arrested, too many good people, better people. Too many had suffered beyond words, beyond his country's capacity to meet their pain and sacrifice with even a dream of justice. A gallery of ghosts held his eyes open, kept his spine stiff and strong. If he hesitated, if he gave in to the threat of indignity, to anger or defiance, he failed them all. His interrogators would have smelled the weakness, one more activist cracking apart, felled by his own fear.

Kyaw Kyaw, though.

That he had cracked was obvious from the instant Nigel laid eyes on him. For one thing, he'd addressed the officers who dumped him into the room after their first night of questioning as *saya saya*, teacher, teacher. It was too sycophantic, preening in the way of one who dared no longer hold his head up high.

For another—he'd had trouble sitting. They had taken a candle in the night to his testes. Twisting and maneuvering into crossed legs, he shouted and gasped. The sight would have been fodder for a roasting among his friends for years to come. But he had terror in his eyes, a jumpiness that spoke of knowing that he had it coming but he couldn't say when or how.

"Don't tell them anything," Nigel had rasped. "Don't tell them about my email account."

Kyaw Kyaw had looked down and looked away. "I already have."

They took him away after that first morning. It was the last Nigel heard of him.

At first they had kept Nigel in a room just beside their central office. It had a window that gave onto a cement mixer and a pile of bricks. Another looked into their office. To relieve himself, he needed to knock for escort to an outhouse. Sometimes he could hear snatches of conversations among the grunts. He learned of the flimsiness of their support for the junta, that their problem wasn't with the Lady per se, nor indeed with her ideas, but with the weak position from which she operated. It wasn't entirely her fault, they might have conceded. She had what it took. But what they secretly yearned for was a firm hand, a solid plan for tomorrow. They needed to know that the call for democracy and human rights wasn't all the stuff of youthful fancy, to be discarded in a few nights' bashing.

He had been offered better food after the first day, a simple chicken or fish curry that he saw they ate themselves. Within days, the captain gave him money for breakfast. On a few occasions, they took him along for their morning visits to a teashop.

The police station in which he was being held, he had discovered, was Aung Tha Pyay detention center. It was none other than Special Branch headquarters, which spread in a grid-like compound with rows of hangars on either side of its central offices. There was space enough to hold and smack around at least half a dozen other detainees. All this time it had perched a stone's throw from the traffic-congested crossroads between Kyaik Waing Pagoda and the Junction 8 shopping mall, a glittering, always crowded tile-and-glass symbol of pseudo–middle class prosperity. The place was a jewel among the handful of new high-rises, with which, in the previous decade, the junta had signaled the city's impending launch into modernity, a new age of liberal capitalism after the restrictive bleakness of Ne Win's would-be socialism.

Later—after he had refused a third attempt to turn him—they had dispatched him to a cell without a window, whose concrete walls were covered in political scrawlings.

Until then, he had continued to address them with the distant familiar, with *Uncle*, *Brother*, or, if he could discern it, their rank. It wasn't disrespectful but it didn't flatter. The way he saw it, the only person in that compound worthy of the title of *saya* would be an honest citizen who belonged to and worked for the people, a real teacher. As far as he knew, that honor fell to him alone.

"Where's your *saya*?" a lower ranking officer asked him at one point, inquiring after the three-star captain.

"No, no, he's not my *saya*," Nigel answered. "He is a policeman. I'm an ordinary man. I'm a teacher. He is not my teacher."

"Why d'you say like that?" the man had answered, possibly a touch impressed, possibly enjoying the opening for a sadistic jab. "You'll be arrested."

He missed his wife.

He missed her determination, the concentrated luminosity of her eyes, the sinewy curves of her body and her long, fine tresses that she plaited down to her hips. The way she would fold her tiny form around his shoulders, as a vine binds around a tree.

His sadness spread like a dark stain behind his sternum. A raven settled on his chest, pressing down, clawing, spreading to full span its moonless wings and beating them in growing panic against his rib cage as if to turn the sadness into agitation, into a white-hot yearning to jump up and cry and rage and scratch the walls and punch them until his knuckles bled and the sharp pain shooting up and down his forearms—into his locked elbows and shoulders, the pulsing veins in his temples—until somehow the physical explosion numbed the anguish, the terrible despair of sitting there, day in, day out, braising in his impotence.

He sat cross-legged and watched the feelings, the violence of the images they yielded, located them in his body, labeled them without judgment, and returned to the coolness at his nostrils, the shimmer of space at the top of the breath, the trickle of his exhalation, the subtle pause. The return of air to the nostrils. The soft movement in the abdomen. The renewed cycle as his body, *this* body, was somehow breathed.

If thoughts carried him away, he pulled his focus back. Always the breath was there, always beneath the distractions of consciousness, cycling through, observable, yielding to perception of the evanescing instant, of the ubiquitous now. The constriction in his chest sat there still, hard, and knotted, but isolated now, its intensity somehow dissolving. His thoughts, just thoughts, passed and popped as soap bubbles. After a time, a peace, a quality of blue, stilled the inner turmoil and he began to free himself in just that way from the ferocity of his emotions and their relentless capacity to hijack his self-control.

The ability was common to the mindful of his country, born and bred in a land that taught from an early age to hone an inward gaze. *Vipassana* meditation, insight meditation, and the concentration it required, heightened self-awareness and mental detachment through the paradox of absolute engagement with the self. To observe the passage of one's thoughts and emotions was to see them then as no more than a parade of images, a *pwe*, an all-night vaudeville that had traditionally kept a village distracted until dawn. Watching them as they rose and dissipated, one would awake to the conclusion that all was sound and fury, signifying nothing.

Practiced regularly, meditation could bring a person to experience directly in that way the three states of existence arrived at by the Buddha, Siddhartha Gautama: the omnipresence of suffering; the impermanence of everything; and finally, if you broke down through observation each passing moment of consciousness to its molecular components, the lack of a continuous self. Such was the pathway to enlightenment.

It was also the route to freedom.

Nigel had yet to graduate into a regular practice, not in the way of the fiercely devoted, the elders of the NLD party or most anyone who learned, in prison or in the prison of the country, to confront their circumstances with the most elemental weapon of all: the ability to face oneself. That he reached for meditation now and found in it a coping mechanism, as it served for so many of his countrymen, was almost instinctive. Meditation, and its philosophical underpinning, was in the very marrow of his culture.

And so, at the moment of his arrest, he had felt acutely his lack of self, and the sudden relinquishment of ego had become his gateway to invincibility. And so the members of his movement, the elders of his party, and Auntie too, had always professed a lightness of heart, and humility, no matter the years of their incarcerations. It had been more than mere platitude. Authorities could hold them physically hostage but never could they contain the essence of their being.

For them, for Nigel, the possibility of achieving that freedom, of mental or metaphysical freedom, was an expansion of the ideal enshrined as a human birthright in the Universal Declaration of Human Rights, which activists found useful to copy down or photocopy and circulate when and how they could as a teaching text; Auntie and the other elders had long since made explicit how compatible its standards were with Burmese goals. With their lives, they wanted and sought that definition of freedom—negative freedom, the visible emancipation from the interference and restraints of autocratic rule. In parallel, they had another goal—positive freedom, possession of the liberty to unleash their full potential—and its attainment depended not only on a system that was just, that encouraged equal opportunity. That freedom depended mainly on personal agency. Attempting it would never grow easier. Every day presented a new confrontation. But it was empowering merely to try.

When he couldn't manage it, Nigel tried turning his sadness inside out. He scored off time's passage on a scrap of paper—five days, seventeen, twenty-six—calculating from the end of his remand. He recited prayers, mantras that could still his mind. The markings of his pen were like beads, for worrying past worry.

They had given him the paper and the pen within a week. It was a rare prize for a detainee. "You are innocent. We will let you go home," one of them had informed him at the end of his four-night questioning. "But you have to wait." To release him, they said, they needed the green light from the "ministry," by which they might have meant the Ministry of Home Affairs, or the Ministry of Information. Just as possibly they meant the ministry of their invention. He knew they were playing mind games, toying with his sympathies. He knew they liked the idea of an educated young man, convincingly quick of thought, who would have the capacity to organize and sow dissension on the state's behalf if or when they returned him to his ward.

One afternoon, the head of the detention center had summoned him for a private conversation. He had allowed the talk to roam free and far, defying taboos that society-at-large could only skirt in whispers. Quoting Grandpa, U Win Tin, renowned as a writer and a wordsmith long before he had become the NLD's de facto strategist, the SB officer spoke of daring to venture beyond convention. If Nigel wanted to fight the good fight, the SB chief told him, he should likewise strive for "an alternative way."

For the gall alone of turning inside out the ideas of an avowed democrat, and a genius of language at that, the point had merited consideration. Nigel had answered: "It's not *me* who has to find that alternative. It's you. Because you are under orders. You do what you are told. I'm not doing what I'm told. I'm doing what I like."

They didn't try to make him one of theirs after that.

Day after day, he penned a letter to his wife. They were simple missives, shorn of poetry, which neither of them had ever read or craved. He couldn't send them—his paper dispensation hadn't come with postal privileges—but how else to fill the blankness of his hours? He told her to reach out to her mother or an aunt. She must be hungry. She wouldn't like to beg, but she was weak and upset.

Do it for the baby, he enjoined. *Please try to make yourself healthy. Be strong.*

Worse, he fretted that she wouldn't be able to keep still. She would find a way to work up some dangerous public stink in the name of their love and their politics. *Please don't tell anything to the media, not in a wrong way.* He meant the exile media. There was no other possibility. But that would do nothing except entrap her, too.

They had met within days of her release from Insein Prison. She had served seven months for leading a march of eleven other activists on the Traders Hotel down Sule Pagoda road, in the heat of the crackdown on the Saffron uprising. Waving a giant placard, she had worn the black and camouflage of the underground student union, a scarf wrapped around her forehead. The point had been to catch the attention of a newly arrived hotel guest, a United Nations envoy, lest he had missed the riot police, soldiers, and USDA thugs who were smashing down on crowds less than half a block away. With authorities moving in, their little assembly had scattered. Khine Sandar Win had ducked into a side entrance, sprinted up a stairwell, and knocked furiously at a random door. A woman let her in, and there she had hunkered a few minutes, twitching to be back in the street, refusing her hostess's increasingly impassioned pleas that she at least change into clothes that were less screamingly activist.

She'd walked out the building into the embrace of the state, and onto the mass detention center at the horse stadium. She had listened for the screams, watched a friend break under the pressure, and witnessed a body—one of her band of eleven—carted out under a white sheet. Somehow she found a moment to charge at another of her cohorts to kick him in the shins, reminding him that even a *girl* could stay strong. Herself? She had fainted briefly from electric shock treatment. But she had kept her word. Stayed mute.

Afterward, they had relocated her to Insein and kept her without trial. They'd released her on May 3, 2008, into a city knocked sidewise and dizzy by Tropical Cyclone Nargis. They didn't give her enough for the bus ride home, and then the buses weren't working and when she finally made it, her home was no longer there. It had vanished with the winds that killed at least 138,000 people.

As was tradition for newly released political prisoners, she had within days dropped in on the NLD office. Nigel had been teaching a class. From afar, in a throng of people, she had struck him simply as a beauty he had to conquer. It took him three days to land a first date, a record of sluggishness. And yet she was no stranger to his charms. She had spotted him first, delivering his speech in the midst of the crackdown. Demure, he'd quickly discovered, she was not. She was an activist's activist, a living spitfire, whose tale of interrogation had made her an activist legend.

And the other thing is, he wrote, *I miss you a lot.*

What hurt most of all was the realization that he had, in fact, been selfish.

He had never subscribed to the informal doctrine circulating among young activists that to fall in love, and thence to marry, was to sell out. Their views seemed narrow-minded, the position of people who didn't have the imagination to see that love of country began from love of family. Against the general disapprobation of his peers, even of his parents whose own marriage had, in a strangely indirect way, landed him here, he had married Khine Sandar Win and never looked back.

They were on their third date when the warning came to disperse on account of a recent bomb attack on a USDA office. In Khine Sandar Win's case, she was barely four weeks out of Insein. In Nigel's, a convoy of police cars had rolled up near his brother's home to inquire about a young man who fit Nigel's description.

Nigel had shot with her to a friend's house in Tamway, but the friend, for logistical reasons, couldn't accommodate them. With few options left, they darted into anonymity in a township just over the river and signed into a random guesthouse, one room for two. Never would a respectable woman have re-emerged with her honor.

It was fitting, if either cared to notice, that the site of the guesthouse was Thanlyin, home to the myth of Burma's great star-crossed pairing: a princess, whose mother's death in childbirth had forever cursed her daughter with bringing misfortune on future husbands, and a young prince from just over the river whose father had consequently forbidden them contact. Of course they had met, of course they had fallen in love, but the prince ended up swallowed by a bewitched crocodile who had previously been acting as his secret chauffeur to visit the princess on the other bank. Within days, the princess had died of heartbreak, and the smoke from their respective funeral pyres had mingled and arched over the river as a great rainbow.

Nigel and Khine Sandar Win had married on December 8, 2008. There was no ceremony. There were no guests, nothing in the way of the traditional marriage, with man and bride decked out in bright silks and attended by a line of revelers with gold parasols.

The clash of their personalities strengthened them both. Where she sought confrontation, he preferred peace. He bent and negotiated; she attacked. But he had outgrown his knee-jerk anger, channeled it early and with skill through the artistry of karate-do. A lone child, and a girl, she had never had the opportunity to find another vehicle for her energy, and it became the source she had drawn on and wielded in the months of her detention.

Now, as he pored over his letters, he saw how narrow his concerns had been. On account of their choices, she was trapped at home.

In the past I didn't take care. But if I'm released, I will take responsibility to care for my family. So please make yourself—the letter registered his hesitation—*please wait for me.*

⚜

ANOTHER DAY, BEFORE AUTHORITIES relocated him to the concrete cell, he thought he had hallucinated. And then it turned out that the entire detention center was suffering the same delirium.

Khine Sandar Win had turned up in the compound.

The officers outside told him they had seen her for themselves: a wraith of a woman with a stomach the size of a football and a demand to see her husband delivered with such a natural sense of entitlement that they were lost for words.

They threw her out, of course. But they couldn't keep themselves from spilling the news to Nigel. As they related the details, he watched them attempt to stifle sheer admiration. A random civilian, and a pregnant woman at that, marching straight into the heart of a no-go detention center! A secret center that had escaped all the prison lists and maps!

When he heard that she'd been turned away, he lay on a bench and felt himself die. He couldn't eat. They took it for a hunger strike and the second time she appeared, disguised this time as a day laborer headed for the center's construction site, they let her through.

He stared. And she stared. And then, with the half hour that they'd been permitted ticking before them, he took her hand, launched with her to the outhouse, and slammed hard the door.

She told him she had found the site after news had aired on the radio that Kyaw Kyaw had been arrested. Shortly afterward, Kyaw Kyaw's home had been raided. It hadn't been hard to piece together where Nigel had been taken, too.

He handed her his letters, twenty by now. And then she was gone.

Now he had only the walls for conversation.

There was defiance in the graffiti. There was sorrow too, the loss of a daughter here, of a beloved there.

They had been marked with who-knew-what jagged fragments, a crust of concrete or a nail. A few were in ink. They told of a room that had been a holding pen for political detainees from 2007, 1998, 1996, and 1988. Possibly they went all the way back to the student protesters of 1964, when Ne Win massacred 130 of them and the next day blew up the Rangoon University Student Union.

Successive generations, in those messages, seemed to trip up on each other, pinballing and echoing around him into a single, great, unfinished song. In this halfway house, this blacked-out axis between agitation on the streets and the prisons, they had all languished. Here too they had been trapped in a state of metaphysical suspension as senseless to Nigel as the nation's trajectory itself.

We started MDC.

He knew it well. MDC, the Myanmar Development Committee, was one of dozens of groups, underground or semi-submerged, and the quickest off the mark to call for nationwide demonstrations against the junta's hiking of fuel prices on August 15, 2007. The group had been founded in 2006 by a friend, Htin Kyaw, from down the road in North Okkla.

Htin Kyaw had attempted to lead a demonstration at Theingyi market on August 22, 2007. It was to be his fourth protest that year. To ensure a measure of press coverage, he had tipped off exile journalists, ducked into hiding, and succumbed on August 25 to a citywide manhunt. Eventually authorities had swept up the core of MDC's membership. It was abundantly possible that Htin Kyaw himself had scratched this message between one interrogation and his next destination. All Nigel knew was that they had confined Htin Kyaw for a few months in the dog kennels of Insein Prison. Then he was tried. Dispatched far north to Khamti Prison in the parched hills of Sagaing, he was half a year now into a twelve-and-a-half-year sentence.

In recent weeks, Nigel had worked with MDC's point person, acting as interlocutor with a big-time exile leader, code-named "Happy." After the MDC point person had in turn vanished underground, the task of communicating with Happy had fallen to Nigel.

He had stepped forward, less out of desire than the compulsion of duty. Always there were new gaps to fill, always the call to keep unbroken a line of activists that stretched backward to Ne Win's coup, to the time of General Aung San even, and onward to a future whose responsibility fell at present to Nigel. Casting his eye around, he vowed a reinvigorated fervor to the task. Had they released him then and there, *when* they released him, he would only plunge deeper into his greatest and most dangerous political investment yet.

And that had been to found and nurture an activist network of his own.

In the bag that he had abandoned behind his computer at the Internet café was the substance of that other life. Never hiding, never denying his own name, he had all the while been fomenting the sort of activity that would have, off the contents of the bag alone, earned him increments of seven-to-fifteen-year sentences, multiplied each time for:

- One USB memory stick, possession of: violation of the 2004 Electronic Transactions Law, Chapter XII, clauses 33 through 35.

- Several pamphlets, unauthorized publication and distribution of, and subversive contents of: violations of the Printers and Publishers Registration Act of 1962; Emergency Provisions Act of 1950, Section 5; Act 505(b) of the 1957 Penal Code.

- A logo for his network, usage and potential distribution: Section 17(1) and (2) of the Unlawful Associations Act; Acts 505 (b) and Act 124 respectively of the Penal Code. Likewise, again, of the Emergency Provisions Act, Section 5.

- And a cell phone. Nway had rented it for Nigel in the standard way—from someone who had rented it in turn from someone else. Sentencing at judge's discretion based on respective SIM-card and handset registration violations.

Nigel could only hope that the bag had somehow found its way into the hands of a curious bystander. It was an expensive way to spread subversion. But at least it was safer than the more typical recruitment method, dependent on time, trust, and the slippery skill of artful political persuasion.

"Our group is not popular, not yet," he had explained to the American reporter he had met weeks before on Kandawgyi Lake. "We don't want to be known. If we aren't known, we have a good shot."

Its membership was difficult to define. Activists liked to keep cells small, no larger than the handful of names that might spill out under interrogations. The tactic had infiltrated the underground from the communists, who had always had the best feel for organizing before they'd definitively collapsed as a viable force amid the conflagration of 1988.

The American reporter had seemed reluctant to take him at his word. Few Westerners would understand. They demanded hard numbers, mission statements, annual reports. They needed tangibles and what they liked to call "proof." They seemed unable to wrap their minds around the notion that dozens of avowed "community-based organizations" and other less formalized groupings in the Burmese underground were of necessity fluid, rhizomal, and capable of evaporating as fast as they could call to the fore their people, on a sudden turn of national fervor, to lead the revolutionary charge.

He had called his network the "Saffron Generation."

At least there was time enough here to plot its next moves.

From the wall, the scrawling by an anonymous peer that most haunted Nigel became now his battle cry:

Even in my dreams I won't say the truth.

3

CITY OF EXILES

FEBRUARY 2009

THE WAY NWAY SAW IT, the trouble with Nigel was that he didn't have a clue.

Nigel concluded otherwise. Simply put, Nway was just a royal shit.

It was about three months before Special Branch agents would hound Nway out of Rangoon; four before they'd arrest Nigel.

The blowup had come on the journey back from their clandestine trip to Mae Sot. But boys being boys, or a lifetime under dictatorship being a lifetime under dictatorship, the issue of contention had reached a roiling boil as they sat stewing in private reproach, staring off in opposite directions from the slimy-wet hull of a hired sampan.

Motor off, the boat drifted down the yellow waters of the Thaungyin, slicing an untraceable path between Thailand and the scrubby fringe of their native jungle. There, to the left, were the smuggling docks. Workers, half-naked and gleaming with perspiration, hustled onto Burma-bound flatboats quantities to fill a hangar of industrial chemicals, crates of soda, snakes of rubber piping, and, piling up behind them, a boulevard's worth of car parts and mopeds or electronic rejects from the junk heaps of half of Asia.

They moved fast, paced to the rhythm of impending apocalypse. The place wasn't exactly a secret. Officials or kingpins on either bank got their cut, though precisely who that was on the Burmese side depended on which group happened that day to control what patch of turf and the corresponding tollgates all down the concrete wall that skirted the river. The current configuration, at least in this neighborhood, was a patchwork of the Christian-dominated Karen National Liberation Army, or KNLA; its breakaway nemesis, the Democratic Karen Buddhist Army, the DKBA; and the Tatmadaw, which had long before designated the area a free-fire zone to wrest control back to the state. And who could predict the next skirmish? The whole crisis, an on-and-off insurgency that dated at least to a Karen near-overthrow of Rangoon in 1949, had left a status quo about as permanent as the winds, a situation not likely to improve, what with rumors of an impending ham-fisted government push to order the more accommodating of the armed ethnic rebel groups—which around here meant the DKBA—into surrendering their weapons, political aspirations, and hard-earned sense of discrete identities into a single, great Tatmadaw-lamed "Border Guard Force."

The virtue of the transnational black market was that it tended to be spared the vicissitudes of civil war. Out poured teak, rosewood, rice, dried fish, precious gems, off-brand hair creams and lotions, and five-a-penny trinkets, or, not too far up-country, heroin, opium, and methamphetamine. In went cigarettes, powdered milk, brake fluid, and all the manufactured gizmos on which everyone above the level of a tarpaulin tent depended. The informal system by now ran to at least three to four times the size of the economy on the official Burmese ledgers. From the perspective of Thai officialdom in bordering Tak province, it had always proven preferable to watch the leakage with one eye shut so long as local businesses stayed greased. Even so, times could get tough: sudden night raids on illegal activity on the Thai side; knock-on effects from whimsical *kyat* demonetizations on the Burmese; commodity prices inflating wildly on account of a massive recession worldwide. And it was always the coolies at the gate who somehow took the hit.

And over there, on a giant rubber tire, a family of Burmese migrants swished and washed their way toward the Thai side, sopping and stick-thin, with nothing left to their name but résumés of cheap sweat.

Tires were standard transport, about a nineteenth the price of a sampan. The bargain rate came with a dose of anxiety because the tires tended to twirl off-target, floating with unfortunate precision directly under the official Thai-Myanmar Friendship Bridge. It took a few commutes to learn how minor the risk; that the chief consequence was the pretty view from the checkpoints on either end and the perpetual smiles of the officials manning them, fattened a little more with each off-book crossing.

By comparison, Nway and Nigel's ride was luxury. But then, their purpose had been altogether different from begging at the gates of a Mae Sot garment factory.

⚜

FROM RANGOON, FIVE DAYS EARLIER, the bus had taken them briefly north, then hooked southwest into Mon state before venturing into Karen state, which skirted Thailand down its western border. If they were stopped and questioned at any point until then, they could claim, without need for elaboration, that the target of their journey was Hpa-an.

Hpa-an, the little capital of Karen state just over the Thanlwin River from Mon state, had been the destination for Auntie's first and, as it had turned out, single permitted trip outside Rangoon after her release in 1995 from her first six years of house arrest. She had headed for a venerable Pa-o Buddhist abbot who oversaw a nearby sanctuary that was renowned for its loving-kindness and peace.

Her pilgrimage, a bone-jolting drive that had ended in a redemptive few hours with the abbot, had served to introduce the country in four "Letters from Burma" for a yearlong series in Japan's *Mainichi Daily News*. The landscape she described was a marvel, as variegated as Burma's multiethnic people. From fields near Rangoon, "dotted with palms and every now and then . . . the white triangle of a *stupa* wreathed in morning mist," it shifted to "the tender green of the graceful paddy plants; the beautiful lotuses, pink, white, and blue, floating in pools and ditches, the dark, violet washed hills carved into rolling shapes that conjured up images of fairy-tale creatures."

In Mon state, they had passed in the vicinity of wondrous Kyaik-htiyoe Pagoda, a giant rock balanced in millennial defiance of gravity off the edge of a cliff, with help, it was said, from a hair of the Buddha. On they drove, past rubber plantations that yielded to "a straggled out place with a slightly battered air," the town of Thaton, which had centuries earlier been a center for Buddhism. It had also been the capital of a Mon kingdom whose monarch had been so mighty that, even forced to kneel in defeat, he caused his Burman conqueror, King Anawratha of Pagan, to break out in a cold sweat.

Finally Auntie and her little NLD convoy had reached Hpa-an, a land of "striking hills that rise sheer from the ground." The contradiction between the brutality of the unresolved war with the Karen people and serenity of the Pa-o abbot's domain seemed to strike her poetic imagination in notes as false as the implantation of a repressive dictatorship on a country so breathtaking. "As we approached Thamanya," the abbot's sanctuary, "the quiet seemed to deepen," she wrote.

It was difficult to imagine that we were close to areas which have served as battle-fields over most of the last fifty years. Fighting broke out between government troops and Karen insurgents almost as soon as Burma was declared an independent nation in January 1948. And there has not been a political settlement that could bring permanent peace to this land with its wild, magical quality.

Nway and Nigel had no thought on their journey to stop for a visit to the Buddhas meditating in neat lines in the Lonebini Gardens. There was no pondering, either, of the meaning of pure spirit, of stupas silhouetted against jungled hills that rose from tropical mists. Nor had they time for a detour to Kyaik-htiyoe Pagoda, that great boulder suspended on a hair, on faith alone, like a golden sumo wrestler twirling on a tightrope. Contemplation of the splendid heritage of their land—the very stuff that arguably made their country worthy of the fight—was an extravagance left for later in life.

Neither of them had enjoyed a chance to meander blithely in that way far beyond Rangoon. Raised in the Irrawaddy Delta about two hours from a vast coastline of wild, untouched beaches, Nway had never before even looked out to sea.

Not that either of them had much care for tourism. As far as Nway was concerned, you'd seen one pagoda, you'd seen them all. Great beauty had proven its capacity to weaken them both at the knees. But beauty of that sort, they would have had to agree, belonged to girls.

What Nway and Nigel saw instead in the blooming splendor of the passing landscape was the seamlessness of the country's poverty. There was no quaint-ness in the endless grass-and-thatch houses on slender stilts; nor of yet another farmer and his bullock cart, man and animal engaged in constant rivalry for who or which seemed most malnourished. It wasn't a pretty sight even if you zoomed out and squinted, and saw it as some delicate, palm-framed bucolic, as if Burma were some time-stopped wonderland designed to arrest the hearts of Western romantics come to escape the soulless industrial advances of the twenty-first century. Always a nostalgic of that kind could catch a pastel scene of water buffalo ambling ahead of a farmer wispy in his *longyi*, or another in a broad-brimmed hat on a sampan, punting with a bamboo pole to the cadence of a field song, down a watery artery interlaced with giant lily pads and bursts of violet hyacinths.

It was fitting that Auntie had long before put out an international call to shut down tourism, a direct response to the junta's declaration that 1996 was "Visit Myanmar Year." Complete with controlled itineraries that would allow visitors no opportunity to stop by the institutions of the detention system, the bid had coincided with the forced relocation without compensation of tens of thousands of inhabitants to clear space for new developments such as the Myanmar Golf Club and a spate of crony-built high-rise hotels in Rangoon.

✧

AS THE PAIR APPROACHED THE THAI BORDER, what mattered still more was the unfurling of the country's genuine political complexity.

Vines slapped at their ankles and mud sucked at their flip-flops and splashed up their calves. The trunks of the trees, chipped with little triangle mark-ings, pointed toward a river crossing that didn't begin at the Burmese town of Myawaddy or the official border posts on the Thai-Myanmar Friendship Bridge.

It had been thrilling in its way to get so far. They were spitting distance, al-most, from the city of exiles, fueled on dreams of revolution—or the resources and knowledge to help them get there. Nway, rarely impressed, had felt some-thing like butterflies.

He knew people who had fled to Mae Sot. There was his old friend from his early days in the NLD with whom he had formed a short-lived "Lower the Price Committee" in the heat of the Saffron uprising. Soon thereafter, the friend had earned his legal license and joined a handful of lawyers who dared the vain defense of political prisoners. When, in October 2008, a clutch of clients turned their backs on a judge as a boycott of proceedings that they knew would end in conviction, Nway's friend had stood by, and was charged in turn with contempt of court. Subpoenaed to face the charge the next day, he had profited from a momentary distraction of the presiding assistant judge to duck out the court-room and never looked back until he had made it over the mountains, through the jungle, and across the river.

Now he worked somewhere in town for the Burma Lawyers' Council, one of at least a dozen exile organizations that had found in Mae Sot the ideal perch. There they could train; monitor the situation in the country and disseminate the information back inside or worldwide; coordinate with international nonprofits and governments; and build connections across ethnic groups vying variously for autonomy, federalism, or a chance to build their temples or churches and teach their languages in schools. At least since the arrival of the Internet, some of the exile organizations had also found ways to make Mae Sot the technological control-center for underground activism inside.

It was a convenient spot, free from cyber-censorship but close enough that in the right patches you could even pick up the Burmese cell phone network. That was helpful for deflecting suspicions that you'd ever left, general subterfuge, or simply because Burmese cell technology—a monopoly of two state-controlled companies—enjoyed the curious distinction of forbidding calls to phones abroad. With enough care to not rub Thai authorities in the nose with their presence, and dispersed among the rest of Mae Sot's riffraff—a fleeting population of missionaries and non-profiteers, rights advocates, and freelance racketeers—Burma's demimonde of economic and political refugees could almost hide in plain sight.

But Nway hadn't planned this trip to visit old friends.

For his part, Nigel had few illusions about Mae Sot. He'd been there before, and last time it had been the way of the migrants. With a mercilessness that still stung, he had understood then how the pretty trappings of parochial success were nothing. The measure of a man was and would always be his character. Back then, he had lost his identity crossing a slip of this same river. Gone was his right to complacency, the easy comfort of knowing who he was and where in his community he might have yet traveled if circumstance hadn't intervened.

His parents had just been arrested, and, at a loss for income, he'd followed his brother-in-law to Mae Sot. He hadn't known that the botched attempt to launch a national uprising on 9/9/99 had its origins among exiles from 8/8/88 who had there found a base. Neither did he learn that the little Thai town had become a prime destination for Western do-gooders who were helping with anti-SPDC advocacy; leading "capacity building" workshops; or servicing, in some internationally connected way, seven refugee camps, mainly for Karen, that ran up and down the border. All he knew was that Mae Sot was a hop and skip by river, or over the bridge, from the scraggy Karen town of Myawaddy, which was periodically shut down on account of shelling, and that it did a thriving business in migrant labor.

It was as if a different sky lit either side. Burma's Myawaddy had seemed awash in jaundiced yellow. Its patched-together cars from another era belched diesel at the trishaw drivers pedaling hard past jagged lines of little huts crammed with renters whose tenancy was as transient as their employment on

the other bank. Atop a hill rioting with palm and peepul trees, a pagoda of faded
frescos and cracked-tile flooring watched over the whole sad exchange: the little
stick figurines on giant tires or flatboats slipping back and forth and back and
forth across the Thaungyin River—the Moei to the Thai—in an eternal cycle of
self-perpetuating dependency.

Where the river edged into the sand and mud on the other bank, the
Burmese figurines sprawled in wooden hovels collapsing around lines of laundry. They fed about 160 sweatshops and factories to a count of an estimated
hundred thousand laborers, revolving through as fast as they could be picked up
by local Thai police, thrown into a holding pen, and, if they didn't have the cash
to buy their way out or contacts in Thai intelligence, spat back over the Moei
and into the dark, straw hamlets whence they mostly came.

Mae Sot, beyond, had exuded a white-grey crispness that reflected off the
tarmac or the mirrored fenders of its trucks and cars. All crisscrossed in electric poles and paved highways, it had bars and restaurants with strange menus
that featured "muesli" or "fry-ups" for the pretty Western girls and the san-
daled white men; chili-spiked Tom Yum for the Thai; and whatever fed the
pleasure of all the smugglers pushing stock from who-knew-what reaches of the
continent. There were warehouses on every block crammed with cosmetics to
last a century. At every corner, a 7-Eleven brimmed with cans and dirt-cheap
SIM-card top-ups. It gave the sense—for all the betel spit of Burmese exile red-
dening the sidewalks and the slapdash lack of charm of a frontier town—of the
irrepressible worldwide progress that had left Burma far behind.

It was, however, a strange sort of modernity. Nigel had never been blind
to the effects of corruption. But the view from the sweatshops, the lies that sustained the marginal economy of the borderland, had brought it all somehow into
focus. He saw his brother-in-law arrested for the transactions of a jade business
that had in its way been honest enough, and with it, learned the price of his own
ignorance. No one was safe, and even the petty criminal, buffered in the black
market by a vast community of the like-minded, was finally not for sparing.
So much for shrugging away all the little legal lines that people crossed, he'd
thought. The whole system was eaten through with rot. It wasn't a sudden overnight epiphany, but thereafter Nigel was living in truth, awake to his life and his
place in a sharper reality in a way that echoed the mindfulness, the moment-by-
moment awareness, that derived from insight meditation, *Vipassana* meditation,
which he, like most every Burmese Buddhist, had been taught from youth to
cultivate. Even as he later embraced politics, and watched and learned as one

who had been starved, he never lost his understanding of that terrible, original contradiction: the facile delusion that it was better to be corrupt and survive, than fight the good fight, for principle, for justice and democracy—as a rights activist or as a politician.

But that was later. Just then, he was nothing, reduced in Thailand to a nonentity, a furtive wanderer in an alien land with an alien script and an alien tongue, ducking in a different way for different reasons a different set of police.

Now again, ankle-deep in the sands of the riverbank, facing east toward Mae Sot, Nigel told himself that this trip would be different: driven with purpose. And with meaning.

Nway's gaze lingered west.

Parts of Myawaddy were off-limits, mined and brutalized in the course of the six-decade-old civil war. The no man's land couldn't be far—at most about two miles beyond the Karen town. Nway didn't have to step into it, into some hapless farmer's booby-trapped acre of paddy, to feel the resonance of unresolved conflict, the country's truest conundrum.

What would he say? How would he respond? Could he find a way to promote unity across the movement: between the NLD, the brothers-in-exile across the river, and the fissiparous ethnic minorities, here and on the other bank?

Burma was a patchwork of peoples. Animist, preliterate hill tribes had for centuries practiced swidden and sought isolation from the encroachment of Mon, Arakan, and Burman. Those three peoples, in turn, shared rich, scriptural traditions; Buddhism; and dynasties of kings who had warred over territory in the flat, central river valley, with periodic spillovers into modern-day Thailand, India, and China. British rule had hardened the distinctions in a textbook imperial formula that included conversions to Christianity, mainly from among the hill tribes, and selective favoritism.

After independence, the insurrections against the fragile new parliamentary government had included a hodgepodge of communists, criminal gangs, and some of those ethnic minorities, clamoring for secession or autonomy. They had morphed across the years into multiple, off-shooting insurgencies, sporadic and driven by a variety of sometimes ill-defined, sometimes competing agendas: desires for religious and linguistic autonomy, territorial claims, control over resources, centuries-old mistrust of the mainland Burmans or each other, and warlordism. Few groups were linguistically, religiously, or even geographically monolithic. Factions that claimed to act in one or another of their names were often self-appointed. In places, dependence on a war economy had created a self-sustaining dynamic. They had entrapped entire generations.

The war with the Karen ranked as the country's most historically intractable. According to some measures, it was the oldest internal conflict in the world.

A documentary on the plight of Karen civilians had lately circulated on the streets in Rangoon. It had made Nway cry. He had watched children stagger about on one leg, maimed by mines. Others, trauma-struck, stared into space, or, tear-stained and in patched-together clothing, chased after mothers who heaved bed rolls or jerry-cans or pots on their heads as they fled from one scorched village to the next, through the rain, through the muck and unsparing heat, up and up perilous mountainous trails, deeper into jungle, on an endless odyssey to nowhere.

No activist from the mainland prodemocracy movement deluded himself that he or she had it worse. In their struggle, they had opted for nonviolence. But never had they reproached the ethnic minorities—the Karen, Kachin, Shan, Chin, Mon, Arakan, Karenni, or Wa, to name the largest groups—for resorting to arms. When soldiers were coming to burn down your village or rape your sister or turn your father into a live landmine-buffer on a forced march, you couldn't exactly fall to your knees in prayer and expect sudden pangs of conscience to stay your attackers.

Exile and foreign organizations had abundant evidence of a longstanding pattern of abuses that included massacres, systematic rape, forced portering, the conscription of child soldiers, and the wholesale razing of villages. It was part and parcel of a counterinsurgency strategy, called the "Four Cuts," that the Tatmadaw had developed in the 1970s to undermine the ethnic militias by cutting off their access to food, funds, information, and recruitment. Its latest chapter had been so devastating in places, and was sufficiently well documented, that activists abroad were calling for a United Nations commission of inquiry against the SPDC on possible charges of war crimes and crimes against humanity.

The push was divisive. Rebel armies too would have to face trials for their share of child soldiers, drug money, and blood on their hands from their use of internationally banned landmines, or the intimate brutality born of existential battles defending patches of territory about the size of a cattle ranch.

It would never be enough to simply replace the military junta with parliamentary democracy without simultaneously addressing the grievances of the minority groups. The NLD's repeat calls for dialogue with the junta had always included representatives of the minorities. But Nway had enough guile to understand that any lasting solution would inevitably require more than a magic reunion followed by a cross-ethnic sing-along.

There had been one great moment of possibility. In 1947, a year before independence from Britain, General Aung San, then head of the interim Burmese government, had convened representatives of the Kachin, the Chin, and the Shan for a conference in Panglong, Shan state, an area of northeastern Burma that at the time was a protectorate of thirty Shan principalities. On February 12, the three groups had agreed in principle to join a Union of Burma, on the condition that they be allowed to retain their autonomy. The Shan were also granted rights to secession after a referendum, which was to be held in ten years. Not all groups were signatories. Among those absent were the Mon, the Arakanese, and the Karen. But even after Aung San had been assassinated, and as rebellions broke out within months of Burma's independence, the "spirit of Panglong" had ever since been invoked as the yardstick against which to measure prospects for a lasting political solution that might one day result in a peaceful, multiethnic federal nation. People every year marked February 12 as Union Day.

Folk dancing and the donning of ethnic costumes on the anniversary of the Panglong agreement had been just about the only official concession to that chimeric future. It had all gone south since 1947. General Ne Win's coup in 1962 had preempted the possibility of a Shan secession, and his Burman-centric rule had exacerbated desires for autonomy and self-rule. Since 1988, one of the more successful policies of the SLORC-turned-SPDC had been to ensure the impossibility of contact between the nonviolent pro-democracy movement of the mainland and the ethnic minorities.

The result had been greater mistrust, and the general ignorance it fomented. It was difficult enough to gauge viewpoints dispersed across a smorgasbord of different languages and remote hilltop outposts far from paved roads, without even trying to get past the British-era "Unlawful Associations Act" of 1908, whose vague provisions the junta wielded with relish to render illegal most groups on the border and likewise inside the country. For their trip to Mae Sot, Nway and Nigel had hurled headlong into multiple violations of the law.

It was worth the risk. Nway, a Burman if he ever thought to class himself ethnically, had understood young that you could travel a lifetime in the mainland democracy struggle and never once encounter the real problems that the minorities faced. He liked to tell people that the difference between the ethnic areas and the Burman-majority central plains was that if you "exercised your rights" in the plains, you'd be arrested and sentenced; in the ethnic areas you'd simply be killed. Without a chance to openly exchange views and perspectives, the main protagonists in the struggle against military rule could never truly forge a united front.

But the exiles—the students who had fled the crackdowns after August 8, 1988—knew more. In the jungle, in this jungle, they had shared with the Karen and the Mon handfuls of rice along with dreams of overthrow. Even the tree markings around Nway and Nigel reverberated with that past, a vestige of the students' pathway out of Burma.

Despairing for another way than nonviolent civil disobedience to rid the country of the junta, tens of thousands had scattered in the early 1990s from the central cities to the border with India, or China, or mainly right here, with Thailand. They'd sought alliances with the rebel Karen forces or the Mon, or whichever other armed ethnic group would care to train them. Here they had formed an army, the All Burma Students' Democratic Front, the ABSDF.

Perhaps here, too, had passed the students who had hidden in 1989 for nearly four months at the bottom of Nway's garden in Twantay. They had arrived one night, tense and bloodied. Nway's parents had arranged for them to hide in a little shack, half-submerged in weeds and twisting creepers. Nway and his three brothers were to provide the young men with constant alibis. They would sleep together: eight boys, with mattresses and pillows enough for only four. In case of local snoops or sudden searches, they could pass it all off as a fraternal pyjama party. At any hint of danger, they were to signal across the garden, back and forth between the shack and main house, using a sign language invented by Nway's father that they transmitted as shadow in shafts of flashlight. The stowaways knew, then, to disappear—scrambling over a wall, across an alley, and into the dark corners of a nearby pagoda. Nway, then only about seven or eight, had lived the entire episode as his first act of grand rebellion.

All four had eventually headed for the border. As a parting gift, one of them had left behind a poem. He had been reluctant to go, acutely aware of how combat in the jungle could ravage a mild city boy's body and a heart that had no deep yearning to shed blood. The only way back was victory or death.

In his poem, his tears fell onto train tracks. It might have been a metaphor for the inexorability of duty, or for the unstoppable march of tyranny, of the SLORC come to run them all down. The anguish of it had stuck with Nway all these years. A single teardrop had stopped the train. And then the young man's tears had dispersed.

He had been prescient enough.

On this border, in the jungle, there had been bickering bitter and fractious between and among the armed ethnic groups and the students of the ABSDF, whom the ethnic rebel forces had been inclined to mistrust because the students were mostly Burmans, tender urbanites whose end goal was democracy, without guarantees for the minority rights that the militias were fighting to achieve. Worse, the students fought among themselves, splintering along lines that derived in part from rivalries that had emerged in 1988 between two student unions. Miscommunication and cronyism had won the day over reason. Even the Karen National Union chairman, General Bo Mya, had attempted to heal their fissures at the ABSDF Third Party Congress with the slaughter of a cow and a pig, and the timely intervention of a Christian preacher, invited to deliver a sermon on unity. There had been greater controversies too: the alleged executions of ABSDF members on the border with China, and elsewhere on charges of espionage. By the mid-1990s, the breakdown of the anti-junta alliance had been multiheaded and messy enough to support the conventional cynicism among scholars and analysts that this was the way of Burmese culture, that no one knew the meaning of negotiation, that there was no hope for anyone to build anything because every disagreement became a personal feud.

Daily now, dozens of former young revolutionaries faced their legacy in a struggle that was no longer theirs to lead, watching from across oceans or from just over the border as versions of the same mistakes played out. Gone soft around the middle with time and the comforts of life in richer lands, they had little left but dashed dreams fermenting behind the smoke-and-mirrors of foreign-funded impotence and infighting.

Or so went the rumors. Nway knew it wasn't entirely their fault. Throughout the 1990s, the military junta had sown dissension, carving out ceasefires with one ethnic insurgent group after the next. They were temporary agreements that did little to address localized political grievances, but they assured a measure of stability by divvying up resources and land between minority commanders and their counterparts in the police or Tatmadaw. The ceasefires had also denied the groups incentives to unite. One by one, they gave up harboring student encampments, forcing the students backward into ever-dwindling zones of combat. The Tatmadaw could then apply the full measure of its growing offensive capability against those few groups that remained restive.

Chief among those were the Karen. But, in 1995, a Buddhist faction had broken from the Christian-led Karen army, the KNLA, and its century-old political wing, the Karen National Union, the KNU. That splinter group, the DKBA, or

Democratic Karen Buddhist Army, had allied with the junta in an act of perceived treachery that had led in December to the fall of Manerplaw, and with it the fatal loss of headquarters inside Burma for both the KNU and the pro-democracy alliance of veteran politicians and the students who had there planted their base.

Then had come a long, difficult period of self-imposed exile, the soul-searching of fast-aging men and women cut off from home, from prospects of normal life or honest income. Adrift in defeat, they were forced at last to see their efforts at armed uprising for a consolatory fantasy, the last-ditch malarial hallucinations of desperate zoology and physics students, half-starved and diseased in the jungle, drilling with bamboo sticks instead of rifles, hopped up on nothing more substantial than the unquenchable absolutism of their youth.

They had planted vegetable gardens, and hacked out training camps. They'd held conferences and planned and organized. But they'd had no resources, and no means of acquiring them. Their turn to violence had meant forsaking, in the eyes of the world, even the moral high ground that had attended the glory of a peaceful "people power" movement in 1988. Against the Tatmadaw—professionalized in years of counterinsurgency campaigns, and fed by bottomless supplies from joint-venture companies, flourishing harvests of opium poppy, China, and wholesale predation on local villages—the student army had never stood a chance.

Later, Nway had found out that his poet friend, the reluctant warrior who had sheltered in his garden, had died. How or where exactly—fighting for the ABSDF or felled by disease or merely from a broken heart—only the *nats*, the spirits in the trees and hills around Nway, could now recall.

But all that lived experience wasn't lost. When Nway had made a contact some weeks before with a mysterious exile in Rangoon, he decided it was a golden opportunity.

People had been stealing over the border for trainings or equipment for years—but the possibilities had narrowed since the border closures and Internet shutdowns in the year and a half since Saffron. Now at last on the edge of a river, almost narrow enough in places to reach across and connect hands, he could assess what there was to know, see the lacunae of contact for what it was, and bring back what he could to build ties with the movement's political center.

He had told himself that he needed to look serious. It meant he needed a wingman, and who better to accompany him than Nigel?

NIGEL AND NWAY HAD MET two years earlier at Open University classes at the British Council, a program with a handful of scholarships that the British Embassy quietly reserved for members of the party who had been chosen through examination.

They had been instant rivals, competitive in the way of young men discovering for the first time they were no longer the only star. There was something almost comically antipodal about them. Nigel was visibly deliberate. Nway's effort always seemed languorous, as if he were well oiled. Quickest off the mark, he had a tendency to twist and turn an argument like the body of a snake. In the split-second hesitation as others pondered a question, he would pounce, divvying up his answer into numbered points that struck one instantly as pithy and refreshingly direct, if, on reflection, lacking sometimes in theoretical subtlety.

Nigel had been warned about Nway. It was the kind of gossip that could delude one into thinking it had a grain of truth even as it wormed its way, mind to mind, from a rich loam of ignorance, mistrust, and fragments of interpretive reality. Nway had the quality of the rich kid and the know-it-all. He always seemed preoccupied with two things at once—an ear to his cell phone, or shooting a thought down-room in the space of a breath between two sentences—as if you weren't important or quick enough of wit to merit his full attention.

Nway was of that species to generate impulsive hatred or adoration. Few, if any, emerged from an early encounter with indifference. Even Maggie had it in for him, and she was their English teacher, a foreigner of Polish extraction with little claim to the darker rumors that circulated among activists.

Maggie taught them the word *manipulation*. But even as she tried to take Nigel under her wing, helping him with meals or field trips, and citing Nway as a prime example of "one who manipulates," Nigel spotted the fallacy. So Maggie hadn't fallen under Nway's spell. Did that really make him an opportunist, a businessman, a two-timer who slipped arrest by selling out his friends? Maggie didn't know anything about politics, anyway. On that assessment, largely intuitive, Nigel would never allow her to correct the substance of his political essays—only the inaccuracies of his English. That he might be wrong, politically naïve in the way he knew himself still to be, was immaterial. He would good and well figure it out for himself.

If it had hurt Nway to be maligned in that way, or to be misunderstood because he had succeeded too well at playing a role that he sometimes donned to conceal tasks of greater import for which he willingly sacrificed the superficial trappings of his reputation, he internalized the wound. He could fold in on himself and seem the more secretive or deceptive for it; and if the pain surfaced as an abscess, he could just puncture it with a joke.

Nway knew who loved him. Alix, his English teacher at the US Embassy's American Center where the NLD had dispatched him first, had fallen for him instantly—Nway and his best friend, Arthur, both. Nway and Arthur were not her best students, neither the most intellectually gifted nor the most attentive to detail in their assignments. But they had a goodness, a lightness of spirit underscored by a purity of purpose. More than Maggie, Alix sympathized with the impatience that could come of sitting through hours of syntax and grammar, when the nebulous and manifold abuses outside demanded a different sort of weaponry. Alix understood, moreover, that Nway had another job, more difficult, on the knife-edge of risk. If he showed up late, it wasn't because he was a slacker. Once, forty minutes into class, he had blasted through the door, dripping from head to toe, as if he had fallen or been kicked into the river. She never asked, and he didn't explain. He apologized with self-recriminatory severity, ducked straight for his workbook, and never looked up until class finished even though, a tropical animal inclined to sneeze at the barest gust of an electric fan, he shivered with increasing violence under the pitiless Arctic blasts of the American Center's functional air-conditioning.

Another day, he had brought along a girl whom he claimed as a cousin, and asked if Alix might teach her English too. With nary a hesitation, no questions asked, and never a thought for pay, Alix worked for weeks, with or without Nway beside her, to pry through her new charge's monosyllabic resistance. It came as less an insult to her relative age than a blessing when Nway and Arthur one day politely asked if they might henceforth call Alix *Mother*.

What Nway was, indubitably, was a natural spokesman.

Auntie had spotted it early, in 1998, within weeks of his first appearance at the party. She had chanced upon a book club—"death sentence for the author," Nway jested later—where a smudge of a thing with the concentrated almond gaze who couldn't have been long out of high school had been arguing with precocious audacity a contrarian position to the elders in the room about the significance of suicide in a famous novel called *Shame*. It must have struck her as sufficiently at odds with the deferential preference for age and the general self-restraint, because she handpicked him for the NLD's Central Youth Committee. In an instant, he had bypassed an age-based and geographic chain of command that ran from township-level committees to the Central Executive

Committee, with a rigidity that was increasingly earning the party criticism for failing to implement the democratic processes it claimed to represent.

Four years later, after Auntie had returned to house arrest, he had attended a lecture at the American Center delivered by two visitors from South Africa. They had shared perspectives on how to overthrow a government through noncooperation and the subtleties of a revelation that Nway henceforth called "spin-doctoring." When the lecture ended with a competition whose victor would have the task of drafting a two-page broadsheet, Nway had felt a twinge of urgency, as if the job belonged to no one else. He scored highest. There was such freedom in the prize—permission at last to express his concerns about the country exactly as he saw them.

His newspaper had reached Auntie, doubtless through the diplomatic pouch that back then she had still been allowed to receive. It was a greenhorn's effort, slapped together with earnestness, and additions from Arthur. Nway thought at least he must have made her laugh. She had that way about her—unabashedly entertained by his amateurism but still inclined to reward the effort. He had come to her another time with a translation of a *Newsweek* article. She had scanned it, giggled, and asked what he meant to do with it. Why, he'd answered, stick it to the wall of the NLD Youth Office for general educational purposes. She had responded by pulling to her side an elder to whom she assigned the task of helping Nway with his English. The man replied that he was busy, but would translate the piece on his own time. That would defeat the point, Auntie told the elder. Better, always, to teach a person to fish. Henceforth Nway had a private English tutor.

His stab at a newspaper had yielded still greater repercussions.

An Uncle soon told him that he would, per Auntie's request, be joining the NLD's Central Information Committee.

It was a serious promotion and Nway took it every bit as seriously. No one as junior in the party had made it to the committee responsible for communication with the media, at least not since arrests throughout the early 1990s had hulled the youth wing of its feistier '88 student revolutionaries. U Aung Shwe certainly had not approved Nway's advancement. The young man could claim the title, the NLD chairman had informed Nway, but he would, in practice, be forbidden from talking to reporters.

"Why?" Nway had fired back. "I'm over twenty. I'm the representative of a younger generation. I should have this right."

"You complain too much," came the reply.

He knew it was arrogant to argue. It didn't respect tradition. But the injustice of it, and the sheer political illogic, rankled more.

The party had never been so passive when Auntie was free. In 2000, between her first and second stints of house arrest, and two years into Nway's arrival, they had attempted to spread membership far and wide. That arrests would follow within hours of the first gatherings of each new Township Youth Committee became a given, the blackest among the black running jokes. The pattern was nearly every time the same: NLD youth members from one or other township recruited fourteen local youths, found a few senior members from the old 1990 chapter, and sought out a willing host. In their first and, as often, their last meeting, the new youth members of the chapters set about electing three among them to act as executives. Just in time for scrawling the candidates' names on a board and a brief stumping by each in turn, Auntie would appear, warm and smiling, with fresh-cut flowers in her hair.

The young organizers knew to expect her, and she knew when to come, because they had told her quietly as soon as they had clinched a quorum. She could arrive apparently unannounced, apparently on the spur of the moment, chauffeured by a loyal young man whose most salient quality was a harebrained disregard for common sense at the wheel and a concomitant genius for outmaneuvering officialdom on motorcycles. In another life, in Hollywood, he might have made a killing as a stuntman. In Burma, between bashings and malnutrition in prison, Auntie's chauffeur ended up blind.

The point had never been to set up yet more NLD committees. The turn of the twenty-first century had been a difficult political period, when perceptions about the junta's villainous absurdity collided near daily with the full measure of its repressive blowback and repression, each time, nearly won. Auntie could never leave her compound at 54 University Avenue without a convoy of state agents revving up on her tail. The NLD kids were by morning scrawling their names on blackboards and by evening crouching in a police van on their way to jail.

The point had been to defy attempts to isolate her. When she came, fear took a holiday. An advance party, the same youngsters who raised a quorum, would have let slip aloud in that market stall or this teashop that the Lady might be on her way.

"Did you hear?"

"Hear what?"

"The Lady! Coming here!"

"When?"

People heard. The news spread. Out they poured to see her. Then she could say a few words, laugh, shake outstretched hands, and accept bouquets. For a moment, possibly for years beyond, the people she had been forbidden from reaching had been touched, again, with hope.

It had been six solid years since the party had abandoned that kind of provocation.

After an attack by USDA thugs on Auntie's convoy in the northern town of Depayin on May 30, 2003, killing at least seventy NLD supporters, she'd been returned to house arrest for "protective custody."

Nway and others from a camp of young members who were informally referred to as "the Lady's youth" had ever since wasted through long hours at the Office, pushing letters across a desk, transcribing a few, but mainly hatching plots and watching them deflate in the cigarette-fogged corner room that served as the youth office. They ached for more productive activity, as opposed to "Chairman Aung Shwe's youth," who inclined toward sitting pretty, holding fast to the law. The divide protracted a difference in approach that had its origins in the NLD's beginnings, between the intellectuals and student "hardliners" and the former army commanders, Aung Shwe among them, who preferred moderation.

For all the constraints on the party imposed by the junta, there were ways to fact-find and recruit. Nway and his friends felt a responsibility to somehow document and broadcast abuses. They had legs. They had so much energy. What purpose the party of people's rights, they mused with ever increasing pique, if its most dynamic representatives only lounged about and smoked?

At least the downtime had given him plenty of time to read. There wasn't much available in the Office. Though the NLD had attempted to tally problems and prisoners, members had learned the hard way that it was best to keep the most incriminating details of their activities inside their heads. What had been set down and filed away in cabinets that gathered dust against the walls, three sets of raids had more or less finished off.

Still, there were party rules to peruse, and meeting minutes, and sheaves of statements. He picked up what he could: befriending some of the senior Uncles, piecing together a narrative of modern history and his own sense of how and why the country had reached its current mess. He had learned as well as anyone how the party worked: its chief players, its challenges, its intrigues. And he knew now how to "spin-doctor" it all, reveling in a rudimentary vocabulary that allowed him to refine for himself a most intriguing new political skill.

The other Uncles of the Information Committee had watched Nway watching, and recognized Auntie's attempt to promote him for what it was. Even
from under house arrest, she was trying to inject the party with new vigor and
sharp political instinct.

Privately, they told him that they would give him his chance. Henceforth he
could act as go-between with NLD local members, and he could take responsibility on issues of special concern to the youth.

Never would Nway admit that he was the son of a nurse who had treated
Auntie's ailing mother in Rangoon General Hospital in 1988, before they had
become friends in their own right. He didn't mention either that his father
had danced with Aung San Suu Kyi as a schoolboy, selecting the daughter of
General Aung San when he picked her shoe by chance from a pile in a formal
ball for their respective boys' and girls' schools in India. Nway would never
mention his father at all. Everyone had his tragedy. Nway would, and had,
earned his place in the NLD fair and square, though unconventionally, on his
own merits.

But for his fast rise he had never since lived down the jealousy.

༈

NIGEL, THOUGH, HAD BEEN DIFFERENT. Fine-tuned to sense peo-
ple's political potential, Nway had seen the possibilities in him at once. Back in
'98, his inaugural year in the NLD, Nway and Arthur had likewise hated each
other on sight. And look where that friction had got them: so close they could
almost finish each other's thoughts.

But then, of course, Arthur had fallen in love. It was an idiotic lapse of
judgment. He had decided to marry the girl, and, lovely though Nway had to
concede that she was, Arthur's girlfriend was no activist. So, actually, it was un-
forgivable. When Arthur married, he would have to take care of her. He would
have to think about an income. He would—criminally—have to give up politics. Nway and Arthur had sworn a pact on it: never to fall in love, never *ever* to
marry. And now Arthur had headed straight for treachery. Nway hadn't talked
to Arthur in weeks. He never made it to the wedding.

Along came Nigel with his clear-eyed way, his avidity and evident intelligence. Bonded a bit by the mishap with Maggie, Nigel and Nway learned that
they shared a vision, a consummate ability to stand back and see it all with ambition as lofty as the country's future and a perspective that looked beyond the
puniness of their particular egos.

They had also felt a mutual outrage when authorities at the British Council decided midway through their four-year Open University degree to reduce it to a two-year certificate. They were told they could complete their degree in Thailand.

Nigel took the certificate. Nway refused it, on principle. But neither of them would venture abroad for the final two years, knowing, with force, that it would destroy their ability to work as activists, exposing them to authorities through passport control and all the attendant paperwork. To their mind, the decision was capricious and unjust, utterly defeating the purpose of secret scholarships designed to educate pro-democracy activists so they could apply their learning to the problems at home.

It was clear to Nway that Nigel had it in him to become a stellar "front-liner." He was a born leader. Without vanity, he was willing to step into the limelight. For all his own surface brashness, Nway had always preferred to maneuver from behind the scenes. His talent was strategic invisibility. The possibility of a partnership yielded thoughts of the creative, one-time interaction between Auntie and Grandpa, U Win Tin, wizened senior journalist turned senior strategist of the party.

From a grain of begrudging respect, and a few rounds of drink, Nway and Nigel nurtured a fledgling trust. Eventually they splashed around ideas for a network of their own. Something small, Nway felt, with "minimal risk but huge impact." Tensions were rising within the NLD youth wing. The Saffron protests of September 2007 had come and gone. The NLD caretakers had failed to claim any measure of political leadership that, in Nway's eyes, might have made all the difference.

Brimming with human evidence, video evidence, photo evidence—and no outlet for any of it—he had within weeks of the crackdown made contact with a reporter from the Democratic Voice of Burma, which operated out of Oslo to edit and broadcast the raw footage sent in by a network of on-ground secret reporters. It meant at last that Nway and his peers had a place to send all their accumulated documentation. Who cared, really, if the exile media station took credit for all of it, never acknowledging that some—most of it, in Nway's eyes—was fed to them not by their own "underground reporters" but by the unpaid rank-and-file from the political party whose representation in the revolution never made it into the headlines?

Eight months later, the NLD executives' failure to respond to the referendum on the junta's new constitution had proven the final straw. Nway, in defiance of his senior leaders' passivity, had gathered a few friends to monitor the voting.

Born in controversy, drafted under duress on and off for fourteen years, and enshrining clauses that seemed unequivocally designed to entrench military rule behind a civilian façade, the constitution had been scheduled for a referendum on May 10, 2008. Everyone knew it would be rigged. Come hell or high water, Nway felt, it was their duty to document the details.

Then hell had hit.

Whole villages had been razed as Tropical Cyclone Nargis made landfall on the night of May 2–3 across the Irrawaddy Delta before cutting a northwestern path that blitzed through Rangoon and swirling apart in Mon and Arakan states on either edge of the country. Peak winds of 105 mph had churned up walls of seawater that coursed up the Irrawaddy to twenty-five miles inland, submerging entire districts, smashing away straw-and-bamboo huts and snapping the *hti* umbrellas atop pagodas like little twigs. There were stretches of land that looked as if they had been carpet-bombed. Monasteries and schools had been just about the only critical infrastructure to survive. Gone too were oxen, water buffalo, and stores of paddy seed, or fishing boats, pigs, and bullock carts on which the smalltime farmers and fishermen of the delta hitched livelihoods that even in good years barely hovered above subsistence levels. A harvest or four of desperate conditions beckoned. Across Rangoon, streets and boulevards were clogged with felled trees and blown-off roofs, and electric power and basic supplies were even shorter than the norm.

International aid workers waited white-knuckled in Bangkok or off the coast for a green light to chopper in emergency supplies. The junta stonewalled, and stalled on what few visas and permits it granted to relief workers from agencies that were already based in the country. But it deployed law enforcement to hustle and scare people across the country to polling sites in time for the constitutional referendum. On the day of the vote, tens of thousands of people were still unaccounted for, their numbers rising day by day to a final official toll of about 138,000. Though conceding that the worst-hit areas in the delta could postpone their vote by ten days, the junta didn't wait before declaring a ninety-eight percent turnout, with a ninety-two percent approval rate.

Nway and his colleagues had been forced to work in the open street. They'd had neither equipment nor any means of organizing a scientific countrywide surveillance. In advance, he had coordinated with acquaintances across the country, near enough to secretly observe polling stations without taking undue risks. They were to stand by with information, to be collected by half a dozen friends in Rangoon, via Nway's single cell phone. Then they would phone in live reports to his contact at DVB.

It was tricky enough to pull off without arrests, but it wouldn't have been impossible, were it not for their leaders' bureaucratic mule-headedness: refusal to open the Office a hair earlier than the usual 9 a.m., refusal to keep it open past 4 p.m., regardless of the fact that the polls that day opened at dawn and closed at 6 p.m.

At least a dozen NLD youth crowded outside the Office, just opposite the little yellow-plastered Special Branch hut. They were violating the prohibitions against public assembly, plus about a half-dozen additional laws with every thought, gesture, and half-step that questioned the junta's "roadmap to disciplined democracy." All they could do for self-protection was to relocate a few feet with every phone call, and pray. Nway had been sorely tempted to wave and say cheese.

He had withheld the urge out of a stronger sense of the gravity at hand— which was to gather and disseminate all the evidence that they could collate about the violations of the junta's referendum, conducted in a country ripped apart by a storm so lethal and so poorly dealt with that the bodies were still floating by the thousands, bloated and rotting in the tide-locked rivulets of his native delta.

Monks and citizens of Rangoon had taken it upon themselves to head from the city with whatever supplies that they could muster, or they were picking the bones from the bracken fields and burning the dead on giant funeral pyres. Homeless, hungry, and without livelihoods, thousands of storm survivors were squatting in long lines down the sides of the few roads of the delta. Nway had only to step out of his house in Twantay, one of very few with an extant roof, to witness the devastation. Everyone had been touched. Kyaw Kyaw, new to DVB, had felt compelled to begin a documentary on the children that the cyclone had orphaned. His eye pinned to a camera lens, fixing the ruin to the far horizon, his brother had accidentally stepped on a cadaver. Cyclone Nargis and the chaos of its aftermath were the strangest visions of all their lives.

Within three months, U Aung Shwe, doubtless fed up by the youths' constant whining and the breakdown of general discipline, was threatening to reconfigure a new youth committee, handpicked from his perceived favorites. Against them, rumors were unleased of bad behavior—misuse of money,

selling out to intelligence, even sexual misconduct. They were allegations carried on a wave of Chinese whispers that, once let loose or even hinted at, could
forever besmirch an activist's good name and fatally destroy fragile filaments of
trust. "The Lady's gang" went on record to the exile press saying they would
have to resign if their views were not heard.

Even for Nigel, a fresh face to the NLD since only 2007, it was time to look
beyond the party.

⤫

PISSY AND SILENT, THEY WERE headed home now: back across the
river to a smudge of a path that snaked through hip-high grasses and tufts of
trees, a Karen jungle trail, to an open-back pick-up that would bump them to
the KNLA tollgate toward which they had been instructed to aim; a palmful
of "tea money" handed over in lieu of Thai exit visas; and then—assuming no
hiccup—the fifteen-hour bus ride via Hpa-an to Rangoon.

"I should tell the Uncles about 'Ko Thu Ta,'" Nway said to no one in particular, gaze drifting with the smoke of his cigarette as it gusted out over the water.

Nigel, finally snapping, engaged.

"No. You shouldn't," he said. "You'll lose all respect."

Five days of listening in near silence to the theater of banter between the
exiles and Nway, five nights of watching him peacock-puffed in the chest and
loosened up with booze, boasting about what he knew and what he couldn't or
wouldn't say, and what their hosts pretended to know and couldn't or wouldn't
in turn divulge and Nigel felt not a hair more reassured about the situation over
the border or its capacity to wreak havoc among activists inside. They'd been
like zoo animals, trapped in the cage of a compound, prodded and displayed
for the sport of a handful of men, who were balding and paunchy in the way
of veterans indulging their nostalgia with reheated reminiscence and too much
beer to drown its chronic ache. And was it not envy that he could have sworn
flickered in their eyes? They hid it well, that or some deeper grief, behind their
bravado, their condescension and surface posturing. In Nway, or in Nway and
Nigel both, their hosts had seemed to mine the experience of activism inside
Burma as if to revive a world forever lost to them.

But Nway had risen to the show, either because he knew and didn't care,
or didn't see enough to know. With each passing day, Nigel's heart had sunk.
He'd had high hopes—for what, he wasn't sure. He'd assumed at least an even
footing with his friend. Instead he found himself silenced, relegated to the wall.

The frustration wasn't just that Nigel had never been a shrinking violet. Like Nway, he had a keen ability to distinguish blind subservience from the ritual necessity of occasional deference. Life in an anarchic brood of nine, with its readymade system of checks and balances on any one sibling's insurgent claims, had a way of providing early lessons about uneven distributions of power. It didn't take a grand degree to recognize the inconsistencies between the natural administration in the little society of his hut and the inequities beyond.

Which meant he had the capacity, when it suited, to break free of feeling *anade*, a sensitivity peculiar to the culture that bubbled up as mingled guilt and shame in anticipation of causing discomfort. It was the height of decency to spare people accordingly; therein lay much of the secret to native Burmese warmth and hospitality. The trouble with feeling *anade*, though, was that it frequently entangled itself within the web of other social obligations—toward parents, teachers, and sages, or anyone above a certain age. That meant it could, and did as often, collide with the urge to stand up to authority, if or when authority proved outrageously or intuitively wrong.

By that standard, there was no reason here for bootlicking. The situation called for politeness, certainly. Reverence, no. By whose appointment had these men earned their veneer of leadership in the movement? Had the fresh air of freedom—the very world theirs for the taking—rendered their sense of themselves too heady?

Worse was the venality. The pair had ventured over the border to plead for money, which was ugly enough. But now Nway was hoarding it all himself, all the cash and gadgets and whatever else "Ko Thu Tha," their host, had given them. Nigel couldn't say for sure how much, because Nway—sitting opposite, flicking his cigarette ash into the river—hadn't let him near so much as a gumball.

Like a sharp slap, the full blow of his first trip to Mae Sot hit him again now: the sudden recognition of people's complicity through inaction with the vast malfeasance of the system. At the very least, it lay at the core of their passivity and fear. It wasn't power that corrupted. It was fear. Auntie had famously written as much. With that realization had come a stab of self-awareness that he was as guilty, because, like the rest of them, he had willingly—until that moment—surrendered to his powerlessness.

Why, then, should he have imagined that this trip would prove different? Why? Because now he was an activist, splashing about in something greater than the sum of his personal needs and wishes? Because he believed in Nway and their shared vision, and thought in turn that Nway trusted him? Why else would Nway have invited him along, on a trip as risky?

Nigel had never much considered himself quick to judgment. But business, or transactions of pecuniary power masked as instances of principle, turned him to stone. In the muggy morass of mid-river, batting away the flies, he brooded on the lesson of this second trip, still more damning than his first. Now it wasn't that people were shying from activism out of passivity, but rather that activists—the very people holding the torch for everyone else's hopes—could be as corrupt as the system they were fighting.

He didn't entirely doubt the sincerity of some exiles, nor their significance in the larger movement. He'd discovered it firsthand some weeks earlier, after the point man for MDC, the Myanmar Development Committee, had vanished underground and Nigel had taken his place to become chief online "fuse" between a cell of the group and the exile who went by "Happy." Until then, he had acted as an unofficial translator, helping the MDC point man send English versions of terse updates on Google-chat to Happy, in exchange for—whatever it was that had warranted the updates. Employing English on Gchat was helpful because informers and spies tended not to read it, but mainly because Burmese script had yet to be encoded as Unicode, the industry standard, and the alternative was woeful miscommunication between computers employing variations.

In their sporadic conversations, Happy's instant messages had exuded an avuncular geniality. With the intimacy of lived experience but without its sneer of superiority, the exile had appeared to draw just enough information from the snatches they sent to offer what counsel he could.

Nigel never knew that Happy had once been a young doctor who drank cough syrup through medical school to numb some doleful filial disaffection and the broader political malaise that had, later, been Nigel's too; that, when the country combusted in 1988, he had, like Nigel in 2007, found himself, stumbling on innate talent as a community organizer; that he too had known the first euphoria of revolution and the terrible disillusion of the crackdown.

Happy never thought it necessary to divulge that he had been one of the two famous leaders of the student army, the All Burma Students' Democratic Front, the ABSDF. Nor could Nigel know from their faceless online interactions about the man's sense of the tragic, how the subtle slump of his shoulders held the burden of his responsibility for the failures that had kept them all in stalemate, because they spilled at least a little from his personal rift in 1991 with Moe Thee Zun, the other brash young leader of the ABSDF, though more ideological and strident. Pragmatic engagement with the here-and-now had always been more pressing.

What had passed between Nigel and Happy in the terse exchanges of their Gchats had drawn instead on the language of "civil society building" and "community development"—the less insidious lexicon of a revolutionary strategy that had developed, since the fall of Manerplaw and the soul-searching thereafter, into a more evolutionary mission among activists to spread education and teach workers and farmers about the meaning of democracy and human rights, the value of the environment, labor rights or women's rights, or resource rights. They were goals to help rebuild a nation that in Happy's breakout day in '88 had been slogans, just words that they shouted with full lungs and slapped on banners without thought for what they meant or how they could, only with effort and particularist focus, take root in their society.

It was safer not to reveal biographical details—that Happy's real name was Dr. Naing Aung, "DNA," and that he had lately assumed joint-responsibility for rethinking the strategy of the wider democracy movement. Since the arrival of the Internet and then the debacle of the Saffron uprising, Happy had helped unite into a single alliance about ten exile groups, and while they were advocating abroad and helping Burma stay on the agendas of distracted foreign states, they were also recruiting and coordinating activists inside Burma. Yet, without the chance to communicate openly in turn, all Nigel had learned of the man and his world over the border was that he was someone significant. It had been enough to trust that Happy had the knowledge and perspective of the forest, and the ability to impart it to the activists stuck among the trees.

But Nigel hadn't met Happy in Mae Sot. Now that he had witnessed the view from the forest, he'd seen only vindication of the worst rumors.

It could have turned out otherwise. "Ko Thu Tha"—their host of recent days—had seemed to want to talk with Nigel. He was a big man, an important deputy for the government-in-exile, the National Coalition Government of the Union in Burma, or NCGUB, which had come together from among the candidates who had won the 1990 elections, then fled to the border after the SLORC had definitively ignored its results. But there'd been troublingly little chance for real interaction; Nway had been poised to interrupt at every attempt.

From the rest of their host crew, all Nigel heard were snippets about international influence. They seemed caught in some vast, transnational enterprise and it smelled of business that was dirty and corrupting. Perhaps the power of all that knowledge and all those global connections, like the choice in Thailand among brands of beer, had proved intoxicating.

"I don't trust them," he said now to Nway. "They were just trying to impose their ideas on us."

Nway, caught in a long, complicated thought, didn't think to answer.

Later, with the hindsight of the frost that came between them, he would formulate just the right response. It was the one point that might have ended the entire argument because he knew that deep down Nigel felt it too or they would never have got this far. "Well, maybe," Nway should have said. "But we must find a way to cooperate with them. Our enemy is too big."

He had also seen ample evidence in Thailand to sense some vastness that he couldn't fully grasp. But where Nigel had smelled a rat, stymied in the way of the blind man groping at an elephant, Nway had apprehended enough to wonder at the shape of that enormous contour.

Sure, the fiscal morality of some exiles was probably rough around the edges. The junta's propaganda had always smeared them as foreign stooges, dancing to the tune of purposes un-Burmese. There had been a time, in the mid-1990s, when the state mouthpieces featured regular fabrications about young innocents, university students who had fled to the border areas, returning home chastened and horrified by rape or other abuses that they had supposedly suffered at the hands of the student rebels. It was cleverly poisonous. These days, the rhetoric had all the clumsy subtlety of a tiptoeing ogre. People dismissed it in the way they best made use of its source, the *New Light of Myanmar*—as kindling for their kitchen fires. But the relentlessness of its message had left an invidious imprint because it converged with a sense that was all too much a part of the culture. And that was that money was unsavory. It bought agendas; it skewed the cause. It got people arrested.

The theory, so far as Nway had discerned, wasn't entirely false. Exile organizations had come to depend for their livelihoods on foreign donors, which meant they had to satisfy an agenda that was no longer entirely their own.

Which didn't mean the exiles weren't worth an audience. They had so much accumulated experience. Reality, besides, was more complex, and Nway hadn't needed to make it out of the country to trust the possibility that his own prejudices could be wrong. Not all exile organizations were crooked, or exploitative, or obsessed with their own inflated importance. Their work included the great success of lobbying Western governments to impose sanctions on Burma. Successive waves of them, through the 1990s and since Saffron, had ensured the surgical encroachment on the assets and rights of travel enjoyed by generals, their families, and their crony kingpins. If they hadn't bankrupted the junta, they had undoubtedly played the leading role in devastating both its international and domestic legitimacy. Other organizations had even managed to embarrass the junta with sufficient international noise about its widespread use of forced labor that it now had to concede to the presence of the International Labor Organization. The exiles had recognized early that the junta's desire for acceptance, including its bid to join ASEAN, was a pillar of weakness that they could shake to the core.

Too well, moreover, Nway understood his movement's tendency toward fragmentation. "Family politics," he called it, with a flaring of the nostrils. He would substantiate the thesis with examples in the long, twisted narrative of broken national dreams between the first stabs at national uprising against the British and the stagnancy of now. He'd start with the power struggle between Aung San and his brother-in-law, Than Tun, one of the leaders of the Communist Party of Burma. He'd pass next through the tumult of 1988, the first great chance to rally together against one-party rule. Instead the veteran politicians of the 1950s went one way and the prominent leaders who eventually formed the NLD went another; and then the troika that had founded the NLD had split.

The history of the students since 1990s had been as bleak.

"We must change this history," Nway would say, thumping a table, referencing some new disagreement that was bringing them all to a standstill.

That only four months earlier he had himself loudly resigned from the NLD along with most of its youth wing didn't seem pertinent; Nway had no intention of defying the party's larger goal. His walkout was a tactical decision, only a touch fired by his penchant for tripwire recalcitrance. But really, it had hinged on the betrayal by sheer ineptitude of that broader final ambition, which was to replace military rule with democracy and, in the meantime, act like actual representatives of the people.

There was wisdom in the broader movement, out on the periphery, beyond the NLD and its effort to achieve democracy within the framework of the law. Only now, emancipated since his resignation in October from the confines of the party, could Nway seek it out.

But in the past five days the opportunities had been so limited. For safety's sake, they hadn't been able to venture beyond the compound into Mae Sot proper. The town was a minefield, crawling not only with Thai police primed to catch illicit migrants but also with spies, a factoid that Nway appreciated with special pique on account of a recent botched attempt to acquire a passport. He'd applied through a broker to whom he'd coughed up an exorbitant fee on a promise-or-your-money-back of fast-tracked paperwork, unlikely enough for the average plebeian, much less anyone with the complication of sometime NLD membership. Summoned to the passport office, Nway had met with a senior intelligence officer and fielded questions that had with sinister exactitude homed in on why and when he had resigned from the NLD, and whether and for what purpose he was still meeting with senior politicians. He'd answered with a sly heaping of honesty, enough to carry the day without actually selling out. Interview completed, the intelligence officer had told him to return within twenty-four hours to collect his passport. All Nway needed to do in turn, the officer had beamed, was to pledge that he would, while abroad, check in with authorities every two weeks and deliver a list of names of all the people he'd met. Nway had thanked the officer, flashed a hundred-watt smile—and skedaddled. He had never even bothered to retrieve the whopping fee he'd funneled to the passport broker.

The junta cast a long shadow. It was hard enough to disabuse people of the complex of deceptions and relationships by which they participated in their own surveillance. Most everyone had a nephew who was a monk, an NLD uncle, a cousin in the military or another working the paddies, a sister in university, or a civil servant taking bribes for pay somewhere therein. Clearly the Burmese diaspora, in Thailand or elsewhere, suffered from the same stressors—the chronic tic in the neck from constantly glancing over the shoulder.

Still, for all its limitations, this trip had proved just as the mysterious contact had told Nway weeks earlier. The man proffering the invitation had been refreshingly demeaning: spot on with a diagnosis that the road to democracy was paved with good intentions but woeful capacity. They needed skills. They needed knowledge. They needed to understand the international context. How often had Nway pondered that same predicament, endlessly holding it to the light?

Nway took it as a given that Nigel didn't understand the significance of cultivating VIP contacts. He saw this as some venal power play, as if Nway were hoarding them for no reason beyond his own distended ego—which, if Nway was honest with himself, he was a bit. Except it was the only way. The interconnections of the movement were everything. If he had the faintest interest in academia, he might have written a tome on the subject. It wasn't charity work. Sometimes it hinged on kinship, or bonds of love and friendship that no interrogation, no matter how brutal, could ever sever. But just as often, the only way to circumvent the toxin of mistrust was through barter, a rub-my-back-and-I-yours expediency. Risks of betrayal and exploitation were par for the course. Such was the nature of a social movement forged and maintained in the half-light of an information blackout, strewn with informers and stymied by communication that could only ever be piecemeal.

For eleven years, Nway had operated at or near the lodestone of the movement, learning from the best. He had befriended the senior Uncles and grown so close to Auntie when she'd roamed free that she had come to call him *Baby*. That they became surrogates for the sisters, fathers, children, whom they could never have or who had vanished or grown into strangers in their long absences—all that was incidental. Nway had profited from the intimacy to become a vital link between the old and the new, connecting the know-how from decades of opposition to military rule with the inchoate savvy of his generation, denied the rudiments of decent education but groping, in the absence of their elders, for a rebellious politics all of their own.

Meanwhile, who could deny their need for resources? Why not milk the exiles? It wasn't as if they had any qualms in turn about dangerously capitalizing on their contacts within the country—the activists who risked everything with every gesture—the better to claim greater influence when they appealed to foreigners for funding. Nway had enough dirt on them, or at least the risks some exile groups had blithely demanded of his friends back home, to turn blue in the face.

But right then, on the sampan, he had no time for appeasement. Nigel was the rookie, new enough to the NLD that he had to play second fiddle. He just didn't get it. Politically, it was important that Nway seem in control—unfair though it might seem to Nigel. To have any platform with the exiles, Nway needed to appear big, bigger than he felt, big enough at least to be told what the Uncles back home needed to hear, and likewise to seem capable of leading a network that might have significance in the wider movement.

They were fatter for the effort by a cell phone and a full five *lakh*, about five hundred dollars. Of course it fell to him to hoard the booty. What good in spreading risk? Ko Thu Tha had told Nway as much: Nway had been the chief point of contact, Nway had sought the meeting and the equipment. To Nway, thus, fell the responsibility of smuggling it back.

But all that was impossible to explain.

Nway was as handicapped from birth as the rest, forced to live among walls that the junta's system threw up between even the most intimate of friends—for all his ability to parse tradition from mere habit, to apprehend the constraints of authoritarianism for how they mutilated his society. Neither Nway nor Nigel, nor anyone else as open of mind, had the language to break through, the permission granted to oneself to come clean and to simply, straightforwardly communicate. Every thought dodged another. Each factoid needed to be weighed for cloaking. Even when he trusted with his life, as Nway trusted Nigel, it was always safer, for everyone, to keep mum.

Still, there was something that irked. Nway felt small. Was it true? Had he been played? Try though he might, he couldn't entirely swallow his own story. Mission accomplished, somewhat. Now they had to focus on returning in one piece. And all for what?

In truth, the trip had proven a grand disillusion. Certainly he had gathered more contacts. He'd learned about the power of international policymaking and how to deploy the "boomerang" effect, appealing to a third, foreign party to exert pressure on the junta. There were hints of still greater innovation, such as the group that ran Radio Blue Mountain, a roving two-way interactive show that broadcast to Tatmadaw grunts serving on the remotest fringes, encouraging them to speak aloud their frustrations. Hundreds of soldiers were rumored to be deserting.

Often it was a question of the right small push. The great American theorists of strategic nonviolent action, Colonel Bob Helvey and Professor Gene Sharp, had taught as much to some of these very exiles about fifteen to twenty years before: you could undercut the structures that propped up a dictatorship—the civil servants, the bureaucrats, the rank-and-file of the army—if only you presented them with a vision of a viable and different tomorrow.

Nway could even live with the sense that his hosts saw him as nothing more than a naïf—a poor player with a pathetic plan for a hit-and-run, flash-mob-style network. Case in point, he had set out for twice the amount that Ko Thu Tha—Dr. Thaung Htun—had given him.

But now he was beholden to an exile. As Nway and Nigel left, their pauperism and dependency compounded the sense that they had all been circling each other like tigers. There hadn't been time enough to break through the mistrust.

And what the exiles knew of the mechanics of the NLD, and who did what, and how and why was minimal. The government had Military Intelligence, the

USDA, and Special Branch. They had eyes in every computer, on every phone, at every street corner. What, at root, could the exiles help them achieve, with all their experience and access? It was gutting to sense—somewhere between the hinterland and home—that the junta might have, after all, succeeded.

Or—had it won? Were activists in Burma and abroad not instead building something that was larger than any individual could perceive? Nway couldn't say. The only lasting outcome of the trip was the immensely depressing certainty that he and his peers could meanwhile rely only on themselves.

4

GRANDPA

Today is March 12, 2010. Today I reached the age of 80. The age of 80
is rather too old. From where I am, I can see the crematorium at the
cemetery. It is not far away. When I say "it's not far away," don't
come asking me if the end of this last journey is getting any closer.
Don't come telling me that the end is still far away.

I know the end of my journey is near. I know the funeral pyre is close
at hand.

I know the time left for me to live is less and less.

I know death closes in.

But beyond the realization of all this is the realization that I still have
a lot of work to do. That is the point of what I want to say here.

—Win Tin, *What's That? A Human Hell*

ALWAYS KEEN FOR GOOD WORDPLAY, Grandpa didn't mince it
pretty about freedom. There was no freedom behind bars; no great epiphanies
that landed in the quiet of isolation; no moments of redemptive mental escape.
No glimmer of justification could or would he find to sanction a quarter of a
life there lost. And when they spat him back out, it was all same same. To a
reporter from Radio France Internationale who came to Rangoon to collect his
biography, none too aware that he had every intention of scratching out his own
within the year in a furious race against his own mortality, U Win Tin called
freedom after his release "a farce."

They kicked him out of Insein Prison on September 23, 2008. After nineteen years, two months, and nineteen days, he had just over nine months left to serve on his full sentence. The sun had yet to burn the morning into a wet furnace when they unlocked the door to his cell. He refused to emerge; wouldn't follow orders to bundle up his few books and bits of old cloth; flipped off the insult of a release that turned on Section 401, the amnesty clause of the Criminal Procedure Code, because it would have meant accepting the state's pardon as if, back when, he had committed an actual offense. Also, it came on condition that he sign a form renouncing all future political activity. They might as well have asked a cow to fly over the moon.

For one thing, he had a track history of turning them down. In 1991, the same offer had landed after they had softened him up with a decent lunch. Then came the temptation of 1995, a delicate opportunity that in retrospect would have allowed him a critical reunion with Aung San Suu Kyi, U Kyi Maung, and U Tin Oo, the other newly released founders of the NLD party. The last attempt had come just seven months earlier. He had been recovering in the high-security ward in the basement of Rangoon General Hospital from a second hernia operation and they must have calculated that the physical weakness or the fog of anesthesia had somehow mangled his brain.

For another, in the entirety of his two-decade incarceration, he had never exactly shikoed in abasement. Already before he'd joined the NLD executive in 1988, his four-decade career as a journalist had been a litany of cutting against the currents of the country's political turbulence. Through and through, after he had graduated from his first job, playing hooky from Rangoon University to pull near-all-nighters collating the latest Agence France-Presse dispatches to break them to Mandalay by sunrise; after he had cofounded a newspaper that pioneered gut-punching editorial audacity; after he had faced his first confrontation with the Tatmadaw for publishing a report about the astounding poverty and isolation he had discovered in a visit to the Kachin people in the mountains near China—he had never shied from the stories that demanded to be told, issues that he felt needed to be discussed and disinfected in the court of public opinion. So be it if it would mean taking a controversial position, risking a jail sentence, or facing off with what he had diagnosed as early as 1958, the period of the Military Caretaker Government, as a dangerous mental rigidity among military officers.

In prison, he'd tried hunger strikes; speeches honoring important anniversaries shouted through the bars of a kennel shared with the prison attack dogs;

and a twenty-five-page denunciation of an exhibition that depicted the 1988 up-rising as a riot instigated by "destructive elements and terrorists." They had taken him out of his cell in 1991 to visit the show at Envoy Hall on U Wizara Road in downtown Rangoon as part of their first bid to turn the national lu-minary into one of theirs. To the exhibition slogan, "Only when the Army is strong will the country be strong," Win Tin, like a patient schoolmaster, had returned: "The reality is that the military comes out of the womb of the people. Thus, the slogan should be: 'The people are the only parents of the military.'" And on he had averred. He wrote, he told them, with self-professed "sincerity and openness," relishing the chance to score his truth across every last, delicious morsel of paper they gave him, in the service of calling their bluff.

His boldest moment had required a different sort of finesse. Paper and pens were forbidden to prisoners; reading material, for the better part of twenty years, was the stuff of fancy. The only relief was release or oblivion, if only the flesh could be numbed to sporadic beatings and the bones to the chill that seeped in from bare, concrete floors. To receive as a gift or as barter a native-made cheroot and not to smoke it; to instead hold its fragrant leaves to the nostrils, blotting out the pervasion of rot; to unpeel those leaves and, with trembling fingers, find the thumb-sized filter, wrapped always in a fragment of newspaper; and then to hold up that fragment to a shaft of daylight and so reveal upon it three strokes of ink, two words, the suggestion of a phrase: that was to discover, or rediscover, the entire world.

Let them destroy the body. Let them debase the potential of each day into a routine of mere animal survival. The grit of the prison encrusted every crack of skin and fumed through every pore. But Win Tin, a man of letters who had lived for free expression, would not abide starvation of the mind. As long as inmates languished in cells together and had their wits still with them, they'd try, and manage, other ways. He had been a ringleader, and the doyen of writ-ing and publishing activities, in what he came to call Insein's Joint Action Committee. The idea for it trickled into form, cell to cell, by tapping messages on pipes or bowls or walls; or in coded strings of pebble or threaded plastic bags or rolled up inside cheroots that they passed through prison staff and petty con-victs whom they'd cultivated with cigarettes, *kyat* bills, or whatever other trea-sures they could hoard. Infinitely more efficient were snatches of real dialogue in the fifteen minutes at the communal trough at bath time, or if they were espe-cially lucky, in an hour or two of exercise outside, dependent on select wardens who knew when and for just how long to turn away.

Somehow, across months, a germ of solidarity had blossomed into a move-ment, defined only by its self-perpetuating defiance, the targeting of injustices in prison life, and the spinning of an ever-widening web that eventually netted accomplices down at least two halls and in over two-dozen shared cells. It had never been the smartest move, in truth, to skim the hotheads from an opposi-tion to military rule that spanned the gamut from rabid communists to armed ethnic guerrilla leaders, to starry-eyed schoolboys, former military command-ers, ministers-elect of parliament, and one wizened guru of national journalism, then dump them all within the perimeter of a few hundred yards. Had the JAC's chief organizers taken roll call at its height, they might have claimed participa-tion from more than three hundred inmates and too many guards and bit-prison laborers to count.

The majesty of it lay precisely in the ensemble performance. Between stabs of anger or expanses of boredom so agonizing that the desire gripped to eat one's own arm, inmates fell prey to that old national scourge: factionalism. It was worse here, as if the sun concentrated its full force into the Petri dish of one walled-in metallic world, and man, stripped to nothing except a prison number, had ever to contend against the dust and the boil in his blood and the temptation to lapse into the easy savagery of dog eat dog.

Here it had been necessary to sniff out and circumvent the spies down the hall, the common criminals among them who could find relief from demucking the outhouses or other of the filthiest of chores if they pledged to inform on the politicians. Here, democracy was only a level playing field for competing wiles: the resourcefulness or cunning to invent an electric contraption from scraps, or, if too poor for bribes, the social skills to build a network, the better to secure an egg, some dried fish, any nibble of protein to round out the grubs in the gruel from which no other nourishment could come. Five unwashed bodies pressed together into ten-by-eight cells had a way of exacerbating and amplifying the narcissism of their small differences, until, sometimes with violence, they'd magnified into matters of life or death. There were instances of "Commies" scaring "Students" silly with threats to "dye them pink;" or life-preserving, bootleg antidiarrheals denied to the sick but stockpiled instead for distribu-tion among one's exclusive ideological club. The grotesque pettiness of it was enough to turn a sympathizer to acid, or into a lifelong enemy, and often as not it did.

And yet, with the overriding focus of a common enemy, those differences had flattened out, until they had built a vast concordance, beginning with a hard kernel of political detainees, through petty convicts, drug traffickers, and the kind of indifferent criminal riffraff with whom they had often been forced to share their cells; then the grunts among the prison staff who had enough compassion, or material need, or ambient animosity for sitting at the bottom of the military caste system. Win Tin prided himself on at least one representative in the JAC for every group.

Everyone had played his part. With serpentine ingenuity, members of the self-named "Media and Information Committee" smuggled in local journals, rare copies of *Time* and *Newsweek*, and—miracle!—not one but two 8-band pocket radios; batteries, too. Squatting in patches of shadow, radios tilted to just the right angles, they could tune in to the illicit exile broadcasts and likewise keep abreast of little turns in state propaganda through the official Radio Myanmar. To disseminate the news as bulletins they turned to the young man with the most beautiful handwriting, who was consequently charged with the oversight of a "Hand-written Periodicals Producing Committee."

The joint heads of a "Medical Assistance Committee," Dr. Zaw Myint Maung and Dr. Myint Naing, NLD members-elect of parliament from 1990, had been practicing physicians. Into their cells went clean syringes or herbs and tinctures, and out came home-fabricated potions—minimal but critical treatments that couldn't cure a single case of hepatitis but that might have been enough to somehow protract hope.

Others drafted sentimental or symbolic screeds that looked outward, into the poetic resonances of a strong cup of sweet tea, or backward into the history of university-sourced agitation. Their verse went something like this:

> *let it be known to*
> *those in the military who hunger for power*
> *those demonic military,*
> *wishing to build a military nation*
> *under a military democracy and military politics,*
> *that we shall resist definitely with the strength of the fighting peacock,*
> *may it eternally be recorded in history!*

They were never going to chisel masterpieces. However abstract, or about as nuanced as a graffiti tag, it was enough merely to entertain a point of view or to indulge the sensuality of forming words with minds that cried insane for occupation and hands that were denied all tasks except the primitive.

For Win Tin, success rested in snatching liberty with each recorded sylla-ble. Truth was truth to the end of reckoning. With avuncular pride, he watched the younger inmates funnel their stifled passions into two new magazines. They called the first *The Tidal Wave*, in memory of the first student to die in March, 1988, and the other, *The New Blood Wave*, timed to the Diamond Jubilee of Rangoon University. They managed 102 pages, decorated front and back with illustrations. Hand-copied editions circulated where and how they could. At least one ended up buried in the dirt outside Hall 4. Someone stashed another between the pond and the officers' quarters.

The overflow included policy papers and weekly bulletins, straight political essays, and personal tributes to the country's greats, including biographies of Aung San Suu Kyi and Prime Minister U Nu, he of the lost era of parliamentary democracy. They filled books two-inches thick that the inmate best skilled with handiwork had stitched from plastic bags, cardboard, wood, and scrap cloth. By November 1995, the hypothetical table of contents of the prisoners' oeuvre was a firebomb of free expression. The likes of the stuff hadn't seen the streets since the halcyon burst of anarchy in 1988 that hovered now like a dream between the end of one dictatorial regime and the dark dawn of the next.

Nor was it the whispered indulgence of specters. If there were little way to pass messages to visitors at the grate, on account of authorities taking notes on either side, there was always the possibility that one among them would be re-leased. Then he might take with him ideas from the "national politics" com-mittee, or the "education" committee, or the committee to whom responsibility fell for honoring anniversaries. It was no irony to concede that time in Insein, outside the punishment cells, permitted, in its way, the longest running political seminar in the country.

For his part, Win Tin kept office.

In the great cast of mind of a man born in 1930—whose boyhood was set against the revolutionary struggle for independence, who had come of age through the fragile years of parliamentary democracy and cut his teeth as a re-porter and editor against the anarchic currents of civil war, the turn to military rule, and then the long, downward spiral of the country to 1988—the neces-sity of somehow engaging with the political foreground had always been most pressing.

As a schoolboy in 1945, he had tripped up on himself, doe-eyed and struck dumb, before the vision of General Aung San, scrubbing himself with focus from waters that the fifteen-year-old had fetched from the well himself. Aung

San, repositioning his army base, had briefly come to rest at the house of Win Tin's uncle, about two hours north of Rangoon. Stumbling for words, the young man had managed to ask the great Bogyoke, the General, if he might join the fight for independence. Already he had witnessed the cold brutality of Japanese occupation, and he was full with nationalist fervor from his uncle, who had been fighting alongside Aung San. The Bogyoke, at first as unresponsive as a mirage, deigned eventually to look up from his task and raked his fine eyes over the boy. "Are you in school?" he asked. Yes, nodded Win Tin, only actually fifteen years his junior. "Then finish your studies," Aung San had answered. "We have enough fighters. We need thinkers."

And that had been it.

Early dabbling with prose in his late teens and early twenties had taught him two things. First, he would never be a poet, nor ever a writer of the literary merit of his friends. Skimming a draft of one or other of their efforts had consistently proved to him the inadequacy of his own. Second, much though he had always placed "real writers" on a pedestal, he realized quickly that he had a hankering instead to be in the eye of the storm. He was, in short, a journalist.

In 1957, fresh returned to Rangoon from an eye-opening tour through Europe as a consultant for a publishing house in the Netherlands, he had launched a newspaper, the *Kyay Mon*, the Daily Mirror, which he and his co-founder had spiked with editorials that slanted toward peace. Nine years after independence, the country was consumed by war. Three communist groups and several more ethnic-minority insurgencies vied for effective control against the military, which still enjoyed a reputation for the valor and efficiency that had won Burma its freedom. Within a year and half, the *Kyay Mon* had the widest circulation in the country. Within two, Prime Minister U Nu declared his administration incapable of containing the violent chaos, handed over the reins of power to a military caretaker government led by General Ne Win, and the newspaper had been forced to shut.

Win Tin had taken up next as editor of the state-owned *Hanthawaddy Daily* in Mandalay. He steered it through the steady downgrading of press freedoms, watching himself move ever further from straight news into the disguise of metaphor and allusion. Inevitably, under his auspices, matters came to head. Inevitably, the *Hanthawaddy* was ordered to close. As he struggled to find outlets for his work, and watched the country's poverty deepen in parallel with his own, he had found solace in talking with dock workers and factory laborers. At last he had time to spend with the ethnic minorities, whose difficulties had largely been impenetrable to a young and busy Burman. In that way, he'd expanded the reach of his connections, and apprehension of society.

One day he had learned a curious tidbit about the capacity of a mosquito to kill a crab by stinging it in the eye. The essay he wrote on the subject became, in retrospect, his most popular. It circulated in an underground rag among students and revolutionaries who had little trouble reading into it a scathing critique of military rule and, if one only looked, its vulnerabilities. In prison, Win Tin had had time enough to ponder whether his arrest on July 4, 1989—early even for the leadership of the NLD—was a case of special revenge against the author of "The Crab."

At least in Insein he no longer needed to employ euphemisms. For the Joint Action Committee, he drafted reports of NLD prison "meetings"; policy papers arguing for cooperation with the Communist Party of Burma and the students' party, the Democratic Party for a New Society; and a plan of action he called simply "Ten Principles of Unity."

When government had ground to a halt in 1988, there had been, for him, little choice. He became vice president of the Writer's Union, one among the syndicates that banded together that August and September under the banner of the professions to petition, or agitate, or grope for societal solutions to the nationwide combustion. They gravitated to the lakeside compound of Aung San Suu Kyi, who, in turn, came to rely on Win Tin for counsel and regular briefings about a country to which she had only just returned after living abroad since her teenage years. It was a short step to his appointment as one of three secretaries of the new NLD party. For nine months, from the party's founding until his arrest, he worked side by side with Aung San Suu Kyi, the party secretary general. He became a key strategist.

It was hardly an office job. The party, even in 1988, was less an entity than an idea—a vast alliance slapped together from the throes of revolution by a basic desire to return to the people their right to be free. It was a mission without borders, without walls. That from within prison Win Tin could find new ways to act against the junta was his greatest counterpunch to date.

The high point of it all was a document on prison conditions. Information had filtered in from every corner: confessions from the six-meter-square punishment cells down Hall 6, or from Hall 5, the "women's block," so named because prisoners were forced to speak and act like women, else crawl or wriggle on their bellies for hours up and down a path of flesh-ripping gravel. With three months of effort in late 1995, they had gathered on a plastic bag more than seventy signatures, including prison identity numbers. They passed it around in the handle of a bucket, care of staff or common criminals for about the price of three instant-coffee mixes.

Then it had arrived for editing at Hall 3, Cell 2. Bleary at first from another surgery, Win Tin lay on a raised block of wood that functioned for an invalid's mattress, squinted through his owl glasses, and sucked his lips over his bare gums. He dived in: correcting, focusing, breathing again to the rhythm of language-as-action that had been the prime mover of his life. When it was done, it was passed to Dr. Zaw Myint Maung, "Dr. Z," to spirit out to a friend, and onward, through a chain of connections, to the United Nations Special Rapporteur on Human Rights in Myanmar, one Professor Yozo Yokota.

At which point, on November 11, the entire operation was blown. A key conspirator cracked under interrogation. An inmate was caught with a version of the letter. Days of digging up the piles of dirt outside the outhouses and the concrete floors of Cells 1 through 18 in Hall 4, and on down Halls 3, 5, and 6 had turned up sufficient contraband—from nail clippers and a ten-foot wire to a pair of felt-tip pens—to heat up the usual mute pantomime of a closed prison trial.

For the bravado of the stunt alone, he wouldn't have traded the extra beatings, the nine months in the dog kennels, nor the difficult years that had followed trying to keep himself sane in solitary.

For the privilege, ten of them had been sent to hard labor. Another twenty-two, including Win Tin, were charged with 157 additional years between them. Sentences turned on themes of solitary, dispersion to prisons on the far fringes, beatings, and forced labor. The spectrum of punishments would steal eyesight, hearing, movement, and, for U Hla Than, life itself. The son of farmers from Moulmein, U Hla Than had become a lawyer and then the NLD's elective minister of parliament from the former penal colony of the Coco Islands. His death certificate blamed pulmonary tuberculosis and a case of HIV, but few doubted the mortal wreckage that punitive sanction had inflicted on his body.

In what had proved a rare study in a political trial, and a more typical instance of leakages the system permitted, an anonymous clerk took dutiful minutes of the trial proceedings, a judge signed off, and somehow it was slipped to someone who slipped it to someone else. Eventually it found its way to the Assistance Association for Political Prisoners, a watchdog set up in 2000 in Mae Sot by a former Insein inmate.

Win Tin, the one-time art critic, had he been handed another turn of fate, might have enjoyed the trial report's review. Its non sequiturs and contradictions, as each testimony tripped up on the next, had all the deadpan of an absurdist script. And yet from fragmentary information, it built a monument to their elaborate conspiracy, testament that people of a mettle to change society would, under repressive limitations, not only refuse to break but instead whet their strategic obstinacy. As an actor in the presentation of it, he had found a different sort of gratification. Here was a chance to write his own script and then deliver the monologue that he had been denied in his first two trials at Insein.

He had been arrested in 1989 on a charge of complicity in the illegal abortion of a young unmarried woman, for allegedly harboring her boyfriend. His father had happened to phone the tapped NLD Office landline to seek news of him. It had been Win Tin's misfortune to fulfill his secretarial duties for the party and pick up. They'd sentenced him summarily to three years, and, as he neared release, they piled on a new eleven-year charge. His second trial had been as throwaway as the first.

Back then, first in 1989 then 1992, he had been caught off-guard, knocked dizzy not so much by the consummate irreverence to an elder or the abuse under interrogation that had smashed out his top teeth and mapped cuts and contusions across his sexagenarian body. The seismic shock had come from discovering how completely the judicial system and basic civility of his beloved country had been bent.

Refused counsel at his third trial in March 1996, he and another twenty-one defendants had been shoved into the secret session one after the next. Each pleaded his own defense and, sometimes, called one another up as witness. All argued not guilty to the charges leveled by fifteen accusers. Turning the 1950 Emergency Provisions Act on its head, which punished citizens for knowingly disseminating false information, they variously testified that everything written was true; that, however, the poems or letters or other accumulated alleged writings either never existed or were not traceable to any one among them; that if they were traceable, they were in fact fabrications of intelligence officers; signatures, if they were not actually fabrications, had been coerced out of them; or, were it the case that one or another draft was alleged to match the handwriting of this or that inmate, they had merely been written for personal reasons.

Win Tin salted his take with a peroration. The précis of his testimony spanned a full page and half of the trial transcript. Claiming to revisit themes from the homework of his earlier twenty-five-page denunciation of the anti-1988 uprising exhibition, he summed up his "five main points": (1) "the Army was working for continued military domination in Burma," (2) he "could not accept the fact that the Tatmadaw was creating a destiny for the country," (3) he "objected to the military intervention during the 1988 uprising, in which a new generation of students and the entire nation participated," (4) he "supported Daw Aung San Suu Kyi's tireless effort to establish democracy for the generation to come," and (5) he called attention to the sufferings of political prisoners, a matter he had raised when he was allowed to meet two foreign delegates, a UN envoy and US Congressman Bill Richardson.

Next he complained about a few of the more pressing problems afflicting inmates. When inmates demanded their rights, authorities only allowed them to heat up their food. No one had followed up on a demand to recognize political prisoners as a separate category; since 1988, the government had persisted in refusing to acknowledge their existence. And medical attention was critically lacking.

Finally—because, why not be a stickler for detail?—he dug into the charges against him. He found a few to pick apart. Frankly, he told them, he could not write poems because he was too old. And just because there was no name alongside an article, didn't mean that he had written it. It didn't seem pertinent to ask if anyone in the courtroom might have seen the other issues raised in the Joint Action Committee's letter on abuses to the United Nations.

It was, in all, a touch elaborate. But no one could accuse him of exceeding entirely the bounds of the system's reality.

The way he saw it now—on that torpid September 23, 2008—if there was any internal logic to their rules, he ought to have been released three years earlier, a date he'd calculated based on the two- or three-month reductions that the jail manual prescribed for every year of a sentence served.

On top of which, he'd played this game before. The worst was July 5, 2005. *This is it*, he'd told himself, *sixteen years and a day purged. I'm done.* He had gathered his few religious books, a T-shirt, and a *longyi*, and handed off the rest to a friendly prison guard: a worn pillowcase, a few dry biscuits, the crumbs of his last care package from a visiting friend. Outside his cell that day, he had joined a lineup of about a hundred familiar faces. Leaping before them, the prison director had launched into a speech, longwinded and somewhat out of tune with the usual grunts and shouts. At one point he had paused to call Win Tin to his side for a photo op, like a star-struck tourist. Baffled, Win Tin had obliged. Then everyone had been frog-marched to the exit. On to the red door, down the prison boulevard, and out the gates into the streets beyond where children laughed; freshly baked naans mopped up spiced soups in corner teashops abuzz with easy human chatter; and pilgrims bowed into the golden light of Shwedagon Pagoda where birdsong caught on the vibrations of the *hti*'s tinkling bells. All that and more for everyone but eight, who had been asked to linger.

For their little group, the prison guards had beamed, authorities had reserved a special farewell: an exit interview with the Minister of Home Affairs himself. They had duly been escorted to an office. Win Tin had been invited solo into another. There he had waited. And waited. Only the cicadas broke the silence, and the crows, and the muffled barks of wardens shouting their orders that sliced the Insein day into its infernal segments. Noon had turned to sunset, sunset guillotined to night, and then he had been taken without fanfare or further explanation back to his old cell.

Damned if four years later he'd fall for it again.

So when they jangled their keys at 6:30 a.m. that morning, he waved away his breakfast rice gruel in disgust and profited from the gaping maw that had been his barred cell doorway to wander out into the shade of the tree that grew gnarly and crooked from the dry dust of the prison courtyard, witness to the whole carnival probably since the time of the British. Wardens pleaded with him, one after the next, but he wouldn't budge. *Nothing good will come of this.* Finally, about 3:45 p.m., they slapped into his arms the few trinkets he'd amassed, together with his prison pisspot, and booted him still in his prison blues out the red door.

Perhaps they'd assumed that in the general confusion of the 9,002 others released on amnesty that day throughout the country, no one would much bother to notice one more old man.

⚜

HE RETURNED TO NOTHING.

Later, in the introduction to his prison memoirs, *What's That? A Human Hell*, he would list his losses: his adopted daughter, forced into exile; his teeth, smashed out in an early prison beating; a testicle, side-effect of his first operation for a strangulated hernia in the barren Insein clinic that the surgeon afterward admitted had come three years too late.

The apartment Win Tin had once kept in Lanthit Yiek Tha had been seized in 1989, even before he'd been tried in the Insein Prison court for his first charge. What few belongings had been his had long since been scattered to the winds.

A sister, his lone surviving relative, lived five floors up a steep stairwell with no elevator. But half a year shy of eighty, with a bad heart and wheezing lungs, he could no longer brave the journey up and down.

For a period that he assumed would accompany him to his ashing, he lived liked a nomad. That first night he had taken refuge in the nearby Insein home of one of his two most loyal friends, a colleague from the old days who had across the years mortgaged much of his own meager possessions to pay for Win Tin's prison upkeep. Thereafter, from Insein township to Yankin township, Yankin back to Insein, Win Tin had to move every two weeks between one distant sub-urban residence and the other on account of the law on sleeping arrangements that was, in his honor, enforced in both townships.

It was a petulant attack. It scratched, but it couldn't cut deep. When vis-itors came, and come they did, they would have to make do with a patch of curb, a teashop, whichever plot of barren land that served as birthright even to a beggar.

In any case, he had always preferred the life of the mind. And it wasn't as if he had much luggage—a walking stick or two; a toothbrush, once he had finally visited a dentist; and a collection of books that grew off gifts and tributes to about the size of half a shelf. Out of solidarity with those he'd left behind, he refused to take off his prison blues. The decision hardened when authorities demanded he give them back. So clothing was not so much an issue, although given the terrible heat, and the fact that he would not shrink from public ap-pearances in the service of his country, it paid to have a few clean blue shirts to spare.

He had never married, an avowed workaholic whose great escape from po-litical journalism had been the arts. Now he could no longer publish, not even whimsical appreciations of music or painting. All his pen names were on the black list. If he found old forewords to books of art or poetry, they appeared under a pseudonym he didn't recognize. And what private editor would risk running an article, even on so anodyne a subject? They were a hardy bunch, the editors who braved the censors every week or month in the clutch of magazines and private journals that had apparently sprung up in recent years. But they played enough with disaster with each new print run.

There had been a time when editions went to press before the obligatory submission to the Press Scrutiny Board. Only then, with thousands of copies readied for sale, would publishers receive instructions to ink out sentences or entire pages, or to glue them together, or to tape little squares of silver over offending paragraphs. Then all copies had to be rechecked, and everything counted. Sometimes the PSB ordered the destruction of an entire edition. It cost a fortune that no one had to each time risk the full print run on a few dicey phrases of veiled allusion. Already a fraction of publishers' budgets went toward government paper rations. The rest they allocated toward black market supplies, which inevitably cost more. There was never much left over for the inevitable, censor-enforced margin of error.

The mechanics had refined somewhat in the years of Win Tin's absence. The censors' handprint had become more insidious. All writing now headed to the PSB before the print run. Problem areas, highlighted in thick blue or red, were simply to be rewritten or replaced with sunnier insertions from the state. Thus had the burden to self-censor passed to the publisher. A sly foe, was self-censorship, Win Tin knew. It was a form of coercion that didn't work just by sapping one's ideals. Rather, as with so much else in the military's system, it broke wills as a matter of practical economics. What with the thicket of rules and ordinances governing everything from the employment of an electronic gadget to the right to use a copy machine, there had never been much chance for native-born samizdat.

Win Tin, besides, wasn't one for gratuitous vainglory. But neither had he risen to the front ranks of journalism only to crawl away, ghost-like, under a rock of cowardly anonymity. And even if he tried, he couldn't much hope to hide his signature flair for punning and syllable-play that had, in prison, lent itself to a slogan that became a personal drumbeat: *Suu Hlut Twe, Suu Hlut Twe*. It was the sound of freedom. *Suu* for Aung San Suu Kyi; *Hlut*, for the People's Parliament, the *Hluttaw*, and the convening of it; *Twe* meant dialogue, between the NLD, the junta, and representatives of the ethnic minorities.

As for publishing in the name of the party: when pigs grew wings. The NLD's press registration permit had been revoked in 1990, a situation that the Ministry of Information had found good to reiterate in January 2008 after a one-off NLD Youth newsletter had found its way to the Internet. The NLD party spokesman, U Nyan Win, had been duly summoned to the ministry where he had been met by the director of the PSB, a Special Branch police major, the township Peace and Development Chair, a township law officer, a township judge, and a lieutenant colonel from the Army. So—that was a nonstarter. Nyan Win was a solid lawyer, sleepy in the eyelids and soft of heart, but tough on technicalities. Patient too in the way of the professionals among them who knew not to squander passions on futile gains, he had opted that day for obedience.

Best, he had felt, to deny knowledge of the newsletter and sign a paper on behalf of the NLD agreeing that it would distribute publications no more. "If a certain road is blocked," Nyan Win had later explained to the US Embassy, summing that overarching philosophy, "you should avoid it and choose another."

Putting aside the looming shadow of his political infamy, the fact that his name had been wiped from the journalistic record, and that he was two decades creakier in the hips, Win Tin faced another problem entirely in his lack of an identity card.

He wanted an identity number. It wasn't even bending to the whims of military rule: the requirement on carrying a card dated to 1957, the days of parliamentary democracy. Back then, he had prided himself that his citizenship was somehow inseparable from ID number CG-068482. In 1989, his number had disappeared along with everything else.

He had no means of acquiring another. Official application was a lottery, rigged in the way of all complex corrupt systems. Some obtained them on the border, others for a fat fee through a freelance broker. Others still had found that years of pushing paperwork or sweetening officials with "tea money" cleared up in a miracle of efficiency just in time to coincide with the May 10, 2008, constitutional referendum. It was thus fanciful to imagine the successful acquisition of another for a man once denounced as Aung San Suu Kyi's puppetmaster. He had borne that smear with more amusement than offense, as anyone who knew her well enough to appreciate her stubbornness, cuss-headed as her father. That he could and did stand up to her and that she, fifteen years his junior, would beat back his arguments by force of wit and intellect was precisely the stuff that made her, to Win Tin's mind, the leader they all needed.

Meantime, his lack of an identity number meant no possibility of renting a property, even were he to have the money; no right to vote, had there been any to cast that he didn't feel an urge to boycott; and no possibility of travel anywhere beyond Rangoon, no matter that he'd be stalked wherever he went and that the most pressing problem areas were the free-fire zones in the ethnic-minority states, which were in any case off-limits to visitors from the mainland.

Of all the slaps, that last might well have stung the most.

Even before his life had taken an inexorable turn toward the political, his curiosity for man's condition had lured him across the world and into the lives of the workers and farmers and hill tribes who formed the rich fabric of his society.

And Mandalay! How he missed Mandalay, sun-drenched and sandstone-carved, with its tough-talking girls and glittering moat and remorseless capacity to stab a man in the heart. The whole city had burned down twice since 1981. About half had since been rebuilt, Chinese-style. But still it managed to confound—a sudden surge of blue crumbling pillars rising from the banyans, a sudden maroon against gold. In Mandalay, Win Tin, the great lover of literature, would again have found the beating heart of Burman culture; and at the corner of 84th and 33rd, tucked behind a cramped bookstore, the century-old presses of the Ludu publishing house, still cranking out pages deep into the midafternoon heat, beside a contraption strung to a generator that rattled marbles to loosen the ink from the plates. He had worked there too briefly, fresh out of university, and the awe in which he had held its long-departed founders, the great authors, Ludu U Lha and Ludu Ahmar, echoed through the disillusions of his maturity.

But what guesthouse or friend could risk his visit were he to hop north on the self-same train that he'd once boarded, brimming with youthful ambition? How could he advocate for the rights of others, when he had none? Henceforth he would have to take the pulse of the people as he had all this time in his cell: dependent on second-hand observations and his own memory.

Without an ID card, Win Tin became, like all the rest, a wraith.

⤚⟡⟞

SO THE JUNTA SPAT ITS AGED prisoner into an enforced shunning. Endlessly packing and repacking his plastic-wrapped bundle, he looked down, gauged his penury to about the weight of his rags, and cracked a smile.

No one could stifle the fire in his belly. Not with so much left to do. Win Tin, at the moment of his release, sprang like a coil and single-handedly upped the game of the entire opposition.

On his first full day out, he took interviews from the foreign and exile press from 6 a.m. to 4 p.m., and then from 7 to 10 p.m. The next day bled to midnight. He hadn't invited them. He had no address. But they knew, somehow, to come.

"Why am I speaking with so many people?" U Win Tin told the *Irrawaddy*, an Open Society–backed exile magazine run by a former '88 student out of Chiang Mai, Thailand. "Because I want dynamism. I don't have time to listen to what I have said to check how much of it is right or wrong. I just keep talking."

He estimated he had about five days' worth of free attention without penalty of rearrest. It was the only way for authorities to mark a break between one sentence and next.

Again and again, he stressed "unity" and "dynamism." His words, broadcast back to a people sensitized for hidden meaning, managed to be at once direct and disarming, transcending the hot air of hope to home in on the fragmentation and passivity that, by general consensus, risked inflicting the final blow on a movement crippled enough by long attack.

"Some may say that the old man is talking nonsense. He is outdated. There are a lot of things he does not understand," he continued, anticipating criticism that would be of a piece with a friend's warning from just the night before that he avoid excess emotion. "That may be true. It is possible there are things I don't understand yet. I try to take this into account. I know I have a lot of flaws. But I am trying to be active. Why do I want to build up dynamism? Because without it, we have nothing."

For fresh-emerging political prisoners, the swarm of reporters had become something of a ritual. They could not be named, much less featured, in local journals. But the international wire services and the exiles were only too keen to tell their stories.

It had always been a bit of a lottery, though. In theory, the junta turned a blind eye, playing with the pretense of largesse in a way that struck participants as transparently self-serving: the biggest prisoner amnesties tended to coincide with visits from foreign dignitaries, specifically UN envoys who were then sworn to mentioning the amnesties in their official documents as signs of "progress."

But unlucky types could just as well be sent straight back to the clapper. Upcountry releases were trickiest because the envoys never made it that far, and the small-time satraps there reigned supreme. And what they didn't know about the world, for want of basic urbanity, and what they didn't understand about high-stakes politics, for want of ability to think their way inside the motives of senior generals, they knew instead about ledgers and ordinances and rules that forbade talking to the press—functionaries, in short, fixated only on the fatter cats just up the chain.

Rangoon, however, was a different stage. And Win Tin was a star. For all his modesty, he knew he was a draw not only to a sizeable cross-section of his fellow citizens, but internationally too. Feted by UNESCO and PEN International for his services defending freedom of expression and the art of truth, even if his years in prison had more to do with his straight politics, he had also earned the dubious accolade, on the global human rights hit-lists, of the longest-serving political prisoner in the world.

At home, that status was a bit of a dead heat. Pulling up close behind—
to draw an example at random—was Dr. Zaw Myint Maung, Dr. Z, the good
doctor-turned-NLD MP-elect whose punishment for participation in the Joint
Action Committee at Insein had included relocation to far-flung Myitkina,
among the embattled people of Kachin state on the border with China. There
the graceful hymns of the Christian Kachin inmates, entwined with the Pali
chants of fellow Buddhists, helped keep alive the innocence of his ideals every
morning into his eighteenth year.

Another was U Khin Maung Swe, who had also signed his name to the UN-
bound letter from Insein. He was among the seven political prisoners released
with the other thousands on September 23, in his case from Lashio Prison in the
Shan hills near Thailand, after a few years in Myingyan, where the humanity of
the wardens was as cracked and overheated as the starved soils of the surround-
ing central plains. He had left behind his faith in the power of mass uprising
along with his right ear's ability to hear anything at all—a few whacks too many
with a sadistically employed bar of soap. But somehow the former geologist-
turned-NLD cofounder had maintained the boyish blush of his cheeks and a
posture of steel. On Tuesday, he had nearly seventeen years to his name.

And what of U Win Htein, also released that Tuesday? The one-time personal aide to Aung San Suu Kyi and a former captain-turned-entrepreneur with
a booming voice, expansive temperament, and a list of prison-spawned ailments as hefty, he had been twelve years into a fourteen-year sentence in Katha
Prison, fresh off another six-year stint.

Alas, he suffered a classic up-country maneuver. They'd rearrested him on
Wednesday and sent him back to Katha. The joke had been better the previous
time, had been his to make, because back in 1996, he had already packed a bag
with soap, toothbrush, and other prison luxuries, in anticipation of the knock
that inevitably one random night, that May, had come.

And best not talk of the terms faced by the leaders, or rank and file, of the
ethnic armies. If they made it to prison at all, they were most often kept in permanent purgatory on death row.

Point was, they were all in the soup. Win Tin, whom Aung San Suu Kyi had
once described as "little given to talking about himself," considered himself not
a hair more worthy.

Still, however one viewed it, he had a panache all of his own. The unruly
mane of white hair, a warm smile on a leathered, broad-cheeked face, and eyes
that twinkled behind those vast, owl glasses presented to the world an image of

genial intellectualism that, together with the sylphlike Aung San Suu Kyi, cast into deeper contrast the blurry shadow of a faceless junta.

A formal invitation to return to the party landed within two weeks. The members of the Central Executive Committee offered U Win Tin his old job. He demurred. First, he said, he had to watch and listen.

But he didn't wait. There was too much to do.

By Saturday, he had made it back to the NLD office for the party's twentieth anniversary. It was as public an event as the NLD could these days muster. Predictably all the Western diplomats converged for the ritual; and all the country's Asian neighbors, including China, India, and the members of ASEAN stayed away. Fresh home from Lashio in northeastern Shan state, Khin Maung Swe, the former geologist, stood tall among the crowds in the crisp white shirt and Kachin *longyi* that had long been the NLD's standard uniform. He too had been an early party founder. He had stepped forward in 1989 to join the party's executive lineup after Win Tin and the rest had been culled by arrests.

Outside the Office, a handful of supporters released birds from their cages and shouted slogans to free Aung San Suu Kyi. Police carted three of them away. Ten others were stopped en route and taken to a detention center for the full length of the ceremony, plus or minus a few hours.

Inside, the members of the Central Executive Committee reiterated a statement condemning the 2008 constitution. Among its most undemocratic clauses, it reserved a quarter of parliamentary seats for the military; and returned full executive powers to the commander-in-chief in case of any vaguely defined national emergency. Any amendment to the constitution required more than a three-quarters majority, which was impossible to achieve if the rest of the seats were allocated to the military, who would vote as a bloc according to their orders. Rammed through in the rigged referendum that had followed in the wake of Tropical Cyclone Nargis, its final insult was that, once it entered into force after general elections to be held at some date to be determined in 2010, it would forever nullify the election results of 1990.

To most people, who assumed that the electoral process would change nothing in their daily lives, the NLD's censures could seem as futile as they were dry. To those more focused on the minutiae of the junta's closed-door machinations—and the potential consequences for the NLD party or wider prospects for achieving democracy—the stakes were existential.

Anyone of age to remember, besides, had seen a version of this ruse already. The constitution of 1974 had similarly offered little of novelty to the country, except to add gloss to the freelance twelve-year despotism of General Ne Win. Henceforth he could change his title to the more semantically appealing president of a newly declared Socialist Republic of the Union of Burma.

If on Saturday at the NLD anniversary Win Tin boiled to say something, he waited, listened, and nodded kindly as anyone of an age to address him as *saya* knelt before him and pressed their foreheads and hands to the ground three times, a tribute accorded otherwise to parents, abbots, and likenesses of the Buddha. Then, like a beloved old uncle at a wedding reluctantly called to make a toast, he pushed slowly to his feet and dived into an impromptu speech that flared into a tripartite manifesto calling for the release of all political prisoners, genuine dialogue with the junta, and unity among opposition forces.

His voice raspy with advanced age, he measured his words with gentility and sincere self-deprecation. But in moments of passion he punched down on his consonants, and his easy smile and open expression turned to a mask of hard focus. Win Tin, when he spoke in public, commanded attention.

At once, he could be homeless and a soldier. The junta had all the riches of the soil. Win Tin had nothing. But, inside, he had everything. So did they all.

His trusty friend, Maung Maung Khin, had tried after a couple of months to rent Win Tin an apartment in the city center. Just as he prepared to move, the deal fell through. They tried elsewhere, with the same result. His would-be landlady and landlord respectively supplied excuses short on detail but heavy with the fume of panic that came with learning the identity of their future tenant. Vague threats, they claimed, had landed but they couldn't or wouldn't spell them out. *Fear*, Win Tin said, shaking his head at his friend. There was no rancor in his assessment, no hint of judgment. Not everyone could take up a cause with so steep a social price. But ever and always, the rub was people's fear.

Eventually, the pair decided on a lie. In the logbook of the local ward authorities, they claimed kinship. If no one bothered to follow up, it meant that Win Tin finally could settle in Yankin. And, actually, why would they? Little mendacities were proving the foundation on which the carapace of the post-1988 junta's state somehow held itself aloft. He would henceforth lodge—and nowhere else legally—in a two-room cabin tucked at the bottom of a garden all garlanded in bougainvillea, a few feet from the bungalow where Maung Maung Khin lived with his wife.

This presumably eased the organization of shifts among his stalkers. Ten agents watched Win Tin round the clock, stiff-backed in their pressed shirts and aviators, or toying in teashops with tea that they didn't drink. They trailed him on trips to the NLD and to private rendezvous, or loitered on the corners and around the stalls of the flower market down the block. They had cell phones, affixed like holsters to their hips, denied by cost to the rest of the population, and motorcycles, denied by law to Rangoon's civilian inhabitants. The sight of their paraphernalia was a chronic rubbing of the nose in the consummate venality that the system had acquired since the junta ditched Ne Win's pseudo-socialism for the bleak benefits of crony capitalism.

When authorities learned that he was on lists of invited guests, hosts were harassed until events were cancelled. Would-be visitors were best to steer clear of meeting him at home, else Maung Maung Khin and wife risked hours of interrogation. That they expected as much hardly made it tolerable, or in any way sit easier on Win Tin's heart or sense of karmic justice.

Tongues wagged in knowing circles that, actually, it was all a ploy. Senior General Than Shwe was playing his old tricks, sowing the field with "hard-liners" ahead of his much-ballyhooed 2010 elections in a fresh version of the divide-and-conquer tactics that had been the defining feature of his rule—that, and his marked absence of evident charisma. Win Tin had a reputation as uncompromising. His policy positions, though admittedly tested only in the turbulent nine months between the founding of the party and his arrest, were unflinchingly assertive. He had been at the core of the caucus of civilian intellectuals whom Aung San Suu Kyi had drawn to the party. Whereas the former military officers in the NLD had cautioned against it, he had argued unequivocally for the Tatmadaw to end all political involvement and retreat instead to their barracks. It had too much blood on its hands to warrant any other option.

In the course of his career, he had traveled to Western Europe, the satellite states of the USSR, and across Asia, including China at the cusp of the Cultural Revolution. They were foils enough to set the mishaps of his country's politics in context. That he knew how to agitate and organize did little to quell rumors that he was a communist. It was a charge that he thought unfair. It was true that he had read Marxist texts and pasted up a few posters in his youth, when communism was all the rage among nationalists who were casting around for revolutionary alternatives to the decadent capitalism that they ascribed to Western imperialism. That socialism became the go-to ideology of mainstream moderates was a direct offshoot of that history. When the Communist Party of Burma, the second strongest political force of the 1950s, resorted to violence, Win Tin had leaned in editorials on the side of negotiation, largely in support of the then-civilian government of U Nu. But his stance had won him few friends in the military. The effect was pernicious enough that in 1988, one of the NLD party's founding troika, U Aung Gyi, a former brigadier general, had accused Aung San Suu Kyi of consorting with communists. It had caused a near-fatal rift.

But that had been the extent of it. In his view, the communists had been wrecking the country. His trips abroad had left him with few illusions about utopian credos. Whereas his host family in Amsterdam had surprised him with the enjoyment of a typical lifestyle that permitted them to buy books, instead of borrowing them or receiving them as gifts, the livelihoods in communist cities from Prague to Peking seemed about as stunted and bereft as those back home.

Even so, years later it was an easy smear to resurrect. To him now—the tongues fretted—would flock the radicals, the disgruntled, the flotsam and jetsam of small-timers and loners who floated around or in parallel or in the bowels of the movement, around and beneath the NLD. The party itself would self-implode, a house all eaten through with termites that a poke of the pinky would cause to crash.

But the tongues underestimated Win Tin's strategic intelligence.

Close observation of man as political animal in the microcosm of prison had only refined his capacity to see three moves ahead. Razor sharp, he had honed his mental faculties through his years of solitary confinement with self-enforced drills every morning. In his mind, or on the walls and floor of his cell, with the stray hairs of a prison cat that he dried out and pressed into the reddish powder of a hand-crushed brick as a makeshift paintbrush, he first set himself problems of arithmetic. Then he turned to words and memory-work until he'd surrounded himself with a chalky pantheon of illuminating forebears. To Shelley's "If Winter comes, can Spring be far behind?" Henry David Thoreau responded: "I never found a companion that was as companionable as solitude." The tenacity of Winston Churchill—"We shall go on to the end"—echoed in a favorite line from William Ernest Henley's "Invictus"—"my head is bloody but unbowed," which doubled in its resonance because Aung San had translated the poem into Burmese himself. And where Win Tin had recalled only the essence of a speech or stanza—the fearful symmetry, say, of a tiger, tiger, burning bright—he riffed off on his own, composing verse that in any other circumstance he would have laughed off as so much sentimental dross, but here allowed himself, lest he should weaken, as a mirror reflecting back the pealing voice of his better self.

Now, in interviews, he could be interrupted by a phone call or a complicated message in the middle of a nuanced proposition and minutes later pick up the thought without a beat, on the diphthong he had left hanging.

A pragmatist through and through with the tough judgments of a newspaper man working to tight deadlines, he had never set much store by scholarly theory nor the superstitions that had become commonplace to justify the foibles of history—the belief, say, that the skies could be relied on, to the point of passivity, for karmic payback; or the mystification of the number nine. That kind of nonsense prevented a more rigorous understanding of measures such as Ne Win's devastating 1987 demonetization of the *kyat*, a disastrous attempt to undercut the black market. It had been too easy, in that instance, to dismiss as Ne Win as simply mad. Better for all concerned to hold a government to account by analyzing its decisions for their rational incompetence.

Win Tin had little patience even for the deeper metaphysics of Buddhism. But he understood the appeal of meditation. In the years after they had installed loudspeakers to blast sacred Pali-language chanting into cells at 5 a.m., he too had found it helpful to sit still and, with a few breaths and a dose of personal control, escape. In that way, like his countrymen, he could find a pathway to a kind of mental emancipation that the junta could never penetrate.

Often, he had allowed his thoughts to drift among the pavilions of Shwedagon Pagoda, basking in the serenity and the play of light and sound. At thirteen, in his first ordination as a novice monk, he had wanted nothing more than to prolong his stay at the monastery. But he no longer had the taste for a pious life, though at times he longed, in that wistful way for lost innocence, to retreat to the monasteries where the only sounds were the murmur of mantras and the soft scuffle of feet on warm, polished stone.

To his mind, taking the saintly route of spiritual detachment could sap the struggle in the hard glare of the here and now. Never could mental freedom substitute for the right to paste a poster to a wall, to travel unregistered, to assemble in crowds of more than five. He had seen one too many a good man, hearts full with Buddhist loving-kindness, felled on one end of his life by a Japanese bayonet and on the other by the disease of a jail cell.

There was no time to waste.

The country he returned to was a disaster.

With the fall of Ne Win's Burma Socialist Program Party, the junta that had ruled through his prison years had abandoned any pretense of socialism. In theory, it had opened the country to market capitalism. In practice, the generals had narrowed the economy into a private dipping pool for their own families and a micro-elite of businessmen who had built vast monopolies of infrastructure, hotels, communication, narcotics, and resource extraction. They built them off favors and licenses that they exchanged with the generals for well-stocked bank accounts in Singapore. Since the collapse of the Communist Party in 1989, relations had also considerably improved with China. It had since become the junta's greatest trade partner. The rest of Asia, from India and Thailand to Japan, tripped over each other to cut deals with the military's joint-venture companies. Off windfalls from sales of natural gas, hydropower projects, oil, jade, teak, and a still unaccounted-for sum derived from opium, heroin, and methamphetamine, the junta had doubled the size of the army and invested millions into its arsenal. It was pouring the rest into giant vanity projects that included a largely empty, would-be "cyber-city," Yadarnabon, that was rising from grey gravel near an old British-built hill station. The capital and most of the country's civil servants had also been uprooted to Naypyidaw, "abode of the kings," and there had the junta's operations become ever more opaque.

By contrast, Rangoon seemed ever rattier and more decayed, its inhabitants gaunt and hopeless. Among the seventy-five percent of the population that still depended on a rural livelihood, farmers were up to their eyeballs in debt, barely holding up against each new monsoon battering. The International Monetary Fund, the United Nations, and dozens of private economists had tracked the plummeting *kyat*, an inflation rate that hovered around twenty-seven percent, the hollowing out of the formal economy, and the flight of foreign investment. The only people who might have disagreed were members of the 0.01 percent— the junta's business cronies and the growing bubble around Senior General Than Shwe, who made it impossible for credible information to make it to the top. No one was ever felled for delivering good news. So far as Win Tin could tell, the only sectors that had truly been liberalized were beans and pulses. By the time he had emerged from prison, the crop had become the chief currency for small-time businessmen trying to do business abroad.

What to do? How and where could they push?

Auntie would one day come out of house arrest, and it fell to Win Tin to lay the groundwork.

The NLD that he found now had been defanged, its landline cut off, its offices across the country shuttered since 2003. In the mildewed mustiness of the cowshed that served for headquarters, everyone now seemed so old.

The average age of the eight remaining members of the Central Executive Committee—excluding two still under house arrest—hovered above eighty.

Where was the resonant energy of the NLD's younger days? What had happened to the plan that Win Tin had sent to Aung San Suu Kyi in November 1988 as she campaigned door to door up-country, suggesting that they hold elections for party officials in every ward, township, and district? If there was truth to the argument that the party had grown too rigid, it wasn't for lack of early enterprise. Before the pre- and post-1990 crackdowns, they had been able to hold elections for local party chapters in exactly two towns.

Within days of Win Tin's return to action, he was paying his respects in hospital to the party deputy chairman, U Lwin, who had suffered a stroke. Chairman Aung Shwe was home with influenza. At his advanced age, the disease could incapacitate him permanently on the turn of a sneeze. All criticism of the party caretakers was, in any case, moot. They had never seen themselves as more than placeholders, waiting out the return of their leader, Aung San Suu Kyi.

Each of the former officers who had joined the NLD in 1988 had rebelled in his own way, in his own time, against the warping since 1962 of the Tatmadaw and the wider country. Aung Shwe and Lwin had as noble a history as the rest, but they knew to be careful in their confrontations with the junta because of a mindset they understood too well. It was true that they had not been as proactive as some young Turks would have liked. Their chief failing was their traditional adherence to strict hierarchical decision making. In its way, though, that mindset had served as a kind of metaphysical Maginot Line, keeping safe behind it whoever still roamed free from relentless state offensive.

In that miniature of the country, the young blood was flailing.

Over a hundred of them had resigned in some disagreement with Aung Shwe, Win Tin learned. The real problem was not their dedication, nor even the spark of passion or ambition that no tyrant could ever quash. What they lacked was skills. Chief to blame was their education. A school system that had in his childhood been the lure of Asia was now a distant memory. The irony of the founding of Rangoon University was that the British had intended it to be little more than a factory for their loyal middle management. The student generation of the 1930s, taking full advantage of its free debate society in the Student Union, had turned the place into a breeding ground for the country's revolutionary leadership, marrying a burgeoning sense of organization with a nationalism that had already found root far beyond Rangoon. Since the 1910s,

farmers and abbots had been facing off perceptions of colonial brutality in localized, wildfire rebellions.

Successive military rulers had spotted the problem. Since 1988, the universities had been open for at most three years in a row. If they bothered to persevere
at all, undergraduates studied at a distance, dispersed to new, faraway campuses and satellite lecture halls that served only as cash cows for final degrees
that needed to be bought. In lieu of which, would-be students had turned en
masse to private tuition classes. Twenty-somethings snaked every day around
the block from the passport office on Pansodan Road. They swarmed billboards
that advertised jobs as carpenters, waiters, or construction workers in the United
Arab Emirates, Australia, or Indonesia. The visa sections of the Singapore and
Malyasian embassies were swamped with applicants desperate for a chance to
find work abroad. Win Tin recognized the social catastrophe.

In prison, he had earned the epithet "Mr. Any News" for constantly egging
on anyone for a nugget of information. But the most credible news came crashing in with each new wave of prisoners. The largest had landed just one year
earlier, after the Saffron uprising, and then again after the cyclone, which had
so clobbered the country that even in Insein parts of a roof had flown off. The
drenched inmates had attempted to light a fire. Authorities had taken it for a riot
and moved in on them with live rounds.

With a cynical bite that wasn't lost on him, Win Tin had been released as the
number of political inmates, floating at nearly two thousand, had reached an all-
time high. Judges were meting out some of the longest sentences in the history
of the detention system, with terms ranging from sixty-five to over one hundred
years to assorted human-rights defenders, labor activists, artists, satirists, journalists, bloggers, and Buddhist monks and nuns.

The tongues were not after all wrong: Win Tin's personality had a mag-
netic pull. Among the activists who flocked to him were the mutineers from the
party youth branch. Concerned about the lack of "young blood" in the party, he
convened a meeting in December. They came without hesitation. All they had
really wanted was to be heard.

But others came to him too. With the cross-societal contacts he had forged
in prison, he surveyed the different parts of the opposition as if they were chess
pieces. The greatest challenge now would be to forge a united front, to somehow find a way to reach the ethnic leaders, the more influential exiles, and
whichever social activists or members of a still-sentient underground could be
lured into a giant, secret accommodation.

The one bright light since 1989, Win Tin surmised, was the relative advancement of technology. The Unlawful Associations Act, the Electronic Transactions Law of 2004, and a half-dozen other prohibitions forbade contact with the border areas or, in some way, made direct communication an offense against the security of the state. So he would bypass them, with messages directed through the Irrawaddy, or Mizzima, or, better still, the radio broadcasts, which could reach even the furthest fringes of the jungle. Playing the same game, the exile press indulged him, in turn, with articles or broadcasts heavy on lengthy direct quotes.

But he needed a more immediate ear to the ground. He needed eyes, to see what his stalkers could not. He needed legs. He needed a different vehicle to pass more sensitive messages.

He needed, as it turned out, young Nway.

⤳

NWAY NEVER DELUDED HIMSELF THAT HIS significance to Grandpa was greater than the other activists who also stole to him by night.

But it was evident to Nway from their first encounter that U Win Tin had a different sort of mind and a different sort of energy. Until Auntie herself was free, Win Tin alone had the right balance of respect, tactical ability, and depth of experience to rise above the petty feuding and the "family politics" that had struck Nway long before as a plague on all their houses.

To Nway, there was nothing hard-line about dynamism. He, too, was a pragmatist for an army of pragmatists, whose direct line he traced back through the most effective political leaders to General Aung San himself. Never doctrinaire, Aung San had had little trouble switching, in the interests of Burma, from an alliance with Japan to another with Britain, from fascistic pandering to the necessity of liberal democracy.

Not long after Win Tin had lured back the NLD youth wing, Nway returned with a friend to the elder's temporary perch, that night in Yankin. He came bearing a message from a prisoner, conveyed to Nway through the prisoner's brother.

Once more, but privately now, Nway introduced himself to the senior activist. Nway bowed to pay his respects, and, rising to his feet with a shy smile, he found himself unknotting the details of his activities, the nature of his plans and hopes, his reasons for diving underground. Despite a loyalty to Auntie and the NLD so visceral that he could scarcely match it with words, he had, he said, quit the party to do the party's work.

In the presence of Win Tin, unbidden, Nway turned to glass. He couldn't, or wouldn't, hide a detail. It wasn't a spilling of his résumé so much as a catharsis, an unsolicited chance at last to come clean in the way he came clean to no one except Auntie. Even that regular confessional had become impossible. He could talk to her only through the distorting channel of her doctor, then her lone interlocutor. The doctor's visits were rare enough, and overfilled with the needs of other agendas.

As the young activist returned and returned to visit the older man, volunteering for ever more risky errands, he never inquired about Win Tin's other "channels." Nway knew enough to sense that the underground was alive, and still active. It was abundantly reassuring to know that at least one senior figure endeavored to put a finger on the pulse of it. To Win Tin, like a great node, all tentacles would lead.

Nway might have guessed, but could not know, that to Win Tin had come one "Glimmer Cliché," younger brother of the leader of a resurrected All Burma Federation of Student Unions with whom Nway had cofounded his six-person "Lower the Price" committee in Saffron; and older brother to another who had grown close as a son to the great '88 student strategist, Ko Ko Gyi, in Kengtung Prison. Now Glimmer was a live wire, working at-large for Ko Ko Gyi and the Big Brothers, the '88 Generation Students.

Nway didn't know that Glimmer had likewise splayed the anatomy of his activities before the hallowed *saya*, Win Tin, he in his prison blues, in age as deceptively fragile of bone as a bird, with a mind that contained universes.

Appealing to the furtive wit of a sage whom he thought a communist organizer, Glimmer had asked Win Tin if he might consider a broader underground alliance. Would he go "hand-in-hand" with all the discrete little networks? Would he think to work directly with the cells that had, with more or less success, all this time been spreading ideas about rights and responsibilities to farmers, factory workers, or in any case *acting*, while the NLD had talked and done naught?

Nway didn't know, but he might have guessed from what he saw and learned from Grandpa, that Grandpa's response to the young Glimmer had been to stay underground and out of view. "It's the technology age, and technology will help us go 'hand in hand,'" he had answered. "Make your activities on your own." *The time will come.*

The disappointment had cut Glimmer to the bone. But the point was fair. It was not yet time.

No one, of course, could know the full measure of U Win Tin's movements. Not even Auntie. But she would sense the subtle shifts, and listen, as Nway hoped the ethnic leaders might, for sly signals through the radio.

In *Saya* Win Tin, whom he came quickly to call *Grandpa* with an unfeigned and growing affection that seemed returned in kind, Nway recognized himself: someone who also understood the power of the shade, the need to keep his cards close to pave the way for a future that he could only vaguely see.

At every opportunity, Nway made himself available to be at Win Tin's side, watching and learning. Almost by accident he discovered that he loved him. When time came for the insertion of Win Tin's prosthetic hip, Nway was at his hospital bedside, talking politics, always politics, but swallowing back a curious lump in his throat.

In turn it helped that he could offer contacts. He knew people in exile, knew of ways to talk to the National Coalition of the Government of Burma. Why else would he have gone to Mae Sot?

To Nway, eventually, fell the most treacherous tasks.

And if it came to it, he knew, perhaps best of all, how to deflect attention.

I still have a lot of work to do.

5

CITY OF WRAITHS

YELLOWING, NWAY'S FATHER HAD GONE MAD.

He'd slipped, not for losing spine or strength but because he knew too much. Bloated and belching, he fought the fog's descent. As a young man and on through graduate medical studies, he'd lived and reconciled far-flung worlds: India and England, the Renaissance and salt marches, David Hume and *swaraj*, modernism, cubism, or postwar existentialism. In him, in Auntie, whom he called *Sister*, that mindset—cosmopolitan, you'd call it—could sharpen the ability to see it all as fleeting and absurd. But if others also endured the years-long incarcerations, the attempted forced removal of the meaning in their lives, there'd been no seepage of the spit into the psyche. For Nway's father, likewise, days that turned to months, then years, and long his sense of philosophical removal had kept him shielded—*the mind* as *its own place* that *in itself can make a Heav'n of Hell, a Hell of Heav'n*—until they'd beaten back at it so much that he realized in the creeping way of blooming agony, the drop that drips down and down and down always on the same spot upon the forehead, that all along it had been a lie, a terrible pageant of self-delusions. This *dignity*—this armor of a distance that kept him safe from the contagion of their system—what if instead it was pure fabrication, and, like his very self, substantively as baseless as the air?

He began by gazing out from atop a promontory and, by the end, he'd shriveled until he could no longer see himself apart from dust.

They put him in solitary, a kennel of packed earth and only a bowl of brown water—for washing, drinking, wiping, and eventually, maybe, confusing with his own piss. Right hand, left hand. He couldn't shut up the voices, constant voices in his head that screeched and laughed and whispered. Right hand, left hand. *A Hell of Heav'n, Hell of Heav'n.* He couldn't remember anymore. Couldn't distinguish which was which. Eat with the right, clean with the left. Clean with the right, eat with the left. Right hand, left hand. And now this filth, this infernal world, *twisted by knaves and made a trap for fools* that he'd kept at bay outside the membrane of his truth, long enough at least to take the hits and tell his torturers still exactly *nothing*, at last, years later, it all contaminated him. Now he'd enfilthed himself. There was no going back.

He'd been too sharp, too ready in Insein with his riddles, a pithy turn of phrase that never failed to mock the *unforgiving minute*, not even when they made him crawl on paths of jagged stone and looked on laughing; nor either when they'd lashed him to a chair and freed him up, only to lash him back another way. He'd lasted long—one year, two, four—well past those early bashings behind the knees and under his feet, the little games they played with pulling plastic bags over his head until the moment just before they knew he was about to go. To relieve the spasms in his back or legs before they'd let him loose just long enough to take a sip of water, then rope and twist him up again, he'd find a kind of ledge on which to lean or rest a limb or section of his feet. He'd reach, then, for a place beyond his Burma, redemptive fables from that colder, Christian land whose faith had once been his, the anatomical imaginings that flashed now in a doctor: how even at the crucifixion a man could find a sill on which to prop his heels until again he cramped and then he hanged. Nway's father's mind had found a kind of balance in a harmony of East and West, ideas rich enough and firm enough to ground him in his wisdom, or into his convictions—more than enough, you would have thought, to keep him whole and hopeful for the life that waited, come the day they'd let him back outside the gate.

Until the moment when it finally escaped him, he'd known exactly how to give his sons his hope. They came to visit one by one. To each of them in turn, he told them—told little Nway—the ingredients he wanted in his first meal home. *Next week*, he'd say. *Next month at most. I don't know when exactly, son, but soon*, and perhaps the son could hear enough through the din of other visitors, or glimpse enough of that old smile through the shadow of the grate to feel again the confidence that his father always knew, just *knew*, was never wrong, the noble U Maung Win of Twantay to whom so many flocked for counsel.

In Twantay, Nway would poke his nose under a threadbare curtain, belly down, chin pressed into his wrists. Always in a cloud of smoke from cigarettes or cheap cheroots, his father would calm his visitors' ruffled emotions, the untamed passions that shook and shivered like palm fronds in a storm. A well-timed thought, a nod, a willingness to hear and never seem to judge: Nway's father weighed their words and somehow everything went still.

Oh, and ginger and river-fish, lemongrass and long beans. That prawn curry your mother whipped up for last year's pagoda festival. You remember? And can you make sure to tell her to set out my blue longyi? *Yes, not the trousers. Don't you forget.*

A heavy rain had been crashing down when the knock in the night had come. Three sons, shaken from sleep, stood close together and huddled near their mother. The eldest was away at university.

"Don't worry," Nway's father said to them. He was smiling. "I'll be right back."

Then he had been led away and his sons hung their heads, sure of nothing except the drumming of the rain and the knowledge that their father would never be right back.

Later, he had been sentenced to twenty years. For what? It didn't matter. Nway knew enough: his father had been active. So had they all. Had they not all? He abhorred the regime. He talked of it every night. He had done many things, knew many people, and the amorphous accretion of his potential offenses would have stocked the docket of a predisposed judge with a fairground of carnival accusations. The least of it had been his family's months-long adventures in their hut at the end of the garden, thickly carpeted in the refuse of jungle, where Nway and his three brothers shared four pillows and four rattan mats with four other boys—not quite as young, bloodied, and scared at first, then patient, then increasingly impatient. His parents would never add a fifth mat, nothing to give the appearance of stowaways, and nor would they let their sons back to sleep inside the house. Not that any of the four boys would have thought to try. Nway, in any case, was too small. They were playing a game, and one of its rules was danger. With the uncomplicated severity of a child's moral judgments, he had felt that what they were doing was right. The real culprit, in any case, had been his mother. To her had come the students because alongside her they had, a few weeks earlier, marched in the streets.

But a man of influence, of *awza*, could not and would not hide in that way at the bottom of his own garden. Nway's father had stature, respectability, a capacity for free thought and a readiness to wield it when and if he felt like it.

Aung San Suu Kyi had *awʒa*. Win Tin had *awʒa*. Nway's father had the kind of *awʒa* that the junta, hard pressed to consolidate its own in the aftermath of the elections of May 27, 1990, was finding most essential to thrash down.

From the sky, Insein Prison stamped itself on the northern expansion of Rangoon like some alien spaceship. A vast, industrial octagon with a central tower radiated halls and barracks to a triple-walled perimeter. Attached was a rectangular tail, dissected with another grid of barracks and boulevards that fed back into the city. A roving population of ten thousand prisoners had been crammed inside its central octagon throughout the age of the post-1988 junta, about four times as many as in the rule of the British, who had built the prison in 1887 as the most secure lock-up of their empire.

Then, as now, the only exit into the wider compound of the rectangular tail was through a little red metal portal that clamped shut inside the red archway of a delicately trimmed red façade, the picture of a pretty nineteenth-century British rail station.

To scrawny little visitors who squatted all day in that gate's shadow, the prison was a world of coiled violence and brutal emotion. It was too saturated in color, at once acutely bright and empty, false in the way of the wooden monstrosities caricaturing human gesture in a puppet show at the *pwe*. There was a snack stall and a padauk tree, and a toothy village of wooden huts where the prison guards lived, which ringed the barbed wire of the octagon's bleached outer wall. The place should have been black and white and smelling of decay. It shouldn't have been approached with street-vendors selling goldfish, calling out for purchases of fresh-cut mango, oblivious to the arrest, only a stone's throw away, of generations, of time itself.

Nway was about eleven years old. After a while, he was no longer quite as frightened to make the trip alone because he had acquired the company of an imaginary friend. The boy was a touch older, about the age of classmates who had, since Nway's father's arrest, been shunning him without exception. He hadn't really understood. He had never before been wanting for friends. It must have been their parents, warning them to stay away. It hurt, though. He couldn't pretend it didn't. In any case, his new playmate proved wonderfully kind. He gave wise counsel, too, instructing Nway not to drink, not to smoke, and always to study hard. There was something about his guidance that sounded like Nway's father. But he was there for play, someone with whom to doodle with twigs into the sand when Nway shivered or quaked at the barks and shouts of the prison guards that exploded up his spine like little bombs, or the insults they cracked and threw like peanuts at the no-good offspring of some two-bit convict.

They might have treated Nway with more respect. He was always well dressed. But the prison compound was a great leveler. His mother tended the clinic alone now, and the eldest hadn't yet broken even from his first amateur stab at raising chickens. For those quarter-hour visits permitted once every three weeks in the first two years, there was never money enough to come with a brother, nor either with their mother. It would have meant double the fare to Dala from Twantay, double for the ferry, and double for the buses that coursed an hour north through the traffic of Rangoon. They needed money to ensure safe passage of a care package; money to fill up that package with a few, select essentials; money that went to the guards at the front-gate checkpoint, at the waiting station, in the final hairpin turn before the outer gate of the inner circle and entry to the visitor's block inside the central octagon. They needed to pack a lunch and snacks for themselves too, enough to last all day or into dusk because, as often, they would be made to wait, to squat for hours in the citrine dust, or if it rained, inside a waiting room that was always half-full with anguish or the static of collective nerves.

He told his mother once about his prison-trip companion. She had expressed alarm. But Nway reassured her. He knew his friend was only there on borrowed time. He had appeared one morning at first light quite like magic, just as Nway left Twantay. There he was still as Nway boarded the ferry, and on the bus. He never left Nway's side even at the checkpoints. Nway would wait with other inmates' relatives and friends. They would mass together in patches of shade, barely moving, not reading, not talking, unable to occupy thoughts or hands with anything at all beyond the peeling of a hard-boiled egg. There was always someone sobbing softly, a young wife, perhaps, wary of perturbing the other visitors, or a daughter twisting away toward the outhouses to hide her face. All day sometimes—he could have sworn it was on purpose—they'd be made to wait for the shout that might as often never even come to call them forward to the final checkpoint and then into the red gate. Nway's friend would disappear just long enough that Nway could focus on his father. He popped back out within minutes, tagging along until Nway was curled up safe on his own mattress.

Then one day the prison visits had stopped.

Hush hush, Nway's mother said, her eyes darting, a little crazy in their movements. No visits, no more, none. *Be still and say no more on it.*

Nway didn't know why. No one that he knew would say. It was a rumor, like his father's death itself, best squelched. But it was true. His father was too good, too educated, too brimming with belief in his detachment for the slow, sadistic breakdown that should have never been and that he knew at last would never end.

Word came that U Maung Win, born Winston Min, had died. He'd had complications of the liver. Watching him jaundice, Nway's mother had written in vain, letter after letter to plead for his transfer to a hospital. Some said that he'd been murdered. It was October 1996. Nway, who had turned the corner into adolescence and was approaching high school graduation, didn't believe it. Why should he believe it? In the punishment cells, inmates had always been forbidden visitors. There had been no body. There would never be a body. It would have been cremated and the consciousness recycled. Perhaps he was somewhere out there, in there, lost, but living.

Nway's father, idolized by all four sons to near divinity, could never die.

⋘⋙

MAY 2009

THE DOGS HAD GATHERED AT A nearby table. One by one they had begun to drop off, bored, or out of cash, or simply clocking out. The young men watched until the last of them had dissolved into the dark, the shared taxis had all puttered away from the Dala maidan, and the price of another round of beer was a surefire dulling of the reflexes.

Best to then spread out. But not yet. It was always possible that a Special Branch agent was waiting for Nway around the corner. Already they'd showed such effort, chasing him from the Office, from one bus to the next, and over the river to Dala, beyond a Rangoon agent's narrow bailiwick. That first tracker had disappeared, but reinforcements had multiplied here, hovering close.

The beer den had proven a decent refuge. And it wasn't as if its manager was in any rush to shut the place down. Business, for once, was booming. Who could say when the government would next hike the fuel prices, or the cooking oil would run out, or, if current rumors had any merit, all the earnings of past weeks would vanish in a sudden overnight wiping out of the one-thousand-*kyat* bill? Who could predict the arrival of another drought, how quickly the drinking ponds would dry or incur an infestation of diarrheal Guinea worm and the earthenware pots would sit empty, mocked by the unforgiving summer sun before the monsoon rains that were breaking later with every passing year?

Darkness normally brought Dala to a standstill, freezing into place a liminal zone that existed almost entirely to service its nomads: day laborers, street vendors, or battalions of children playing hooky from school because they had enough guile or good sense to have picked up early the general assessment that formal education was a fruitless endeavor, especially when you could seduce a tourist, just over the river in Rangoon, into a purchase of postcards, and earn a free language lesson with the sale. They were people who passed through fast and disappeared without trace, bound by the thousands for the crack-of-dawn ferry and the fishery or produce markets of riverside Rangoon, then back by dusk to homes in hamlets between Twantay and Khamhu or Kunyangon.

The commute was one of decades, unevolving as the township. With no overland route to the city, just two creaking riverboats alternating in five-minute drifts against the muddy current, the place had never stood a chance. Even the empty field that had been Hlaing Thayar on a far bend of the river had made it to the status of an urban "industrial zone," complete with functional factories on account, eventually, of a bridge. In Dala, the only structures built to last, aside from an orphanage and a school, were the pagodas. They stood on either end of the township, jeweled *htis* capping the gold-leafed domes, shuddering their bells in sudden gusts of hot air, framed with bright painted curlicues and liongryphs, swept and cleaned and tended with the intense devotion that had always been the anchor tethering the majority of society to the straight and narrow. Most everything beyond was flimsy and frail, wobbly bridges over ditches of sludge to huts patched together from bamboo and thatch, slabs of corrugated iron and tarpaulin for roofing, and alleys that twisted through the dust to piles of trash.

It was a sore on the city, a mere hop and a skip away, and a constant reminder that the country beyond subsisted in a state of improvised habitation, of delicate limbs salvaged from nature or endlessly recycled parts, barely holding up against the daily threat of a collective death sentence from another bad rain storm. The bars themselves were testament to the perpetual uncertainty, patchworks of bamboo poles and tarpaulin sheeting with a bank of bricks to hold back the sewage.

And so on one particular night that May 2009, in a beer den suddenly crowded with young revelers at one table and, at another, with sober-faced mid-aged men, a store manager anguished between shutting down operations for the night and prolonging his sudden, possibly karmic turn of fortune's wheel when, as fast as he could blink, his clients were already gone. Vanished in a thunder of motorcycles.

The plan was simple enough: the burden would be on the tracker. Outside Rangoon, motorcycles were a free-for-all. Seven wispy, black-maned figures powering forward for an hour on the sinkholed road toward Twantay in the thick gloaming, past a seamless stretch of paddies, or, if need be, out into them: it would take a feline's eyes, or a convoy of functional SUVs at least, to pierce through the darkness and discern one from the next. Ah, the merits of no street lamps! Like poverty and its discontents, electricity or the lack thereof could prove a potent ally.

Nway turned for his ride to a friend, a motorcyclist he had first hired in the weeks after he had sold his own to buy a computer a few years back, in theory for his home but in practice for the party. Riding back to Twantay one evening, he had slipped up, taking a call from an NLD Uncle and leaking just enough without his usual veil of codes and metaphors. What was he *thinking*? Sometimes he was just tired. Then again, it had been a while with this particular driver; after a time, if you were feeling it, you had to tiptoe in deeper with each acquaintance. That was just part of the job description, if not strictly by the party playbook. The young man had understood immediately. He had grunted something back, and the deed was done, bond of trust sealed. Most every night since on the Dala dock, he waited. And there he was tonight, dependable like good Man Friday, instantly alive to the urgency for Nway with scarcely a word exchanged.

❦

THEY LOST A FIRST MOTORCYCLE, then a fourth, then two more, and finally they were cruising alone.

To the left, in a passing black blur, spread the field where authorities had blocked Auntie's car in late August 2000 for ten days.

She had been bound for the town of Kunyangon in the Irrawaddy Delta, for the opening ceremony of a party youth chapter. It was to be the first of three beyond Rangoon since she'd launched the initiative earlier that year. The midnight sweeps that had followed each opening had, by then, become so predictable that even Nway hadn't known if or when Auntie would brave the trip, despite the fact that Kunyangon was near enough to Twantay that he had been partially responsible for its preparations. He had wanted to be kept in the loop, but she had answered that she didn't need him for the ceremony. He was too young, she said. It was enough that he had assisted in the preparations. She had meant that there were only so many sacrifices to contemplate. *Deer gives birth to fawn and tiger eats the fawn*, or so the proverb went, and it had played again and again in his head with each new felled friend.

To help him build the Kunyangon quorum, he had conscripted Arthur and another friend, who, in a comedy of mistiming, had both ended up stuck in Auntie's convoy too. They had slept the previous night at Nway's house in Twantay and were heading that morning to the Office via the Dala jetty, just in time to spot the ferry making its return trip. It was curiously free of paying passengers. Security forces had swarmed the area like ants. The skiffs too had been diverted to a different jetty. It meant Auntie herself was in the vicinity, testing the limits of her permitted movement, and she was right then headed over the river, together with Grandpa Tin Oo, party vice-chairman, her doctor, her driver, and ten other NLD youth who were acting as her security detail. Security forces, apparently, had little problem with the river crossing, so long as the party didn't venture beyond Dala.

But Auntie had them fooled. Her driver had hidden a couple of vehicles in the Dala monastery, and, faster than police could catch up, out they came and in she slipped. Arthur and friend had joined her about then. Nway, given his familiarity with Dala government personnel, had opted instead to play messenger boy. In an age before cell phones, it meant dashing back and forth, using the diverted skiffs, then the bus north through Rangoon to the Office, to keep the Uncles informed. Which was a good thing, as it turned out, because eventually it fell to him to secure provisions, enough to sustain the whole marooned crew beyond the single packet of dry biscuits and whatever water they'd stocked, on which they had survived for four straight days. Auntie—accustomed to the organization of deprivation with unpredictable end dates—had played ration-mistress, doling out two biscuits a person a day.

Eventually, after her vehicle, and the accompanying van with the NLD youth, had been forcibly lifted and tugged into a side road; after police had slashed the wheels, a first donation of bananas had landed and the peels devoured together with the fruit; after the youth had built a nighttime shelter in the field from stray pieces of plastic sheeting that did nothing to keep out the mid-monsoon malarial mosquitoes or the rising wash of mud on the nights when it poured; they'd dug in for the long haul, thoughts of Vimy Ridge and trench warfare possibly playing in the minds of the European-educated elders amongst them.

"Due to threats of violence by armed insurgent forces, travel by prominent persons to some parts of the country is at present inadvisable," the government had said in a statement released on the first day—which was funny because the only real dangers in the delta were attacks of dengue and diarrhea. Meanwhile Aung San Suu Kyi and company were declared to be "resting" in Dala, where they were later invited by Foreign Minister Win Aung to take in the delightful scenery, and offered "beach umbrellas" and a "mobile toilet" in a series of statements that hinged on a theme of Aung San Suu Kyi and company as on a kind of country picnic, protected by the state.

In the field, Auntie and company refused the junta's token offerings. But water, rice, and other elementals eventually trickled in from the NLD in Rangoon, passing through a hut-load of police officers who acted now as gatekeepers. While Auntie stayed calmly tucked in her car with the Uncles, or with her nose buried in a book, a few of the kids went into town to purchase bamboo with which they built a more impervious shelter. Arthur and friend, somewhat younger than the rest and not much given to carpentry, had preferred to employ a couple of bamboo pole cutoffs as fake binoculars, which they turned on the police officers who were, in turn, watching them with a real pair.

By the time they had started work on an outhouse and begun planting a vegetable garden—Auntie's initiative—the situation had become something of a global diplomatic incident. Increasingly antsy at a time of critical economic outreach, the junta was running low on fresh excuses. It accused Aung San Suu Kyi of a "well-orchestrated plan" to give the country a bad name in time for the United Nations millennial summit, which was scheduled to begin within days. At which point, toward 11 p.m. on September 2, 2000, about two hundred riot police had moved in. The night was so black it was impossible to see one face or flying limb from the next. Arthur was seized by his *longyi* and kicked into a corner of the hut. Winded, and stupefied, he felt a jackboot pressed into his thin chest. A couple of ribs seemed ready to crack. Out of the dark came a voice telling whomever was beating him to stop right there. It must have belonged, he'd suspected, to the policeman with whom he'd been exchanging waves and smiles and fake binocular inspections. Auntie, meanwhile, had been seized from her car. There had been a tug of war with a policewoman whom she had initially confused in the dark with Arthur's friend. Thinking she was rescuing him, Auntie pulled with all her might at a leg. Then she faked a fainting.

With Auntie and the Uncles loaded into a separate vehicle, the rest were piled into a police van and driven the long way back to Rangoon, winding through Arthur's slum of Hlaing Thayar. They passed Kyaik Waing Pagoda and the shopping mall at the crossroads of Junction 8. Arthur could think of no more jokes. His throat dried up. They were heading toward Special Branch headquarters, the detention center at Aung Tha Pyay. He could see the gates, see the nights of torture that stretched beyond.

The policeman grunted something to the driver. The van turned right.

Arthur exhaled. They were headed toward University Avenue. The van pulled into Auntie's compound, and there they were unloaded and kept under house arrest for two weeks. The Office, meanwhile, was shut and raided.

As it had happened, the whole standoff had a repetitive quality. Four times already, between June and August 1998, Auntie had been stuck in her car on her way out of Rangoon. The final incident had triggered Nway into an action that had cost him his medical degree.

The first, on June 7, 1998, had ended after about thirty soldiers lifted up her white Toyota sedan and set it down 180 degrees, facing back toward Rangoon. In the third incident, six nights on a wooden bridge about twenty miles west of the city, she had been blocked by barricades and sandbags; she wouldn't turn back and they wouldn't let her move and so she had slept in the car with a driver and aide, until her supplies of water and food had dwindled, her dehydration had mounted, and international outrage had risen to a such a pitch that the Philippine foreign minister—in a first for the otherwise tepidly condemnatory ASEAN—urged the Burmese to rise up against the military regime in much the way that his countrymen had ousted Ferdinand Marcos. Eventually Auntie had been pushed aside by armed police, and, sprawled semiconscious with fever on the backseat, forcibly driven home. Weak for days thereafter she couldn't commemorate the tenth anniversary of the Four-8 movement; couldn't attend the August 21 conference that she had called for in June, in an ultimatum to the junta to convene the parliament of 1990; couldn't even find the energy to sit upright at her piano to tinkle out tunes that normally had the salutary side effect of announcing to supportive bystanders that all—at least with Auntie—was quite well.

Her health was still fragile when she had set off again, a fourth trip, as with each previous attempt, to test her freedom to move. She was trying for Pathein, a town on the west coast of the delta. The plan was to meet ministers-elect from 1990, whom authorities prevented from traveling to Rangoon to meet instead with her. At least that fourth trip she had opted for a van: roomier for sleeping, and likewise for provisions.

New to the party youth wing, and just returning home to Twantay after rare attendance at a lecture at the Institute of Medicine, Nway had assessed with a newbie's self-seriousness the relative gravity of Auntie's latest situation, convinced an entire busload of fellow students of the same and led them in protest out of the bus and straight for her blocked van.

They never made it much beyond the road ditch. The instant effect was twenty-odd detentions, though temporary, and as many university suspensions. In Nway's case, he had been offered a paper to sign informing him that he could pursue his medical degree on condition that he went straight from home to class, and class to home, with no stopping en route even for a quid of betel.

There had been a momentary stab of satisfaction in telling them where to stick it—that, and their good-for-nothing university degree, drained of quality in the way of all the attributes and institutions that had once ensured the country its scintillating future. He resigned barely halfway through his first year.

Truth was, he had genuinely wanted to become a doctor. There had been, foremost, a yearning to follow in his father's footsteps. Of all his brothers, he had been the only one to have the requisite examination marks for medical school. Sometimes still his father came to him in dreams, hard at work in his rural clinic. In and out of the good physician's surgery in childhood, Nway had honed a natural sensitivity for the hard luck of people's circumstances. But none of that mattered so much. Choice, personal ambition: these were the luxuries of the free. In politics, besides, he had discovered a correspondence between the art of healing and fixing the body politic, or what he was fond of diagnosing as the thornier problems of the "social structure."

Mainly though, Nway recalled the stillbirth of his career only when he considered that the inciting incident revealed his dimwit lack of strategic sophistication. "Stupid, no?" he'd say, in stitches about it now, even though, were he to rewind the clocks, he'd probably do it all over again.

Speeding past tonight, he caught a whiff of that battleground field. It had since been converted into the Dala landfill. That had been a clever ploy: getting people to collude in the dumping of their trash on the memory of it. Nor could you fix a commemorative plaque to shifting dunes of plastic bags, empty bottles, the sick-sweet fermentation of an entire town's detritus. Not that many remembered to make the association. But Nway knew. Lest he ever lose his confidence or the twisting of his humor, he only needed a sniff of the place, on his daily commute between the city and Twantay and likewise tonight, and for another week he was good to go.

⁂

GOOD MAN FRIDAY PARKED FOR a moment by a ditch.

Nway pulled out his packet of Ruby Reds, shook a cigarette toward his friend, and lit himself another. It was impossible to say where the field ended and the sky began. The silence was as bottomless as the night. Only, if you listened for it, an insect fidgeted sporadically, and beneath it all, a heaving, long and slow, as if the land itself were breathing. They burned down to half a butt each, heaped themselves back on, and revved up anew.

The road from Dala to Twantay was long, straight, potholed, and empty. There was time to cloak himself in night. Time to regroup, breathe a little, and think.

The way Nway saw it, the pro-democracy movement was like a car. To function, it took all kinds of pieces of machinery, from the tiniest nail to the internal combustion engine. Everyone mattered, everyone had a complementary role to play, and only then, with each part in place, screwed tight and well oiled, could they move toward their goal in great, humming harmony. But like the brain that conjures consciousness, it had to be more than the sum of its parts. It needed a magic ingredient, an ineffable *je ne sais quoi*. To rev up with all else in place, what the movement needed was a *spark*.

Everyone was always talking about the spark.

The spark didn't actually depend on idealism. Idealists were all over, ready with a handful of pamphlets to scatter from the roof of a bus, the poetic gesture of a trial defense, the sudden angry naming of the Lady in a public marketplace—aloud. Small wonder that the students dived in first. They were the ones who were raring to go, jumping at any signal, always attempting to organize. However successful the implosion of the universities, a critical mass could be relied on to stand tall, cognizant in some hazy or hyperspecific way of how they had always starred in the narrative of the country's struggle for freedom. Time, aided by repeat university closures, was their most fungible commodity.

But no matter how far back Nway scoured for the cause of a nationwide uprising that captured a wider cross-section of society, the immediate trigger had always somehow been economic. People needed to feel it, not in their hearts but in the pits of their stomachs. There was a delicate balance to be struck. Things had to get just bad enough to believe that you had nothing more to lose, but not so much that you no longer had the energy to thresh the crop or forage in the fields for roots.

Nway recalled the most tempestuous days of 1988 as snapshots—flying his fighting kite in the middle of Sule Pagoda Road, innocent to the eeriness of the boulevard's absence of other life. His mother had come to claim him in a panic; he must have stolen out of his grandfather's house, a few streets away, during the curfew. Or he was elbowing a path through people's hips, lured by cries and shouts at the sight of an old man bleeding from the skull into a gutter, and a car exploding in flames.

The image that had pricked deepest, though, like a shard of crystal, were the adults at home, tensed and huddled around the radio, listening to the impassioned railing of the university students and the student union president, who had taken the nom de guerre, "Min Ko Naing," the Conqueror of Kings. His speeches alone carried the nation on the wings of his poetic cadences. *That's what I want to be,* Nway recalled thinking. *A student leader.* Only in his country was the fervor of campus activity as synonymous with perdurable historic change.

But protests or strikes were, at best, one tactic among the dozens. It could only be thus in a strategy that had as its end goal—in all honesty—a veritably colorless, institutionally rooted democracy that could one day pass from one leader to the next on the basis of elections, rather than accidents of birth to martyred independence leaders.

Nway never stopped thinking about it, even now, as he bumped along the road to Twantay on the back of Good Man Friday's motorcycle, speeding away from arrest.

To dismiss one or other uprising as a failure, in the way of the cursory observer, was to reject the possibility that the collateral effects of a crackdown didn't actually create the long-term constructive changes that would somehow advance the movement's cause. He had read the manuals. *From Dictatorship to Democracy,* by the American political scientist, Gene Sharp, had been a favorite of the underground since Sharp had written it on the request of an exiled Burmese journalist in 1993, as the students who had fled to the jungle were struggling with the idea of turning violent. From Mae Sot now, running clandestine workshops in what Sharp had dubbed "strategic nonviolent action" or "political defiance," a handful of them drew on his synthesis of revolutionary methodologies to supplement their own history and personal experiences. Revolutions, the kind to definitively topple governments, were not the stuff of accident. The idea, as much for the exiled '88 leaders as Min Ko Naing and the rest of the Big Brothers who had stayed behind, was to plot a map toward democracy with the kind of planning and precision that belonged to military campaigns.

From the vantage point of those who didn't understand the "strategic" in strategic nonviolent action, Saffron was a failure. But it was simply too early to say how far-reaching its effects.

For a year, the junta had been nipping attempted protests at the twenty-minute mark or less. Even the first protests in August had begun to die down, broken apart by security forces. It took lashing a monk to a pole and beating him on September 5 in Pakokku, an important monastic center, for the viral spread. Within four days in nearby Mandalay, in the tradition of the old underground groups, a group of senior abbots with experience in 1988 and a hard core of younger counterparts had founded the All Burma Monks' Alliance. Their first stroke of genius was to take a name that presented to the country the grandiose claim that it represented the entire *sangha*, the monkhood. Their second was to deliver an ultimatum to the junta calling for an apology by September 17. Failure to act by the deadline would result in excommunication of the generals and their associates with a *sangha*-wide overturning of their alms bowls. It was the highest form of punishment that the monkhood could impose against lay citizens.

The junta had ignored the threat, underestimating the connections within the *sangha*. Almost every Buddhist male at one time or another in his life passed through the monkhood as a novice. At about four hundred thousand, the sangha was as populous as the army, and at least, as it turned out, as tight. Monks studied at the same university, shared the same Buddhist rulebook, and, crucially, passed through different monasteries in the course of their vocations. The senior council of abbots had long before succumbed to the regime's co-option, dependent on its patronage. But scrambling communication at the lower levels was always going to be more difficult.

It wasn't hard to gauge how the All Burma Monks' Alliance had achieved it. In the growing countdown to September 17, its younger leaders hopped between Internet cafés, dispatching messages to monasteries across the country and coordinating with civilian activists: friends of friends of Nway from the NLD, the Big Brothers, or other, looser groupings. The monk whom they chose for spokesman on the radio, U Gambira, had made it to Mae Sot for a clandestine training in strategic nonviolent action. It gave him contacts and entrenched him firmly within the movement's wider web. There must have been a mole—the junta found good to use the factoid of his Mae Sot connection against him when authorities caught him in November and sentenced him to eleven months, later to become sixty-eight years. Proof, if ever Nway needed it, that Mae Sot was as rife as home with spies.

But even that brazen alliance could not have foreseen the popular explosion out of the monasteries. Nway had felt his heart swell each day with their growing numbers. It had been wondrous, truly enough to bring the country to tears. In his wildest dreams, he had never imagined it possible.

What had happened next was a study in how a crowd could turn—on nothing, on a hairpin, at some self-enforcing moment when sufficient perceptions shifted from defeat to victory, imperceptibly at first, then inexorably into a groundswell that would crest before, just as fast, everything went to hell.

On September 22, the demonstrations had taken a decided turn to the political. A group of monks were permitted through the police checkpoints on University Avenue, past Auntie's house. She appeared at her gateway in tears, hands clasped in prayer—her first public appearance since 2003. Thousands more people poured out thereafter, cresting to a high of 100,000 in Rangoon on September 24. In a country so repressive, the achievement was colossal.

And for being led by monks instead of students, it had signaled a paradigm shift. It had also benefited from modernity. In 1988, the only foreign witnesses to the crackdown had been a handful of diplomats. The final death toll, though many times higher than in Saffron, had never been settled. But in 2007, the world had watched in real time as security forces fired into crowds. Even without contacts at CNN or the Democratic Voice of Burma or whichever other outlet could focus world attention, scores of his compatriots had each managed to upload and dispatch a few seconds of grainy footage, before the junta had slammed the servers shut.

No longer could it hide behind its empty carapace of "Asian values." Still less could it lay claim to its hallowed Buddhist piety. No amount of diamonds on a pagoda's *hti* or fresh gold-leaf on the bodies of Buddha statues could fix this. When the generals attacked the most revered members of society, it was an assault on the very cosmos. They had raided and emptied ancient monasteries, forced the commission of blasphemies against the *Vinaya*, the *sangha's* sacred Buddhist canon. There had been mass disrobings, beatings, disappearances, and mysterious cremations. Images circulated of monk's bodies, unidentified, abandoned, face down in rivulets, snagged by branches, their robes billowing around them in pools of blood. It was a crime so egregious that the members of the SPDC, already excommunicated by the *sangha*, would be rewarded with rebirth in the realms of *Naraka*, Buddhist hell.

The junta had tried to redeem itself, disseminating word that the monks who had participated were bogus. Some were dupes. But others spotted the omens. Pagodas, or pieces of them, were crashing down. So too, shortly, would the sky. By way of celestial retribution, Cyclone Nargis had landed within eight months.

There had been rumors of defections from within the officer corps, and a handful of demotions for failures to follow orders. If it was true, if a crackdown so blasphemous had chipped the ranks, then it wasn't all for naught. The movement had always had trouble infiltrating the army.

Where the junta really lost, though, was with the young. Years of deliberate effort to sabotage the education system or starve it of funds; the accumulation of falsehoods that percolated through propaganda and single-source textbooks; the omnipresence of fear; and people's radically diminished access to independent sources of information had together resulted in a rising generation with no memory of one-party rule and the national rebellion against it, no understanding of their own history, and, so Nway heard the lament, few interests beyond painting their nails if they were girls or, for boys, whiling away the hours at gaming stations in the Internet cafés. Long before, Nway had made it his mission to perforate their apathy.

But the events of August through September 2007 had changed all that. Untold numbers within a cohort that stretched from teens to thirty-somethings had been politicized. It had taken only a few days for the student movements to surge anew from ash. There again on the streets was the peacock, the emblematic bird of the last royal dynasty, which the young nationalists of the 1930s had adopted, altering its posture from "proud" to "fighting" in a symbol of resistance against colonial rule. There again it blazed gold on a scarlet backdrop, on the flag of the underground All Burma Federation of Student Unions.

Nway could step back from it now and parse it all with analytical detachment, but the truth was that the Golden-Yellow Revolution—Saffron to foreigners, or, to Nway, "James Bond" when he was referring to its events within earshot or writing about it—had left a personal trace. It had been his first mass uprising as an adult and as an activist. He bore little nostalgia for it, beyond his awe for the monks and the lingering thrill of participation in the collective, a community of the likeminded that until then had largely been imagined.

A politician foremost, forced by circumstance to behave like an outlaw, he understood the vitality of striking a balance between leadership and invisibility; between the underground and over-ground; between hard-line revolutionary work and its diminished role in a wider struggle whose ends depended on the more prosaic drudgery of keeping alive and transparent a viable political party. There were moments for playing the part of the nail or the part of the wheel. And there were moments for somehow taking the time to put the car together, as a mechanic. Democracy, Auntie had always said, was a process. Getting there, Nway knew, was only ever going to be a small, though passionately charged, stage in the nation's rebirth.

But at the time, he never had limbs enough to be everywhere at once. As far as he'd been able, he had marked every critical turning point with his presence.

He had been among the activists who had, together with the Big Brothers, launched the first, peaceful march after the fuel hikes down Sule Pagoda Road.

They had used the opportunity of the annual memorial on August 19 for Kyi Maung, a former NLD chairman. Sometime between the ritual speeches and the polishing off of the luncheon feast, one of Nway's cousins had suggested aloud that they march in protest. The Big Brothers led about a hundred of them that day down the same busy artery where Nway had, as a child, in a previous era of mass protest, stared up instead at the sky. Along the way, bystanders enlarged the procession to more than four hundred people. On they walked, for five miles. No one raised a placard or shouted a slogan. Unity and discipline: these had been the hallmarks of the pro-democracy movement. When questioned by police, they claimed they had no other choice but to proceed on foot. It was too expensive now to take public transport.

Nway had never met directly with the Big Brothers, though he had followed closely their White Prayer and Open Hearts campaigns. Up to 2004, and for a few months between 2005 and 2006, they had been in prison. Chairman Kyi Maung's memorial provided Nway's first glimpse of their storied revolutionary aptitude. They saw the urgency of the fuel hikes for its political potential. They knew just where on a street corner to position themselves, for how long, when and how to scatter. Like good soldiers, they preplanned the expansion of protests beyond the moment when, inevitably, they'd be arrested. Within days, most of them were.

And Nway had been at a final, brutal showdown on September 27 outside Tamwe Township High School No. 3. He had lost his flip-flops; his camera, fresh stocked with video and photo evidence; and a friend.

Shoulder to shoulder, they had been walking in a column of peaceful demonstrators. His friend had borne the revolutionary red flag of the students, emblazoned with the peacock. Nway and others, denied the possibility of wearing the sign of the NLD, had tied the peacock insignia about their biceps or wrapped it around their foreheads, ninja-style.

They had been surrounded by armed riot police and truckloads of soldiers, rifles at the ready. No one believed that they would open fire, not into an unarmed crowd, certainly not one full of adolescents and parents come to pick up their children at the end of the school day. His friend had been felled by a single bullet whose whisper Nway recalled still with a shudder. It must have been a sniper's shot. There had been no other warning. Then the soldiers had let loose. Everyone had run for their lives.

"You are a hero," they had written by way of tribute under the young man's photo that they tacked to a patch of wall in the Youth office at the back of the NLD. There was no further adornment.

A UNICEF calendar was stuck nearby on an arbitrary month from a year gone by. No one had thought to flip it to the present, or take it down, not because time had stopped but rather because, by that point, time simply didn't matter. By now they might have turned the Office into a great sarcophagus; at times, it could feel like one. They did what they could for the families of the fallen. Beyond that, no one had much patience for picking at individual wounds.

But Nway had felt responsible for the young friend who fell beside him. Thet Paing Soe was sixteen years old, and Nway had lured him personally to the party, steering him straight from an aimless adolescence that he had been smoking into a coma. He'd come to Nway after a local USDA boss had tried to employ the boy's affection for weed to stir up trouble; the USDA man offered to supply the young man with enough marijuana for at least a dozen friends, who were encouraged to smoke to their hearts' content, so long as they did it somewhere public. They were also to wear T-shirts, care of the USDA, that bore the image of Aung San Suu Kyi, which in all other instances was banned from the streets. It would have provided solid fodder for the state mouthpiece: "Aung San Suu Kyi's Youth Supporters Aim for High!" The Press Scrutiny Board might even have permitted an exception, just that once, to publishing her name. Perhaps they would have placed the story, with accompanying photographs of twenty or so stoned-out kids, astride the usual back-page warning: "Skyful Liars attempting to destroy nation: BBC lying, VOA deceiving; RFA setting up hostilities. Beware! Don't be bought by those ill-wishers."

But the lad had turned against the plan. Nway, upon hearing about it, had fed him a means of sabotage, and then an escape route into the warm embrace of the pro-democracy movement.

Doubly painful was that his new friend had been, on that fateful September 27, 2007, carrying the wrong flag. Thet Paing Moe belonged now to the NLD, and it was exasperating enough that U Aung Shwe had forbidden them to bear the colors of the party, but it was still more unjust that a young man should have died for a group on which he had at most half a morning's claim.

But what was that to a sniper? When he'd aimed, the bearer of that scarlet flag of revolution had been the most symbolic shot.

༄

THE BOTHER, THEN, ABOUT THIS sudden spot of trouble in which Nway found himself—hounded out of Rangoon by intelligence agents—was that he needed to be back in the action, not in some pigshit rural boondocks where you could barely get cell phone reception, and connection at the lone Internet café was as hit-or-miss as an exile's honesty.

This was no time to be arrested.

It was never the right time. But right now there was a major crisis. Police had seized Auntie after an uninvited American tourist had swum across the lake to her house on the evening of May 3. For giving him overnight refuge, she had been transferred to the Insein Prison guesthouse to face charges that she had breached the terms of her house arrest. The trial had begun May 18. How long it would drag out was anyone's guess.

From what snatches of information Nway had gleaned, the American, John Yettaw, wasn't so much malicious as touched in the head. According to his wife, Yettaw appeared to have been driven by some messianic mission premised on "peace and forgiveness." With his homemade flippers, he was easy to dismiss as one more kook on the extreme end of Auntie's global cult of personality.

He seemed, on first analysis, just the kind of nuisance to make life tricky for activists. As a rule of thumb, Auntie's devotees, abroad or within the country, didn't much skew the cause to the negative. The adulation she generated ensured at least a slow burn of concern for the general situation. Complications could arise when they achieved that pipedream of participatory democracy. At that point, the country needed a citizenry capable of understanding their responsibilities, willing to engage in the day to day of parliamentary politics, not crowning a queen and ceding their responsibilities accordingly. That such a prospect would be antithetical to every molecule of Auntie's body was of little consequence.

There were those at home who even revered her as a spirit *nat*, the hallowed "Angel of University Avenue," a female *bodhisattva* whose rise to the forefront of the movement in 1990 had coincided miraculously with the swelling of the breasts on Buddha statues. So far as Nway was concerned, she could frankly use all the magic powers that they would give her.

But was Yettaw really so innocent?

Grandpa had first heard the news of Auntie's arrest when a phone call from a journalist in Japan had shaken him from sleep for predawn comment. He had been horrified. Digging where he could for all the facts to hand, he'd learned that Yettaw had tried this odyssey only a year before. Why, then, had the authorities given him a visa? How was he able to bypass officials on the lake? They had chucked stones at his passing form as if he were a duck. In Grandpa's view—and Nway agreed—Yettaw's history in the country had been more than sufficient to earn him a lifelong sentence on the visa blacklist.

Most suspicious was the man's timing. He had crawled wet and exhausted and somehow—how?—made it through the security gate at Auntie's compound and onto her doorstep within days of the end of her latest five-year detention.

It was clear to Grandpa, and to Nway, that the generals needed a pretext. Attempts to sever Aung San Suu Kyi's ties to the people in an isolation so complete that she had been denied letters, visitors, any interlocutor at all, save her doctor and house assistants, had done little, ostensibly, to assuage the generals' anxieties, or the ferocity of their wives' jealousies. The West, for one thing, never shut up about her. Ahead of the 2010 elections, the prospect of Aung San Suu Kyi roaming free and yapping with her unstoppable mouth undeniably kept the generals awake at night.

Every day since, Grandpa had been holding a vigil at the gates of Insein. Nway, when he could, stood beside him, snapping photos or phoning in reinforcements, then heading to an Internet café to relay their numbers, exaggerated by a few dozen, to the exile press. For an issue as emotive as Auntie's fate, inaction risked broadcasting the paralysis of the opposition, and the twilight of long-nurtured fantasies of toppling the junta from the streets.

The verdict, when it came, would be inevitably summary, dramatic, and arbitrary, hinging probably on the degree of force of General Than Shwe's next postprandial hiccup, or more likely, given her rumored jealousy, his wife's.

Already it had coughed up a slew of international condemnations. But at home, people were sloughing the whole thing off, anguished with vicarious empathy for Auntie, or turning their faces away in disgust. Nationwide reverence for her could not outweigh their resignation to the trial's outcome. Auntie's sentencing, however unjust, was a given—a battle to lose within the wider war.

But dreams of revolution died hard.

At large, the armed ethnic rebels had hunkered into defensive postures. Strengthened by intensifying competition between its Asian business partners for newfound offshore gas fields and the pipelines to channel them, the junta was full with talk of its elections. The movement, if anyone had faith that it existed outside and around Auntie, appeared to be flailing. Nearly two years since the crackdown on Saffron and eight months since Nargis, the country—until Auntie's trial—had lacked even the consolation of world outrage.

An old friend of Nway's had put it best just nights before, in the backroom cubicle of a downtown bar: "2007 to 2009 is not a long time—it means people are weak, confused, and generally putting their efforts into finding food."

The friend knew whereof he spoke. He had spent the previous months immersed among fishermen. Of the four students who had hidden in the back of Nway's garden in 1989, he was the only one with whom Nway had been able to keep in touch. Ever since, he had led a peripatetic existence as a professional revolutionary. But he had passed through Twantay at times, meeting with his young friend in teashops and passing on dribbles of thoughts, and eventually pamphlets and books that had fired Nway's curiosity and his sense that rebellion, in some secret way, was the only way to change the world.

"If I organized a demonstration, we must know our power first," he'd continued, his voice rising to a shrill pitch in the dark well of space that functioned as their periodic secret meeting hole, though designed for paramours. "If our struggle is to be the junta's failure, we must get people to love their rights and make them unite."

He was right. But it was the work of decades.

Meanwhile, on June 19, Auntie would turn 64. She deserved some mark of solidarity, a small gesture that she might hear of, if Nway worked it well, through the radio.

Perhaps, the color yellow—

❧

AT THE TOP OF TWANTAY, THE PAGODA cast a nighttime glow. Twin shafts of lights crisscrossed at street level. Hitting a downward slope, Man Friday cut the engine, and coasted. "Who d'you think—?"

"Can you get reception on your cell?"

But Nway already had his handset pinned to his ear.

He phoned his eldest brother, only to discover that one of the two lights ahead belonged to the motorcycle on which the very same was perched. The other belonged to a cousin.

"Go, go!" said his brother as their motorcycles rolled up side by side. "They're looking for you all over town!"

꧁꧂

WHEN HE WAS CHILD, NWAY HAD been wild in the way of the third in a litter of four, unburdened from the responsibilities of maturity. He liked to filch mangoes from the field that a grandson of Senior General Than Shwe had stolen some years back from a local farmer. He liked to tear through his home, scattering trails of dried mud from his skinny calves, or capsizing vats of steaming rice to reach for a handful of powdered chili for who-knew-what new-invented caper.

But he had the sensitivity to know that when he risked his limbs by leaping across the gullies between the sampans and the cruisers to fasten them as they bumped together, and when he honed the monkey-grip to hug his way up a coconut tree for the fat, green fruit that mocked him from far above, he did it mainly for sport, for mischief, or on a personal dare; whereas his friends, whom he followed or competed with in a continuous game of chicken with no care for their relative age gaps, were as often driven by necessity or the omnipresent tight little knot in the pit of the stomach that regular heaps of his mother's rich curries could never permit. He watched, too small to help but not so helpless that he couldn't hand over some tool or instrument, as yet another toothpick-thin neighbor landed on his father's surgical gurney, felled by scarcity. It was a raw education, lesson enough to learn that his life was built on the freedom of small luxuries.

As likely an early inculcator of such lessons was the mindset of his father. Nway could no longer remember specifics. But ideas resonated and carried forward in each brother long after Winston Min had gone.

Most—including Nway's mother—blocked the memories out of duty. It was better that way, to stay silent, to respect the peace of the dead. Only once a year, on a day in October, would they gather to honor his passing. Nway, when he talked of him, referred to a fictive uncle. But the thoughts surged when Nway least expected them, in the recognition of a few lines of a Rudyard Kipling poem or in the example of his father's tolerance that echoed in Nway's open-mindedness. It underlay Nway's sainted patience for the sort of popular cluelessness that he took upon himself, discreetly, and person by person, to re-educate.

If Nway's real name indicated as much, he was born on a Saturday. Saturday belonged to Saturn, to a southwesterly direction, and to the Dragon. It was the day of a child who was highly intelligent and quick of wit. This child would find it difficult to work in a team, but with patience would turn into its leader. Most parents saw Saturday's child as the bringer of ill luck. But there had always been exceptions. One Saturday, on February 13, 1915, in the central dry zone town of Natmauk had been born a boy who would more than any other person shape the imagination of the country: Aung San. Another Saturday in 1978, in the northern Rangoon slum of North Okkla, had seen the arrival of Naing Ngan Lin, "Bright Country"—Nigel.

But neither of Nway's parents had cared much for astrology. He never learned his exact birthdate. Later he understood that the loss of it was an attempt by his parents, in the eccentricities of Ne Win's waning rule, to bank their children's future in study abroad. Only after a certain age could young men and women leave the country for further education. The certificates of all four sons were burned, the ashes discarded, likely into the meal of a neighbor's hog.

Later Nway would find himself berated for the imprecision. Rivals would use it against him to suggest he had whiled away his better years, that he should demonstrate, if he was *that* old, more personal maturity. As he flew through school, one year after the next, a squirt by comparison with the growing heft of his classmates, it might have become increasingly obvious that his age had been, in the local schoolbooks, considerably cooked.

After 1988, his family had moved definitively to Twantay. Until then, he would spend the school year in his grandfather's house on 31st Street in Rangoon. A stern man who had pressured his father into medicine, Nway's grandfather had built a booming joint venture in textiles under British colonial rule, then lost it all, together with a garage full of classic cars, in the nationalizations of the 1960s. In his parents' self-enforced banishment to rural backwardness, Nway had seen nothing less than a return to paradise, a playground that stretched to the far horizon. The Irrawaddy coursed by, rich and heaving, spotted with fishermen on sampans trawling for an endless treasure of aquatic delights. Water buffalo collapsed down the muddy banks and lolled about in the cooling currents. There were sudden thickets of jungle and at every turn, heavy branches of tamarinds and peepuls that twisted outward and upward, demanding to be climbed.

His parents had met at Rangoon General Hospital. Neither of them given to bureaucracy or strict tradition, they had never bothered with a wedding. They had picked Twantay for their medical practice out of a shared sense that it was just the kind of backwater that needed them most. There was enough for a lifetime's work against tuberculosis, diarrhea, and a half-dozen other afflictions that would have been preventable in a better-managed system. And it was close enough to the city to send their growing family back for school.

Whip-smart as a flag snapping against a pole, Nway played hard, wrote his own rules, and laughed off any attempt at discipline. And discipline, if there had ever been much under the liberal-minded watch of his mother and his socially distracted father, had unraveled in the days after U Maung Win disappeared.

Nway's eldest brother tried to step in. Of all his siblings, he had loved Nway best. A teen by then, Nway would fix the wires in the family car, gun the engine, and career down the muddy paths. Another time, he took money from the parental stock and dispensed it on friends or random bystanders in an afternoon on the town. Untamed, he seemed easy prey for drugs, disseminated among ethnic rebels in the border areas as a weapon of war, and easily purchased even in the mainland. Nway fought in gangs, and ended up in hospital, bleeding from the head.

But the eldest had other duties now. Three or four years Nway's senior, he was a softened, more scholarly version, with the same shade of skin that they two, of the four, had inherited from their father. A first-year chemistry student who cherished his studies, the eldest had been in Rangoon when news landed that they had come for his father. The world lost its shape. He could not remember how many hours, days perhaps, he had wandered without aim through the streets of Rangoon. He should have known the map of downtown like the lines of his palm. Long walks with his father through those very streets had become something of a treasured tradition.

He had permitted himself that single indulgence. Soon afterward, he dropped out of university, as if the endeavor had been nothing more than childish fancy. Then came an attempt at raising chickens. It was a farmhand's job, dependent on roughhewn skills not easily acquired for a doctor's book-fed son. He tried, and failed, and turned to carting ice cubes for fish farms in the wild seas beyond

Pathein. Later, he moved up the chain into management, and slowly built up a steadier income for his family.

He needn't have worried about Nway. The boy had a fire about him. All he was wanting was a purpose. The day had come, not many moons after they had stopped visiting prison, when their mother assembled her sons together. She told them—there was never really much of a question in it—that one of them would henceforth have to work with the Lady.

The youngest was still a child, and the two eldest had their work and new families. The universities were shut again. Nway, fresh out of high school, seemed to be wasting at the beer dens. He was the most obvious choice. The fact was that Nway had always known that his mother would one day ask. It wasn't just because she had admired Aung San Suu Kyi for ten years, ever since she'd tended the Lady's mother at Rangoon General in 1988 and noticed in the daughter a rare managerial thoughtfulness.

He had taken to the Office like a fish emptied back into water. Overnight he clipped his hair short and shouldered the discipline and the uniform of starched white shirt and Kachin *longyi* with a pride he had not yet known. Within weeks, he had met Arthur. A tight circle of about ten young members knit around them. Together they had journeyed through their first, tumultuous year, graduating from their first terrors, navigating the secret courtships of different factions. The Office was no pristine monolith. From within its ranks, they'd strained against the competing pull of everyone from the most legally circumspect to the hard-line dynamos who moonlighted in the underground.

Nway's eldest brother had briefly joined him at the Office. But the vocation that gripped Nway never caught. He stopped going after a handful of visits. There were other ways to help the Lady. Henceforth, he would watch over his little brother, and in the steady flow of cash, ensure that he was never hungry. And so Nway came to rely on his elder brother for the majority of his finances.

One by one, as Nway's friends exited politics, buffeted by the hardships of their lives, Nway rose up the ranks. Endearing himself to Auntie, and at the kernel of a new generation, he never relinquished his erratic originality. Early in his political life, he had understood that there was no reason to presume that anything would change should he hesitate to make a move. A decade more, perhaps two, and people would plummet deeper into desperation. Boys would be press-ganged, girls tempted into prostitution. History weighed on him, and it stretched forward as endless and unchanging as the rice paddies. The Buddhist impermanence that was rooted in the soils infused him with the knowledge that when it was time to go, when arrest caught up with him or the elders of the party failed, he, like them, was nothing more than a drop in the ocean.

And so he powered forward, aboveground or semi-under it, undistracted, never stopping to consider as one year bled into the next that his actions were somehow self-sacrificial. Foolhardy, certainly. "Stupid," he would call some of them. The idea that he or any of them were manifesting a kind of courage, moral or otherwise, was a joke. "We are just doing what we have to do," he would say, and only when pressed. That justification became a refrain. It might as well have been his motto: transactional, pragmatic, deceptively uncluttered with sentimentality. It was a shrug of resignation, of duty shouldered, as natural to him as air to lungs. It might even have suggested jadedness if you heard it in vacuo, without the context of absolute effort, of muscle and mind constantly, relentlessly, for eleven years, primed for getting Burma to democracy. Once he had set his course, definitively, he would not stop for anything less.

⤛⤜

PEOPLE JESTED THAT RANGOON WAS a city of house arrests. The numbers ebbed and flowed according to the whims of the junta and the less variable laws of biology.

There was Auntie, of course, at 54 University Avenue. Technically, she had been sleeping since May 14 in the "guesthouse" at Insein Prison. But, confined in it for thirteen of the previous nineteen years, the grey blur of her villa on the far side of Inya Lake had acquired the quality of a lodestone. Some accelerated near the barricades on either end of the street or dared not turn their heads as they drove past. But people still felt her presence, as if they had compasses in their hearts.

There was Grandpa too—not Grandpa U Win Tin, but the other Grandpa, U Tin Oo, former army chief of staff and defense minister turned convict turned monk turned lawyer turned NLD vice-chairman. In the summer of '88, together with Brigadier General Aung Gyi and Aung San Suu Kyi, he had formed the original troika of the party. At eighty-two, he was getting on a bit, though hardly inclined to retire. He couldn't much afford to let slip the physical discipline of a longtime army man nor his daily diet of tea and meditation that kept him nimble and light in mind and morale. Even so, house arrest was a healthier option than yet another run through the detention system. For alleged knowledge of a foiled coup attempt on his one-time boss, General Ne Win, Grandpa

Tin Oo had served from 1976 to 1980, and then again for service in the NLD from 1989 to 1995. That last had been hard labor.

At least this third stint, after nine months in Kalay Prison, he could spend with his wife and family. Which didn't make it a cakewalk. Incarcerated at home without charge since he had attempted to fend off murderous thugs in an ambush on Auntie's convoy in 2003 at Depayin, Grandpa T and family had fast descended into such dire financial straits that, in December 2004, his wife had secretly reached out to the US embassy for three hundred dollars a month, to be laundered through rental of a vacant family property. It was a mark of their desperation that they should risk it. Taking funds from a foreign government meant walking headfirst into the oft-recycled charge that the NLD had never been more than a foreign import, the bastard child of a woman who had spat on her heritage by living her adult life abroad, marrying an Englishman, and spawning two half-breed sons. But the Embassy could be relied on for its discretion.

Then there were the fallen generals—Ne Win foremost, "the Old Man," or, for a long while, simply "No. 1." He had actually died under house arrest in 2002. But if you didn't discount the fact that the country seemed somehow suspended in time; that progress was a function of decay; and that attempts to give the city a facelift with a handful of shiny new high-rises were cancelled out by the triumph of mildew and accompanying material depression, then the fact that the strongman who had brought them all to this impasse was no longer with them was somewhat immaterial. As if to vindicate the sentiment, when he'd finally passed, no one had bothered with official funeral fanfare. He had been a shadow for years, if for a while after his resignation in July 1988 with the outsize back-door influence of a senior officer to whom the chain of command would always pay respect. A foiled coup attempt against Senior General Than Shwe, a last hurrah allegedly plotted by his family in March 2002, had offered just the pretext to finally eclipse him. He had died within months, confined to his villa with his favorite daughter, Sandar Win.

Now only his ghost endured, and it haunted the military, the economy, down to the cellular structure of society. You could quibble that the country had never materially recovered from the devastation wrought by World War II, that the seeds of ethnic division and civil war were sown in the nineteenth-century British imperial proclivity for censuses. But fear, military rule, and a hermetic, Burman-centric chauvinism came compliments of the man who had seized power in 1962.

Still alive, though severed from his capacity for malice, was General Khin Nyunt. He was confined just north of Inya Lake inside the Defense Services Compound. Speculation had been rife that his arrest in 2004, in the name of some petty corruption scandal, was more about the consolidation of power of No. 1, Than Shwe, and likewise No. 2, Maung Aye, then the commander of the armed forces. Khin Nyunt had been too wily, too adept with realpolitik. He had single-handedly forged ceasefires with seventeen ethnic minority groups from 1994; finessed openings that made him seem a peacemaker with Aung San Suu Kyi; and, in 2003, announced the "seven-year roadmap to disciplined democracy," which did more to confuse the international response to the junta than any of its previous attempts at scrubbing its image.

But generals, like revolutions, ever devour their own. Down with Khin Nyunt, the former Secretary-1 of the SPDC, protégé of Ne Win, one-time prime minister, and longtime arch-spymaster, had come crashing the entire military intelligence apparatus that he had been credited with building and had used to spy on his peers. Hundreds of trained intelligence officers had been arrested with him. Now they were serving sentences from Insein to Putao. The rest had scattered: some on mercenary motives to the borderlands where they ran little businesses helping exiles ease the cross-border traffic of underground activists.

For others too, Rangoon had become a ghost land, a place to abandon one's identity and drift for weeks at first, then months, and eventually the years—undetected, wraithlike, forbidden from contacting relatives or returning to native towns.

"We are internally displaced people," joked an elderly man one afternoon to his visiting half-sister, except he was not actually joking. For different reasons and different imperatives, he had been forced south in 2002 to Rangoon from Pakokku, and she, in 2005, from Rangoon to Naypyidaw.

A warm-hearted community leader and civil servant, he had never entertained a thought to leave Pakokku, the town of his birth that rested on the banks of the Irrawaddy as a Buddhist scholastic center, its soils baked to the shade of monks' robes. He had less trouble leaving the one-party constraints of the Burma Socialist Program Party. In 1988, he asked to be fired rather than follow orders to denounce agitators among his employees. With uncanny foresight for the darker age to come, he raided every last tome on government from a vestigial bookstore. And then he had joined the NLD.

Ever since, his twin joys had been his politics and his ice cream parlor, Everest Ice Cream, top of the world and talk of the town. It wasn't the first in

Pakokku, but it was the best, the setting for novice ordinations, pagoda festival celebrations, and wedding parties. Daily offerings—pandan and coconut, mango or vanilla—depended on the smooth operations of an adjoining ice factory, which meant electricity, which meant state rations of fuel supplemented by black market stock. In his devotion to the NLD, he felt he was cheating on his wife, and he once admitted as much to her in a sly letter about his other, clandestine love. It ended on a punchline that revealed his passionate mistress to be politics.

But then he was kicked out of the NLD for talking to the media without permission from headquarters in Rangoon. Next, not much caring a fig for the technicality of his firing, local township authorities came to clip his electricity. A young captain who had fallen in love with his daughter was rewarded for his association with the local NLD sahib with a commission in a brutal, free-fire zone on a far frontier.

Once an agitator, always an agitator, or so it went, according to the local town commander. He let it be known to his underlings, who let it be known to the servicemen, who took their snippers to Everest Ice Cream's wiring. The financial success of a ranking member of the NLD was provocation in itself. The ice melted, the factory shut, and its owner sold his house and business. All that remained of the parlor were four chairs and a checkered linoleum table that served as a dining room in the single-bedroom apartment in Rangoon that he shared now, at sixty-nine, with his unmarried daughter, his wife, and their dog, Baloo. Never with his spirit intact could he hope to return to Pakokku.

As for his half-sister—a judge—she had been seconded like most civil servants to the all-new capital city, Naypyidaw, on little more than a few weeks' notice. In the law, she had found her life's purpose, strengthened with a graduate fellowship in Japan and the hard work it took to climb to a judgeship by forty. She relished the mental gymnastics of the legal system and knew as well as anyone how it was pockmarked with inconsistencies. The judiciary wholly lacked independence, but it wasn't, to her mind, entirely irredeemable. For a while, she filed paperwork because she had privately told her superior that she could never take a case of a political nature, the kind that might hinge on a nonpolitical charge but that came with orders, always from the highest reaches of government, to convict. The only possible wiggle room was in the length of the sentencing.

What had done it for her was the discovery that her other brother was a pro-democracy activist too, and had been arrested for it. Her boss, who happened to keep a stock of banned books on Burma on his home coffee table disguised in paper wrappings, had assented. Political court cases were rare enough, he'd surmised, and depending on the locale to which she'd be posted when she eventually recovered her ruling privileges, there'd be more than enough controversy to keep her busy. There were endless Tatmadaw land thefts to litigate and delicate corruption charges against drug lords who might have protection from high-placed local commanders.

So really—and she sometimes tossed under her mosquito net at night for it, or poured herself for solace into her Buddhist practice—the judge lived torn between her mind and her heart. She worked in a bureaucracy whose leaders gave orders that she knew to be terribly wrong, and opposed on pain of death by many of the people she loved best. Of her two brothers, one of whom had been an NLD ranking member before they fired him, she inherited the work of the second. He had been an avowed independent whose civilian leadership from Pakokku during the events that triggered Saffron she had discovered when she recognized his voice while tuning in to an illicit Radio Free Asia broadcast from her new office in Naypyidaw. After his arrest, and then his death in prison, she had quietly taken over his informal job as a prime source for a reporter at that same exile radio station.

The reporter was a Burmese doctor based in Washington, DC, whose career choices since 1988, and the use of his byline, had forever cut him off from chances of returning home. Every week now, he checked in with the judge for leakages that only someone with her high-placed insider knowledge could supply. Tidbit by tidbit, conversation by conversation, their secret compact had turned emotional. He felt guilty for the arrest of her brother; she felt guilty for her day job, and, in a more slippery way, for also deceiving her superiors. Each of them was lonely, but no longer so much alone, and their hearts quickened with each chance to talk, the charge intensified by a renewed hope inside the impossibility of it: the cross-continental, politically tangled complications of a love that tried to bridge the chasm between discrete islets of wraithlike limbo.

Another ghost in Rangoon was Nway's first English teacher at the NLD.

Once the vice-chairman of the NLD local Irrawaddy Division branch, his mild manners, mild voice, and mild vision of the world belied a life of accidental adventure. This teacher was, like the proprietor of Everest Ice Cream, of that generation for whom prospects of a return to parliamentary democracy was not an adrenaline rush premised on mass uprising so much as bottled common sense. By now he should have been cooling his heels surrounded by his grandchildren.

Instead, he had been on the run since 2000, the only member of a group of five NLD colleagues to duck arrest. Their trial two years later saw them each sentenced, and in his case, in absentia to seven years, with hard labor. They were charged under the 1950 Emergency Provisions Act for meeting on September 10 and 12, 2000, right after the incident of Auntie's car in the Dala field. The headquarters had been shut and raided. But Nway's teacher's group had printed a statement that called for a variation on the usual menu of themes: the release from house arrest of Aung San Suu Kyi and other party executives, permission to reopen the headquarters and the local Rangoon chapter, and "urgent tripartite dialogue" between the government, the NLD, and ethnic groups. They had typed it up, and sent it to Voice of America through the US Embassy.

There were ways, after a time, to carry on life with a semblance of normality. If you were small fry, like Nway's teacher, like Everest Ice Cream's proprietor, it was never entirely evident if authorities had an eye on you for the long term, tracking your maneuvers to see whom you would meet, why, and where. Then again, why ascribe to malice what could just as well, in a bureaucracy of underpaid, poorly educated minions, in a city of millions, have proved incompetence and incapacity? Which functionary would have the ideological tenacity to check an identity card all the way to the requisite, dust-caked ledger in the township of your birth?

What ideology?

More to the point, wherefore the need for greater investment of effort by the state if your life had been suitably scuttled that you now lived like a rat, moving by night, always surreptitious, always looking over your shoulder? The longevity of military rule in Burma had less to do with foolproof organizational rigor than its capacity to keep fear at a simmer through the bogeyman of possibility. Auntie's most dangerous offensive, and lastingly destructive, had been to help people steel themselves against it. The theme ran from an early essay, "Freedom from Fear," and through the laughter and relaxed ease of the weekend talks of 1995 and 1996 that she, together with the Grandpa T and U Kyi Maung, had held from the gates of her villa.

Nway's NLD English teacher surfaced time and again to help out old friends at the Office, such as, for instance, a supreme court advocate, who had of late become a ghost as well.

After twenty-seven years of defending political prisoners before judges who would sentence them regardless, the advocate had been charged with contempt of court for passing on the message to judges on October 29, 2008, that his clients refused to recognize the trial's due process. Doubtless the notoriety of his clients had something to do with the charge: they were nine of the most prominent members of the '88 Generation, Min Ko Naing, and the other Big Brothers, and each had been held without charge for about a year. For that, he had ended up in a cell of Insein himself.

He served his full six-month sentence. They had treated him, he felt, decently enough. It was nothing compared to the beatings and other abuses that he had spent a career documenting. Still, he emerged rangier, hollow in the cheeks, his shock of white hair razed to a convict buzz-cut. Then his law license had been revoked. Now he could no longer practice.

How to rebuild an identity? Previously a member of Auntie's four-person legal team, he had been a pioneer in the defense of political prisoners. Case after case, year after year, it had been an endeavor only as futile in its visible impact as self-belief itself. Even in a closed trial session, he had succeeded— as Auntie's spiritual mentor, Vaclav Havel, had defined it once—in shattering the world of appearances, exposing the emperor as naked, living outside the lie. He acted and breathed instead according to what Havel described as "a truth which might cause incalculable transformations in social consciousness, which in turn might one day produce political debacles unpredictable in their consequences."

There were legal professionals who had turned their backs on the lie of the system after one or two such provocations: the judge, for example, out of family loyalty, or the government prosecutor assigned against Win Tin in his first empty trial in 1989, who had been suitably revulsed with himself that he became, thereafter, one of the NLD's staunchest legal loyalists and Auntie's personal attorney.

Less obliquely, the supreme court advocate had established a notoriety that inspired a handful of younger up-and-comers. And even as he failed to secure dissidents from lengthy sentences, he was well placed to quietly pass details to the sharp-toothed exile press whose reports might otherwise have been muddied with speculation.

At his desk, in a basement on 41st Street, under his retired black court gown that swung now from a hanger like a phantom, the advocate stuck to the same rigorous schedule. He printed new business cards that discarded the proud stamp of "Supreme Court Advocate" for "legal advisor." The agent who monitored his office, at an angle from just over the alley, had been, it seemed, relieved of duty.

And yet, it turned out, there was so much to do: compiling case information on land requisitions, or forced labor, or instances of press-ganging. Now he found a new life passing it all to the two-person staff of the International Labor Organization liaison, on the twelfth floor of the Traders Hotel on Sule Pagoda Road. There was almost more latitude in it. If the advocate was careful, he could steal out to the villages himself, slipping between checkpoints, scouting for information. No longer did he have to waste precious energy shuttling back and forth with the same fruitless arguments to the Insein Prison court.

Biggest site of all for wraith-spotting in Rangoon, though, was the underground.

The list and flavor of its characters would here grow long. Often as not they were so given to employing pseudonyms, switching up cell phone numbers, and tripling their fake identities that confusion, mistrust, and self-deception could be as rife as double agency.

Take, for instance, the most potent in name, force, potential, and multi-generational experience: the at-large members of the '88 Generation Student Group, otherwise known to Nway and company as the Big Brothers (and a few Big Sisters). Several among them had earned their activist credentials as leaders of the straw-flame protests that yielded the '96 Generation and the '98 Generation. The '88 icons had all been swept back into prison, most on August 21, 2007. The rest had been hunted down in hiding within months.

Without the disadvantage of comparable face recognition or notoriety, their affiliates and rising rookies had maneuvered in their stead, after 2007, according to friendships, strategic savvy, reputation, or sheer luck.

Among them was "Ko Taw," a toothy thirty-something who, at an expensive coffee bar that he would never normally be able to afford, enjoyed startling an American reporter with the claim that he was looking forward again to prison—time for meditation, for push-ups, for relief, really, from the constant juggling of identities.

"I have so many identity cards," he grinned, tucking with ease into a plate of fries, as if he were the sort of crony's son with high-topped sneakers and a pretty karaoke girl who frequented these spots. "Sometimes I am a teacher, sometimes a student."

The previous night he had met to discuss where and when to spark "guerrilla strikes" with a motley crew variously claiming affiliation with the All Burma Monks' Alliance, the Young Monks' Association, the 2007 Generation, and

MDC. He had a personal tie to the All Burma Federation of Student Unions, but the finer distinctions between groups didn't much matter. Later in the week, he and one among them would head to a factory and pretend to be workmen. They had ideas to pass on about striking for better conditions and pay.

Another, "Soe Tun," chose to hide in the most unlikely spot of all.

When authorities learned that Soe Tun had grown too reliable as the '88 Group's at-large leader, he heard the news and then scouted for a room and a willing accomplice in the heart of a military compound.

Soe Tun, lanky and given to modesty, had risen into activism as a '96 Generationer, yet another university student who suffered from the irreversible ailment that came of briefly but conclusively expressing aloud his desire for change. He'd been arrested, released, arrested again, and, after Saffron, had worked in parallel with young Glimmer, who had appealed to Win Tin for leadership, and whose brother knew the great Big Brother strategist, Ko Ko Gyi, from Kengtung Prison, and incidentally worked with Nway in Saffron and his lawyer friend now in Mae Sot. The best-kept secret of the underground, and likewise its most dangerous, was that the Big Brothers were never actually more than two or three degrees of separation away.

Soe Tun had also worked of late with a private tuition teacher who went by "Phoenix."

Silver tongued, with strong eyebrows and a sense of nuanced strategy that dazzled foreigners for its intelligence, Phoenix had in 1988 fended off a lynch mob from an unbridled attack on an intelligence officer and applied the same principled cool to recent campaigns. In the weeks prior to the 2008 constitutional referendum, he had, with Soe Tun, organized activists across the country to vote "no." Anticipating serious irregularities, they recruited watch groups, people previously unknown to authorities who would plant themselves beside local precincts to surreptitiously observe the count. It had been difficult to pull off, because it violated local electoral rules, though less so people's sense that to keep a vote clean was the greater responsibility.

Phoenix was adept at keeping Western embassies informed with analysis and updates of his activities. He also had the rare ability to ask for money.

Shortly after the Saffron uprising, when authorities shut the borders and help from the exiles had been squeezed to naught, he had secured a small embassy grant. It didn't go down well. Later, among the exiles, there had been talk that the money had been misused. There was a rumor of an activist in hiding whom Phoenix had phoned, and within minutes—not coincidentally—she had been arrested. Another allegation circulated, still more damaging, that he had committed some unpardonable offense against a girl.

Underlying it all, there was the sense that he had usurped his privileges. He claimed a leadership in the movement that had not been his to take. He was no friend of Min Ko Naing, the Conqueror of Kings, the Poet-Leader of the Big Brothers. Nor either of Ko Ko Gyi, the strategist; Htay Kywe; or Jimmy, Grandpa's dashing neighbor down a few cells and over a hall in Insein. Phoenix had never made it out of doors to participate in the Big Brother's civil disobedience campaigns. He had embellished his role in their successes and exaggerated the significance of his personal ties. All he had ever been, his would-be colleagues pointed out now, was their interpreter.

And why was he not in hiding too? Why could his voice, even as a whisper, rasp with an actor's clarity across the second floor of a downtown bar, waxing lyrical about politics? Why indeed, they asked, had he never been arrested, or never suffered more than a dubiously short detention, in years gone by?

When the suspicions caught up with Phoenix, he defended himself with substance, pushing forward with pro-democracy petitions and other tangible actions. He had a little daughter. He had a wife. For what possible trip of ego, he argued to whomever cared to listen, would he put either of them at risk? Who cared, really, if he wasn't famous and had no group with whom to claim association, so long as he pursued the cause among the very people who were best placed to shake the system? He had accumulated new recruits, fresh-faced voices, people beyond suspicion of the state. Besides, on what democratic vote, he wondered, had anyone anointed the Big Brothers?

But when he lost the ear of diplomats with the arrival of new batches who took the at-large skepticism at its word, Phoenix eventually melted into shadow too.

ᨆ

THE CITY ITSELF SEEMED HAUNTED, a carcass of its former self, abandoned back to nature and to a peculiar urban leprosy that ate at the sculpted façades with baroque formations of mold in five shades of turquoise. Cyclone Nargis had felled so many of its ancient trees. But the humidity, the fecundity, and the cockroaches and mosquitoes had a way of indefinitely fermenting in the lakes, creeping through the piping, and piercing into brick, upturning or forever cracking apart the sensible grid lines and sturdy walls of Victorian Britain as if it might, in a few snatched years, have ever tamed the native febrility of a patch of Orient as far removed from the temper of pallid, drizzly London as a primal roar from a whimper. At times, in the operatic downfalls of high monsoon, or at the cusp of another deep indigo dusk, Rangoon seemed less a city emerging from jungle than the jungle itself, black and spiking against the sky, punctuated in brief spots with crumbling stone and mortar that sagged and heaved under the dead gravity of all that tropical life.

A cacophony of crows had the monopoly on sound, even above the din of twenty-year-old Nissans and Toyotas and cast-off Japanese buses that sputtered by day along the cratered boulevards. At sundown, they yielded to the sonar of a thousand bats—tens of thousands, even, shooting out from the West Gate of Shwedagon Pagoda and cresting above the city in a great arc against the violet light before they dispersed to who-knew-what vampiric expeditions.

And where they went, and what they saw or smelled or touched of places closed now to the eyes of men, it was a wonder to imagine. Did they fly five in a line through the forsaken People's Parliament on the far side of Resistance Park, or pour through the smashed-out windows of the Ministry of Foreign Affairs? How many of them hung from the crenellated turrets of the Secretariat, still red, still standing tall, which had once stamped proud the colonial authority over an entire downtown block between Anawrahta Road and Maha Bandoola to the north and south, and Theinbyu Road and Bo Aung Kyaw to the east and west? Now its clock faces stared down at old Rangoon, broken on two sides, like the curled-up lips of twin toothy crones, sneering at a city whose inhabitants scuttled past like roaches, or squatted in the gutter beside its unscalable gates ribbed in barbed wire, unashamed to defecate but too skittish to affix a plaque or lay a wreath in remembrance of where the great Bogyoke, General Aung San, and his proto-cabinet had, on July 19, 1947, been gunned down.

People said that the junta, in 2005, wrested the capital north to Naypyidaw, to the barren site of a ragged little town originally called Pyinmina, out of an astrologically motivated fear that an invasion would come from the sea. The counsel that generals sought from astrology, numerology, or mystical ways of knowing ran counter to modernity's worship of scientific rationalism; though a point of disdain for foreign observers who saw them as backward orthodoxies, they could offer clear lines of hope for the people too. And military policies were never far removed from serious strategy. There were solid reasons for the new capital, of a piece with the autarchic, inward-looking gaze that had defined military rule since 1962. The British had felled the last king with a flotilla that had headed up the Irrawaddy from the Andaman Sea. In the days after

Cyclone Nargis, naval vessels belonging to the Americans, French, and British had hovered again in the Andaman. How were the generals to know that the superpower that had invaded nearby Vietnam or, two years before Naypyidaw's ground-breaking, had overrun Iraq, would hand-wave their remote tropical dictatorship as a "boutique issue"? Was it not tempted by the teeming richness of their country's resources that had made Burma a magnet for meddlers from all over Asia?

Brand new Naypyidaw centralized control of the six army group commands, including Northern Command out of Kachin state, and North Eastern and Eastern in Shan state, with 105 battalions between them patrolling the zones of active combat. From Naypyidaw, the junta had better access to the ethnic areas, and, likewise, to the pipelines and hydropower stations on the river systems, whose yield had been divided between their joint ventures and Thailand, Yunnan Province in China, or anywhere else but back home.

The junta's legitimacy had always been contested. Religion and history were battlegrounds for the taking. The new capital, with its giant statues of ancient Burman warrior kings and its royal pageantry, had been built with unfeigned symbolism to recall a mythical past of golden supremacy. It had also provided contracts to the general's business associates—Tay Za and Steven Law—whose firms constructed its eight-lane highways and colossal edifices, clean, wired, and, with three layers of street lamps, well lighted enough that it seemed to a visitor's eye an orgasmatron of electricity, as if to blast abroad the news that Burma—Myanmar, to its inhabitants—was as modern as Manhattan, as if it meant, in its hubris, to blot out the very stars.

Still unfinished, devoid of life beyond its construction workers and civil servants, it was a tabula rasa unsullied by a messier past. Senior General Than Shwe could look around and, if he didn't peer too closely through the monumental arches or see the weeds already impaling the concrete of the deserted sidewalks, he might for an instant believe the hype of his yes-men that he had created a Myanmar all zigzagged in bridges and roads and bound for the future—though, according to engineers on his projects, leading from somewhere to nowhere at all.

But, really, it was as if one morning, a general had squinted out his duct-taped window in Rangoon, thrown up his hands in despair, and simply upped sticks. Discarded with the city were its masses suppurating on the streets, the ethnic stew of the Indian quarter, the aggressive offal hawkers in Chinatown to the east, and the mangy crawl of all the mildew, stench, and filth. And always the hidden menace in the covert glances of people behind their *thanaka* sandal-wood cosmetic paste, which they dotted on their cheeks like masks of clownish false cheer. At every corner, a trishaw driver or an ice-block vendor picked at his teeth or a wiry dough vendor fanned to naked flame his wok-heating char-coals. Urchins flitted among them, auguring chaos, and shady brokers sidled up unbidden with syncopated bargains of fresh *kyat* loaves concealed in newspaper wrapping, special rates for crisp US dollars, or Thai *baht*, or Euros, *if you will only follow me please.*

At night, they spilled anew into the streets, gathering for a game of im-promptu *chinlon*, an artful local volleyball, perching on generators, or curling up on the concrete islands between the lanes. Anything to breathe free of the torpidity of heat and cat piss in their cramped apartments; or to catch the last, free shafts of halogen light; or to find a bit of peace to tune in to the evening's illicit shortwave broadcasts from the Burmese services of Radio Free Asia, the BBC, or Voice of America.

The thing with turning against your own people was that you always feared that your people were ready to turn on you. If bombs exploded in Naypyidaw, no one knew, because no one saw it by daylight, because the coaches bound for Mandalay from Rangoon, or Rangoon from Mandalay, were scheduled to pass through it at night.

And if by chance you tarried there, to visit the new Uppatasanti Pagoda, the Royal Pagoda, pillared in polished bricks of jade and a foot shorter than Rangoon's twenty-five-hundred-year-old Shwedagon; or if you stopped in on the penguins at the zoo in their air-conditioned pen; or to take in the jewelry museum, a trove of such earth-mined distinction to shame Ali Baba and the con-tents of his little cave, you couldn't really move beyond. There was no walking in Naypyidaw. Distances between its islands of aspirant fantasy were so vast that they demanded wheels. There was nothing yet between the construction sites but mortar and scrub.

But in Rangoon, the poltergeists threw hissy fits on anniversaries and the living, though preoccupied with the drudgery of daily survival, never left a patch unpeopled. In Myaynigone Market, in northern Rangoon, in June 1998, the spirits of the dead—possibly belonging to bodies recently exhumed against the laws of faith from a nearby cemetery that authorities had reportedly sold off to the drug lord, Khun Sa, or possibly related to the seventy students and twenty policemen killed in the market on June 21, 1988, precisely ten years prior—at any rate, in Myaynigone, some dark force threw plates and cups off teashop tables. At a nearby appliance store, televisions levitated and collided in midair. A passerby reported watching one flash to life with images of splattering blood.

❧

INTO THAT RANK OF GHOSTS, Nway disappeared one night.

He was a fugitive now, and a "UG" activist—underground, among the hidden many.

Turned away at the pagoda in Twantay, when his brother had warned him of roving authorities, there had been nowhere to hide except under their very noses. He had taken refuge that night at the home of a childhood friend, who was not incidentally the richest scion in town. For the sin, Nway and a band of mutual friends had nicknamed him the "tycoon." For the purposes of more pressing anxieties, it meant his family owned a three-storied house, roomy enough to disappear within.

There, Nway had sheltered for three nights. With suspicions rising in the household of a stowaway in its midst, Nway had relocated to his friend's uncle's home, under cover of a conveniently timed funeral wake. They wrapped him head to toe in cloth. A passing glance would have mistaken him for a pious Muslim woman. It helped that he was passably androgynous.

That night, the tycoon, Nway, and another childhood friend, a poor poet whom Nway had once inveigled into his tight circle of ten NLD youths, profited from the ongoing distraction of the funeral party to share a drink. Caught between grief at the tycoon's deceased relative and the dread menace of a shared arrest, it was hard to say whether they had laughed or cried more into their lone flask of cheap Myanmar whiskey. Veering between emotions, they even shared a fleeting moment of philosophical detachment. In Buddhism, everything decayed. All was transient. Moments such as these were all they had to snatch.

Alone again for the greater part of the next few days, Nway had fidgeted, cooked up new jokes, worried about the necessity of hiding out at all. With each passing hour, the boredom grew until it threatened to eat him alive, joint by twitching joint.

Inevitably, always, his mind wandered back to politics. He thought about his "Ten-Second Network," which he imagined now as a battalion, fifty-strong, one thousand-strong, dependable and disciplined. He presented them to Auntie, and she was smiling a little, free again from house arrest and with that old twinkle in her eye.

Mainly he tried to think about the color yellow.

Yellow was Auntie's favorite—or gold, if you cast it through the local linguistic prism. It was the color of the *padauk*, the national flower, whose fragrant sprays opened once a year, for a day or two at most, with the first monsoon rains. Auntie, always keen on fresh-cut flowers and ever mindful of symbols, would wear a sprig of *padauk* in her hair. In people's eyes, her unabashed feminine grace married her with that sprig to the New Year. She had always had that way about her—a freshness carried in her smile that didn't seem to wilt with age.

His Ten-Second Network would converge at a junction. At the designated signal, everyone would pull out something yellow: nothing overt, perhaps a hat, a patch of cloth, a rubber duck. Nway, or someone else, would snap a photo, everyone would disperse and he'd hustle to an Internet café to send it to his contacts in the media who would, even though they couldn't show faces of those involved, spread the news back inside.

Inspired in part by the "white" color campaign for political prisoners of the Big Brothers, the idea was akin to a flash mob, the second-generation street tactic that had become fashionable among other UG activists. Less demanding than full-blown protests, they were easier to coordinate, safer, and, for all their evanescence, as potentially lasting in the minds of unwitting bystanders as pieces of theater.

The effort could end up as little more than a stab-in-dark show of solidarity with Auntie or—oh, how he'd like to dream!—the trigger for that elusive spark. There wasn't room for failure. Failure, in these instances, didn't exist, unless, of course, no one showed up or braved the seconds. And there was the rub. Months of cultivating friends or fresh recruits would culminate in an instant. But if they succeeded, they would have proven to themselves and to each other that they had the stomach for more.

He liked to dream that his Ten-Second Network married small risk with huge ambition. It was half the reason he'd made the trip to Mae Sot with Nigel, seeking funds from someone he had no reason to trust, on pain of a life sentence.

He liked to dream that his idea was not pathetic, not a drained imitation of the Big Brother's thousands-strong successes.

Most of all, he dreamed he could talk it out with Nigel.

But he couldn't. Nigel had branched away to form his own network, and he was calling his the Saffron Generation. They were scarcely talking. For all Nigel's invitation to join a reporter at a restaurant on Kandawgyi Lake a few weeks earlier, you could have cut the tension between them with a knife. It must have been a matter of the money. Always the issues between them came down to money. It hadn't helped that Nway had been careful to fudge his biographical details on account of the other two activists whom Nigel had also invited. Nway couldn't say why, just a hunch that one of the others had something to hide.

Crouched into a rheumatic posture of cyclical daydreaming in a dust-caked closet at the tycoon's uncle's house, word had landed from Nway's poet friend that authorities had stopped in on his brothers and his mother.

To make his getaway, they would need a decoy. The simplest, and the best, was a brawl.

Nway's brothers and cousins gathered a few friends in the teashop near the mango tree and, whether they only pretended to drink themselves silly or slipped a few on the way, the plan worked. Punches were thrown, and police were called, speedy to the scene of too much loose testosterone after dark in the middle of a quiet town.

Time to move.

With another convenience that hadn't been entirely coincidental, the parents of the tycoon owned a construction business, with several trucks. The tycoon called the family driver, bid Nway a fond farewell, and headed, fists at the ready, to the teashop mêlée. Nway crawled into one of the vehicles' cargo loads, hunkering among tires, and bumped back the long route through Arthur's Hlaing Thayar into the bowels of Rangoon.

It wasn't yet midnight.

It was too early to head to Nandau, the Palace, his old safe house. He had to wait for the house checks to subside.

But few would have recognized him. Through his friends, his mother had suggested that he don a wig. It had felt just this side of absurd. But he had ceded to a hairnet. It flattened his hair into a scholar's cap. His thin form floated inside an anorak three times his size. He felt himself shrink. His very gait turned timid.

From a new cell phone number that he had swapped out in Twantay for his old, he called the reporter who Nigel had introduced to him at Kandawgyi Lake. The work of a politician could not end with a personal crisis. Grandpa had reminded him of such days earlier, fielding a call for an interview about Auntie's trial on a landline that had been clicking intermittently with the usual markings of primitive wiretapping.

Inquisitive in that Western way, the reporter was also the rare person who would challenge him to think. Nway liked that. In any case, she'd make a decent alibi. They wandered along the empty sidewalks, then headed to a karaoke parlor. But the place struck him as too loud, too humiliating, even as evidence to present to a foreigner of the country's moral degeneracy. It was painful for Nway to witness the parade of girls, innocents from the provinces, in their Thai-tight dresses and garish face paint, proffering themselves in catwalk formation to the highest male bidder.

They moved to a late-opening beer den. Nway poked a chopstick at a plate of fried chicken feet. He deflected questions about personal heroism into a catalogue of favorites. Auntie and Win Tin took first and second place. He tried and failed to translate untranslatable puns by his Hero No. 3: Zaganar, the country's greatest living satirist, who had been sentenced in November 2008 to fifty-nine years for public order offenses related to speaking to the media about millions left homeless after Cyclone Nargis.

On ticked the hours, past the moment when the waiters slopped cloths over tables and stretched out where they worked, dozing to the buzz of mosquitoes and the intermittent caterwaul of the dogs. Far to the slums, and dawn was close at hand. No buses now, in any case. Too tired to head home. Might as well stay.

The reporter headed back to her hotel at about 2 a.m.

Nway, again, was alone.

There was a silence to Rangoon then, an innocence almost, as if the cruelty of small-minded men, the conditioning of fear could be pressed to sleep. Bereft of traffic and nighttime footballers, the broad boulevards around Sule sat empty as in curfew. Only the stray dogs stirred. They slunk past and gathered in clusters, waiting out the time until the click of 3 a.m. and then they bayed, a wild chorus that rose across the city, howling at the cloud-blotted moon.

He drifted to the jetty. A hot flurry rustled the fronds of the coconuts. A cigarette in hand, he gazed toward the pinpoints of light across the river where Dala stretched, and the Irrawaddy Delta beyond. He could touch it, almost, if he stretched out the length of his arm into the inky dark.

Forevermore, he didn't know for how long, Twantay was closed to him. In the end, it had taken a village to save him. It wasn't a lesson that he would be quick to forget. For Auntie, for the movement, he could fight until death, one more anonymous soldier ready to take the hit. But for Twantay, and the efforts of friends, he would have to remain free. There'd be advantages to staying in the city, with closer connections to the Uncles and to Grandpa. He could dash between them into the early morning. But he'd have to adjust his other methods. No more could he rely on young Snow, and brilliant Paw Paw, and wise

Acca—three sisters who had become something of his aging mother's adoptive daughters in the absence of filial care.

Where to go?

He decided against the Palace. He wanted to save it for the Uncles as a space free of eyes for meeting beyond the Office. Better that he vanish, one more punk among the hundreds in the grid of boulevards down by the river, among the booksellers and deserted jetties off Strand Road, round Sule, and on towards the offal stalls and one-time opium dens in the back alleys of Chinatown.

At 4 a.m., on his first night in Rangoon as a fugitive, there was nowhere to disappear but into the darkness itself.

PART II

6

THE STAKEHOLDERS

APRIL 10, 2010

THE ACCUSATIONS WEREN'T PRETTY. In fact, they were downright dangerous. Employing the Internet for any purpose beyond a late-night session of cryptic Gchat was crapshoot enough. But to use it for spamming all and sundry with the details contained in this particular email, at this precarious moment, verged on the criminal. Word would travel. Rumors would take flight and offer pretext for legal sanction.

Now the Uncles—Nway's Uncles—were in trouble. The official NLD youth were in trouble. The democracy movement itself, revealed at a moment of direst national necessity to be as fractious and factional as it had ever been: ditto. And the whole complex edifice upholding the military regime could see it, the whole country, the whole world. Senior General Than Shwe in his fortified villa in Naypyidaw must have been rubbing his hands in glee. They might as well have checked the box on half the vague offenses that the supremo had sprinkled through his speech days earlier at the annual Armed Forces Day military parade.

Never in his life had Nway imagined that he would have to manage a crisis as self-mutilating. He had thought by now that they would have learned. He had wanted to believe—in the way of a willful naïf, the new lover who walks on smiling down a corridor of red flags.

The call with news of the email had landed as Nway was strolling by night with Nigel past the dead zone of Strand Road to the jetty beyond Botataung Pagoda. The place would be far from earshot, and breezy too, freed from the heat of the day that the city sucked down into its joints and concrete arteries, only to blast it back by night. Beyond a second-rate karaoke bar and the bustle of nighttime pilgrims at the pagoda, life thereafter would be sporadic, at most a few young couples come for the rare patch of privacy.

They had much to catch up on: comparing notes, primarily, on potential "second-line" members for an election-monitoring network. Priming it to capacity was becoming daily more urgent. The rumored date of the elections kept shifting—all anyone knew for sure was that they were to be held within the year—but the electoral laws had finally been announced on the official Myanmar TV on March 8. These had confirmed everyone's worst fears.

Lest anyone miss them, they were spelled out across the next few days in the state mouthpiece and in forced supplementals in the private journals. Then the countdown had begun. The deadline for re-registering as a political party was May 6. Failure to do so by that date would mean dissolution.

It had been a difficult few weeks for the party. Without clear lines of communication between Auntie and the Uncles, barring the sporadic intercession of Nyan Win, her lone interlocutor since the Yettaw incident, who could visit only after seeking permission in writing from Naypyidaw; with few opportunities to consult far-flung party members and none at all with the wider public; in a chronic state of talking by periphrasis if party members weren't in a back room that they trusted not to be tapped, the decision about whether the NLD should register to participate in the election had hung for some time in the balance.

The divisions among the executive committee members had been hard to hide. There were twenty of them now, since an expansion in January to include some of the younger Uncles. With the platform of the headquarters, they could officially engage with visiting diplomats and take calls from the exile media, who were apt to press for answers on the highest-stakes battle that the NLD had faced since 1990.

Khin Maung Swe, the half-deaf geologist who had been released from Insein on the same day as Grandpa, favored participation. To the media, he'd made a point of measuring his words. Taking care not to unnecessarily antagonize the junta, while keeping firm to party positions, he was intentionally conciliatory, although it could take a subtle ear to hear it. To him had fallen much of the credit for the finessed line of the Shwegondaing Declaration, which had set down the party's preliminary position a year earlier. Grandpa was a favorite for the colorful quote. He wasn't one for daintiness and had little trouble openly expressing why it was that the 2010 "elections" were a dangerous sham.

Chairman Aung Shwe was more discreet. But it was clear he was of a like mind with Khin Maung Swe, in his case to secure the party's legal survival. As for the vice-chairman, Tin Oo, Grandpa T, fresh released from seven years of house arrest on February 13, he'd kept largely silent too, but everyone knew that he wanted to wait until he'd heard Auntie's view. At least they had all agreed that the whole process was indeterminate until the electoral rules and regulations had been issued.

In the end, the NLD's decision had come down to a gathering at the Office of more than a hundred members of the Central Committee, the party's second-tier leadership, convening for the first time in more than a decade.

"Hey, look!" said Nway, pointing at an empty shrine that they were passing on their left.

Normally it belonged to the Lady of the Emerald Palace, a *naga* or cobra-headed dragon deity, a spirit guardian *nat* endowed with formidable powers. In life, she had been a wealthy patroness, a generous donor to Botataung Pagoda, who had died in the ruby mine region of Mogok in 1955. As spirit, she knelt just opposite the pagoda in the form of a smiling woman, hands clasped in beatific prayer, with a headdress of snakes, a cloak of green, and fresh tides of coconuts, green bananas, and baskets of flowers that lay devotees presented daily in exchange for treasures received, ruin averted. Among the dozen of spirits in the official *nat* pantheon, she was not the most ancient nor even the most treacherous or vindictive if displeased. Still, or perhaps for that reason, the Lady Mya Nan Nwe had the distinction of finding herself every night, between 9 p.m. and dawn, mysteriously shackled at the wrists.

Analysts and astrologists had circulated the theory that she had appeared in a dream to Senior General Than Shwe—him or his wife—and that the hand-cuffing was a means of pinning her down, preventing the sidereal punishments she had threatened for the sacrilege of the junta's crackdown on the monks. Just as likely the general saw her as an avatar for the real Lady, for Auntie. In either case, the timing of her ordeal, every night since early 2009, seemed apposite. Nway preferred the theory that it was actually the work of prisoners' families or friends, come every night to appeal for help or merely to register their protest. Nigel inclined to agree. It was a cunning ruse, if true. Mya Nan Nwe radiated an aura of sufficient might to scare off retributive sanction from local authorities. Than Shwe and his wife were famously vulnerable to the occult and feats of *yedaya*, black magic. As long as the *sangha*, the Buddhist monkhood, kept them excommunicated, they would be loath to cross a *nat*, too.

And yet, tonight—

"Where'd she go?" said Nigel.

Pilgrims by the hundreds padded barefoot among the pavilions of the pagoda opposite, sat in meditation, or worshipped and lit candles at their cardinal points, apparently unperturbed about the gaping hole just over the lane where normally the Lady of the Emerald Palace sat enthroned in her vast, now featureless sea of fruits and flowers.

"Maybe we should start a network to protect the rights of *nats*?"

They laughed, first one, then the other, and the sounds crested, lost their hinges, and tumbled into each other as a single multiheaded eruption. At times like these it was almost impossible not to admit that under it all they had a solid, fraternal affection.

After months of tension, Nigel and Nway had reunited into a working partnership on the heels of a conversation that Nway had with Auntie via the lawyer. It was more a one-way instruction along the lines of Nway passing the message that he had been working away from the Office, and she in turn saying that he should focus on election monitoring. She had, actually, asked that Nway return to the party. Nway, who took it as his primary duty to keep her up to date, had managed to persuade her that he had never been more committed, but working on the periphery of the party—from the street, even—was invariably more productive.

One evening, over several beers and a chili-spiked papaya salad that Nigel had mopped up and Nway had inevitably coughed up the cash for, Nigel had dropped specifics about similar intentions, by which he'd meant a network with a clear goal to direct the energies of youth who tended to lose faith, as had they all within the Office, out of inaction. He wanted a target for his Saffron Generation, or whichever fresh talent he spotted among his students.

Nway had seen his opening and dived in, enjoying the realization that he was directing an amorphous idea into something solid that aligned at last with the compelling needs of the party. He had finally conceded defeat on his Ten-Second Network. The last straw had been a "blue campaign," to be triggered across half a dozen towns in solidarity with Grandpa, detained briefly for a September 2009 column in the *Washington Post* in which Win Tin had explained to Americans how misguided were attempts by a recent visitor, Senator Jim Webb of Virginia, to convince the NLD to run. Two or possibly three activists had managed a few seconds of something blue, or so Nway had confirmed afterward. Beyond that, it had proven impossible to coordinate, more difficult to show what it was, and, even worse, he'd had no means of gauging its effect.

To Nigel, he'd signed off his latest plan not as his but Auntie's, whose word was always the clincher. Next thing you knew, they were hard at it, the more engaged and even-keeled in their partnership because of a newfound complementarity: one maneuvering from aboveground, a respected face in his community and known to colleagues as to local authorities; the other, flitting among the senior politicians or morphing between various guises to finger, in his nebulous way, untapped layers of society.

Privately, Nigel had conceded—to himself and to his wife—that Nway had been remarkably generous. They had barely been talking since Mae Sot in February 2008, but as soon as Nway had learned of Nigel's detention that June, he had somehow ensured that Khine Sandar Win had money enough to stay fed and clothed, no questions asked, and never mind how long or indefinite the incarceration. The couple had a healthy son to thank for it.

Nigel's release from Aung Tha Pyay had been timed with precision: August 14, 2009, the week after the verdict on Auntie's trial and the very day that the US senator, Jim Webb, had been scheduled to land in Naypyidaw to negotiate the release of the American swimmer, Yettaw, who had been facing seven years in jail himself. It had been a cheap trick. Tradition demanded that Nigel head straight to the NLD office to register his news—and authorities knew it. Word would travel to Senator Webb, probably through the embassy, that an activist had been released in good faith. Two months in detention, free at last, and Nigel had been livid. The junta had made him its pawn. A week later, Khine Sandar Win had given birth to a very vocal son.

It had never occurred to Nigel that Nway might, at about that precise period of time, have been in a spot of trouble himself. Nway had thought it wholly unnecessary to bring the matter up. For one thing, it was safer for everyone to keep the early details of his fugitive existence to as narrow a circle as possible. As for helping comrades, no matter how deep in the mire, he had a duty, plain and simple. The only thing that would keep them all afloat was to share everything—a bowl of soup, a textbook, a sudden windfall of *kyat*.

There had been days, back in his early months at the NLD, when he and Arthur and giggly Su Mon, or whoever else from their tight-knit circle of ten NLD youth, had only enough between them for a single cup of tea—a smoky oolong from the Shan hills, with a dollop of rich, condensed milk. It had never tasted so sweet.

They were still doubled over with laughter when Nway's phone interrupted. "Go ahead." It was a friend, an official NLD youth member. "What? Where? And this was when? Who? And—say that again . . . yes, bad connection . . . A gang of *what?*"

An email was circulating on the Internet. And its contents were devastating. Nway shot a dark look at Nigel. *Listen to this.*

He had to make some calls. He'd visit the Uncles if he could. He was intimate with each of the Central Executive Committee members whom the email's author had expressly accused of being part of a corrupt and controlling NLD "Gang of Four." First Nyan Win, the lawyer, who happened to have let Nway into the Information Committee back when; then Han Thar Myint.

But tonight, it was already too late. Nyan Win, soft about the eyes but never more alive than in a good legal tussle, would probably just shake his head, somewhat droopy but philosophical. Han Thar Myint would take a moment to remove his glasses, screw tight his eyes in his tiny face, rub at the deep furrow above the nose, and then say something witty with an accompanying blip of laughter. He'd have a plan by the morrow, though, doubtless subtle and surprising in much the same way that he had worked in backdrop all this time, unobtrusive, and few except the Uncles, Auntie, and Nway had any notion that he could matter quite so much. With Ohn Kyaing, the third named of the "gang," Nway was also close, although in a more formal way. He'd always looked up to the senior journalist, who had been a newspaper colleague of Grandpa's, though of a younger generation. It had been in Ohn Kyaing's newsroom that Nway had briefly sheltered a year earlier, when an agent had been on his tail.

Worst hit was Grandpa. Ringleader among ringleaders, he was—the email accused—"receiving huge amount of funds from abroad but he doesn't turn it over to the party." And Grandpa, Win Tin, was a night owl. His energy never seemed to wane. Perhaps Nway should hop it to Yankin.

But actually, the damage for now was done; it was enough that they were smeared, the party's true dissension revealed, its inchoate plans for after May 6 broken apart and strewn about like a smashed watch. Nway, besides, had a midnight appointment with the punks. They were a band of about seven young men, middle-class, mild of manner, and searching desperately for expression that for now they seem to have explored mainly in their haircuts. He had befriended one of them at an Internet café some weeks back and inveigled him into a regular conversation that had eventually netted an entire circle of shock-headed Internet gamers into an informal weekly discussion group. They would meet at the BBQ stalls down 19th Street, then decamp at about 2 or 3 a.m. to whatever teashop around 35th Street was still vying for road space with the rats. He would ease them in with some thoughts about "death metal" bands, then turn gently to issues of development and the economy. He left it to them, really, to ask whatever bubbled up. And then he would answer, patiently unpicking the half-truths and filling in the blanks until they'd found the essence of their wider, societal frustrations all on their own. They were of age for university. None of them had bothered to matriculate, but not always for lack of buried curiosity. Already they looked up to Nway as something of a *saya*, thirsty for the opening to learn and think, though never turning intrusive questions back at him. It was still early days—"Isn't it true that Aung San Suu Kyi was offered the post of defense minister?" one of them had asked him just last night. There was much to re-educate. But at least the directness of the question and the use of the Lady's name, unprovoked, signaled a measure of progress. They were a touch out to pasture, but they had good hearts. He had high hopes that the three most responsive among them might turn into serious activists.

Onward, then, with his workday—beyond midnight and the constraints of an ordinary schedule. And so it was to have been for the National League for Democracy. Nway's methods and those of his party had seemed at last to be converging.

If only whatever grains of truth this email revealed hadn't thwarted that possibility.

MARCH 31, 2010

DAWN MELTED PINK OVER the sun-bleached ruins of Amarapura as Dr. Zaw Myint Maung—Dr. Z—descended from a Rangoon red-eye into a crowd of nearly ten supporters. They waited among the usual sweaty clamor of peanut sellers and moped drivers at the coach station, angling for a fresh haul staggering off a night bus. "If you vote to run, don't bother coming back," one of his number had privately thrown at him a few days before. He meant the NLD vote, about registering for the elections. "Stay in Rangoon."

It hadn't entirely been an empty threat. No one could ever accuse the citizens of the central dry zone around Mandalay of a deficiency in conviction. Amarapura stretched a few miles to Mandalay's south. Though a small backwater with pony carts and trinket-sellers lining the sands that fed into a seasonally dried lake, the "City of Immortality" had served as royal capital for seventy years. Its inhabitants lived among constant reminders of that former glory. You could see it in the old city gates; in the vast, white dome of King Bagyidaw's Pahtodawgyi Pagoda, which looked out from atop a hill over the expanse of fields that had once formed a fragment of great kingdoms; or in U Bein Bridge, which lost itself in the winking horizon somewhere far across that desiccated lake basin where oxen ambled now before a farmer's plough. Wonder among the country's wonders, world's longest teak footbridge, its 1,060 columns had been salvaged from King Mindon's palace in 1857, when he had first relocated his court seven miles north to Mandalay. From that new capital, Mindon's successor, King Thibaw, had been defeated in 1885 in the third and final Anglo-Burmese war and sent packing from his fortress in a bullock cart, to India, never to return. The humiliation—the original wounding from which all else could be mapped—had left its traces generations later, feeding a liongryph pride in shared nationhood, the sense of a people whose idiosyncratic way would, *must*, prevail long after the power-hungry and the opportunists had passed into dust.

The heat, too, had its effects here. It was hot and dry and parched in a way that amplified the passions, exacerbating rage, turning Myingyan Prison, just north of Pakokku, into the worst of the worst, where reddened criminals smashed the politicians and the wardens looked on laughing. So anything that smacked of political surrender was a betrayal and the offender deserved something like disownment.

But Dr. Z had kept his promise. The news had landed faster than he could make the journey back. And so they came to greet him, men and women both, beaming, thumbs up, pressing through the crowd of roustabouts to squeeze his arm or slap him on the back. There wasn't much more aloud that they could say. Solidarity in silence carried him across the coach station and homeward to his clinic. Only those who thought to wonder could see in a local doctor's parking-lot popularity the enduring vitality of the people's political aspirations. Not for them the critics' viewpoint that the NLD had in fact, in an act of globally historic myopia, just committed suicide.

Dr. Z had yet to adjust to the traffic on the boulevard outside his house in central Amarapura, the furious bleatings that drivers employed in lieu of traffic lights or road signals, or because to honk en route from somewhere to wherever else was merely to say hello. He'd had less trouble with the snoop who positioned himself over the road and at an angle of about sixty degrees from the open window beside the couch where he chatted with his constant stream of guests. It wasn't as if the country were a snippet freer than when he'd last seen it in 1990. He had expected to be spied on, what with diving back into politics within two weeks of his release. But of all the effects of eighteen years and three months of incarceration—the awkwardness of dinner, for instance, with his daughter, who could not say *papa* when they'd arrested him and now a strong-willed woman about to earn her graduate degree—he would never have imagined that he would sometimes miss the silence of his cell.

Not so, though, in that overnight bus from Rangoon. He had slept well. The gentle rocking and hum of the air vents that gusted in the dry heat of a midsummer night had proved as hypnotic as nibbana; that, or the equanimity that came of duty fulfilled.

He had just returned from the March 29 meeting at party headquarters of the Central Committee.

Twice in the past twelve months, senior NLD members had been able to gather. The last instance was in April 2009, for the two-day party congress that had ended in a vote for the Shwegondaing Declaration, the preliminary party position on the elections. Dr. Z had made it to both. Never exactly the seat of opulence, the Office had seemed still more cramped, with barely space enough to accommodate the nearly 150 party members who had converged on it these last few days. It had made for a gay reunion, if heated with the personal convictions that they were to put to the test. Four riot trucks had rolled up outside, and intelligence agents overflowed from the hut over the road, snapping photos, taking notes, as apparently gleeful with the surge in activity as the party members themselves. They faced no other interruption. It would have been self-defeating, in this instance, for the junta to deny a legal political organization the right to decide how to play within the goalposts of its electoral game.

Not since 1996, when hundreds flocked every weekend to the gate of Auntie's compound for the talks that she alternated with then-party chairs Tin Oo and Kyi Maung, had they been able to assemble in such numbers. Even then, there were sporadic interruptions, harassment of visitors, roadblocks, and USDA toughs, with handkerchiefs tied round wrists by way of uniform, manning barricades with batons and sticks, or, memorably on one occasion, pounds of overripe tomatoes. Photos were taken, visitors traced to their home villages. Meanwhile, plans for strategy sessions for the countrywide party leadership or to commemorate the anniversary of the 1990 elections had always been thwarted. They counted 258 arrests alone in 1996. Taking up the challenge, they had broadened the plan from an hours-long anniversary into a three-day party congress. They scheduled it to coincide with another weekend gathering outside Aung San Suu Kyi's house, which that time drew an audience in numbers that she declared the highest yet on record, adding that they came "in spite of the inclement weather," by which she might have been punning on the climate of repression or actually referring to a deluge of monsoon rains.

In June 1998, she had issued an ultimatum: the junta had sixty days to convene the 1990 parliament. By the deadline, the party had tallied 884 arrests, MP-elects, and party workers. That was the summer in which she was four times blocked in her car. They went ahead anyway, convening a skeleton parliament of ten, which they called the Committee Representing the People's Parliament.

By then, it had become standard daily fare in the *New Light of Myanmar* to list NLD defections and resignations in far-flung towns—a hodgepodge of fiction and reality, as members were whittled down by emotional fatigue, loss of business opportunities, property evictions, and the need to safeguard themselves and their families from explicit threat. Of 392 NLD candidates who had won seats in 1990, 112 were no longer "active" or had fled abroad. With about 11 members left, the Central Committee had been abolished in 1991. It had only been re-created in February, largely on the impetus of Khin Maung Swe and Grandpa, who had both seen the dire necessity of reinvigorating the party for the indefinite future. In practice, they would have liked to hold elections. But the inability to campaign or assemble freely had always stalled attempts at internal party democracy. The executives had selected its 108 new members off nominations solicited from local chapters, which made them, for the most part, known quantities.

So it was a formidable crew of holdouts with whom Dr. Z had been chatting and patting backs just forty-eight hours earlier. Among them were comrades he had in brief but cavernous lows across the years assumed he would never see again. Others he had come to know better by name or face in prison—in his case Insein or Myitkina by way of the transit center at Mandalay. Too many were old enough to have retired into the monasteries, or a more peaceful way of life, or simply into boredom, with honor inscribed in their hearts. But what honor in failure? Here thus were they in droves, afflicted with the same crack-brained ambition to somehow fulfill an unfinished promise.

In a roomful of homespun salmon and ochre *pinni* jackets worn in ode to the clothing of anticolonial nationalists, that lone shot of defiant blue in the second row, complete with a slash of scarlet for a shoulder bag emblazoned in giant NLD lettering, was none other than Saya Win Tin. Dr. Z had landed in Insein a year after him and they had come to know of each other's intensity of commitment through the fragmentary complicity of their Joint Action Committee. It had been Dr. Z's misfortune that the copy of the letter to the UN that ultimately blew it all up had been on his person. It had landed him twelve years extra on his first six-year sentence, two and a half of them in solitary, and the rest served after his prison transfer about 740 miles north to the remote capital of restive Kachin state.

There too was good Khin Maung Swe, transferred out of Insein on similar charges. Dr. Z had known him better from the party's founding days, a geologist whom Aung San Suu Kyi had appointed on the day of her house arrest to take the place left open by Win Tin and other front-line civilian intellectuals.

And what a relief this time to have been joined by Tin Oo, Grandpa T, the vice-chairman, freshly released from house arrest on February 13. He sat in a *pinni* in the row behind Win Tin, tall as a wing-bean, with a thick mop of hair and the focus of a seasoned meditator. Something of a chameleon whose pre-1988 life demonstrated a consummate fearlessness for reinvention, the onetime protégé of General Ne Win married a natural affability with stern self-discipline, which had made him a rare bridge between the former military officers in the party and its intellectuals. He was a good man for the job of steering the party back on course, in the glaring absence, as yet, of Aung San Suu Kyi.

For his part, it had been scarcely a year since a chronic gastric ailment in Myitkina had degenerated to the point of preventing him from swallowing more than the thinnest rice gruel. His wife had suspected stomach cancer; the Assistance Association for Political Prisoners, which carefully tracked these matters from Thailand through an extensive underground network, had cried foul about the threat to his life as he entered his second month of near-starvation without due medical attention. As it turned out, he had been released within weeks. He had toughened and leathered with age. But he had lost none of his boyish animation, framed in freckles. It might have been a matter of purpose newly availed, or the excitement he felt among the NLD sympathizers of his hometown who hadn't a thought that he might have cause to abandon political activity.

Everyone was struggling, that much was clear. Some of it seemed linked to the global recession, but to extract people's economic and social woes from government malfeasance was delusional. "Every issue comes back to politics," his longtime friend and Myitkina cellmate, Kelvin, used to say, and he would know—he'd always been more focused on economic development and humanitarian relief than the civil and political rights demanded as first priority by most

members of the democracy movement. The complaints to Dr. Z on his first day
after his release on February 22, 2008, had startled for their thematic repetition.
From early morning to about 9 p.m., friends and acquaintances had trooped in
to pay respects to a man they had last seen at thirty-eight, and found him now,
at fifty-six, exuding a relaxed empathy that rendered them instantly at ease.
There must have been something about a hero's return after long absence that
permitted, for once, the indulgence of catharsis in the name of catching him up.
If he harbored any doubt that it might all have been for naught, that it was time
now to step back from politics and make a priority of his long-neglected family,
his sense of vocation had returned with a vengeance.

. His wife had clinched the question with a single nod. A doctor too, she had
run the clinic and raised their two sons and daughter, head held high through
the subtle little banishments inflicted on a prisoner's family and the dayslong
complications required for fifteen-minute prison visits once every three months
on whichever end of the country he happened then to be. As if authorities had
found the two furthest possible points on the map, Amarapura was about equi-
distant between Insein and Myitkina. Like so many who were attached through
kinship or sheer affection to more visible activists, she had also been a crucial
conduit for trickles of information that made it in and out. So—now? They
could manage. He would not have to abandon the cause for which they had long
before reset the course of their lives.

In 1990 Dr. Z had been one among the scores of NLD candidates whose
only qualification for elective office had been his relative education and the
status that came with a thriving medical career. He had acquired a few years
of managerial experience as head of a hospital. But it had been a personal failing that had ultimately driven him to politics. In medical school, he had taken
a keen interest in social questions, but he had never felt the freedom to join
his classmates in periodic student rebellions, in part because he had a greater
responsibility to his father, who, as a professor of medicine, was government
staff and would have suffered for it. And so he had stood by, sick to his stomach but weak at the knees, as two close friends were beaten and arrested in
the unrest around the burial of U Thant, UN secretary general, in 1974. With
time, his self-reproach had grown. He saw himself missing every new out-
break of national discontent, even as he encountered more evidence of the
injustices and impoverishment of one-party rule in his patients' pathologies
of privation and the increasing material difficulties of trying to provide them
with adequate care.

Come 1988, he had marched, and become a representative of the Mandalay Doctor's Association. Reprimanded, he asked to be fired from the city's Institute of Medicine, paid back the full amount of an unfinished biochemistry scholarship, and joined the NLD. He had run in his hometown of Amarapura. On May 27, 1990, he had won it for the NLD with 21,119 votes, or sixty-six percent.

Arrested on a train bound for home from Rangoon that December, he had been charged with treason and sentenced to six years. The crime involved a gathering of fellow electees at Rangoon's Gandhi Hall. On July 28 they had called on the junta to convene the Pyithu Hluttaw, the People's Parliament, to which they assumed they had been elected. The Gandhi Hall declaration was a response to Announcement 1/90, which the State Law and Order Restoration Council had issued the day before, exactly a month after the elections. This had stated that the elections were never meant to result in a parliament. No transfer of power to civilian authorities could take place until a new constitution was drafted. Until then, the SLORC would maintain sole executive, legislative, and judicial authority, with help from low-level institutions.

The turn of events was absurd, though not out of a keeping with a military council that had seized power the previous September and proceeded with a nationwide vote while clearing the streets with gunfire. Arrests of key NLD leaders preempted their subsequent attempt to gather as a provisional parliament in Mandalay. This persuaded the elective parliamentarians who were still at large to endorse a parallel government, the National Coalition Government of the Union of Burma, in the SLORC-free border areas. Aung San Suu Kyi's cousin, Dr. Sein Win, was appointed prime minister.

On Dr. Z's head, though not his alone, fell accusations for its establishment at Manerplaw, Karen headquarters, on December 18, 1990. Fifteen years later, ten after the fall of Manerplaw to Tatmadaw forces, it relocated to Washington, DC, and though it had never professed to be more than a symbol for the real thing, any suspected contact with it threatened to bring down the junta's full measure of repressive sanction.

For all that, Dr. Z had no regrets. The NLD had valid reasons to throw in its lot. As now, people had debated participation on the merits. By May 27, 1990, all but four of the party's executives had already been incarcerated. Martial law was in effect. The terms of a transfer of power from the new junta were never spelled out in advance, a point of contention that the NLD had tried to bring up with the SLORC. The future, undoubtedly, was uncertain. Faith that the vote itself would be free and fair was difficult even for the most idealistic.

But the electoral laws of 1990 had flung the field wide open; 230 parties of all sizes had registered, some with sincere political intent, others more eager for the priority access granted them for telephone lines and extra gasoline rations. Minorities earned separate status for the first time since the British had classified the population into 135 ethnicities. They put forward representatives, taking their chances with a less-violent platform than the war zones of their burning villages. Most powerfully, hints of future foul play seemed conclusively outweighed by the millions-backed mandate that had made itself manifest since March 1988. It was the mission of the National League for Democracy, the greatest alliance of citizens his country had ever known, to honor their perseverance, to guide the impulse for change from spontaneous and freewheeling, passing through the organized phase of strike committees and directed action, and into the slow-bore construction of institutions and democratic processes.

Dr. Z had been able to travel without restriction to all ninety-nine village tracts in his constituency. Crowds had poured forth to listen. There had been no interference. People were uncowed.

Whereas: the elections to come struck him as unequivocally unjust.

He believed in compromise. He believed in the need for dialogue. He'd had more than enough time to meditate in his cell on the needs of his country as something more complex than a rookie politician's early calls for mere "change."

In the dry zone of Upper Burma, as all across the rural spread of the country, the growing chatter of diplomats and foreign analysts—that the party was an obstacle to progress, that the elections were the only way, that Aung San Suu Kyi herself had lost her relevance, that she was too "stubborn," too much a moralist—resonated not even as a whisper. What mattered were the granular needs, problems of drought or forced land confiscations, and the hard-knotted fact that nothing had changed for the better, nothing would change, and the fault lay not with the NLD, whose great, red sign rusted on shopfronts and homes that had been shut since 2003, but with the regime that had shut them down. Even the most parochial and least educated around him had little trouble rooting the decay and decline of their livelihoods in the corruption of their rulers.

There were thirty townships in Mandalay division, and each of them could claim fifteen active members. It meant a readymade base of five hundred supporters. There were always ways to engage each other: conversations at weddings, pagoda festivals, or ordinations. The local youth had even dared a poll.

And Dr. Z had again taken up his medical practice, which allowed for intimate conversations. It wasn't hard to gauge the general resolve.

It was hard for anyone to imagine that the SPDC would in good faith and at the height of its powers unilaterally set in motion a process to dissolve itself and make way for a new legislative: an upper house, a lower house, and fourteen regional parliaments, according to the 2008 constitution. Trust in the generals had been the greatest casualty of years of lies and broken promises. To doubt them was as much common sense as insurance against fresh disappointments. The White Shirts, the mass social apparatus better known as the Union Solidarity and Development Association, the USDA, that the military junta had created in 1993, had long been primed to turn into a political party. In the past year it had been stepping up its charitable activities, establishing medical clinics, agricultural loan programs, and other barely disguised stunts of public relations. Most of its twenty-six million members had been coerced into joining, by virtue of being civil servants, teachers, or high school students. Others were lured by its fringe benefits, such as avoiding conscription in local forced-labor projects. But the USDA was undoubtedly the home for high-placed officers to relocate as politicians once they had removed their uniforms. Rumors from Naypyidaw were rife that No. 1, Than Shwe, the USDA's unofficial patron, was about to order No. 4, Prime Minister General Thein Sein, to take over its chairmanship.

Exile media, quoting anonymous government sources, were likewise fingering a spectrum of current senior officials as likely candidates for forced retirement from the military. Uniforms removed, they could then take on leading portfolios in the new civilian administration, the idea being that they would occupy all positions beyond the twenty-five percent bloc of seats that the constitution explicitly reserved for those still wearing Tatmadaw khakhis. Among them was No. 3, General Thura Shwe Mann, and, likewise, Major General Htay Oo, the current USDA secretary-general and minister of agriculture and irrigation.

So why would people invest in the fantasy that these elections would somehow bring about genuine change? There was more promise, frankly, in the purchase of an illegal three-digit lottery ticket and better distraction down at the corner teashop, catching the latest game of Manchester United versus Whomever.

Then had come the announcement on March 8 of the electoral laws. These had seemed specially designed to once and for all torpedo the NLD.

The Political Parties Registration Law banned anyone serving a criminal conviction from voting, contesting public office, and forming or joining a political party. In any other country or context, it was a reasonable caveat for high office. In Burma, it meant the forcible ejection of about 430 incarcerated NLD members, and of Aung San Suu Kyi, the unchallenged leader of the entire movement, who was serving out the additional eighteen months of house arrest with which she had been sentenced in August 2009 for sheltering Yettaw. And what of the hundreds more, strong-minded activists whom Dr. Z knew personally to hold the torch for the country's future? From the bright strategists of 1988 to the great comic Zaganar, languishing in a cell in Dr. Z's very own Myitkina, the good doctor could not imagine such a betrayal.

Moreover, to register meant colluding once and for all in a vast, national nullification of the 1990 mandate. The 2008 constitution would enter into force after the elections, and then there would be no turning back. Parties would have to pledge in writing that they would obey and protect it and abide by its election laws.

On the bus ride down to Rangoon, he had combed through his already well-thumbed copy of the brick-sized constitution. He knew by heart the clauses most famously offensive to would-be democrats. The previous April, his colleagues had unanimously voted, and he along with them, for the Shwegondaing Declaration, which called for the junta to revise the constitution before the party would consider participating. Reading it again, he had stopped cold at a new discovery. Article 409 of Chapter 10 read: "The Pyidaungsu Hulttaw"—the people's assembly—"shall enact necessary laws concerning political parties." Dr. Z was no lawyer, but it meant, so far as he could discern, that even were the NLD to register, and win, and be allowed to take its seats—which was fanciful enough—the members of that chimeric assembly in any case had the power to ban it on a whim.

The party, he concluded, had been given no choice.

The NLD's sworn purpose was to rid the country of military rule. To bow before the restrictions of the junta's electoral laws, to agree to abide by the terms of its flawed constitution, to trust in their haphazard, abusive legality, was to give it all up. There was too much at stake. The principle was everything—it was all the people had left. Over time the NLD had been shorn to little more than its essence, a hope of freedom—quixotic to some, but a guiding light for everyone else.

Failing which, they would succumb to karmic acceptance, as if this government was all they deserved. Already too many had turned away, nauseated by politics, fleeing with their fear, searching instead for nibbles of joy in communal

moments such as the glory of a *shinbyu* novitiation ceremony, or through meditation, the intimate detachment from their worldly dissatisfaction through truest
devotion to Theravada Buddhist practice.

But in that same set of Buddhist values, the achievement of freedom, political or mental, was the quest of a lifetime. Fundamentally, Buddhism was
premised on personal agency; the Buddha himself counseled rejection of all
doctrine. Only through self-discovery were the great truths arrived at, instances
of clarity found and lost and found again in the experience of meditative insight.
Only through pursuit of the Eightfold Noble Path could a person gain lasting
release from suffering and achieve self-awakening.

Those fundamental tenets permeated the air. For a time, they had found
strongest expression in socialism. But when socialism had failed utterly as a
model of governance, impoverishing a country that should have raced ahead
as a paragon of regional modernity, people had cried aloud instead for the freedoms of liberal democracy, even if—like Dr. Z in 1988, like so many students of
that time—they had no full understanding of what it meant.

But the yearning for recognizably democratic values was far from exotic.
Burma was no China, forced to invent an ideology from scratch and tack it on
a culture with no memory of such. Here democracy was as much in the foundational myths as in the shared history, in the literature as in the pamphleteering.
People had only to look back to the struggles of their own parliamentary period.

It was the basis for the millions who had flocked to join the party or voted
for it in 1990. Aung San Suu Kyi had waxed eloquent on the subject, explaining repeatedly how universal standards that the military authorities dismissed
as Western imports emanated instead from within the culture. Senior General
Than Shwe and the generals of the SPDC professed a connection to the ancient
warrior monarchs, but failed utterly to measure up to their ideals, enshrined as
the Buddha's Ten Duties of Kingship, which any child who had passed through
a monastic school might have enumerated—morality, self-sacrifice, kindness,
and even submission to the will of the people—duties that were not wholly different from the universal justifications for elective government. The desire for
just government was as culturally rooted, in that sense, as spiced fish paste.

Dr. Z had headed to the gathering of the Central Committee in Rangoon
without a shred of hesitation about how to vote.

Two members from each state and division had stood to speak. Not a single
voice had been raised in favor of re-registering. And then they had voted, one
hundred men and women. No. The NLD would not re-register.

They had decided for the ethnic minorities' future, for their people's future, for the nation's future. It had been a beautiful show of unity.

Aung San Suu Kyi herself agreed with the decision. Days earlier, Nyan Win had read a statement to the press, conveying her thoughts from their last meeting. It was up to party members to decide, she had said, but personally she would not participate under the election's unjust laws.

Now they had thirty-six days left.

They knew the likely consequences. There would be nothing to stop a raid, the shutting down anew of the few party chapters that had been allowed to re-open in the past two weeks for the first time in years. Whereas they had always stood tall with the rhetoric of legality, they could not now even depend on that flimsy protection.

If some among them planned to register for the vote as independent candidates, Dr. Z would support them. He respected their reasons. But duty of a kind that the National League for Democracy owed to the people was larger than the sum of any one among them.

Today, reinvigorated by the shockwaves of local support, Dr. Z might as well have been plugged into an electric socket.

FRIDAY, APRIL 10, 2010

THEY HAD TWENTY-SIX DAYS LEFT.

Nway knew the likely consequences. Within days of the March 29 decision, Grandpa T, the vice-chairman, announced the convening of a committee of seventeen to organize the clearing out of all the paperwork and furniture from the Office. Already, authorities in Mandalay had pressured a landlord to evict the local division chapter.

Grandpa warned publicly of the impending crackdown. It didn't stop him from penning a strong column on the NLD decision for the *Washington Post* the next day, his second in two years denouncing the elections. He had held back even less for domestic audiences. In an interview with *The Irrawaddy* earlier that week, he had likened the junta to a political rapist. "They want to strip us of our 1990 election victory so that we are like a 20-year-old girl, naked and exposed. We cannot allow ourselves to be raped."

The party's decision had plentiful detractors, mainly among the analysts and diplomats who had not lived their history. They preferred the more conciliatory approach, which meant, to Nway, accepting whatever crumbs the junta threw at them.

Let them be dupes. There might be value in a few independents slipping into the parliaments. But he had little faith that their efforts, even five years down the road, would amount to much.

He had been open to being persuaded otherwise. Asked by the Uncles to tap opinion, he had conducted a poll—not exactly statistically significant, although he'd tried. It had depended on a careful selection of recruits, trained to ask the right questions of the right people, which meant with enough gusto to dare to ask in the first place; sensitivity to bypass people's reluctance to answer; and talent enough to spot informers or to dodge suspicion that they might be working for a political organization. Altogether he and other NLD youth had managed to secure 530 questionnaires, gathered from among party members and ordinary folk in towns across the country.

For the rest, he felt the NLD's act of self-sabotage had done more to stain the election's credibility than any discrete gesture thus far by the junta.

On Monday, the executive committee had held another powwow. They had circulated a couple of papers. From one emerged a three-page apology to the people for their decision. It was both a *mea culpa* for the NLD's failure to achieve its ends and a historical synthesis of why that was, detailing how they had persevered since 1990 "for the emergence of democracy and national reconciliation while enduring arrests, punishment, intimidation, disturbances and all sorts of restrictions by the authorities. Nevertheless these efforts were to no avail as a result of one-sided suppression and annihilation by the authorities. We would like to sincerely and earnestly apologize to the people of Burma for these vain attempts."

But, the statement explained, the electoral laws were "unjust, undemocratic and not in line with the basic characters of the law." And, "forcing parties to pledge to obey and abide by the 2008 Constitution is a violation of democracy and human rights. These laws ignore the demands of an all-party inclusive election made by the U.N. Secretary General and the international community."

They ended with a pledge. The party would never turn its back on the people. It would continue "to achieve our goals for democracy through systematic peaceful and nonviolent means, guided by Daw Aung San Suu Kyi."

What that might involve the Uncles had pondered in the second paper at their meeting. Nway took a certain pride in knowing that he'd had a hand in it, an idea he had passed on to Uncle Han Thar Myint. They were due to hold a follow-up on the idea just after the weekend. They would have to be careful not to divulge details for security reasons, and Nyan Win had said as much to reporters. "We will firmly stand by our decision," he had told Agence France-Presse on Wednesday, relaying a message of support for the NLD decision from Aung San Suu Kyi. "We have our future tasks. But we cannot reveal them at this moment because of our country's situation."

So much for that.

The author of the unfortunate email that Nway had just been informed about, outside the shrine of the vanished *nat*, had just revealed that the secret paper "said something about replacing the vertical/hierarchical structure with a network or horizontal model but the moderates see it as cover for underground work and rejected it. They see it as acting as though it had the HQ's approval. They said the NLD won't be around after 6 May anyway, and if the proposers can't take responsibility they can go ahead on their own."

Later that night, Nway had opted to be late for the punks who were waiting for him in Chinatown, and stopped en route at an Internet café. His source had forwarded the email in full. Dated April 7, it described a long, private discussion between the author and the "moderates" of the party—three disaffected NLD executive committee members who included U Khin Maung Swe, the former geologist whom everyone knew to have been in favor of registration.

"On the matter of the NLD moving into social work," the email went on, "we agreed that it is inadvisable to do so. There would be negative repercussions on all concerned, not least on the NGOs that are doing real work and target communities."

What the email had managed to show, in sum, was that the NLD—or at least its "gang of four"—were about to do something illegal, which was to use "social work" as a cover for the kind of diffuse, rhizomal underground network that Nway, Nigel, and other activists had been trying to develop for years.

The rest of the email was a thoughtful, even brilliant, commentary. Nway had no argument with internal dissension. He didn't even know the email's author. That was the tragedy—the author clearly meant it for a private audience. He was a democrat writing with sophistication about the problems of democrats, analyzing a central problem of a democracy movement that couldn't be democratic in its methods. But there was nothing democratic, or private, in a world of spies and surveillance. Nway had been forwarded it from his young source, who had been forwarded it in turn.

What really irked, though, was the sense that the people this email most took issue with had abrogated their duty. All of them. Including Auntie.

"She is taking her house arrest situation too passively as they see it," the email went on. "It's like implying 'keep me in that house: I can work through Nyan Win.' She didn't seek out and use opportunities. Instead she let herself be manipulated by Nyan Win. She knew that she was going to be released soon. And yet she allowed the Yettaw incident to happen. By doing so she showed no consideration for the Myanmar people."

It was nothing in the least bit new that Auntie should be accused of self-inflicted martyrdom. It was also flat-out wrong. To Nway, this was the bitter accusation of someone who had no channel to reach her directly and didn't approve of the statements she made through her lawyer, Nyan Win.

To have come of age in the Office after 1998 was to apprehend a truth heard in a dozen little revelatory anecdotes from senior Uncles that whatever might be their internal differences, they must reveal nothing except common cause. There would come a time for airing disagreements, for acknowledging what Nway knew already firsthand: that Auntie was but a comrade among the many, someone with whom they could, and had, behind closed doors, joked and negotiated with, debated and dissented from. But not now. Not yet. Not for as long as the struggle lasted. To face not an opponent but an enemy for whom no tactics had proven too low, there was no other way than unity.

The duty of unity, a duty necessary to achieve democracy, was the very last obligation any of them would neglect.

APRIL 29, 2010

KHIN MAUNG SWE, THE FORMER GEOLOGIST, felt aggrieved. He didn't know how it had happened exactly, but somehow, at the eleventh hour, everything had fallen apart. Everything that they had held forth for, everything they had promised and left unfulfilled—gone. Dissolved. And into what? Into an organization for—what was it that U Nyan Win had told *SnapShot* journal just that morning?—"picking up plastic trash." That was what.

"You know, that kind of party, it was born out of an uprising. We never can have that again. Dissolution of a party is very easy. But establishing a party in that way is very hard." The people would start to wonder who was left to trust.

He was speaking to an American reporter in the far corner of an empty restaurant at one of the fancier Rangoon hotels. He had arrived early, and waited, stiff of spine, on the edge of a fat armchair in the marble lobby, his name on a piece of paper that he held up before his chest. It wasn't the sort of place he was accustomed to frequent; it belonged to businessmen from China or Singapore and a trickle of Westerners who larded the moneychanger in the lacquer shop down the corridor with amounts of cash impossible to imagine among his compatriots.

Nor was it in his nature to suppose that the reporter might have recognized him without his sign. At sixty-seven years old, he had maintained an innocence from self-conscious affectation, a gentleness and purity of purpose. It was partly on account of it that the young inmates who had shared his cell in Myingyan had come to adore him like a father. Still, in a starched shirt and deep green *longyi*, his thick hair neatly parted, his body lithe and taut, he conveyed to the outsider the spotlessness of a man of stature, or at least of one who had learned too well that when they took the rest away, all you had left was dignity.

And yet he was undone. Only days before, he would have tried to hide the party's fissures. At least he might have masked the personal anguish that even now rose into the pink of his cheeks, more pinched than usual, or consonants that he punched out with greater force. At moments in the interview, he fingered the rim of an upturned water glass, switched around the position of a fork with a knife, the knife with the fork. A cup of coffee sat untouched beside his elbow, tepid now. The waiter hovered with a pot of steaming refill, unnecessarily close, too close for comfort. Khin Maung Swe's voice never dropped to a whisper in the usual way when someone circulated nearby and the subject, as now, touched on taboos—on history, the NLD, Aung San Suu Kyi, democracy. The foreign reporter fidgeted. She wasn't meant to be discovered doing journalism, talking politics. It could mean deportation and a ticket to the visa blacklist; worse, for the senior politician seated opposite.

At this point, Khin Maung Swe didn't much care. He had nothing more to lose.

At the Central Committee meeting on March 29, he had not been allowed to talk. Nor either had any one of the handful of colleagues who had in recent weeks argued alongside him that it was better to register, that the only real option left was to fight from within the new parliaments. They owed it to the people who had voted for them by the millions in 1990.

They had a duty. With every breath of life he had left, it was all he could do to see that through. He knew it would have been an uphill battle to persuade the would-be boycotters, but they had been trying, he, Than Nyein, and Chairman

Aung Shwe. Since his release alongside Win Tin on September 23, 2008, they
had made sure the executive committee met with greater frequency. They were
talking, disagreeing often heatedly—but talking. Wasn't it the definition of the
pluralism they were fighting for to be able to exchange opinions?

The effort had begun to bear fruit. There had even been a moment when
exile media speculation, ever alarmist about a potential party rift, had tipped
the decision in his direction, on the sheer anticipation that the party would opt
above all for its own survival.

His silencing, thus, had come as a complete surprise. There was no prece-
dent for it, and no warning. Minutes into the meeting, Chairman Aung Shwe
had summoned the twenty-man executive committee to their upstairs meeting
room. They were to hold their tongues, he informed them. The rules were hard
and fast: only two Central Committee members from each state or region would
have the right to voice their opinions. Confounded, Khin Maung Swe had said
nothing. But something had felt terribly off.

That not a single one of the hundred Central Committee members had then
raised a murmur of disagreement against registering seemed almost conspira-
torial. And then they had voted. He knew the picture across the country to be
murky, that he and his colleagues in Rangoon were hardly the only longtime
devotees to democracy to have pondered the weight of either of two bad options. Not everyone had the clarity of absolutism that U Win Tin claimed.

But U Nyan Win, the lawyer, had chosen a few days before the meeting to
publicly relay the latest communication from Daw Aung San Suu Kyi, in which
she had said that she would agree to whatever decision the committee arrived at,
but were it up to her, she would not and could not run under these unjust laws.

No one would think to contradict her and everyone placed high in the party
knew it. Even in her state of near-total isolation, her pronouncements had that
kind of power. They knew it so well that in an executive committee meeting on
March 22, just days before the gathering of the Central Committee, they had
agreed that Aung San Suu Kyi didn't want a split decision and that the result of
the party's vote would be relayed to her only after April 1. She would not weigh
in definitively until then.

If only he might have had a chance to meet with her. The picture she had
acquired was necessarily fragmentary—and biased. The exile media, default-
ing to the simplicity of principle and free to advocate it without living the consequences, had sung a relentless chorus against the elections. Only a very few
had reported on the opinions beyond the conventional wisdom, and that wasn't

always complimentary. They told of a handful of avowed independents who had been variously labeled the "third force."

A few of them were friends. They were afflicted with money or military connections and passports, which meant a relative freedom of international movement denied to most. It made them, invariably, suspicious. About them was the whiff of apologists. In truth, their ideas didn't entirely concur, and they varied in the nuances, but what they shared was a willingness to break through, however they might, injecting fresh voices and approaches between either of two hard lines. It was for that reason that one among them, Khin Maung Swe's old friend and fellow Insein inmate, Kelvin, preferred to call them "the stakeholders."

At the very least, Khin Maung Swe could have offered Daw Suu an argument for why it was that gaining a foothold in the parliaments was the only viable move. He would have told her that the people needed a true democratic option, that anything less was to leave millions hopelessly in the lurch. He would have suggested that to boycott was to deny the possibility of unintended consequences, the sense that after twenty years of stalemate, the creation of a parliamentary system, however flawed and fraudulent, was proving, as some of the stakeholders were saying, the "only game in town." With their uniforms removed, forced each day into routine interactions with civilian representatives, who was to say how many retired soldiers in parliament would begin to change?

He would have emphasized especially that however naïve it was to presume a sudden change of heart on the part of the generals, that there was a larger geopolitical game afoot. They had an undeniable yearning to make the country a full participant in ASEAN, to rebuild economic ties with the world on a more equal basis with India and the rest of Asia. Most urgently, they wanted to scale back China's overbearing gravity. Together, those inexorable economic changes could pry apart the door that political confrontation had only slammed them into.

Trust building was such a fragile exercise, opportunities for dialogue so testy. But it was the only way. Antagonizing the generals with the sort of inflammatory diet that Win Tin had been feeding the press since his release was precisely not.

Khin Maung Swe had managed to convey only that in a single message to Aung San Suu Kyi. Her brief reply had sunk his heart: she had emphasized the need to keep up pressure alongside compromise.

But all they had to show for pressure was stagnancy. It was time for different tactics, which meant an ear for the subtle signals. Perhaps that was his advantage: deafness had been beaten into Khin Maung Swe some years back. He had adapted by listening from a different angle.

But he had every faith in Aung San Suu Kyi's adaptability too. In recent months, she had been at pains to bend and reach out to the generals. She had written a letter to Senior General Than Shwe in September, expressing her willingness to cooperate with the authorities and suggesting that they work together to lift economic sanctions. It was the one great lever of influence she could yet exert. Always quick to blame sanctions for the problems of the country, the junta knew that the West would only lift them with her dispensation.

Her letter had been a success, at least as a tentative step forward. The junta had deigned to let her meet twice with its liaison minister for about half an hour to forty-five minutes each time. Whether much of real substance had passed between them was hidden even to the Uncles. She would say nothing officially, until both sides agreed to a press release.

In November, she had sent a follow-up letter, reiterating the sanctions offer, and asking again to meet directly with Senior General Than Shwe. She had asked also to be allowed to pay her respects to the three ailing NLD caretakers. This the junta had granted, and she had been able to kneel before them and offer fruit and tea with the affection and unfeigned deference of a surrogate daughter. But the junta had denied her other request, which was to meet all the members of the NLD executive committee.

It was nothing new for the junta to appear more sensitive to the NLD and Aung San Suu Kyi, to give a crumb only to take it away. General Khin Nyunt had been particularly adept at playing that game. But every opening was worth nudging. The Supreme Court had even agreed in December, after multiple rejections in district courts, to hear the NLD's final appeal against her house arrest.

Then one of Aung San Suu Kyi's two letters had been leaked to the exile press—a regrettable error on the part of a party member who had seen it lying around the Office photocopy machine.

A column in the state mouthpiece had used the leak to ridicule the letters as "insincere" and "dishonest," charging Aung San Suu Kyi's offer on sanctions as nothing more than a cynical ploy at the behest of the United States, which had, not incidentally, recently changed its tune from freezing off the junta completely to trying, under President Obama, to engage it. Aung San Suu Kyi stood accused of revealing the letters herself.

Khin Maung Swe, as NLD spokesman, had downplayed the charges. They weren't necessarily official policy. He had always been so careful. For months as the Information Committee's front man, he had weighed his words against their potential effects, holding firm to party positions but cognizant that whatever the illicit press chose to quote was as yet the only means of relaying messages to the generals.

His loyalty to Aung San Suu Kyi was boundless, grounded in reason and the passage of time. She had the trust of the borderlands, and she was shrewd and brilliant, with an integrity that had struck home when he had first met her in August 1988. "If you join us, you will face a life of hardship," she had warned him. "You will never again have a promotion or an important position."

If he was honest with himself, the call of public service had always been close at hand. After General Ne Win's coup, he had seen soldiers crush and kill students no older than children. The images had never left him. Later, as a senior exploration geologist with the state-owned Burma Oil Corporation, he had grappled with the injustices of poverty. For all their sweat and toil, the workers he supervised could barely cobble together enough for a solid meal. In 1988, he became secretary of the oil workers' union. Its strikes were among the most strategically paralyzing. Word had traveled to Aung San Suu Kyi, and so had he been summoned by her to Rangoon.

He had returned to the oil fields, requested that he be fired, and joined the party. Only forty-five when he joined the executive committee, he was the youngest. In 1990, he had run in Sanchaung, a township in Rangoon, and won it with seventy-seven percent of the vote.

In hindsight, he could see their mistakes.

They had swept the elections. From their position of strength, they should have reached out to the SLORC. But the former military officers of the NLD knew only communism, socialism, a pablum of theory and army values. They imagined that the junta would transfer power. He had a scientist's feel for pragmatism, and the common sense of the street. It seemed to him that the SLORC would not budge unless they reached out. He had offered suggestions. But either he had been too meek or no one had wanted to hear it. And then he had been sent to prison.

But his incarceration seemed of narrow consequence to the trajectory of the country. He harbored no burning animosity toward his jailors—no yearning

for justice that he wasn't ready to sacrifice for a higher need. He was no popu-
list. The worst to suffer for his decisions, in truth, had been his wife.

All the years of his absence, she had held strong, on edge for some fresh
calamity, some new episode of solitary, or traveling for days up-country for
fifteen-minute visits only to find him absent or disappeared to locations unknown. Months that he spent in the punishment cells and in malarial conditions
without a mosquito net or urinal or basic hygiene had contributed to chest pain,
hypertension, piles, swollen face and feet, and heart disease. He wore a hood for
days on end. The effect of repeated beatings to his head was never adequately
addressed.

From 1990 to 1992, then again from 1994 to 2008, his wife had chased him
across the country. He had been moved, without warning, ever further north,
from Insein to Myingyan, from Myingyan to Oh-Bo, then Oh-Bo to Lashio.
They took him in the back of a public bus, shackled and blindfolded and surrounded by four armed guards, as if he had ever had a thought to grasp so much
as a pebble and throw it back at them. In Lashio, he was allowed two fifteen-
minute visits a month. It was six hundred miles from home, and a twelve-hour
train followed by a seven-hour private hired car. She had only been able to
make the journey twice. Now at last he was free, her grief had unspooled. For
months, she had not been able to get out of bed at all.

He had given everything to the party. No one believed more in its need for
unity and the rigor of discipline. At the first party conference, in April 2009, in
which they voted on the Shwegondaing Declaration, thirty members had made
public an open letter calling for the resignation of party chair Aung Shwe, and U
Lwin. However Khin Maung Swe felt about Aung Shwe's flaws as the leader of
the party, he informed the US Embassy that he thought the letter "ridiculous."
Whatever their internal differences, they had a larger goal, and there were times
for complaints, and times for consensus.

They needed loyalty. Aung Shwe, now ninety-two, was living on borrowed
time. He deserved respect. And that ill-discipline, splayed for all to see, wasn't
just wrongfooted. It was dangerously mistimed. In January 2009, the exile
Mizzima claimed to have secured the minutes of a high-level officer meeting in
which the head of the Northern Military Command had told colleagues that the
NLD would splinter: one faction pro-election, the other against, and that would
be the end of it.

He was not a writer, easy with the fiery rhetoric like Win Tin, nor even a
comic like Zaganar, who made only jokes, but who piled up the accolades and

awards, as if their opinions were more weighty, more apt for translation into the difficult, complex task of rebuilding a nation. He was only a politician, and anonymous, and so lacking the advantage of disciples by the hundreds and the limelight of sycophantic attention. But what if the real sacrifice was daring to fade into backdrop, to take a stand that bent and bowed, that rejected the transient flare of self-affirming heroism for progress based on compromise? What if taking the weaker position, as a moderate, was stronger than the hardliners could comprehend?

He had been dreaming for so long. They had all been dreaming for so long.

Once, back in 1988, he had been of a like mind with Win Tin. He, too, thought the route to freedom was a matter of people power. They had overlapped in the NLD for four months, but they had barely known each other on account of frequenting different professional circles and different regions in the general chaos. Later, in Insein, he had signed his name and prison number to a document they were passing around in the handle of a plastic bucket. What he knew of the effort was fragmentary—bits of information snatched in moments when they could move outside their cells. He knew it had been Win Tin's idea. But how quickly that had all come crashing down. In prison, conditions could change in the blink of an eye.

Not so in the country. Across his various jail cells, he had come to realize that a breakthrough would depend on more than the quick hit of mass protest. After the International Committee of the Red Cross had passed through the prisons, he had been able to get hold of copies of *The Economist* and *Time*. He devoured scraps of news that permitted him to imagine freedom as an outgrowth of economic development, not the vicious cycle that turned on mowing down students in the streets.

So this decision was a failure. And the failure was substantive. They had no future plans beyond May 6. They had never discussed it at their weekly executive meetings. This talk of turning the NLD into a humanitarian organization—Nyan Win's suggestion to *Snapshot* journal that, on the twentieth anniversary of the 1990 electoral victory, they would convert their mission into environmental cleanup, picking up litter—it was nothing less than a betrayal of the people.

"I feel shame," he told the American reporter. He switched the knife with his fork. The fork returned to its home by the spoon. "Because we formed the NLD as a political party. . . . On the background of peacock symbol, all the students dead since August 1988. So now they are using that symbol for street cleaning . . . picking-up-plastic work. I feel shame for the NLD."

In the end, he had met with a few colleagues from the NLD. They talked of what had come to pass. They considered where to go next. They would stay away from the Office until May 6 and meet quietly at one or other of their homes.

And then they would announce themselves as another party. Aung San Suu Kyi would remain their leader, at least as a figurehead. He hoped, if or when she was freed, she would join them in practice too.

Already, the agent who had been tracking him daily had vanished from his post. That was only logical: Khin Maung Swe had agreed to play within the rules of the junta's game.

It was the only way.

APRIL 25, 2010

NWAY CURSED HIMSELF FOR VISITING GRANDPA BY DAYLIGHT.

He had an appointment that night with Arthur, his best friend, on the far edge of town, but responsibilities beckoned first. The party had thirteen days left now. So much for his passing dream of a cold shower—a splash of water, at least, from the trough that passed for a bathroom at Arthur's downtown apartment. It was searingly hot, and he and Nobleyan had spent the last three hours crammed into public buses chasing down a phone shop that might fix another network member's handset on the cheap. They were sticky dirty. And even if by some miracle the water supply around 42nd Street had kicked back to life since a cutoff the day before, Arthur was visiting his mother in the far suburb of Hlaing Thayar and Nway had no keys to his apartment.

There was, moreover, no reason to suppose that whatever agents might be hovering in the vicinity of Grandpa's home in Yankin would mistake their get-ups for the formality of NLD youth members. Young men visiting someone with suitable seniority would scarcely arrive with a punk's indifference to sartorial tradition: Nobleyan in a pair of jeans and Nway in his trademark cargo pants, rock-band T-shirt, and—crowning achievement of the style—a new, asymmetrical haircut that his friends had to his dismay pronounced "gay."

Only a few days earlier word had come from Twantay that two men whom no one could identify had hovered near his mother's home and inquired after him. Afterward, he had studied himself in a mirror. The face that stared back had sharper cheekbones than he remembered, and hollow, blood-shot eyes. He traced a line of blemishes across his chin. Strands of hair hung limp and greasy from the ponytail that kept the heat off his neck. Perhaps this life of vagabond-age had after all taken its toll. For the past year, he'd lived chiefly off nicotine and cortisol. Sleep was for the dead. He looked unkempt and gaunt, and his skin had lost its smoothness, for all his careful post-shower daily applications of clar-ifying *thanaka* paste. He was ugly. There were no two ways about it.

The thing was, he had made his peace with the darkness of his complexion. On and off, it had always generated accusations of being a *kalar*, a term of abuse hurled at people of evident Indian extraction, or Muslim Rohingyas, or Muslims more broadly. In their early days together, his tight circle of ten NLD youth had made it his pseudonym, which had been hilarious in the way of the demean-ing jabs that mark the intimacy of siblings; none of them had been spared a nick-name hazing. Of late, his coloring had even turned into an advantage, helping him slip more easily among different ethnic circles. Even in these days of com-mon purpose and fluid urban coexistence, the minority religions, and Muslims particularly, had a preternatural sensitivity for undercurrents of hostility from the majority Buddhists.

That the authorities had been asking after him in his hometown was likely nothing more than rote harassment. Best he take the warning seriously, given his responsibilities to the Uncles. The news of the inquiry had landed with Paw Paw, along with his biweekly change of clothes. Nway knew her to be as fine-tuned to informers as a walking antenna. But there was always the possibility that she'd been tailed. With that, he'd bit the bullet and headed to a hairdresser in Olympic Tower, who happened to have an artistry for sculpting mohawks and death-metal heads from thick, black mops.

"I want a new look," he'd said simply. Then he shut his eyes and pretended to meditate.

He liked his hair. And he preferred it long. Cascading to his shoulders on the encouragement of no less than his mother, it had done a fine job of making up for his face. Already he didn't like the damage he'd inflicted on it when he'd streaked it red a year earlier, the one concession he had made to his appearance after he returned to Rangoon into clandestine life. Off it had all come now, or some of it, the rest swept leftward with a handful of gel. Set against his fine-boned features, the effect was just a hair this side of delicate. Even he couldn't help feeling a bit like a rock chick. But at least it would endear him to the group of punks he'd been cultivating in Chinatown.

As Nway and Nobleyan made his way to Grandpa that day, everything about them shouted the affluence of punks who wasted their days at the game stations and after sunset headed to the nightclubs, heads full of karaoke girls and hits of No. 4—heroin, as distinct from the junta No. 4, Prime Minister Thein Sein.

They turned past the flower shop into Grandpa's street and spotted three motorcycles. In Rangoon, they were always a sign of roving state agents. These three didn't budge, but Nobleyan could have sworn he saw one of them jump forward just as he and Nway turned hard into the compound.

It had turned out to be worth the trip. "We must dam the water up," Grandpa told them, explaining what he saw as the necessity of preventing further leakages from the party. Nway and Nobleyan had just told him all about their latest network activities, explaining the spread of their talents and responsibilities among a leaderless core that included Paw Paw and her sisters, Nigel, and a brilliant young literature professor whom Nway had only just discovered. *Good, good*, Grandpa had nodded. *Keep going*.

The situation, as Saya Win Tin told it, was that U Khin Maung Swe and associates were busy picking off old NLD members to join what was sure to become a new, splinter political party. What that left to the rest of them was a work-in-progress. For now, they were going ahead with the idea to dissolve into a social movement, with a creative array of programs or committees to build up pressure against the regime from different angles.

In public, they would continue to say little more than that they would devote themselves to social welfare efforts, such as environmental cleanups. Meanwhile, with what time they had left, he and the other Uncles would scan forty or fifty townships to select the best qualified to head subcommittees on strategic coordination, boycott campaigns, legal aid, help for the families of political prisoners, a division for HIV/AIDS work, and whatever else seemed pertinent to the ultimate replacement of military-dominated government with a socially minded alternative. Several of the issues were already longstanding concerns of NLD party members. But now they were to be managed as a semi-underground network. The trick was to stay just linked up enough, but without the crippling hierarchy and headquarters that might as well have been a neon sign pointing authorities toward their more insidiously political ends.

The idea echoed a strategy paper sent to the Uncles in late December by a Polish strategist called Ivan. Nway had just received Ivan's follow-up email. It offered a long refresher, commenting on the options for the NLD after the May 6 dissolution. Ivan had pointed out how similar the situation of the NLD was to Poland's Solidarity after martial law had been declared and the anti-regime trade union had been forced to disband. Instead it had found ways to transform itself, Ivan wrote, to penetrate ever deeper into society, claiming, at one point, one-third of the total working-age population. Some programs were open and transparent, but many more were carried out with greater discretion. "I understand that there is some suggestion to transform into a human rights organization and apply for legal registration," Ivan had written. "It is not realistic and the *greenies*"—the Tatmadaw—"will not accept it." What he suggested instead was richly innovative and surprisingly apt.

To that end, Nway and Nobleyan offered themselves to Grandpa as a youth committee whose savvy was in the way of technology. They were good with research. As for working without a leader or a central office, therein lay the secret of successful UG activism. Their responsibilities would come. Eventually, Grandpa had agreed, they would prove critical.

Trust Saya Win Tin to think outside the box. The plan seemed exactly the shock to the system that the country needed. Elated, the young men knelt before him, pressing hands and heads to the floor in respectful farewell. Time to head out to Hlaing Thayar to confer with their honorary, at-large network member, Arthur, whose mother had incidentally given Nobleyan shelter when his parents had kicked him out years earlier after discovering that he had joined the NLD youth.

With instructions to print out Win Tin's latest medical prescription, Nway and Nobleyan prepared to head out when in walked Uncle Ohn Kyaing, NLD executive and member of its so-called "gang of four." Just behind him trooped in two more young men in the standard NLD uniform, the Kachin *longyi* and starched shirt. It was tough to imagine that the sudden appearance of prominent politicians at U Win Tin's hadn't alerted roving agents to an official meeting. And U Ohn Kyaing's face was almost as recognizable in certain circles as Grandpa's. He was sure to be tracked all on his own.

No matter. There was an exit to the side of the compound.

They cracked apart the door.

A man stood waiting with a camera at the ready.

—*Flash!*—

Nway's hand shot to cover his face. Nobleyan was caught mid-blink. His mug was now on record, snapped walking out of the compound of the NLD's senior strategist.

Heads down, not talking, they shot down the street, past the teashop, past the flower shop toward Yankin Junction. Motorcycles revved up in the rear. The first to overtake them swerved to a halt, blocking their path.

Out came a camera. The man pointed it into Nway's shielded face.

"Why are you trying to photograph me?"

"Because that's my job."

"No. It is not your place to take my picture. This is a public place. So if you want it you need my permission. And you don't have my permission."

He didn't wait for the answer. Hand up, he swerved around the motorcycle and carried on with purposeful gait, Nobleyan in lockstep. The urge gripped to break into a sprint. They reached the intersection. From their left a taxi rolled languidly toward them. A hand shot up to hail it, the car slowed near the curb, and they piled inside.

"Yankin Center!" Nway shouted at the driver. They slunk deep into the backseat. Hearts raced. Seven, perhaps eight, motorcycles wove through traffic behind them. They turned a corner.

He punched out a text message to a friend.

"FINISH BEING CHASED."

The taxi pulled into the driveway near the shopping mall. They jumped out and flew up the stairs into the mouth of the doorway, braking for the metal detector and the security guards checking bags and waving wands, scanning for bombs they probably didn't have the juice to detect.

To their right a supermarket, to their left a bakery, and somewhere ahead an escalator crammed with customers sailing to the second floor. Somewhere in this maze of shops and corridors there had to be another exit. They bounded forward, elbowing their way up the escalator, into a shop, through aisles of shoes and bags and T-shirts.

Shit.

Cul-de-sac.

Turning heel, they launched back toward the main shop intersection, flip-flops squeaking on the faux-marble floor. Eyes darted up to the escalators, back down, around tight groups of girls holding hands, into a coffee shop. Nobleyan pointed toward the restroom, hard right in a space between a bookshop and a Korean restaurant. They crashed toward it, found the stairwell, flew down two floors, the door flapping behind them, paused before another heavy windowless door, slammed down on its handle, and landed outside, in an adjacent street.

All was quiet. Litter lined the gutter. A crooked old man pushed a cart plastered with lottery tickets.

It wasn't the first time one of the city's new shopping centers had served for a disappearing act. Modernity had its advantages.

Panting like dogs—smokers' lungs, the pair of them—they chased down the road and prayed for another free cab. One stopped, they tumbled inside, and directed it to a bus station.

Nway sent another text.

"Yes still running."

The friend replied something about standing by. *Anything I can do.*

"Thank I may need." [sic]

They neared the bus stop, threw the fare at the taxi driver, and hopped on the next departing bus. Not a motorcycle in sight.

He texted again: "Now we are on the bus."

Nobleyan turned to Nway. He too would have to think now about changing something in his appearance.

MAY 6, 2010

ON THE NLD'S LAST DAY AS A LEGAL PARTY, Uncle Han Thar Myint took out his keys, held them up to his nose, found the right one, and rattled open the shutter of the Office, as he did every morning. He wasn't much ruffled. All this fuss, as if any of them were going to give up.

People started crowding in by mid-morning. They surged to 100, to 150. Some were crying. Others broke into song.

> *The world is like that*
> *The Earth will never change*
> *We will never forget what you have done*
> *That is the history, which is written by our blood*
> *The revolution, the people who die in the war for democracy.*
>
> *Awwwww, my heroes*
> *The country where the martyrs are living*
> *Mr. Aung San, the history is so rude*
> *Awwwww, my grandpa*

It was an old revolutionary song.

People had always been breaking into song in the Office in moments of re-membrance, moments of desolation. Nway had sung his in 2000, after authorities had swooped in on a gathering to see Auntie off at the Rangoon railway station. He had been jammed into the back of a police truck but he'd jumped out instantly, clutching the hand of a friend. They leapt over a bridge, camped out for a night beside the rail track near where they landed, and eventually made their way back across the city to the Office. There they found a third straggler, sorting through the debris and scattered paperwork left behind by a raid. The only option, with impending arrest hovering for all of them, was to hit the streets—and alone. In the interim, what other choice had there been but to sing?

Uncle Han Thar Myint had been hoping recently to compile a history of the party. He had searched for archives that predated 2003, but there were none. The best archivist of the party had died. Han Thar had tracked his son to Singapore, but the papers were lost.

Grandpa was busy autographing copies of his prison memoirs. On the NLD's final day, he had only meant to bear witness with his presence. But people kept coming at him with pens and pirated versions of his book. *What's That? A Human Hell*, on his seven thousand and twenty days in prison, had been smuggled to the Assistance Association for Political Prisoners in Mae Sot, for publication the day he had turned eighty, just under two months earlier. Already it was circulating back inside in the old way, photocopies that people passed around, wrapped inside blank covers or gift paper. The most pleasant surprise was that people had found ways to circumvent the cyber-censors and download it from the Internet too.

But this was a day for the party, and its history. Win Tin had kept a diary in 1988. He had entrusted it to a close friend, but the friend, concerned that he was about to be arrested or raided himself, thought it best to place it in the most untouchable site of all—in the home of Daw Aung San Suu Kyi. Whereupon, in the next raid on her belongings, Grandpa's diary had vanished too.

It had been better in the end to keep notes of history in heads. Han Thar Myint's own recollections were deliberately confused, as if even his brain had defended against a raid. He had only briefly passed through an internment camp, but it was all the same. The son of a famous communist, he had told his wife in 1990 that his newfound interest in democratic politics, and the struggle itself, would only last about three years. Then he would return to engineering.

And here he was now, twenty years later, watching an end, nurturing, in the young activists he knew, another beginning.

No one could definitively say what would happen next. After the election, military rule would remain. But the shape of it would change. With a spread among the new parliaments to appear after the 2010 elections, Han Thar foresaw chaos, the loss of the chain of command. It meant, somehow, that there would be political space, somewhere between the competing new islands of influence. Such was the nature of man, the nature of power. Somehow, as Grandpa was telling everyone, they would find a way.

They had organized the paperwork for clearing out. But come the day itself, Tin Oo, Grandpa T, made a very long speech that signaled a different strategy. The headquarters would stay open every day, he said. People were welcome to visit and stay, without restriction. Until the government shut them down at gunpoint, there would be no effort to leave, no taking down of signs.

And so not a poster was unpeeled from the walls, not a single old canister of tea removed. Never had the cowshed been so well loved.

Even the clutter remained.

7

CITY OF KINGS

MAY 2011

SOMEONE HAD LEFT THE FRONT DOOR AJAR.

It was just a hair, but enough for a gust from the elevator shaft outside to rock it open on its hinge; enough for the neighbor on the other side of the landing or a passerby arriving on the floors above or below to catch the burble of multiple voices.

The others were laughing, chatting, scooping up the last grains of lunch from the tiffin box. One of the boys was strumming Minus's guitar. No one else seemed to care. Worse, no one else seemed to notice.

Paw Paw in a seamless gesture sprang up and across the room, pressed the door shut, turned the lock, added the chain for good measure and, on reflex, peered out through the peephole. Then she exhaled and settled anew in her slice of shadow on the far edge of the room. She pulled her knees up tight under her chin. Her eyes returned to her notebook and instantly darted back up and over to the young man who had been the last to walk in, a gaze of concentrated coals whose smolder he didn't catch.

They weren't serious enough. Enthusiastic, certainly, and dedicated, but they hadn't honed the instinct for the gravity of small mistakes. How often had they been told to stagger their entrances and exits, two or three at most in the elevator at any time? That much they had grasped—and that it was critical to defuse suspicion of regular gatherings. Their network was an outgrowth of the underground election-monitoring group that they had begun the previous year.

Even the betel-toothed old security guard, who only seemed to leave his rattan mat beside the front gate to relieve himself in the gutter, must never know.

She would have to tell Nway.

He was pacing between the living room and his bedroom, on his cell phone, cigarette in his other hand. He was a good *saya*, strong on discipline, in his way, and quick as a salamander. Since childhood, Paw Paw had thought the world of his talents. But he could be too permissive. He had so much on his mind. He had been lashing out. It wasn't like him. She had a vague idea that his evident stress had something to do with the contents of the black computer case he had been carrying around. Day by day, he shrank from talking, even as he seemed needier for her counsel, and from his other "cousins," her sisters, Acca and Snow.

The others were so young—though only an average of four to five years younger, if she was honest. Certainly they were no younger or more sheltered than Snow, who had more common sense in her left pinky toe. Already, with Auntie free from house arrest at last, they seemed to have been born in a different time. There was Zin Zin, with her newly red-streaked hair that had just got her suspended from her engineering degree, pantomiming some story that had silly Angelay in fits of giggles along with the fair-skinned, sometime computer teacher whom they referred to privately as "the Korean girl," though Korean she was not.

A young man with a curiously ancient face that seemed chiseled from stone, whom they'd accordingly nicknamed "the Professor," had curled up on the lone armchair, drifting in and out of a post-reading-circle catnap.

Nobelle, whose advanced sense of fashion presented today as an urban-cool variation on her "Western girl" look, was writing in her notebook. Inclined to sit apart, graver of demeanor than the other second-liners, she was the daughter of an NLD township officer. Nway had taken a particular interest in her tutoring. He liked to chide her that she had been the Office pack-dog, yapping at the heels of the Uncles when she was small enough to crawl. The sobriquet "Nobelle" had been a creation of her parents, in 1991, the year of her birth, in tribute to the Nobel Peace Prize awarded to Auntie. Bearing that name alone should have been enough, Paw Paw imagined, to make her more circumspect.

Paw Paw expected more from Minus too. Six months earlier—within days of the national elections and Auntie's release a week later—he had been dispatched to Malaysia for training in Internet encryption. He had returned with the sophisticated silences of a seasoned activist and a device to conceal all their sensitive data. For all the striking novelty of his hip-length hair and underground-rocker clothing falling off a body as flat as a stick of chewing gum, Minus had Acca's graceful capacity to fade into backdrop. As important for security purposes, he had the jumpiness of a tick.

Aung Thura Phyu, the culprit, was about sixteen. He was leaning his head against the wall, Minus's guitar cradled in his lap, and smiling with devastating oblivion. How could he be so clueless about the potential dangers from leaving the front door open? Did he really not understand the need for secrecy, or, for failing to maintain it, the consequences?

Did none of them?

It rankled. And, strangely, it made her think of Doe Doe—her dear friend, so strong and so committed. And gone. Paw Paw tried not to judge them. All of them were here to learn, a dozen "second-line" members now. The curriculum that Nigel and Nway had designed for them included a regular reading discussion group and a Burmese class, to study the formal, literary language of their history. There were also one-off lectures, which Nway was organizing from the growing trickle of visiting illuminati to Auntie and the Office. Foreigners had been rushing into Burma to meet with Auntie ever since her release.

The second-liners were then to take all their teaching and fan it into their local communities, permeating their lessons with ideas about nonviolent civil disobedience. It was up to each among them to figure out how. Some initiated new reading circles. Others taught basic English or basic computer literacy. The "Professor" had organized a pagoda-cleaning service; another had formed a group to help at an orphanage. They were to encourage blood donations and water distributions. Social work was an end in itself. It was also the best cover for political subversion.

What they were not to do was admit aloud that they were loosely affiliated to the NLD nor that they had a direct line to Auntie. Authorities could not touch her for now, not with the world's attention trailing her every move. But they would be less delicate with the NLD party itself, which had been operating in a risky legal limbo since the decision to boycott the 2010 elections.

All of them were scheduled to teach in the NLD's free schools. Under Auntie's honorary auspices, these had expanded in a few short weeks from fifty students to eight hundred, in eight locations across the city. Among them was the school that Nigel and his parents had for years been offering to the ward children of North Okklappa.

Paw Paw's personal fardel had always been to feel the weight of the world, and to see it in the intense shades of one endowed with a sense of the tragic. She didn't laugh lightly. She didn't cultivate her charms in the way of the other girls. There were reasons, she assumed, that Nway or Nigel had selected each of them for their network.

Still, the general laxness made their goal seem that much more distant, and, meanwhile, it trivialized the legacy of those who had sacrificed.

Doe Doe would have turned twenty-three years old by now. She was half-way past the one-year mark of her twenty-seven-year sentence. After discovering that she was an active NLD member, her parents had disowned her in the state newspaper. She had relied for a time on one friend after the next. The Palace had helped too, their longtime safe house, down the road and a block away. Eventually, casting about for a job that didn't require giving up her ideals, she had found the Democratic Voice of Burma. Nway had put her in touch. She had taken to reporting with alacrity. Who wouldn't want to see the immediate impact of her actions, instead of the slow-burn patience that Paw Paw had learned to cultivate, waiting out the wider, more creeping results of education?

Then Doe Doe had visited Mae Sot for a DVB training. When she came back she had charged head first into a sensitive story. She was in Pakokku on the second anniversary of the crackdown on Saffron. But something had changed in her, some new bravado that approached arrogance. Paw Paw hadn't liked it. Neither had Nway. Paw Paw had also visited Mae Sot, dispatched by Nway for a brief training in nonviolent strategic action. In her case, it had wound her still more tight. And love and respect Doe Doe though Paw Paw did, it didn't strike her as clever to be openly brandishing video equipment. After 2007, the repression had grown so severe. It was reckless.

And yet Doe Doe *was* brave. Always Paw Paw wondered if in the heat of confrontation she, too, would have the nerve to stand as tall. And so young! So brave and so young, and so many years ahead of her, lost.

Her eyes suddenly stinging, Paw Paw ran for the kitchen, hoping the supply of water was working, if only just for a splash at the sink.

"Hey! Paw Paw!" Out of nowhere Nway had loomed behind her.

A sharp intake of breath, a blink and—there. No tears. It never relented, though, this surge of sudden grief for absent friends. She turned around and smiled.

"Can you stay a little, after the others leave," Nway said, less a question than an instruction. "Or do you have to go back immediately to Twantay? I have something I want to tell you."

꧁꧂

NWAY, CRUSHING THE BUTT OF HIS eighth or fifteenth cigarette of
the day into the neck of a plastic bottle, turned tail from the kitchen and surveyed the scene at his apartment. It was roomier than the Palace, with a bus-
ier entrance downstairs. It made for a better hiding place. *Naypyidaw*, he had
dubbed this one. City of Kings.

He liked the codeword—and the added kick from the confusion it sowed
among sometime eavesdroppers to name the apartment after the new capital.

He liked it, too, when his "second-line" activists lingered after his reading
circles. It helped thaw the ice between them, although this tendency to lapse
into gossip wasn't exactly the point. Predictably, it was Zin Zin, holding court,
stage right. They had picked her—he and Nigel—because of her confidence.
She was sparkling with life, and people flocked to her. The effect was staggering. In three months alone, she had managed to net three university students,
two company staff, and one civil servant for Nway's book circle—fresh recruits
from a healthy societal cross-section to tempt henceforth into activism.

Each of Nway and Nigel's second-liners brought different talents. Minus
was loyal and low profile, quiet for hours, then out would pop something very
very fast that suggested his mind had been whirling like a circuit board. He was,
incidentally, Muslim, which brought a welcome viewpoint and a tentacle into
the four percent of the population that Nway felt the Buddhist-majority NLD
was rightly faulted for not adequately representing. Also, Minus could teach the
guitar. That was a good thing because his was always lying around, Nway was
compulsively tweaking its strings, and it would be nice to turn the noise into
something approaching music.

Nobelle, plucked from Nigel's English classes, had been an obvious "YES."
She was diligent, not shy with questions, and highly insightful. She had just
graduated university, which, in this crowd, was rare, and with an academic distinction, which was still rarer. Anonymity was excellent. But beauty never hurt.
Nway liked to tell himself that she was the spitting image of a long-lost cousin
who had emigrated to Australia. But really, she had it in her to a stop a man's
heart.

Then, of course, there was Paw Paw. Stoic, though not always, and au-
todidactic, she was responsible and loyal enough that it was easy to imagine her as the network's second-in-command. All three of the sisters—Paw

Paw, Acca, and Snow—had been canny and bright since childhood. Their parents, timorous civil servants in Twantay, had more or less abandoned their upbringing to a loving neighbor. They had none of the advantages of the Rangoon recruits, most of whom were the coddled only-children of professionals. Every minute they had free now, when not slipping away to some fresh political assignment, they were back in Twantay, dutifully pinned to the running of the family noodle soup shop, or the care of baby cousins and grandparents. They had even taken over Nway's filial responsibilities, in lieu of his mother's four sons.

Such was the lot of the rural female. Nway couldn't change it. But he had taught them everything he knew. Acca, closest to Nway in age, had, some years back, managed the lie to her aunt that she was commuting for two years to university. Instead, she had been heading to classes at the American Center as a scholar for the Office. Snow was nearing graduation from law school. Nway had conscripted her as an alibi in some of his riskier errands for Grandpa, partly because she was quick, but mainly because she looked Chinese. It meant, in the prejudices of roving authorities, that she was rich and powerful, ergo, not to be crossed. Her apprentice legal talent had also brought her to the eye of Uncle Nyan Win, the NLD lawyer.

Paw Paw, the middle child, had graduated with a degree in economics, rising at 5:30 a.m. for the two-hour commute to one of the satellite university campuses that the junta had built with intent to preempt unions and disperse students far from each other. She liked to joke that she had actually earned her bachelor's in satire. Her textbook, a classic of state-sanctioned agitprop, had been a study in straight-faced farce, peppered with reversals such as "sanctions open up the economy." She had learned more from pirate DVDs.

Scouting for chances to give her a dose of quality, Nway had taken her to Alix, his beloved teacher at the American Center. Paw Paw had been sullen and silent, and Alix never really knew what to make of her. But the girl had soaked it all up. Lately, Nway had been submitting the essays of his second-liners to Auntie as proof of their evolving education. "Who wrote this?" Auntie had asked, flicking fast through the pile but stopping over a fluent, substantively complex submission in fat, loopy pencil.

"Paw Paw!" Nway answered, not holding back his pride.

Nway's nominations for his network had been largely intuitive. He would sit at the back of Nigel's classes and pretend to be a student. Suddenly he would lob a provocative thought into the students' midst and watch for those who angled to catch it. Nway and Nigel had liked the double pair of eyes. It made their choices more democratic.

Nway liked to think of their group as the NLD's secret youth network but it had no defined name. It was safer for now to keep it fluid. There were reasons for choosing anonymity and reasons for branding. The best model of recent times was Generation Wave. Founded after Saffron by four friends, and restricted to membership of under-thirty-fives, the network had punched above its weight in the consciousness of local activists, banging into action with a graffiti-and-poster campaign across Rangoon in February 2008 that blazed three words: "Change New Government." No one would have trouble reading it as a play on the acronym of the state-owned CNG, for Compressed National Gas. Members had opted to brand subsequent campaigns—and there had been several—with a red, stenciled fist. They had patterned themselves on the Serbian student resistance movement, Otpor!, to which credit fell for pushing out the regime of Slobodan Milosevic.

The red fist made them instantly recognizable, effortlessly imitable, and dependent not on any one leader but on whomever stepped forward. The CNG campaign was as frontal an attack as activists could dare. It was savvy, and it had made them darlings of the exile media. Within a month, the group had been infiltrated, homes had been raided, and nearly half its members had been arrested, including two of the group's cofounders. Activists deduced that they'd all been traced to a single cell phone.

It was partly to avoid such a fall that Nway and Nigel had preferred discretion and lack of centralization in their previous networks. The trouble with their latest version was that they needed a home base, and, increasingly, funding. It meant they would have to define themselves to appeal to donors. Paw Paw had suggested they publicize their social wing, and hide the political, calling it "Togetherness."

For Nway, Togetherness had become a full-time job, to add to his other full-time job tending the affairs of at least two Uncles, a Grandpa, and now an Auntie. Prime duties included troubleshooting a half-dozen little unforeseen fires; chaperoning the girls, which meant counseling their parents; or herding the boys—who were frustratingly apt to wander off tasks. He preferred girls. They were more diligent. They followed orders. They didn't say "yes" only to undercut his ideas.

They were also crippled by the constraints of tradition, expected home by 5 p.m, living with parents until marriage. He had spent the previous afternoon reassuring the Korean girl's mother that her daughter was not about to elope. That evening, he had been at pains to convince Angelay to skip her classes later in the week and spend a day, *just a day*, with her ailing grandmother, who had phoned Nway to say she was coming to town from Pathein, on the Andaman Sea, and might Saya Nway be able to spare her granddaughter for the time it took to meet at the bus station?

Angelay had refused. "She's too extremist," Nway had complained to Nigel over beer that night at the Golden Crow, packed with men drinking their day away. His black computer case was safely tucked at his feet. "She's been here in Rangoon a whole year, just taking classes and teaching. Of course she should skip one of her classes. We can find a replacement. Family should matter. You know?"

Nigel had shaken his head, preoccupied by a more urgent question than the particularities of one young woman. He valued commitment, writ large. "Personal lives," he responded, "should not be mixed with the political."

There was an edge to his answer, as if he were attempting to make a different point. He was fishing.

Nway, five beers in and falling asleep where he sat, chose to ignore it.

❧

NWAY WAS RARELY ALONE NOW. Vanished like a strange dream was his previous year of lone-dog "freelance" activism.

In retrospect, he'd had space to think, to travel down theoretical cul-de-sacs. At times he had even lapsed into wondering what it was all for.

It was good to have a mattress of his own now, and a roof, although he still rarely managed more than four hours of rest at a stretch.

Run out of Twantay in May 2009, he had been homeless for months. When he could no longer resist the call of sleep, he had taken shelter in Internet cafés. For a while, he had secured an arrangement with one particular café owner. As long as he avoided consecutive nights, he could stay past closing, 2 a.m., sometimes until dawn. The manager had eventually relocated to a far end of the city. Roving thereafter from one café to the next, he allowed himself at most an hour or two to sink back into his chair. He made a point of never slumping over the desk, although sometimes it was hard to say if he'd failed. His neck alone told if the chair or the keyboard had functioned for a pillow.

On a few smoking breaks and a can of Chinese-imported Dragon fizz, he could sometimes cruise until dawn. Plus or minus the energy drink, it cost three to four thousand *kyat*, or about four USD. An Internet café wasn't a hotel, exactly, but at least it had electricity. After midnight, the junta's bureaucracy took a holiday, and he could relax into his work, uninterrupted, switching into a flow of multitasking.

Exiles, if they weren't hitting their desks in some faraway time zone but instead just over the border, tended toward insomnia too. He drafted articles, conducted six conversations at once in as many open Gchat windows. A few of his network members had been recruited in that way: Angelay, for one, who had been in the soup of a random email trawl that he had mass-blitzed. She had written back, falling into his trap of induced curiosity. At a critical juncture in conversation, he would send his new friends an ebook, often a short story set in an Indian slum. If they read, and engaged in online conversation about its themes of poverty and injustice, he had the first hints of a recruit.

Sometime, because spy software caught messages in transmission, he shared email log-ins with select people, who would then exchange their most sensitive messages through the "draft" box. One account alone he reserved for the correspondence of senior politicians, letters from UN officials, foreign "friends," or other requests that needed to bypass the standard party *info@*.

When the cafés shut, he'd head for a teashop. All he really needed was a little plastic chair. In that way, he had befriended the society of night, a world of disaffected youth and would-be rockers strumming underground lyrics that would never pass the censors.

Alone and wanting for sleep, he had tried nightclubs, thinking, with earnestness, that he could find a patch of shadow in which to block out the beat of the music and nod off. But the ambiguity of its denizens only churned his moral sensibilities. He hated to see the women pressured to swap their honor for paychecks inconceivable in factory work or other, less tainting pursuits. Worse still were the young men. In quieter settings, he might have tried to solicit them into service for their country. It irked immeasurably that the rising generation of the affluent, or at least of the urban classes, were growing up without passion for their citizenship, or sense of responsibility, or sense of anything at all.

He didn't fault them for it. It demonstrated instead, and viscerally, how deeply he and his ilk were failing. Never had he felt such a sense of loss. It was ineffable—an itch under the skin about his own futility. What did they have to show for any of it? What if they never succeeded? Night after night, all he could do was tell himself that the feeling would pass, in the way of all phenomena. His self, in the Buddhist belief, was no self. That his personal results felt suddenly so petty was of little consequence. Suffering—*dukkha*—was the default state of existence.

Let it be, he would tell himself. Because what did it matter what he really felt?

He would try to console himself then with the old story of the starfish thrower that an Uncle had once related in a similar moment of shared despondency. A man saved starfish stranded by the tide by endlessly throwing them out to sea and the waves endlessly coughed them back to shore. And yet the man stood there, eternally throwing them back, not because he was mad, but because, to him, every starfish had value.

⁓⚜⁓

ARTHUR UNDERSTOOD FUTILITY.

Later in Nway's year of homelessness, as the first hawkers began spreading out their wares into the lanes of the streets in the blue light of early morning, Nway would head to his best friend's apartment on 41st Street.

At eleven years old, on three days' notice, Arthur and his neighborhood in Insein township had been forced onto Army trucks and dumped with whatever possessions they could carry into the mud field that became Hlaing Thayar. He had watched his mother lose everything: their home, and the little retail business that had kept his family afloat since his parents had divorced and his father had died. In the field, there were no schools, no clinics, certainly no electricity. Around the plots of dirt allocated to each household they planted flags to avoid getting lost when they returned by dark from school or jobs over the river. His elder sister was an early NLD member. In childhood in the 1990s, he had played messenger boy for her secret dispatches, terrified but taken by the adventure. With a band of fellow high school friends during the brief student protests of 1996, he had scribbled slogans inside outhouses, excited but achieving precisely nothing.

When the NLD came calling in 1998, recruiting youth in his township after the decimations of the mid-nineties, he'd made a tremulous first visit to the Office. Ever since, Arthur had been the one person in whom Nway had always felt complete and unadulterated trust. But they hadn't been speaking, not since Arthur's decision to wed. To Nway, Arthur had been the best and the brightest, worthier than him. Auntie had adored him. Together on regular all-night security duty at her compound, he and Nway had almost grown up under her wing.

But marriage had stolen him from the struggle.

After a time, during his months on the street, Nway's yearning to talk again with Arthur—and for access to a water supply with which to wash—had prevailed.

In truth, Arthur had been as sincere as Nway about their no-tolerance-for-sweethearts pact. But life was life and love was love. He had made it through university. He had grown up. And all of it had seemed the height of silliness the moment he had seen straight through Nway's repeat requests to borrow his bathroom.

At which point, he'd offered permanent refuge. Nway was grateful, and had bowed before his best friend's offer.

Sometimes, in whimsical moments, Nway had dreamed of finding love himself. He had imagined the apparition of her form drawing an hourglass under a bed sheet, someone with whom to steal time, to share golden days, and he could just stop, just let go, and come the burst of monsoon, he would climb a *padauk* tree and pluck her the first flower of the new year, and she would wear it in her hair as Auntie wore it in hers.

But to love a girl, as he knew he ought, was to offer her protection. And to protect her was to marry her. How could he ever hope to provide for her? And even if she were an activist, someone who hailed from the party itself, there would be complications. If he went to prison, who would bring him his food? The very question was ridiculous, and he would flick it away then, laughing at his idiocy, as if it were a scab. He had made his choice.

At Arthur's, he wouldn't think of imposing a moment earlier than 6 a.m. Beside the risk of spot checks for house guests, it was a delicate matter to share a cramped space with a pair of newlyweds. Gentle as a moth, he would slip off his flip-flops, clear any leftovers from dinner off the little round table, roll it against a wall, and, on the dusty, laminated floor of their living room, unroll a mat on which to stretch out a few hours. He'd have an hour or two until the phone calls began, about a dozen network members across the country checking in from first light, per his orders.

It was worse now, in Naypyidaw. His contacts had quintupled with his responsibilities. Everything had accelerated since Auntie's release. He was good about swallowing the urge to tell his callers to go away and do pushups until 10 a.m., although he'd almost slipped on one recent occasion. Crashing at last onto his foam mattress at 5 a.m., he'd been woken within minutes by "Mi Mi" who was phoning to say she was sick and couldn't come to class that day. He told her to check in with Paw Paw. Paw Paw phoned ten minutes later to tell him that Mi

Mi was sick. He fell back asleep, someone else phoned, and on Nway sent him to Paw Paw. Paw Paw phoned in the issue ten minutes later. And then the same routine again, at which point he very nearly threw his phone off the balcony.

Rewinding a year, he had been both more and less constrained. Even the question of food turned treacherous. First Arthur's wife, a Muslim, had banished pork from her kitchen. Next out, on similar religious grounds, went prospects of a slug from a bottle of Myanmar whiskey that the boys reached for on sporadic occasions. Finally, Arthur's wife had decided she could no longer cook for Nway at all. The message came transmitted through Arthur, who evaded contact for the first few days, then, finally cornered, delivered the sentence with a sheepish apology and a hefty dose of *anade,* that omnipresent admixture of guilt, shame, and anxiety triggered by having to impose or inflict a hard truth.

Nway made sure to pay them enough to cover meals for all three, and their shared moments around the table were most often an affair of laughter and play-ful jokes. He grew to love Arthur's wife, and rely on her cooking. But the couple were sinking, and the young bride, usually a picture of rosy-cheeked good cheer, found herself too bothered by it all to spend her days shuffling between the market and the kitchen, plucking and stewing and chopping and scraping. It was time that Arthur unpeel himself from his football computer games to search for the jobs that had evaded them for a year, since she had lost hers and his Cyclone Nargis–related contract with an international nonprofit came to an end. Time also to cut Nway loose.

Too *anade* in turn to plead his case, Nway had left the isle of warmth that was their household and returned to life on the street. At least this time he had enough to get by, because his brother sent it to him, care of Paw Paw, Snow, or Acca, along with a day's supply of clean clothes that he was to recycle for a week, or until his next package delivery. Free to eat whatever his heart desired, he would ration his cash, deflecting hunger with a nicotine fix until weakness struck sometime in late afternoon. Then he'd sniff out restaurants offering decent crab curries. With a hand on his cell phone and the other snapping a claw, the thought occurred a week into his new culinary regime that he really ought to learn how to boil a vat of rice. Ideally, each day he would have to find another restaurant to spare the risks of a repeat visit, because there, for an hour or two, he would anchor his office.

It wasn't, in truth, such a terrible existence. He had known hunger. During the mass sweep of NLD supporters who had come to see Auntie off in 2000 at the railway station, after he flung himself over a bridge and camped out for a night beside the rail track, he had roamed without shelter for days. Young still, he had been too wary, excessive with his *anade*, about returning home or endangering friends who might have helped. Arrest loitered in the Office. His handful of *kyat* notes had dwindled fast to nil and he had found himself sharing the sidewalk in Chinatown with vermin. He had almost blocked the memory— four days at a time without food or no more than a few sips from a street-corner water jug. He would fall, then, on the kindness of street vendors for a little cup of leftovers, some weak brew with a few strands of noodles. The worst episode had ended with an attack on a thin soup that a cook had supplied after he had bumped by chance into an NLD acquaintance, weak and tattered and lost, like him. Between them, they had not enough for a bowl of rice. They told the woman at a corner teashop as much, and never praised the stars so highly as when she reappeared from a backdoor kitchen with a bowl of steaming broth.

He might have fallen now on the kindness of Arthur's wife. She had nothing at all against the idea of struggling for democracy, and even less of working directly for the Lady, whom she idolized. Mug shots or hand-sized portraits of Aung San Suu Kyi were tucked throughout their apartment: into the corners of the mirror, behind a bookshelf piled in folded *longyis*, between the pots of creams and blocs of *thanaka* sandalwood bark that she would pound and grind into a paste with drops of water and jasmine petals.

But the trials of a young couple ready to start a family were fraught enough without the burden of working in politics. The couple had just overcome the cross-ethnic prejudices of their relatives. Arthur was Buddhist, and had managed a half-hearted pretense of Islamic belief to make it through her family's premarital inquisition; she had told his mother that she was Buddhist. Now her parents were badgering them to get hold of passports and emigrate. With nagging frequency, they sent letters from their new home in Germany, affixing photos of couches and neighborhood houses, and endlessly promising that life there was easier and healthier. And running water! Jobs! Electricity!

Arthur resisted the pull of material freedom. For love of his wife, to make an income, to contemplate having children, he had left the NLD. But never could he abandon his country or the pain of his people. Exile, he knew, would anesthetize him.

As for politics, he could work vicariously for as long as his friend flitted in and out of their apartment. Even as Nway cultivated an existence fuzzed into a blur in the night, Arthur knew enough to guess that when Nway said he had to go, or gathered his flip-flops and the front door slammed, minutes after a few nondescript grunts on his phone, or he delivered that night's promised takeout curry hours late and with the grease congealed—in those instances Nway was in all likelihood meeting with someone senior, significant, and well-watched.

Together, they had typed out chunks of Grandpa's prison memoirs. "In this human hell, this hellish whirlpool, we are still struggling, swimming upstream, downstream." No one had managed to publish anything yet quite like it—nothing as soaring and rich in the darkness of its details. About prison conditions, most people knew, but it took a great prose stylist, driven with vehemence, to pull the filth free from polite obscurantism.

But of Nway and Arthur's activities, Arthur's wife knew less, and guessed less, because they told her less. Beyond the bald fact that she had willfully agreed to harbor a political fugitive, they kept her out of the details for her own safety, but mainly because she had only lately and with reluctance come to accept that the university classmate who had become her husband could never entirely let politics go. To tell her more than the essentials now would likely fan her fear just as it was diminishing.

All that, though, was before the seasons changed from hot to monsoon to cool, and everything and everybody would demand Nway's attention at once.

⤙⊱

GOOGLE CHAT, JULY 2010, between Nway ("Nwe"), from an Internet café in Rangoon, and "Soe," somewhere in exile:

> NWE: *pls notice that NELC education center is located in BAK Tower at Boaung Kyaw Street.*
> *The son and daughter of the owner of the education center is working for our network.*
> *not very actively.*
> *Then, they own the whole 12 floor.*
> *in 1 floor there are 8 rooms.*
> *if we want to rent 4 rooms it is ok.*
> *But we must negotiate them.*
> *Regular for 4 rooms is 250000kyat for a month.*
> SOE: *1st, I am concerned about security.*
> NWE: *There, we don't need to worry about electricity.*
> *more safe. BAK Tower has four exits*
> *one at Boaung Kyaw street.*
> *Second from Central market.*

Third from 40th street.

Fourth from ground floor.

at the 1st floor there are café, market and internet center.

it means always crowded.

SOE: *What is NELC Centre? Is the Conference Centre rent for meetings and workshops?*

NWE: *no no. it is an education company which sent burmese students to abroad.*

SOE: *Do they organize Toefl classes?*

NWE: *yes, many things, many training. we just rent. . . .*

SOE: *If the security is OK, you can rent.*

[*sic*]

❧

THE APARTMENT THAT NWAY AND Nigel eventually found was Naypyidaw.

In May 2010, not long after Auntie had green-lighted the idea for an election-monitoring network and just after the NLD had technically been dissolved as a political party, Nway had raced to Arthur's apartment. Fresh from a follow-up with Uncle Nyan Win, the party lawyer who had been visiting Auntie as her lone interlocutor, Nway had been bursting to share the news that she had just allocated a wad of cash for them, enough to cover six months of classes.

Nigel had been there, too, offering a window into Office activities denied to both Arthur and Nway: photos of the NLD Uncles celebrating the mid-April Burmese New Year's Day with an abbot's sermon and the release of fish into ponds by a pagoda.

All three were elated. Finally, a chance for progress. The money meant they could cover expenses for paper and pens, food, and even bus fare for new second-liners. They could recruit beyond their immediate vicinity, searching for participants from across the country. They needed people from all spots of the map and walks of life, to spread among the polling sites and back into society.

Online, Nway sought out powerful exiles with updates and requests for counsel, trying for added financial help. Landlords wanted six months in cash, up front, which would have swallowed the total given to them by Auntie. They would have to rent in the name of someone who wouldn't raise eyebrows.

Scanning through their contacts for the most trustworthy, they settled at last on Nway's mother.

The last time Nway had seen her had been a few weeks before. It had been their first meeting since he had fled Twantay the previous year. She never came to Rangoon. Since her third son had become a wanted man, any visit would raise instant suspicion from neighborhood informers or local Twantay authorities, who were tracking her every move. All she could do was pray for Nway, every night, kneeling before her home shrine with hands clasped hard on her prayer beads, pressing them to her forehead and heart.

I've given up my son. Let him escape his father's fate.

But duties of citizenship—in the mother as in the son as in the father—always took precedence. And her eye had been in need of surgery.

They had arranged to meet a few hours in the clinic. Paw Paw and Snow had been deployed as scouts and, on a signal that all was clear, he would enter by a back entrance. On the way, his phone rang. "Change of plans," said his mother. He met her instead at the home of a senior politician, an old friend. Thirty seconds into their greeting, barely pausing for him to raise himself to his feet after bowing before her in filial tradition and love, she launched into her mission: Nway must support the friend as an independent candidate in the 2010 elections.

He had left in a state of turmoil. This was the end. To his mother, as to Auntie, it was difficult to say no. But to support an independent candidate, just as the NLD was choosing to boycott the elections, would smear him as a traitor.

Her latest visit was to be similarly hairy, but only because they had to devise a scenario in which she could stay overnight at the apartment, in the way of any new tenant. The place was barely furnished, a tatty piece of foam for a mattress, a fat armchair, a sofa. It would do.

Her health was unraveling. Her legs shook in the heat, the electricity was out, and the betel-toothed security guard hovered too attentively by the frozen elevator. So Nway and Nigel lifted her onto their shoulders and staggered up the stifling stairwell to the ninth floor.

That night Nway ate his first home-cooked curry in over a year. His mother had packed it specially. He had missed her curries. He had never appreciated them enough. It had been a source of endless exasperation that she would reheat and serve the same dish for lunch and dinner for a week. But what he wouldn't have given through his recent meanderings for a heaping of her seafood dishes, bathing in oily puddles of ginger and chili. His hankering for crab curries, in its way, had been a search for lost time.

After she left, Nway had made the apartment his. If he could manage to be discreet, steal in after midnight, he could officially tell himself that he was no longer living on the street. When one or other activist needed a place to crash because the commute home was too onerous, they would lock in from 6 p.m., lest a neighborhood gossip wonder if a late-night visitor was breaking the rule on overnight visits.

Naypyidaw was vast. It had a kitchen, a spacious living room large enough for a comfortable group of thirty seated cross-legged, fifty if they pressed up against each other. A balcony looked down on a busy street, so there were plenty of passersby at all times to blend into, when they shot in and out. Best of all it had two entrances at the front gate, and a few other private tuition schools scattered among the other apartments.

It was better than the Palace for the secret conferences of the Uncles, too, especially given the omnipresent legal ambiguity of the Office.

Their classes had revved up slowly, with basic computer training and English lessons. Each lesson hinged on a question. On market economics: "What do you think of the Burmese economy and the difference between a liberal market economy and the Burmese economy?" On death, from different religious perspectives: "What is the point of death? What will you do as your life's work before you die?"

Three or four weeks in, with the students duly heated up, they moved onto their real business. They introduced an Uncle, Han Thar Myint or Ohn Kyaing, or any willing senior NLD politician. They started with a vote: whether to monitor the elections at all, whether to help the candidates among the few non-NLD pro-democracy parties that were registered, or whether to boycott the process entirely.

It was about then that the junta started getting serious too.

In August 2010, it finally announced the date of its coming elections as November 7. *The New Light of Myanmar* threatened twenty years in prison to anyone caught "disrupting the electoral process" by urging a boycott, which was exactly what the NLD Uncles were just then roaming the country to encourage.

Follow-up columns in the *New Light* in September went on to decry those who would follow such urgings as "irresponsible opportunists."

Next came arrests. In late September, agents rounded up a handful of students in Rangoon in connection with an electoral boycott campaign that included pamphleteering and rare sprayings of political graffiti on a bridge. A week later, for the possession of anti-election flyer templates in his laptop, a Buddhist monk was handed ten years under the Electronic Transactions Law, four years under the Printers and Publishers Registration Act, and one year under Act 505-B, a provision of the penal code that predated the exile of Burma's last monarch, King Thibaw. It was harsh, but the monk had the misfortune of being sentenced on the three-year anniversary of the crackdown on Saffron.

The Uncles had wanted Nway and Nigel to hold classes for seventy, at least. With weeks to go, the needs were ever more pressing. But security considerations forced them to whittle the numbers to five at a time.

Then, one dawn in October, a young participant had been hauled away.

The Dogs interrogated him for twenty-four hours. Trembling still just after his release, before he had yet made it home, he phoned Nway. Over and over, he said, he had repeated to the Dogs that they were only holding English classes. But—he added, his voice breaking—he had not been able to withstand the pressure. He had revealed Naypyidaw's address.

No one ever admitted that they had cracked under duress. It was brave of the young man to come clean, and so fast. Nway had been thankful. That night, he had headed to the jetty and gazed out into the Stygian gloom, contemplating options.

How many hours before the Dogs came sniffing? Would they pick off another, one of the younger students perhaps, still half-formed, still innocent of all this stuff of politics? There was no time to find another apartment. There was no money, none from the stash he had secured from Auntie. A month remained before the first elections in twenty years, a month and a week before the end of the most recent term of Auntie's house arrest. If the junta dared, it would release her. But who was dumb enough to think she would then be truly free?

They shut down operations, bracing for a raid.

It never came.

Slowly, quietly, carefully, they began again.

⚜

ON NOVEMBER 7, 2010, THERE WERE no bomb alerts and no instances of mass picketing.

From 6 a.m. until the close of day, citizens trickled quietly to the polls. The indoctrination of years, of decades, yielded its effects. The elections were peaceful and orderly. People were shooed out of homes and off fields by mega-phones positioned on circulating vehicles and corner street poles, instructing them to show up and mark a ballot.

It was wise, then, to vote for the candidate who represented the local ward boss, because the local ward boss had all the power to make your life a misery. On what evidence of recent times could anyone expect anything else? The Lady might have given them a different sense of possibility. But the Lady was still under house arrest.

Official results emerged two weeks later. Turnout, the government an-nounced, had reached seventy percent. The great winner was the Union Solidarity and Development Party. Headed by the junta's No. 4, Thein Sein, prime minister and now retired as brigadier general, the USDP had been known weeks before, and ever since 1993, as the Union Solidarity and Development Association, the mass social apparatus whose patron had always been No. 1, Senior General Than Shwe.

In the Upper House of the national parliament, the USDP swept seventy-five percent of the seats. It took a near-total landslide in Burman majority ar-eas, and sixty-five percent in ethnic districts. In the Lower House, the USDP took eighty percent. In all the parliaments combined—national and fourteen regional—the USDP won a grand total of 875 out of 1157 seats.

Added to the twenty-five percent of seats that were constitutionally reserved for the military, the victory of the Union Solidarity and Development Party handed the junta a parliamentary rout.

No one was fooled.

On all non-official fronts, reports poured in of systematic polling violations and massive vote-count manipulation. People were turned away from balloting. Coercion and intimidation had been the order of the day. The main tool of the rigging was the use of advance votes: boxes upon boxes stuffed with thousands of uncounted ballots. Some of them arrived with officials just in time to over-turn computations in local polling sites that opposition candidates were actually winning.

Khin Maung Swe, the former geologist, had steered his breakaway party, the National Democratic Force, into the election's biggest pro-democratic op-tion. They fielded 161 candidates. At five hundred dollars per candidate, and with little time to raise funds, that was the most they could afford. In prior weeks, the founders had been slammed as traitors and apologists for the junta and its flawed constitution, denied interviews or censored outright when they gave them. There had been a rift in the ranks over a smear of financial impropriety against the party's cofounder, Dr. Than Nyein, another former NLD MP-elect and political prisoner, whom they accused of receiving illicit donations during trips abroad to Singapore, when actually he had been seeking treatment in Bangkok for complications from eleven years in prison and terminal liver cancer. Khin Maung Swe himself had been disqualified from candidacy at the eleventh hour. Ever the diplomat, he had pleaded the need to spend more time with his family—with cause, privately, on account of his wife's depression. In reality, authorities had found a legal technicality with which to force him from the playing field because of his prior conviction for treason.

But among the people who inclined to vote their conscience, if indeed to vote at all, Khin Maung Swe's NDF represented their best parliamentary hope.

They won only sixteen seats.

Combining forces with five smaller pro-democracy and ethnic-based parties, they prepared a legal challenge, risking prison if they lost.

Even the most sanguine felt robbed.

Some even died from it.

Nay Win Maung had been a "third force" intellectual, publisher, and entrepreneur at the heart of the handful of internationally influential "stakeholders." For months, he had been churning out columns in his journal, *The Voice*, in favor of the elections, calling for participation. He had batted away the flurry of controversy that surrounded his nonprofit, Egress, whose freedoms seemed, to most people, entirely out of keeping with the constraints inflicted on the average local organization. He had the ear of diplomats and foreign academics. Through his international contacts, he had without apology secured a shocking one million Euros from the European Union. Through Egress's booming classes on governance and civil society on the second floor of the downtown Thamada Hotel, he was producing hundreds of young men and women who were rejecting the old revolutionary ways of the democracy movement, preferring economic development first, not civil and political rights, as the path toward the future. His ambition was for tens of thousands to graduate with that vision, or at least with knowledge enough to parse the arguments for themselves.

To members of the pro-democracy movement, Nay Win Maung was the Pied Piper, spiriting away new generations to some far off hell of compromise with military rule. He had been raised among the military elites. His best friend was the son of the fallen spymaster, General Khin Nyunt. For years he had profited from his military ties for the licenses and wherewithal to build his empire: Living Color Media, *The Voice*, and now Egress, whose other executives were as well-connected in business and military circles.

But through and through, enamored with his nation, daring to break free of convention, he had sought to use his privileges to find another way. As the elections had approached, he couldn't sleep. Subsisting on cigarettes and instant coffee, taken black, he was too wired, too excited for the great reforms he foresaw.

On November 10, 2010—three days after the electoral violations had torn away his optimism—he published an apology in *The Voice* under his pseudonym, Aung Htut:

> We climbed a slippery pole, knowing it's slippery. I don't think we were wrong. I thought just by climbing it the first time, we would go rather far. That opinion was wrong. I am ready to take any blame for that. . . . I am not reluctant to apologize to the readers for giving them hope, and therefore, I would sincerely like to apologize to the readers.

In the months that followed, he grew puffy around the middle and beneath the eyes. But he didn't give up, not yet. In the first speech by the country's new president, former No. 4, former prime minister, and retired brigadier general Thein Sein, in March 2011, listeners heard that there had indeed been a shift—of tone if not yet substance. For the first time in living memory, a Burmese high official acknowledged "rural poverty" and "corruption."

The speech was an echo of a column Nay Win Maung had run in *The Voice* just the week before. His words, and his influence, had made it into the writing of the speech. So there was promise. But it would be slow.

On January 1, 2012, Nay Win Maung died of a heart attack. He was forty-nine. Some said that it was the miscalculation of 2010 that had killed him. His country, after all, gave too little sign that it was genuinely changing. He died, it was said, of a broken heart.

The great gamble of those pragmatists who had opted, not for a rapid change from military rule to parliamentary democracy, but at least for the chance of an evolutionary, multiyear transition, was bust. They had, it turned out, been had.

But a colder pragmatism had belonged to the less sanguine.

On November 7, 2010, Paw Paw sat from first light in her control center in Twantay, a dusty room tucked above the family noodle shop, scribbling down reports from friends who were strategically deployed about her ragged little town. All of them had trained in previous weeks to look for irregularities, to ask the right questions of the right people, to stand in the best places.

She sent the results to Nway, who sat in his Rangoon control center, in Naypyidaw, compiling reports from dozens more control centers. That night, to all his contacts abroad, he fired out seventy briefings, each of them detailing a list of local electoral violations.

Scores of others, from on-ground reporters of *The Irrawaddy* and *Mizzima* to avowedly independent citizen-monitors, had gathered evidence from all across the map of the country and blasted it out, in real time, to a watching world. The evidence was damning. The world, barring China, rose up in condemnation.

And then another bit of news within a week dynamited it all to the bottom of page 27.

Auntie, the Lady, Aung San Suu Kyi, the eternally incarcerated Nobel Peace Prize laureate, on November 13, 2010, was released.

She had spent fifteen of the previous twenty-one years under house arrest, and the previous six completely incommunicado. It was a brilliant sleight of timing. The world forgot all about the junta's mass rigging. Cursory observers assumed that her release was the first grand gesture from the generals as they prepared to dissolve the State Peace and Development Council to make way for the new government.

For anyone else, the move was nothing more than more of the same. Her house arrest, extended for eighteen months after the American swimmer's incident, had been set to expire on exactly that day. Always concerned to do its business sometimes according to its own legal playbook, the junta had merely followed its own rules.

Come November 13, Nway had been among the very few to not hurl himself at 54 University Avenue. First he assembled his activists. He instructed them to dampen their elation.

"Be wary," he counseled, his voice darkening, his body tensed. "Now the junta is invisible. We don't know when they will show their hand again."

As the hour of her rumored release approached, they spread around her compound. At a nearby junction, Nway waited, cell phone at the ready, and attempted to triangulate the numbers.

He didn't need it to gauge her relative popularity. He had never been among those, mainly foreign analysts to speculate that, with such a span of absence, she might have lost her magic. He wanted a sense of the crowd's size, rather, to measure relative levels of fear. How many people were daring the plainclothes agents and cameras that they knew could later be used to round them up?

It turned out to be thousands. Among them were so many young people, waving cell phones with cameras poked into the air, that Aung San Suu Kyi was seized with the compulsion to encourage their future participation. In the same way that Saffron had politicized a new generation, Nway had his pick of new recruits from the fresh waves of young enthusiasts whom Auntie's release had volcanically unleashed.

He hoped to find even one among them with half the qualities of Minus.

It was on the periphery of the punks' circle that Nway had met Minus, barely twenty-two, biochronologically vampirical, resisting parental pressure that he take the hours he spent with his guitar and invest them instead into productive work at the family electronics shop. Minus had deliberately failed his high school leaving exams to sabotage entry into university. He didn't see the point. The pair had hit it off so well that by the time Nway considered Minus ready to hear the truth about who he was, and what he did, and why, Minus had already signed up to be his brother.

Within days of Auntie's release, they had fallen out.

Minus had been readying for his trip to Malaysia for an Internet security training. He had been nervous. It was always tricky to fly out of a police state. But to venture abroad on a subversive mission, as an activist, tipped it into real peril.

Two days before he was due to fly, he met with his music teacher, the man for whom he had always borne the greatest respect. His *saya* told him not to go. He had heard from an NLD youth member that Nway was no good, that Nway's claims to friendship with Auntie were nothing of the kind, that Auntie had frozen him off. Again, the story went, it had been a question of misused funds.

That night, Nway had called him, and called again, and then again. Minus didn't pick up. It had been devastating. Minus had become, in his way, an extension of Nway, someone whose ideas aligned and expanded Nway's own, his ambition to choreograph it all from behind the veil, like some invisible puppeteer. With Minus, there was none of that abrasive competitive edge that had always defined his relationship with Nigel. Minus was raw still, but already they were twinned in spirit and heart. Who knew what magic was theirs to conjure?

Nway had tossed and turned on it until, sometime in the early morning, he had jolted upright on a call. "I have something to tell you," Minus croaked. "I'm really sad. I'm really sorry. I can't sleep."

Nway shot out to meet him.

Minus told him all. Nway answered: "You can believe what they say. But don't give up your political feelings. Doing politics doesn't just mean being my friend. Do politics, engage in politics with another friend. It doesn't matter. I don't know who told this story to your friend. But don't hate politics on account of it. You're already doing politics. You are an activist. You take huge risks. Who you do it with is unimportant. Engage with anyone you believe in."

"I believe you. But I don't believe you," Minus had answered. His music teacher wasn't someone to contradict, nor either did he lie. "This is my life. I'm willing to sacrifice it. But I want to see the Mother"—the new title that people had bestowed on Auntie since her release. "If I have a chance to see her, before or after I go to Malaysia, I'll believe you."

Nway told Auntie and Auntie didn't hesitate. She would, she said, see Minus before his trip.

It was a short meeting. But it was enough for a lifetime.

"You must take responsibility as a youth," she said.

Minus could only say: "Yes, yes, yes, yes."

And that had been that.

Within a week of Aung San Suu Kyi's release, the Press Scrutiny Board suspended nine local journals from publication for printing her photo or covering the event in any way. It was a broad trawl, netting *Myanmar Newsweek*, *First Eleven Journal*, *7 Days News Journal*, *Venus News*, *The Snap Shot*, *Myanmar Post*, *Pyithu Khit* (the *People's Era*), and the *Hot News Journal*, even Nay Win Maung's *The Voice*.

She paid a visit on Wednesday November 17 to an HIV/AIDS clinic, the only one in Burma, excepting a wing of a single Rangoon hospital, to diagnose and treat patients from a nationwide epidemic of 240,000 people. It was run by a famous NLD youth leader, Phyu Phyu Thin, who had slyly secured antiretrovirals from the international nonprofit, Médecins Sans Frontières. In previous years, Phyu Phyu Thin had sometimes been so overwhelmed with the need that Nway and others had filled in as unofficial HIV/AIDS counselors.

About five hundred people gathered to see Auntie appear, brandishing bouquets and messages of love and admiration. Two days later, local authorities informed the clinic manager that the monthly resident permits required of its eighty patients would not be renewed. The clinic would have to evict them. Even monasteries could not accept them as hospice patients, a policy that had been in effect since Saffron.

Everything was different. And yet nothing had changed.

❧

SIX MONTHS LATER, ON MAY 11, 2011 just after 11 p.m., Nway, Nigel, and Minus were sipping beers that Nway could no longer afford at his favorite spot down crooked little 19th Street in Chinatown.

The chiaroscuro from street-level halogens carved the façades on either side of the alleyway, catching maroons and greens and shuttered windows whose slats had once fumed with opium. Shadow had siphoned off slices of their table too, and there they had parked their fatigue and pressures that they would never confess aloud.

Nigel yawned. He stared down at his phone at the last picture he'd snapped of his son. He was almost two years old now, a tyrant already, and Khine Sandar Win had thought it funny to spike up his hair with his father's gel.

Nway poked a chopstick at dishes that kept coming: a plate of corn, shavings of fried beef, skewered pork, something white and sizzling on a stick. Another landed with fist-sized red globules in a choppy sea of orange jelly. He glanced at it for a moment, then got up to tell the waitress—the one with a slight weakness for him, conveyed with repeat twirls of her hair strands and the little dance of her knees—that he really hadn't meant to order the kitchen's full spread. How he would pay for any of it, he had yet to figure out. Minus, besides, wouldn't touch a thing; when he ate at all, it had to be *halal*, under Islamic law. Even Nigel didn't seem to have an appetite. Nway plopped back down on his stool, picked at a sliver of fried beef, ate it, and fell asleep where he sat.

And Minus? For Minus, it was practically breakfast time and some chords were playing in his head, beating out the brouhaha of late-night diners still packing the barbeque joints all up and down the alleyway. He tapped at the table with his phone. Boom. Bu-boom. Boom bu-boom.

They waited. There was nothing else for it but that.

It had been a long day. Nigel had spent half of it on buses. He had taken three buses alone from Dawbon to reach his first class in North Okklappa. Sometimes he went direct, but he liked to make life difficult for the seven agents who waited outside for him, scattered among two or three of their usual posts. They had doubled up in recent weeks, an increase that was ever so slightly flattering if troublingly paralleled to the surge of students to the free schools that he and Nway and other NLD leaders had been operating for some time now under Auntie's honorary patronage.

He would have liked to be home by now—all three would have liked to be home—but word had come through a reliable network member that authorities were planning a sweep of activists' houses. There was no real reason for it, only that it was 11 p.m., May 11, 2011, and authorities would think it clever to mock protests that might have been triggered in tribute to 9/9/99 or 8/8/88, though no activists they knew were planning anything of the kind.

May, June, July, August: these were the months when the rains heaved into a fixed gloom of leaden clouds, confounding light with dark. The sun heated the wet world to a boil by midmorning and, by noon, concealed behind the gathering vapors, it pierced them through with torrid shafts. Then it poured. It ripped down with a mercilessness, a violence battering greens so deep and unnatural, so ambitious in their riot, they suggested some chaos from the beginnings of the world. It was the time of malaria. It was the time of anniversaries, which meant as many ceremonies for authorities to preempt.

And it was the worst time to be a politician.

"By the way," said Nigel, "the other day, my father read my palm."

"Oh?"

Nway perked back to life. Nigel's father could look a person in the eye and just know. He had predicted his son's detention and release almost down to the date. From time to time, whenever Nigel was in need of counsel, he would present his father his palm. Now, his father had said, Nigel was to go to America. He needed to be far from his wife.

Nigel hadn't liked his father's reading. There was, it was true, some latent tension between Nigel and Khine Sandar Win. For one thing, she was bristling to get back to the activism she had abandoned with their marriage. And Nigel had been distracted, his head a little full with pretty women who took to him too easily.

About three weeks earlier, in the middle of the Water Festival—a three-day national shutdown in which drunkards and children threw water at anyone; teenagers danced all day in open-back trucks before giant, street-side pavilions from which ticket-holders hosed them down with filthy lake water; and everyone who was sane fled for the monasteries—Auntie had summoned Nway and Nigel for a chat.

She informed them that she had just been offered two scholarships for a four-year degree at an American liberal arts college. She offered them to Nway and Nigel. Democracy would be a long, ongoing process, she said, the work of a lifetime. The country needed their leaders to be skilled and educated. She wanted them to invest the time and return to the country with the world at their fingertips and all the deep learning that they had been denied.

They had smiled and tried to look flattered. Privately they were horrified.

The entire country was partying. Nigel wanted the much-needed break to cool his heels and reconnect with his wife and son. Nway's plans had been to smuggle himself back to Twantay for his annual New Year's joint, smoked with his old friend, the poor poet. Instead, to secure the scholarships, they had to sit exams.

There was an English test and a personal essay on a theme of "Who Are You?"

Nway opted for sabotage. "I'm just an ordinary guy," he began his essay, "And I want my country to be free." Then he tore through a list of reasons of why it was a terrible time to leave, that he could do better work at home, and how his young network members, brave, "grassroots" types who hadn't had even his narrow educational opportunities, needed his guidance at this particular convergence between their evolving political maturity and the country's precarious emergence into a parliamentary system.

His strategy had backfired. Deploying every rhetorical and debating device he had ever honed, he had managed to not lie his way through an inadvertently brilliant, passionate screed on politics, activism, and the universal struggle for freedom. Doubtless, whichever earnest American admissions officer read this young activist's essay must have asked herself if she was, in fact, reading the work of Burma's next Nobel Peace Prize winner, at the very least of a future luminary. The next question to Auntie from the college was more or less: when can they start?

They couldn't say no. No one could say no to Auntie. Instead, they plotted, they'd offer her a bargain: they would alternate. Only one would go. Meanwhile, the other would stay to incubate their secret NLD network. Nigel also had to preside over the United Front of Burmese Activists for Democracy, UFBAD, a secret league of protest-hardened revolutionaries that he had formed in the weeks before the 2010 elections.

And then there were the other responsibilities, the kind that couldn't be spoken of openly, that pressed on the desire to sleep and stole the chance for it at once.

It wasn't a perfect solution, and they didn't even know if Auntie or the college would agree. They were almost at the point of drawing straws.

A palm reading might be just the thing.

꼭

MAY 23, 2011

"NOTHING HAS CHANGED. NOTHING, I TELL YOU." Nigel's taxi driver, breaking a general taboo about talking politics to strangers, was giving him an earful.

Nigel chuckled to himself. He was taking a taxi to his parents' school, a giant, open-air hut on bamboo stilts above open sewage in North Okklappa. Lately, there'd been scarcely elbow room. They were calling it the Mother's School now, in honor of Auntie.

His family had built the school from the refuse of their home, which had been flattened by Cyclone Nargis. With the monsoon season upon them, they had yet to conjure the funds to roof it. A taxi was pricey from downtown, but two potential donors were waiting for him. And, to lose his seven trackers, it was a better bet than the bus. They were always complaining to Nigel when he took a cab—as if it were his problem that they couldn't afford a comparable fare to chase him across the city. Sometimes, for sport, he indulged them by taking the bus. But not now.

The taxi driver had it spot on. Nothing had changed. But Nigel had never been more convinced that it was time for action, before the new parliament had a chance to find its footing. It was early days yet. The junta had dissolved itself in March. The massive work of installing the new bureaucracy was sure to create a void that it was the moment, right now, to exploit.

The system had only grown more insidious. The military regime was smarter, learning and evolving off previous mistakes. Institutional memory was an attribute shared on both sides of the civilian-military divide. Used to be that they would sweep up all the activists. Now they were just targeting the high leadership, or anyone they could identify as capable of management and organization. Why else would the state invest so much manpower into Nigel's personal detail?

He arrived in North Okklappa to hear the worst.

There were no donors at the Mother's House. Meeting him instead was frantic urgency, and news that two Military Intelligence agents and a ward authority, formerly USDA turned member of the USDP, had approached his sister-in-law in a teashop, just over the alley from their school. They told her that her family would have to shut the school down.

They had moved on to his parents, inquiring after Nigel's national registration number, where he lived, and what he looked like. It wasn't information they needed. They had it already, and many times over.

It was standard harassment, almost to be expected. Nigel, hearing the news, tasted a strange bitterness on his tongue, as if he'd just bit into a green gourd. The world thought Burma was changing. But the real trenches of the ongoing struggle were in the slums and townships, in the grassroots, among people too poor to risk everything and too powerless to know how to defend against it. Places the tourists and businessmen would never see.

His family had maintained their school for years. In recent months, its popularity had soared—one hundred students in Nigel's English class alone. They had packed the primary school too. Since his parents had changed the name to honor the Mother, since it had become clear that Aung San Suu Kyi was directly sponsoring the school, there was no curbing its local significance.

Shaded by the tarpaulin awning of neighboring huts, his feet firmly rooted in the mud at the entrance to the school, Nigel's father punched back.

"No, no," he said to the men in plainclothes, "this is none of your business. We are just giving free education. It's not political. What would you have us do, education or politics?" The country was supposedly a democracy now, he reminded them. They were to be allowed to discuss politics. "So which will it be?"

The men in plainclothes had seemed more sheepish by the second, visibly wilting at the force of his words.

Nigel had to hand it to his father. In moments of crisis, he was a rock. It was a family trait. After Saffron, seven of the nine members of his family had landed on the ward list of "sensitive" local types to be watched.

In times past, the confrontation would have chilled the neighborhood, scattering people into homes and far from evident danger. Now a half-dozen were loitering close, wringing out their laundry or tossing out trash, trying hard to pretend they were not actually listening in. Best of all, Nigel's students crowded the school's entranceway, unabashed witnesses to the whole scene. Ha! Let authorities try to evict them now. This was a lesson in boldness that no amount of lecturing could equal. He forged ahead with his class, and his students—all from the neighborhood—made him proud.

"How do you feel?" He asked them. "No problem," they answered. "We aren't afraid." "We will try, we will try." "We'll go ahead with classes."

"Do you have the courage to stand up?"

Again came the answers. "Of course, yes." "*We don't care!*"

They would ignore the authorities and keep coming. There was no feeling quite like the warmth of collective mischief, conscripted in the service of freedom.

And now it wasn't just his family on the local list of "politically sensitive" types. Nigel had managed in the space of five minutes to add to it an additional hundred people.

But this was no laughing matter. They were facing eviction from not one but three locations. Nway hadn't managed to convince the tenants of another school in another part of town to resist the pressure of authorities. And now, Nway had recently admitted, they were about to be kicked out of their headquarters, their City of Kings, Naypyidaw.

It made him furious and Nigel was rarely furious. Nway seemed to have all the money in the world, but suddenly he was saying that he had none left. Just the other day, Nigel had spotted him in the Office, handing out a wad of cash to a young man, someone from a different network. The scene was confusing. But Nigel hadn't confronted Nway. Nway didn't even know that Nigel had seen him.

But it was vindication, to Nigel, of what he had stopped wanting to suspect: that Nway was siphoning off funds, or using them however he wished. The old rumors surfaced. Nigel knew Nway to be kind, to be generous. It wasn't fair that people were whispering that he had set up Doe Doe for her arrest. For goodness' sake, Nway was the one who had helped her find a job when she had been desperate.

But Nigel also felt that there was a grain of truth in Nway's reputation for wanting to hoard the goods, that he had liked to live in the air-conditioned rooms, and surround himself with girls. Nway didn't share; he controlled. Even Nigel's phone had been rented by him.

It was tough to trust Nway as they risked losing everything.

༄

NWAY LAY FACE DOWN, SPRAWLED on the bare floorboards of his network headquarters as the landlord's movers came to strip it.

Out went the white leather armchair.

Ten minutes passed.

They came back for the sofa. Nway hadn't moved. It was midafternoon and he couldn't move. He couldn't think. Didn't want to think. Everything was falling apart.

Sunlight streamed in from the balcony. Acca sat in a shaft of it, pressed up against a wall and watched him, smiling a little, saying nothing, just a soft, angelic presence.

The furniture didn't belong to them anyway. They could live without. The only objects they owned were the books, a full three shelves'-worth. They had amassed a mishmash of comics, three-year-old academic journals, and dog-eared translations about Nelson Mandela and Barack Obama and China. They had used a library system: two people were to sign off before anyone checked something out. They had papers too—humid piles of photocopied stories and pamphlets, boxed up already.

Where to go? They had a week left. Then the landlord would be within his rights to boot Nway back to the street. The six-month lease had elapsed. Nway had managed to extend it in March for two months. But as they approached the end of May, he had nothing left. He didn't have enough either to pay for the Palace, Nandau. His cash had clean run out.

He had resorted to phoning his eldest brother's business partner, claiming that his brother was out of commission and had given Nway instructions to take out a sum from their stock. What a dumb move. It had only been a matter of time before his brother had found out, his dear brother who had been helping him all this time. Now they were not speaking. Any day now, Nway expected him to appear and land a punch in his face.

Even Nigel had just cut him loose from his commitments to UFBAD. The group was a big, bad secret alliance comprising the underground leadership of the All Burma Federation of Student Unions, the Myanmar Development Committee, NLD youth, and whichever other serious, battle-hardened revolutionaries Nigel had connected. They had launched with a press release the previous September, on the anniversary of Saffron, in time to denounce the elections. They were tough and witty, and easy with the dangers. Come the revolution, these were the young guns to lead it. All in their twenties and thirties, they had already amassed twenty-seven years of prison between them. The Togetherness organization and its baby activists looked, by comparison, like a child's tea party.

At least, Nway told himself, Togetherness had served a different purpose. As it had grown, they had given it structure, assigning roles and dividing into committees, for teaching, finances, and information. They had lobbied and campaigned for positions and held an election. Nigel was voted leader. Paw Paw and Acca were to take charge of logistics. Nobleyan became chief of communications. Nway was elected financial chief.

It had stung not to be voted to overall leadership. He had nursed the defeat for a full minute. Then he let it go. They were moving forward. And it made sense. He had always been good at organizing the money. Everyone knew it. Partly it was because he appreciated its necessity as few others in his movement, in his culture. Money, they'd been told, was dirty. Money, they believed, was corrupting. Money, Nway understood, terrified them.

But Nway also understood that for the first time in their lives they faced the prospect of complex organizations that depended for survival and development on more than a pocketful of peanuts. Now—and only now—had come the moment for proliferation, for a full-time staff of activists, and for political ambition that had expanded beyond the walls of the Office to the size of imagination.

Even the exiles didn't understand. "We are a political organization, not a social network," one of them had shot back to Nway by Gchat after he had reached out recently for two hundred dollars, or a hundred even, to help a network member, a young woman from the provinces who had just given birth to an infant without an anus. The sum was just about the minimum she would need to cover the surgery, which was available in only two hospitals, and that didn't include additional expenses for latex gloves, cotton wool, medicine, gauze, bottles of blood, and other basics that hospital patients were required to supply for themselves. The response had been crushing.

The saddest thing, Nway felt, was that he and Nigel had always agreed on the merits: now was the time to seize the momentum, as the old government was reshuffling into the new, as the centers of power were breaking up and reconfiguring. It was a precarious moment in which anything could happen.

He couldn't blame Nigel for mistrusting him. A second-line member had reported to him that Nigel had spotted him in the Office, giving a wad of cash to someone else. The timing had been appalling. Nway had just admitted to Nigel that he had none left for the network. But he couldn't come clean, couldn't explain. He had sworn himself to silence. There was too much at stake. Nway couldn't admit to his creative partner that on Nway's shoulders alone had fallen not one but two national tasks of gravest risk.

Only the Uncles knew.

They had taken on board the full measure of Nway's secrets. And yet they weren't making life any easier for him. They didn't permit him to salvage funds for himself, for his network. There were, from the Uncles' vantage point, so many other needs.

All Nway could do was keep his head down, and his black computer case close.

And then had come news from Twantay that his mother's blood pressure had shot to critical heights. She was weakening. A friend had called to tell Nway that she wouldn't last a month.

Already, when they had first rented Naypyidaw, it had unnerved him to see her health so diminished. The realization had scrambled the fine-tuned moral arithmetic behind the financial deal his family had struck long before. Nway had pledged a life of service to the Lady; in return, his three brothers would tend the family business, help him in times of financial necessity, and take responsibility for their aging mother. To show reverence to one's parents and to care for them into their waning years were cardinal duties. It had been humbling, but he had been able to push it aside.

Now it made him cry.

He felt no pride in his choices. His philosophy of activism began from empathy. Concentric circles of it fanned outward from a core of trust between the politician and his family, expanding to include close friends, his network, and finally the population, in whose defense he purported to operate.

"When you have six hundred *kyats* and you are together with three of your friends," he had written recently in a lecture for his activists, "you each need two hundred *kyats* to take the bus home. At this point, you must be the one who has nothing. Instead of taking the bus, you walk home. It is a kind of political action because they will think you are great and that you care for them. Hence, if your community accepts as the truth that you are struggling just for their sake, they will naturally consider you . . . a moral and ethical person. And that is politics. If you achieve this, we can say that 'well, you are doing politics.' . . . You can start this within your family, because your family is your closest community."

With time and experience, he had forged a personal politics as antithesis to the coldness of bureaucracy and the negligence of his rulers. But how could he sense the pain of another, advocate on his or her behalf, document an abuse, when he felt himself incapable of acting on behalf of his most significant relationship of all: his own family? The torture, prison sentences, years denied the chance to talk with loved ones, or to fall in love at all—the palpable consequences of life as a dissident—contained within them this subtle, slow-acting toxin, the constant sense that somehow, for a futile struggle with no obvious end date, you might have become a bad Buddhist, a bad son, a bad human being.

Even Auntie had faced as poisonous a test.

Her speeches were peppered with heart, with emotion, with political aspirations as more than abstract participatory processes or the often detached, individualist exercises in power of Western democratic doctrine. For her, and, by extension, for the young men and women who had grown up steeped in a way of thinking that aligned with the messages of loving-kindness and compassion of Buddhism, the great struggle for their rights and the building of the nation thereafter was a spiritual enterprise. There was nothing abstract about it. In practice, it meant daring to make a personal journey.

But how?

The generals had attempted to be rid of Auntie by refusing to grant visas to her husband, Michael Aris, a British citizen and Oxford academic, and their two sons, even, brutally, in January 1999 when Aris learned that his prostate cancer was terminal and that it had spread to his spine and lungs. He lived in their home in England, which she had fatefully left eleven years prior, in 1988, to tend to her mother in Rangoon. After several rejected visa applications, the British Foreign Office intervened with Burmese authorities to plead on Aris's behalf. They offered to equip him with a medical airplane as a means of calming the junta's claim that he might overburden Rangoon's hospital facilities. The junta would not relent.

Auntie's telephone, monitored since 1995, began cutting out when Aris was on the line. Were she to leave Burma for a brief visit to England, the pair had long suspected that the junta would make it impossible for her to return. Already they had cancelled her sons' Burmese passports. Still more troubling, she told the British ambassador at the time, authorities would take the opportunity of her absence to round up activists and treat them with greater abandon then was their habitual wont.

Aris had died early on the morning of March 27, 1999, half a globe from Rangoon. It had been less than three months since his diagnosis. The couple's final reunion had lasted two weeks, in 1996. Theirs had been a love that, as one eulogy put it, "tyranny could not crush." The strength of their twenty-seven-year bond had famously hinged on an understanding that the daughter of

General Aung San might one day be called upon to take up the project that he had never been allowed to complete. That in the end she had been true to that impulse, that in the face of personal tragedy she had chosen her country, had proven the ultimate sacrifice. In the eyes of her supporters it had only brightened her star.

Some—government loyalists, the local state mouthpiece, even an early foreign biographer—had vilified her as unloving.

But Nway knew better. Not long after Aris's passing, on overnight security duty in her compound, Nway had watched her emerge from her room, walk with a fixed expression down the corridor, and dissolve to her knees before a wooden board marked in chalk with her husband's name. She covered her face with her hands and wept, great heaving sobs that rocked her back and forth.

There could be no other scene, only the long, private thought of a woman who shouldered the hopes of her people. Moments later, she had wiped her eyes, risen—and caught Nway's gaze. The next day her mask of serene composure had returned intact. To the outside world, her personal loss had to be nothing.

But he hardly considered himself a grain of rice on Auntie.

He made plans for a secret visit to Twantay to see his mother.

But it was no use. It didn't matter that his mother had asked him to do this, that he was, in some visceral sense, honoring the memory of his father. He had made his choice. He wasn't able to live with his family. He was selfish.

∼≫∽

THE FINAL GATHERING OF TOGETHERNESS—before the network splintered—was meant to have been a meeting to decide who would take an internship in the Czech Republic.

They splintered because of miscommunication, because of mistrust and pretty girls, but really, in the end, because of money.

The issue bit them all, but it bit Nway worst, because of his ease with it and of the largesse he could display with shows of it. His reputation for love of money had trailed him since childhood, since he had filched cash from his parents and run off with it to treat half the town.

From the naked floorboards of his stripped apartment, three days shy of eviction, Nway stood to lobby hard for Paw Paw. On the merits of her dedication and the intelligence of her brief stumping, she had earned her place as the clear favorite for the internship in Prague.

Zin Zin stood next to speak.

"You aren't neutral," she declared. Then she accused Nway of a love affair—with Nobelle, Paw Paw, Acca, and Snow.

It was ridiculous. They were like sisters. And for the women, it was shameful.

There was an awkward silence, then fits of tears. Then people left.

There was nothing more to say.

Perhaps he should have come clean to Nigel. Zin Zin had been closer to Nigel.

The truth was, Nway had never been able to rely on his family alone. His brothers had their own families to care for. The family fish ponds only brought in so much. They never had enough. For months, Nway had been scrambling to make his payments. In the interests of a larger cause, he had long since learned to swallow back the shame that came of taking people's donations.

And so Nigel never knew, because Nway never revealed it, that his sometime sisters—Acca, Snow, and Paw Paw—were not his lovers, nor even his disciples, but his creditors.

And there was something more.

Nway would have liked to tell all, to be transparent and held accountable for it in the way that nonprofit workers divulged all to their donors, or businessmen to their shareholders. He would have liked for Togetherness to be a model for the open, democratic ideals that were its goal. But it wasn't yet the time. Nway wasn't even sure he knew how. Conditions in the country meant that revealing all, even to Nigel, was still too dangerous.

And this was why:

Some weeks before, Nway had been asked first by Grandpa, and then, unbeknownst to Grandpa, by Auntie, to be the conduit for funds that each of them had been separately offered from abroad: Grandpa from an exile group; Auntie from the aid wing of a foreign country.

Contemplation of such a possibility would in the past have felled them in an instant. But the NLD had, on May 6, 2010, been legally dissolved. Neither Grandpa nor Auntie was part of a legal entity, a recognized political party. They had every right now to justify taking in money as individuals.

But the technicalities didn't make the act of receiving funds from abroad less deathly risky, less clandestine, or less demanding of absolute trust in whomever they picked to receive it. Still active, and still actively enforced, were the trove of laws that had always been used to suppress dissent.

Nway had been sworn to secrecy. He couldn't tell Nigel. He couldn't tell anyone.

He had found a way. After collecting the money, he held it in his black computer case, then dispatched it back to Twantay to a secret member of his extended clan: someone who never surfaced, never showed her nose to authorities.

The Uncles knew, and signed off on the use and dispersion of every last bill.

Nway had pleaded with them to spare a few hundred dollars for Togetherness, and for Nigel's UFBAD. He pleaded for enough for a month's worth of rent. It was in the interests of the NLD that its new "secret youth network" expand into something greater, the research wing that the party had never had. Grandpa had seen the importance of a diffuse social movement as soon as the NLD had contemplated its dissolution. With Togetherness, Nway argued, they had been nurturing the future.

But there were so many other groups now. Uncle Han Thar Myint and Nyan Win would not play favorites. One afternoon at the Office, they had instructed Nway to hand off an amount to another young man, from another underground network. It was that handoff that Nigel had seen, hours after Nway had admitted to him that there was nothing left for their network. It was that handoff, just as they faced eviction from two schools and their headquarters, that Nigel had wholly misconstrued.

Yet Nway could admit none of it when Zin Zin had, minutes into their final meeting, thrown a hammer into everything.

8

THE ROAD TO NAYPYIDAW

MARCH 4, 2012

AT ABOUT 11 P.M. IN A BARREN HOSPITAL, on the far edge of a barely inhabited metropolis of monumental architecture and half-built mansions encased in bamboo scaffolding, a young parliamentary candidate wiped the blood from his palms onto his jeans and slammed toward the exit of a hospital.

"This," declared Naing Ngan Lin, aka Bright Country, aka *Nigel*, slum kid turned street hawker turned dissident turned politician running for a seat in parliament, "is the *real* problem of our country."

Arms akimbo, a forelock of thick hair falling out of his coconut-oiled parting, he narrowed his gaze and cast it across the dereliction. The junta had touted Naypyidaw as a vision of the future. Into the city it had poured millions of dollars from the windfall of sales of gas and oil, teak, jade, and rubies. And yet here in its hospital there was no running water, no soap, no doctor—and two patients, bleeding and unconscious on gurneys. They had been delivered from Nigel's pickup truck after he and his campaign team discovered them forty minutes earlier by the side of an unlit eight-lane highway, in a mangle of shouting bystanders and smashed motorcycle parts.

Nway darted toward Nigel from the patients and three nurses in white headdresses who stood listless between their gurneys.

"All they wanted is the addresses," said Nway of the nurses.

He scratched his head. Even in a country as befuddled with rules, this was absurd.

The NLD team stormed the lobby, searching for a doctor. Nway shot back to the nurses, who had roused to attention with all the urgency of late-night bar-flies when the pickup had rolled in with the two casualties. To them, he gently suggested that instead of inquiring about the names and addresses of the acci-dent victims and the NLD people who had rescued them in lieu of ambulances, or instead of staring blankly at the patients, they probably ought to think of performing a basic airway-breathing-cardio check and running their hands over the bodies to rule out serious injury. Half a year of medical school and a long lost childhood in his father's clinic, and he still knew more than the nurses.

After thirteen years in opposition politics, three of them underground, Nway might have thought that he had seen it all. He and Nigel both had made it their vocation to break through the cowed and uncritical mindset of their society. But each fresh encounter with it and the countrywide indigence it helped per-petuate still managed to astound. Nothing, it seemed to them, had changed—even now, in the midst of a cascade of reforms that had in the previous eight months appeared to crack apart some new measure of political space. The world had largely lauded the changes as signs of transition from authoritarian rule. At home, they didn't so much suggest the end of the beginning or even the begin-ning of the end. "We are at the beginning of the beginning," Nway was telling the foreign journalists who were openly pouring into the Office for the first time since a brief window before the elections of 1990. The thought echoed consen-sus among dissidents that the sudden loosening of state controls, for being so precarious, came only with greater urgency to push as they had never been able to push before.

At the site of the motorcycle accident, miles from the ecstatically overlit roundabouts of Naypyidaw proper, on a stretch of road whose edges had al-ready returned to scrubland, the pickup's headlights had carved about thirty on-lookers out of the night. They were yelling, talking over each other, walking in circles. Nigel had heard them out, one by one, and consulted with his men. Nway marched straight through the dillydally, past scattered metal and pools of blood, to the two unconscious motorcyclists and a police officer who was cran-ing over them with a flashlight, insisting into its shafts that the bodies cough up the details of their identity cards.

"I work for Naing Ngan Lin, and he is the NLD candidate for this constit-uency. We are taking these injured people to the nearest hospital. If you have a problem with that, phone him," Nway said, thrusting his cell phone, lit up with Nigel's number, in front of the policeman's nose.

To be clear, Nway worked with, not for, his old friend. Technically, he even worked above him, troubleshooting and coordinating the national campaign strategy for all forty-eight NLD candidates who were contesting for as many available seats in a parliamentary by-election on April 1.

The by-elections, for less than ten percent of the total seats, were the first the NLD had contested since 1990. Nigel was vying for votes in one of four constituencies on no less than the generals' turf: ersatz metropolis in the style of neo-Fascist meets Home Depot, with mirror-windowed ministries hulking over empty eight-lane highways, garlanded in three rows of lights (lamp poles, fairy, and threads of neon), all built atop North Korean–designed bunkers. One of Nway's contacts had told him as much, and reporters had confirmed it with photographs and documents from military deserters.

Auntie herself was running in Kawhmu, a network of bamboo-and-thatch hamlets in the Irrawaddy Delta, an hour's drive southwest of Twantay. Days before she had settled on the constituency as her locus operandi. Nway had mapped it out for her by motorbike to gauge political awareness among its villagers (feeble to nil) and basic logistical accessibility (nil to disastrous).

But he wouldn't pull the Aung San Suu Kyi card with the police officer. Deferring to the local candidate, not the Lady, would be less painful for the agent of the state, and better for Nigel's nascent political reputation. Nway had long since learned to calibrate his story to each new circumstance. Ego mattered less in this instance than simply saving two innocents from quick death at the hands of a bureaucrat. This was why they were fighting. This was why they had made the sacrifices: dropped out of university, given up on love, revoked chances of ever earning a regular paycheck. "*This*," as Nway had put it a few nights earlier to Minus's raging music *saya*, ending an argument with a flourish, "*this* is our struggle."

As the pickup had careened down the highway toward the hospital, Nway conscripted Nigel and the team piled around the casualties to shout through their comas that they were okay, they were in good hands now, they'd make it through. One was a solid young woman, to all appearances a scion of Burma's narrow middle class. The other was likely a day laborer from masses too poor for meat more than once or thrice a moon. He had alcohol on his breath, bones for hips, and torso and limbs, beneath the tattered shirt and blackened sarong, as brittle as eggshell.

In the hospital, a scrum formed around the cell phones as the NLD team—a crew of local activists who had collected around Nigel in past weeks—traded contacts, phoned other NLD members in three neighboring constituencies, and worked the lines to get through to a doctor, any doctor, pronto.

A fourth nurse, older, with a sour matron's expression that seemed to suggest that disturbances of this kind at nighttime at a hospital were not approved by local authorities, stood behind a reception desk and methodically tapped her ledger with a wooden ruler. "Name? Address?" she called out, as NLD team members blitzed past.

From the middle of several rows of plastic chairs that functioned as a waiting room, a child with cheeks dotted in bright *thanaka* watched transfixed, swinging his legs beneath his chair, a spoonful of rice hovering between his tiffin box and his gaping mouth.

It was pushing toward midnight. Just under a month remained until the April 1 by-elections. Nway had a red-eye bus to catch for a crack of dawn meeting with Uncle Nyan Win, now the NLD campaign manager, in party headquarters 250 miles due south in Rangoon, mildewing on the Andaman Sea. Nigel had a final check on a stage that his team had been building against the clock in the middle of a parched field for a much-anticipated campaign stop the next morning by Auntie. Perhaps somewhere between, they could all think of dinner. The day had begun at sunrise for Nigel; at 7 p.m. the previous night for Nway.

But no one was leaving until a doctor showed up.

⋰⋱

NIGEL HAD BEEN THE FIRST OF the candidates after Aung San Suu Kyi herself that she and party elders had picked to represent them in the April by-elections. Now thirty-four, he was the second youngest. He was respected, passionate, and, as friends, colleagues, and family members unanimously declared him, "honest."

It was his own fault, Nway told himself. He could have been a candidate, too. The last time he'd seen Grandpa T, the former general and NLD vice-chairman had pointed at him and joked: "Hey. You married yet?" It was his standard opening to the young, decidedly unmarried Nway. Then Grandpa T had pulled Nway aside and told him he should run in the real decider: the nationwide elections in 2015, when all the seats would be up for grabs.

But back when Auntie had summoned Nway and Nigel, only Nigel had stepped forward. Nway had asked explicitly that he remain in the shadows. For one thing, he preferred backdoor strategizing. For another, he couldn't bear the thought of having to wear a *pinni* jacket.

The pair of them might have formed the perfect radical. But their destinies had at some point to diverge. It was the nature of impermanence. And Nway still had Minus.

⚜

TWO DAYS BEFORE THE ELECTIONS, a reporter asked Aung San Suu Kyi to rate Burma's progress toward democracy on a scale of one to ten.

"We are trying to get to one," she answered. She spoke at a press conference on the grounds of her lakeside villa, a deceptively elegant exemplar of colonial-era Art Deco in peeling grey paint. There was a time when the lawn, now manicured and rimmed in an explosion of tropical flowers, was a wilderness of unkempt, hip-high grasses. There was a time when, cut off from postal deliveries, she had so little cash for food that she began to sell off the furniture—museum pieces in their own right if only for their association with her family. But the challenge today was entirely less tragically purgative. For nearly two hours, until she almost collapsed with the heat exhaustion that had nagged her as she zigzagged the country on her campaign tour, Auntie stood under a blistering midsummer sun, firing back witticisms and shrewdly diplomatic rejoinders to an unprecedented gathering at 54 University Avenue of reporters, diplomats, and international election observers.

The press conference was a marker, already, of a certain kind of triumph. Twenty-three years since the NLD won its landslide victory, it had again scored a historic coup. Through sheer participation, it had succeeded in turning a legal technicality in a constitution whose legitimacy it did not recognize into the most significant and well-watched act of political theater in Southeast Asia's recent history. The government had eased up for the occasion on visas to foreign journalists and hundreds had poured in for front-row seats, or simply an undiminished view of the fine-boned icon. Would the parliamentary by-elections of April 1, 2012 prove free and fair? Would an enigmatic military-civilian hybrid government that had in the final weeks of 2011 and early 2012 wowed the world with its fast-paced reforms readily concede even a few seats to the popular might of a party it had brutally repressed since 1990? Only seventeen months shy of her latest stint of house arrest, would it really deliver a perch in government to the *Lady*? The prospect quavered as an ending to Burma's shame if not exactly worthy of Hollywood's most bittersweet, then at least of a velvet transition last seen under the guidance of Auntie's spiritual forebear, Vaclav Havel.

But the NLD's greater achievement, even before voting day, was a double whammy: exciting the passions of a people long since inured to politics. It also began transforming itself from the rigidly hierarchical fossil it had become in the previous two decades into the byword for democratic government that it had always promised to be.

By late March 2012, to be cool in Burma was to join the party with a rap song theme tune set to a colonial-era revolutionary poem, "Wake Up, Myanmar!" To be cool was to support the party whose offices were tucked into private bamboo-and-thatch homes, down mud lanes lined in banana trees, in villages devoid of running water and electricity. To be cool now was to tie across your forehead, ninja-style, a strip of cloth with the sign of the NLD—the fighting peacock flaming gold against a scarlet backdrop—that only months before had belonged to the underground students and come most often with a one-way ticket to prison.

By late March 2012, too, a new generation of dissidents had bubbled to the surface, a toxic alliance of activists who had honed their skills in exile, in jail, or underground. Ragged, informal networks of activists could operate now in the light of day, and the infusion of visibility and relative legality had intensified and accelerated their ambitions.

꧁

IN THE LITANY OF NATIONAL POWER reshufflings, this one offered slim pickings. "This is our test, for the 2015 elections," said Nway's boss, Uncle Nyan Win, meaty and freckled and always sharp with a legal rejoinder. After long stints as NLD spokesman, then Auntie's mouthpiece during her final months of house arrest, he had recently become the party's chief campaign manager. "We need experience under this commission law. There are many limitations and we are trying to, practically to know about this. Practically, we want to know."

Limitations and irregularities ahead of April 1 had become U Nyan Win's bread and butter. There were problems with the voter lists, candidate disqualifications, and venues for rallies denied, blocked outright, or relegated to the middle of remote fields. There were defacements of posters and localized smear campaigns, including an old stalwart accusing Auntie of whoring it with a foreigner—her late British husband—and predictable bribes to entire villages of electricity and paved roads. There were even sporadic threats of eviction or arrest if one or other citizen refused to vote for the military-backed Union Solidarity and Development Party, the USDP.

U Nyan Win, who had fought almost singlehandedly to salvage the party's legal standing after its forced dissolution on May 6, 2010, had just the right credentials for the current battle—an improvised, legal push-and-pull between the government and the opposition, in which the government would concede just enough to the NLD to be seen abroad as conducting a fair election. The NLD, preternaturally sensitive to foul play and just as aware that the lifting of Burma's pariah status depended on how it fared, would fight back at every turn.

Only 48 seats out of 659 were in contest as parliamentary representatives moved to other appointments in the government, vacating seats that they had held since general elections in 2010. The NLD's decision to compete, and to register anew as a political party, had come only after evidence of concrete reform.

Not long after the cobbling together of the first parliament in decades, the changes had begun. By the parliament's second sitting in August 2011, an artifice of awkward legislative procedure had yielded to genuine draft legislation on a raft of national injustices and problems. Reforms treated, *inter alia*, the right to form labor unions, the nefarious consequences of having six national exchange rates, and the 2010 electoral laws that had deliberately excluded anyone with a criminal conviction, which had meant Aung San Suu Kyi and all other political prisoners.

The handful of parliamentarians who had won seats from Khin Maung Swe's breakaway National Democratic Force introduced draft after draft, including a vitally relevant land reform bill, and found that they were taken seriously. They began to develop a sophisticated plan for the complex woes of the country's economy.

And then came the hat trick. On the heels of swelling popular opposition that had simmered for years on the fringes of the war with the Kachin and that had built to crescendo in the blood-soaked lyrics of a national poet and under the weighty pen of Auntie, President Thein Sein had unilaterally suspended a $3.6 billion, Chinese-backed hydropower project that would have destroyed the source of the mighty Irrawaddy River above Myitkina, near the Chinese border. He had followed within weeks with a landmark ceasefire hastily signed with the Karen National Union, pausing the oldest and most intractable of Burma's ethnic minority insurgencies. A day later, on January 13, he finally sprang hundreds of prominent dissidents. Never before had Aung San Suu Kyi roamed free alongside the ringleaders of uprisings in 1996, 1998, 2007, and, most potently, of 1988. Released at last were Min Ko Naing, the Conqueror of Kings; Ko Ko Gyi the strategist; Htay Kway; Jimmy; and the remaining core of the Big Brothers, the '88 Generations Student Group who had almost as great a hold as Auntie on people's hearts.

The clincher for the NLD had been a private meeting between Thein Sein and Aung San Suu Kyi. Both declared the encounter substantive, and Aung San Suu Kyi told her deputies—Grandpa T, Han Thar Myint, Nyan Win—that she had faith in the president's sincerity. Partly to endorse the reforms and partly to take advantage of the new political space, she would lead the party back into the parliamentary process. Even with less than a tenth of the seats, even if victory for the NLD could see her enter a parliamentary gilded cage in which her popular power would be drowned out in a quicksand of severe constitutional constraints, the terms of the democracy struggle in Burma had irredeemably changed. A twenty-three-year face-off between a military government and the party would return to the realm of law. Now they would fight from inside the system.

Thus did a meager seven percent stake in the parliaments allow the country, at last, a collective exhalation.

One demurred. Grandpa, Win Tin, argued that the party was too weak, crippled by the years of repression. If people were suddenly unafraid to attend its rallies by the thousands, putt-putting to remote sites aboard tractors or hanging by a limb off the packed roofs and backs of trucks, it was only to catch a glimpse of Auntie. True, they were "voting with their feet." But the long-term gains would be few. With typical modesty that didn't fit with the evidence, Grandpa argued that they certainly weren't coming for him. So many were the visitors to his home in Yankin that they were double-and triple-booked. He had yet to slow down, even as he relied on a cane and hobbled between surgical procedures on his hip and heart.

In the end, he had relented, yielding once more to the power of Auntie's persuasion. At almost sixty-seven, he'd calculated, she couldn't have many more years of politics ahead of her. If she won her seat fair and square, she might even have a hint of a chance at the presidency in the general elections in 2015. That would of course require an unlikely amendment to the 2008 constitution—clause 59(f) had been written as if to deliberately stymie Aung San Suu Kyi's prospects. It denied the presidency to anyone with a spouse or offspring who owed allegiance to another country. Both her late husband and two sons were British citizens.

Meantime, the by-elections of April 1 allowed the aging NLD leadership to make room for a new generation.

⌘

NWAY HAD ARRIVED IN NAYPYIDAW from Rangoon at 3:30 on the morning of March 4. He came with nothing more than the clothes on his back and his black computer case, which he touched reflexively throughout the seven-hour journey.

Inside was a speech that Auntie was due to deliver within days in a historic turn on Myanmar Television. Coming from the leader whose ability to articulate the people's hopes had for over two decades presented the greatest threat to military rule, a woman whose every gesture since her release from her third stint of house arrest in 2010 had conjured awed attention from the masses and much of the world beyond, the pages in his briefcase might as well have been spun gold. He had typed them up from her notes, then hopped an overnight bus to hand a hardcopy that morning to the Union Election Commission, an appointed panel of ex-officers, academics, and senior civil servants. Their pronouncements on all matters electoral had in past weeks become the barometer with which people gauged the government's sincerity.

To Nway fell the task of pleading her case should the members of the commission quibble, then returning to Rangoon with the censored version. He had been told it would be a matter of an hour or two. Small surprise that the commission deferred immediate approval. Defer and deflect: this was their new strategy.

Someone would be poring over every word of the speech, someone higher even than the commission's chairman, a retired lieutenant general who was on the sanctions list of Western governments and who compulsively rolled four fat gold rings with green and red gems the size of his knuckles. Even the most optimistic of outside analysts were wary of describing the body he oversaw as independent. After politely insisting that no, he could not wait three days in Naypyidaw for the commission's response, Nway had spent the rest of the day with Nigel in the back of the campaign pickup, working his cell phone, fielding complaints of electoral irregularities and obstructions from across the country, planning election-monitoring trainings, and updating U Nyan Win, who was back at headquarters in Rangoon.

The pickup, its driver pumped up on betel nut juice, sped down Naypyidaw's highways from one of Nigel's pit stops to the next, mostly bamboo-and-thatch hamlets rising in tufts of coconut and palm trees between vast tracts of unfinished villas.

⤜⤛

THAT DAWN, NIGEL HAD THROWN A PAN of well water over his face and carefully parted his hair. Then he planted a kiss on the cheek of his squirming two-year-old son, squeezed Khine Sandar Win's thin shoulders, and sped off from his local campaign headquarters. His wife had yet to find her role again. It was a matter of time. For now, she was his most dependably irreverent sounding board.

That day, March 4, it wasn't yet time for campaigning door-to-door, delivering speeches, or taking tea, cross-legged, in the huts of his constituents. It wasn't yet the moment for reinventing the wheel, improvising, and landing on a campaign strategy rooted less in deep erudition than on the freewheeling, participatory tactics that he and Nway had come of age honing and perfecting in their various networks. Today he had only to prepare for Auntie's visit.

He didn't need her endorsement, Nigel insisted to Nway in the pickup between campaign pit stops. He almost didn't want it. "This time, in my opinion, is an opportunity for the youth leaders." In his head, he toyed with tweaking his stump speech to ask farmers if, given the choice, they would honestly buy an old cow. When it was suggested to him that this might sound disrespectful, he laughed. "I respect the elders but I don't do what they say when they make mistakes. I am not a slave to tradition. I always tell them: you have to respect the elders, but you should do what you want, you should have your belief. I have my belief."

Nigel dashed to an Internet café; to a print shop pumping out a giant campaign poster depicting the young candidate smiling over the shoulder of a beaming Grandpa, Win Tin. Then he was onto the middle of a field where his team was hammering and sawing together a stage as music blared from a megaphone that someone had positioned in the branches of a giant tamarind tree.

He took a call from a monk who offered information that a sympathizer of Nigel's opponent from the USDP was planning an arson attack as a diversion from Auntie's impending visit. The conspirator had allegedly hatched the idea in the monk's monastery, out of a myopic miscalculation of the monks' likely sympathies or some latter-day confidence in his fear-mongered silence. Nigel took the information and gleefully phoned it in to local Burmese law enforcement, with a chuckle and a twinkle-eyed appreciation for the palpable irony of a dissident suddenly employing the services of the very intelligence apparatus whose agents had only weeks before monitored him from teashops or on buses on his daily commute between his home in Dawbon and his subversive political classes.

Back he stopped at his headquarters to pick up some campaign pamphlets. Finally, he headed down a banana-tree-lined path in one of his constituency's villages. Children kicked up dust as they chased past goats and chickens. Leaves hung limp in the midafternoon swelter. The only sign of something afoot were the motorcycles stuck with NLD flags parked outside a bamboo house held up by slender stilts. As Nway chucked a clementine at a scrawny village boy then stretched out in the pickup to snooze off the effects of the previous night's red-eye, Nigel and eight members of his team powwowed for an hour under the house in the cool shade of a mud-floored room.

An old man, withered as a walnut, dozed in a bamboo chair. An old woman chuckled softly as she stirred a pot of curry bubbling over burning coals. The team had less than twenty-four hours to compile lists of eligible voters from twenty-seven villages and present them to the Election Commission or face consequences from accepting the flawed version that the government had compiled in 2010. The mistakes, as they pored through a thick mound of papers, were legion: here were people who didn't actually exist, there were people who weren't registered, those had moved to another constituency, these had died a few years back, and that batch were migrant laborers whose home was somewhere else entirely.

Off sped the motorcycles. A family of chickens scattered.

⤙⚬⤚

NIGEL'S CAMPAIGN HEADQUARTERS WAS A two-story concrete shell, with an outhouse and a well, which a local purveyor of bottled fizzy drinks and other dust-covered trinkets had donated for the space of the campaign. It hunkered among a neighborhood grid of huts and shacks patched together from bamboo, corrugated iron, and concrete. Its signpost, giant and red, faced out over the road to the construction site of a mansion belonging to no less than arguably the most powerful man in the country—General Maung Aye, the former SPDC's No. 2 and still the commander-in-chief of the Tatmadaw.

The brick-and-mortar face-off could have been a symbol for the country's current juncture: the NLD, party of the people, poor as their fly-infested out-houses, rising once more to challenge the entrenched might and facile wealth of senior military officers whose monopoly on all aspects of power had for five decades ensured Burma's ranking among the poorest, most corrupt, and most repressive countries in the world.

By now, the NLD required not much more. Time and the harshness of circumstance had denuded the party to little else than an idea. Its light, a still-burning hope, emitted from the very refuse of the poverty it was fighting to overturn. "We were not in the business of merely replacing one government with another, which could be considered the job of an opposition party," Auntie had recently written. "Nor were we simply agitating for particular changes in the system as activists might be expected to do. We were working and living for a cause that was the sum of our aspirations for our people, which were not, after all, so very different from the aspirations of peoples elsewhere."

In those days, dissidence in Burma had become what Vaclav Havel had once described as "the experience of life at the very ramparts of dehumanized power." Auntie's popularity transcended the NLD, and the NLD had never been more than one arm of a diffuse and ragged coalition of pro-democracy ac-tivists, whose membranes were prison walls, national borders, and, eventually, the Internet.

When time came in December 2011 to register anew and present credentials to the Union Election Commission, the NLD jettisoned its old sign, a farmer's bamboo hat. In any case, there had been a kerfuffle with Khin Maung Swe's National Democratic Force, which had adopted a similar symbol. Accused, again, of treachery, the genial former scientist had pointed out that actually, the farmer's hat had been his idea in 1990, and it had been a strong choice, because the country was still seventy-five percent rural. The hat was an easy sign for people to see when candidates campaigned in the paddies and hills. He defied any party member of the time to prove him otherwise. For that reason, the NLD had taken up the fighting peacock, the old sign of the All Burma Federation of Student Unions.

~⚜~

ON MARCH 5, A HAZE OF COAL DUST hung over the evening rally. The red orb of the sun dissolved through the soot into a crenellated landscape of rising concrete. Laborers covered in white dust trucked down the vast highway, past a fenced-in slum of flimsy straw huts in a grid of alleyways all hung with laundry. Beside a teashop where business this evening was booming, young men in white T-shirts bearing the green lion logo of the USDP—the military's party—played football, indifferent or feigning indifference to the onslaught of trucks and hundreds of motorcycles pouring toward them, each bearing the red of the National League for Democracy—red flags, red logo, red stickers. Foreheads were bandanaed, faces stuck with stickers, open-backed trucks and SUVs bedecked in vast, fierce laminated signs. Over the arid immensity of Naypyidaw the flag of the National League for Democracy on this day flew proud. With Aung San Suu Kyi in town, the NLD was suddenly the party to beat.

The crowds here, at the evening rally, were fewer than the hundreds who had danced and jiggled to the beat of NLD songs in the field where she had come to endorse Nigel that afternoon. Viewers in Nigel's constituency had waited for hours for Auntie to appear in her convoy. They squatted under parasols or squinted back at the sun from ruts of hay-strewn cracked earth, as close to the stage as they could manage. NLD volunteers dispensed little paper NLD flags. Impromptu restaurants and fruit stalls sprang up. At one table, a sun-leathered farmer leaned over a mug of fresh-ground sugarcane juice and waxed lyrical about the marriage of Auntie's father and mother. Trucks piled thick with supporters, dancing, singing, and clapping, had pulled up from Rangoon, from Twantay, from hundreds of miles across the country, zigzagging in tow to her convoy as she ricocheted from one constituency to the next. They came, and came again, because:

"I remember 1990."

"The speech never gets old, never."

"We want democracy."

Onto the stage that Nigel's supporters had built through the night, her team had pulled her up, arms first, caging her in for protection from hundreds of grasping hands that would willingly have lifted her to the sky.

"May Suu! May Suu! May Suu!"

Auntie, a fusillade of white roses in her hair, began hoarse, her voice overworked from her punishing countrywide schedule of public engagements. But seconds in, after she had cracked her first broad smile, her voice honeyed and she mellowed into a relaxed camaraderie with her massive audience, as if each among them were an old friend. Beside her stood Nigel, wearing his traditional *pinni*, solemnly nodding to salient points in her speech, the picture of a young man playing by the rules in an old man's game. She slapped his shoulder, and the crowds clapped; she tweaked her stump speech to talk of the land seizures that affected his constituents, and they roared.

It was all over in less than half an hour, and as Auntie, Nigel, party elders, and the three other Naypyidaw candidates drove back across the field from the stage, they stood through the roofs of their SUVs, high-fiving rapturous bystanders, shaking fists with a promise of victory, or bowing to be draped in garlands of flowers.

On drove the convoy to the evening rally for Sandar Min, the NLD candidate in a neighboring district of Naypyidaw. In the heart of the military's administration, down the road from a gem emporium that had stocked the hotels with Chinese businessmen trading jade and rubies, the NLD's supporters and a few random bystanders coughed back the coal dust to listen, mesmerized. A sinewy day-laborer watched from behind a tamarind tree, a hammer and cloth sack slung over his shoulder, staring at the stage a few hundred feet away, frozen in mid-stride. And there she was, the Mother: a distant blur in green silk on a red-decked stage, the singsong of her voice buoyed by sporadic cheers.

No one—not even the Uncles—expected victory from all of the relative newbies running for the NLD in four constituencies in the new capital, Naypyidaw. There was Nigel, green as an unripe mango; Sandar Min, a strong-willed forty-four-year-old entrepreneur with more university degrees than Nway and Nigel combined, and a track record of student activism that had landed her in prison twice after 1988. Min Thu too had been an '88 student and a political prisoner, released on January 13, and the only candidate in all the country to face a slingshot attack, which had briefly felled a young member of his security detail. Least favorable, at least in Nway and Nigel's informal polling, was Zayar Thaw, the party's youngest candidate at thirty-one and a nationally celebrated rapper and musician, whose notoriety had turned political when he cofounded the fist-branded dissident youth group, Generation Wave. For that, he too had eventually landed in jail.

Even in their scarcity, the forty-eight constituencies measured the country's spectacular geological variety, the breadth of its multifaceted emergencies, and the extent of recent changes. They crisscrossed the Burman-majority stronghold of the great central plain and climbed to the foothills of the Himalayas near China, where fighting between the Burmese army and armed insurgents from the Kachin people had, according to the United Nations, displaced fifty-five thousand people since June 2011. They plunged into the southern dagger of land that bordered

Thailand to the east and, to the west, the Andaman Sea, highlighting an environ-mentally controversial Italian-Thai venture to build a multibillion-dollar deep-sea port near an industrial "Special Economic Zone." To reach a constituency just off the coast, in the mangrove-and coral-dense Myeik Archipelago, local authorities refused to lend Aung San Suu Kyi a speedboat; the slow fisherman's vessel that took her to and from the islands ran aground. Marooned for hours in the relentless tropical sun, she had fallen ferociously sick.

Support in other constituencies seemed given in advance. The HIV/AIDs activist, Phyu Phyu Thin, was running a campaign in Mingalar Taunt Nyunt, a neighborhood of Rangoon. Rowdy, spiced with the scent of cumin and the sound of Friday chanting from its mosques, it highlighted the plight of the country's sidelined Muslims, and, by extension, the other religious minorities who had been denied the rights enjoyed by Buddhists. In constituencies near Thailand or in the parched mainland that the British had dubbed Upper Burma before invading it, anti-government sentiment proved so strong, and crowds so thick, that a twenty-minute journey from the airport to Mandalay took Aung San Suu Kyi's convoy a full six hours.

Dr. Z was running a hefty campaign in Kyauk Padaung, a few hours' drive from Amarapura, his hometown. In nearby Pakokku, where the Saffron Revolution had been triggered, it seemed to play out all over again. The NLD candidate, U Pike Co, confronted a local official, now with the USDP, whom he called responsible for the fateful decision in September 2007 to tie a monk to a pole and beat him. Pike Co had been among the local lay leadership whose participation had quickly turned the protest political.

But Naypyidaw had another problem altogether.

Nigel's self-appointed driver who sped down the highways chewing betel nuts had proved less a chauffeur than Nigel's wingman. A former shipman with crabapple cheeks, Thant had been among the vanguard of local residents who had latched fastest to the party's young candidate from Rangoon. His loyalty stuck even after his wife decided they should separate for the next month or two, to protect herself and their children, at least until the campaign was over and Special Branch had had its chance to sweep through.

Dissipating such anxieties had been among the major obstacles for the NLD across the country as it sought to build back its base. If Sandar Min's rally drew smaller crowds than Nigel's, her parcel of the city, like Min Thu and Zayar Thaw's, was dominated by government bureaucrats whose already shaky likeli-hood to vote their conscience was doubly thwarted by close proximity to senior officers. Many quietly pledged their support to the NLD candidate, but they would have more trouble showing it openly, afflicted by rumors of harassment or arrest if they refused to cast their ballot for the USDP.

Nigel's constituents, whom he estimated at 16,900, were largely drawn from rural stock, which didn't necessarily diminish the challenge. When he had first arrived, people hadn't liked him. He was not famous, not a former political prisoner. He could see it on their faces. In eight weeks of campaigning, he had not once made it to any of the city's monuments—the giant water park, the towering Uppatasanti pagoda plastered in cheap jade, the massive People's Assembly fronted by gargantuan bronzes of three ancient warrior kings. It was partly out of contempt, but mainly because he had busied himself with meeting, greeting, and listening.

Thant sped him from one village to another. Many complained of having lost their farmland to big companies, typically owned by officers and their handful of notorious business associates. Most had fallen into migrant labor. The work was erratic, often physically risky, and paid barely enough to afford more than a plate of the cheapest rice, without curry. Some had been so traumatized by the loss of their livelihoods that they went mad. The depression was often so severe that they would shut down, or lock themselves up for days, or drug themselves into the afterlife. It was possible that the brittle man with alcohol on his breath whom Nigel and Nway had rescued unconscious from the accident site had faced just such a fate.

In previous weeks, NLD offices had sprung up anew in private homes in villages and towns across the country. Fear, depending on the place, had evaporated. Even the drunks of Rangoon knew they could chase away policemen if they threatened membership in the party that was again taking the country by storm.

Nway and the campaign team found themselves dashing between rival groups, attempting to defuse tensions as old-timers competed for prominence with new members, and both groups vied with an insurgent third: activists who had for months or years operated underground. In Twantay, the upstarts had set up shop just opposite the dilapidated storefront of the veterans, sticking it bluntly to what they perceived as twenty years of inaction. Incompetents! Opportunists! Lily-livered double agents! Against each group stood accusations and acrimony. The first had let the party die, the second were fair-weather activists. As for the third—if they were so adept at secrecy, who was to say they weren't playing for the other team?

In the critically decisive Kawhmu, where Auntie herself was running, Nway pretended to defer to the authority of a former NLD security man who seemed particularly taken with his past service, then schemed with a lawyer who, he deciphered, had better contacts, and greater willingness to think beyond the past to educate the population ahead of voting day.

Auntie, tasked with intervening in instances of particular recalcitrance, proved rather more Solomonic. To each their right to join the party, she had said. For now, they needed red-meat followers. They could deal with structural issues later, if and when they made it into government.

Nigel played the rivalries off each other. In Naypyidaw, to get anywhere at all, you needed wheels, which meant you needed fuel beyond the weekly rations, which meant you needed money, and plenty of it. Two camps from separate wards happened to compete over which would earn the right to open the official NLD office. Each group conveniently included several wealthy members who plied the candidate with services in an ever-intensifying race. Nigel, his wife and their son, whose material possessions barely filled a trunk, could rely on the generosity of Naypyidaw's rival NLD activists to meet all their needs.

The breakdown in party tradition was proving a boon. Candidates began to depend less on Auntie's aura, and in its place, improvised. Phyu Phyu Thin's team, in Mingalar Taunt Nyunt, unleashed head-bangers into a busy street market for an impromptu rock concert. Phyo Min Thein, an '88 activist and Insein Prison JAC veteran, who had nourished his mind in his cell with books on Vietnam and still rose at 4 a.m. to meditate at Shwedagon Pagoda, opted for the rough equivalent of a town hall meeting. That translated to a gathering of farmers in a field. With five days left until April 1, on the day that the military celebrated as Armed Forces Day and everyone else as Revolutionary Day, about a thousand men, women, and children from over a hundred villages danced, held an unprecedented minute of silence to commemorate the fallen of revolutions past, and cheered as Phyo Min Thein and members of the local party offices took turns declaiming the central themes of the NLD party manifesto: rule of law, internal peace, and amending the 2008 constitution.

The hooting and partying and honking aboard trucks and tractors continued hours after the meeting ended.

Watching the revelry from the side of the road, Minus professed himself gobsmacked. In a constituency renowned for housing the headquarters of the Air Force, and possibly a top secret North Korean–supplied missile factory, the wild abandon of people's celebrations seemed from a different planet. Nway had sent him to the spot, along with Aung Thura Pyu and a handful of other activists, on a dry run to polling sites to check that they would be adequately monitored on the day.

They could tap into this energy, Minus surmised. He would enjoy reporting as much back to Nway. He had become to Minus something of a sorcerer, greater than a strategist, watching and prodding from afar the little play of actors performing in every town and village.

Their greatest test yet was only hours away.

⤙⤚

SUNRISE CRACKED ACROSS RANGOON ON April 1 as people were already streaming toward polling stations. In the "war room," the executives' meeting room that occupied nearly the entirety of the NLD office's second floor, the campaign team had set up seven phones. They rang without interruption from minutes before polls opened at 6 a.m. until dusk. Nway, whose cell phone had long before become the NLD's unofficial after-hours hotline, had taken calls throughout the previous night. He spent the morning beside his research team—Nobelle, Snow, Angelay, and several Uncles—passing news from across the country to Nyan Win, whose furious hand penned one official letter after another to the Election Commission. April 1, 2012, was the busiest day of Nyan Win's life.

At each increment, Nway discreetly phoned the information to his savvy, sometime whiskey-drinking mate, "U Min Min," for instant dissemination on his Facebook page; it quickly became the day's must-read for four thousand (and climbing) "friends" from across Burma's transnational sliver of wired political insiders.

The rest played catch-up: exile media outlets, the Big Brothers, Generation Wave, and all the groups that had proved their activist credentials in recent years tensed beside phones, computers, and makeshift citizen call-in centers. After the fraudulent referendum of 2008 and then the fraudulent election of 2010, the entire opposition braced for another massive deception.

Crisis hit by midmorning. A litany of complaints poured in claiming that the names of the NLD candidates were waxed over on hundreds of ballots. Nyan Win fired off a legal alert for urgent delivery to the commission in Naypyidaw, but there was no fax machine in the office, no functional fax in the hotel of the Chinese tourist whom Nway had conscripted to help a few days earlier, no fax anywhere.

Nway considered for a moment. Then he phoned Nigel.

"What? I can't hear you! What's that? I'm busy!" Nigel was somewhere between polling stations, furiously circling with Thant to oversee his two-hundred-odd NLD volunteer polling representatives. Just the day before, they had crammed into his campaign headquarters, spilling out the door and down the steps, for a final pep talk and a question-answer session with a Rangoon legal advisor.

"You're busy only for your constituency!" Nway shouted back, "I'm busy for the entire country!" With a final impassioned plea, Nway persuaded Nigel to dash to an Internet café, print out Nyan Win's letter, then screech down the highway for hand delivery to the commission.

As soon as polls closed at 4 p.m., the counting began promptly, one basket at a time. International election observers, who had been invited in too late to witness the full campaign, were quick to offer their verdict on the day: "clean," "pretty smooth," "transparent." Minor fudges on ballots and voter lists were understandable, they said, in a country with near-nineteenth-century infrastructure and the machinery to match. But these did nothing to mar an election that on polling day, at least, had been shockingly, remarkably, free and fair.

As 4 p.m. hit, Nigel headed for his local election commission and as his polling agents rang in the results, he marked them down on a scrap of paper that he later folded up and tucked into the breast pocket of a new shirt, starched white and collarless, that he had purchased for the occasion late the night before from the local hypermarket.

⋞⋰⋟

FOR ALL THE TENSION HE HAD EXUDED on March 31, Nigel might as well have been playing marbles. Information had just landed that the USDP candidate had bribed an entire village with electronic transformers and that day handed a hefty 8,000 kyat, about $8, to each of twenty-five young men for no purpose more fathomable to Nigel and his team than to hire them as thugs. He knew already that he would win. His wife and parents too shrugged away the notion that they should manifest any emotion beyond relaxed confidence. A day later, his father would proudly wipe away a tear as he thanked the universe aloud for the gift of watching his son take on the political promise that his own generation had failed to fulfill. His mother would smile knowingly at her third child, whose starry destiny she had trusted to unfold ever since he had first appeared to her in a dream when he was still in the womb: fully grown and dressed in white, heroism and goodness personified.

They had headed to the hypermart in search of stamps or sticky notes or something expensive and papery that Nigel couldn't quite name but knew he needed for his official accounting. No one had recognized the candidate as he and his family tripped past row upon row of shining cans, fat bottles, and plastic-wrapped riches. The exoticism of the place dizzied. Never before had they encountered such abundance.

"This is a shop for thieves," said his father, shaking a fat dragon fruit from a fridge display with a price tag large enough to cover a hefty meal for a family in North Okkla. Much discussion centered around the frozen meat before they settled on a small packet of papaya salad for dinner that night. Only later, as he passed a clearance shelf stocked with *longyis* and white shirts, did it occur to Nigel that he could use a fresh set. His stock of the wraps, all three of them, were worn through and dirty. For a freshly elected parliamentarian, they simply would not do.

Less than twenty-four hours later, he stood beside the legal advisor come from Rangoon, waiting to match the results from his polling representatives with those of the official election commission. Village one: 386 to 192. Village two: 318 to 217. Village four: 580 to 281. And so the victories began.

⚶

BACK IN RANGOON, FEW TEMPTED FATE with Nigel's confident nonchalance. No one, not even the veterans of 1990, had ever imagined anything like it.

By 6 p.m., the gentle civility of the first few visitors to the party headquarters had swelled to a street party themed in NLD red—red T-shirts, red bandanas, red flags waving off bamboo poles. Minus squatted on the roof of the headquarters, feeding the results to a video screen that had been lent to them by a foreign nonprofit, beside a megaphone blasting the NLD theme songs. The roar that greeted the announcement of Aung San Suu Kyi's victory in Kawhmu must have shaken the bells atop the golden dome of venerable Shwedagon Pagoda. By 9 p.m., the dancing and hooting in the sea of red had spilled down the neighboring blocks with such excess that Grandpa T had muscled his way out of headquarters and shouted that Aung San Suu Kyi was calling for discipline and self-restraint. By 11 p.m., with hundreds of supporters still pouring toward the uptown party outside the NLD office, Nyan Win decided it was time to disappear. If the NLD team were seen to have incited as uninhibited a rally, the army had every right to accuse them, to borrow the usual parlance, of disturbing the general peace and security of the state. To the surprise even of its own members, the party had won everywhere except the ethnic Shan stronghold of Lashio, near Thailand. For all their exhilaration at the victory—even in the four constituencies of Naypyidaw, even in constituencies that were predicted to vote military—they could not risk tripping any wire that might provoke 1990 redux.

Out the team slipped, through the crowds, one by one, ducking into the car of Han Thar Myint, the more wiry and discreet of Auntie's deputies. He dropped them off each in turn and on their rattan mats or mattresses by midnight they had crawled, exhausted, humbled, vindicated.

∾≯∾

THE UNITED STATES, AND MUCH OF the Western world that had long held Burma in financial and diplomatic exile, began easing sanctions in earnest. With sufficient foreign aid and investment, the country, to many, seemed on course to join the economic might of the wider region.

But dissidents saw a long and difficult road to the general elections in 2015. The people's response had been less a rally than a "silent demonstration," according to Ko Ko Gyi, the Big Brother strategist—explosive words from a man who knew something about demonstrations. Even Grandpa admitted shock. On the day of the vote, he had run the NLD control center in Mandalay. "*Really*," he said, "we didn't expect that much." Khin Maung Swe's National Democratic Force had fielded eleven candidates. In the surge of attention and support toward the NLD, the NDF had a crisis of money, a crisis of media coverage, a crisis of defections. It lost everywhere. Yet he had no regrets. Democracy had earned itself a mandate.

Days later, as the triumphant candidates gathered in Rangoon for an intimate back-patting all of their own, and the Uncles began planning for an army backlash that never came, Nway wondered why he felt so numb. He had achieved more in past weeks than in years of previous work combined. Everything before had been mere prologue. But something inside felt cold and inexplicably bleak. Nothing of the general jubilation could seep through.

Auntie, invited by world leaders to Oslo, London, and a half dozen other world capitals, asked him along. The last time he had tried for a passport, authorities would grant it only if he turned spy. When he applied anew, days before Auntie boarded her first international flight since 1988,

Special Branch stonewalled. The Uncles weighed in. Still the answer was a resounding—ambiguity.

The broadened political space had opened the floodgates to general defiance. The censorship offices still shut down news stories on subjects such as the monkhood, the effects of the fighting in northern and still politically outlying Kachin state, or the corruption among the tycoons whose closed-door deals with the senior generals and counterparts across Asia had locked down much of the country's resources for an indefinite future.

Still, journalists ignored reprimands from the Press Scrutiny Board and published anyway. Factory workers held days-long strikes for better pay and conditions, secretly nudged on with food and pay from dissident groups. Popular opposition swelled against various dam and oil projects, empowered by the success of the campaign to suspend work on the hydropower project at the headwaters of the Irrawaddy.

Names were still recorded, photos still snapped, and some of the toughest laws had yet to vanish, even layered under new reforms. They included prohibitions on free association, on registering with local authorities when sleeping overnight away from home, and communicating with vaguely defined "illegal groups."

"Old habits die hard," said U Ye Htut, director general of public information at the Ministry of Information, by way of explanation. Even as President Thein Sein's agenda hardened into undeniable reform, the government's motives remained enigmatic. "People say we can see the light at the end of the tunnel," Grandpa was telling visitors. "But we are still in the tunnel."

⌘

THE FIRST HICCUP CAME FAST. Auntie, reading over the constitution one more time in anticipation of attending the next week's parliamentary session, noticed a clause that required new parliamentarians to swear an oath in which they would promise to "safeguard" the constitution. For a party that had stumped on a trio of pledges—rule of law, internal peace, and amending the constitution—agreeing to stand by that wording could backfire later. To change the constitution, already difficult, would prove nearly impossible.

With Nway beside him, Nyan Win shot back to Naypyidaw. No time for a bus, they hired a cab. Short of a concession from President Thein Sein, the new parliamentarians would boycott their first session.

The move might have been a brilliant gamble. Auntie and the NLD could do no wrong as Thein Sein hovered on the verge of returning Burma to the fold of acceptable nations. "The NLD Stumbles Out of the Starting Block," cried a headline in *Mizzima*, the influential online exile journal that had formerly operated out of New Delhi but whose publisher, an '88 activist, had lately opened an office back in Burma in a decisive symbol of conciliation. The political stalemate divided supporters and froze cold some of the foreign observers who had been salivating about the impending end to sanctions, which meant a free-for-all into the country's virgin markets. Once again, they suggested, the NLD had proved its political ineptitude.

In the end, the NLD backed down.

"We are," Nway said, "at the beginning of the beginning."

EPILOGUE

WHERE WAS HEAVEN? It was supposed to have arrived within days.

A year earlier, Minus had been sure of it as he squatted on the roof of the NLD office, feeding the results of the by-elections into a video screen to blast out to the madding crowds, wild on the sense of tangible possibility.

Instead he was waking every night, shaken to the core by his mother's shrieks.

"Aye, aye, aye! Are they coming? Are they coming?"

The mobs, she meant; the same hordes, perhaps, who had hooted and cried at the NLD victory. Laughing, petrol-bombing her home, they would watch her burn—with her husband and two sons.

"Are they coming? Are they coming?"

Raddled and sweating, jolted from her mattress by every bump or creak or the diabolical 3 a.m. chorus of Rangoon's baying strays, she'd appear at Minus's bedside, a shadow of a woman, flinging pieces of clothing into piles along with their few trinkets of gold, their pots and gadgets and electrical cords, and whatever they could salvage for wherever it was they were to relocate next.

269

They had no insurance. They had nothing. One match to their home, to their downtown electronic shop, and to its cramped, wooden offshoot that Minus oversaw now in the slum of Dala five minutes across the river and it would all be over.

She had seen this before, in 1967. She had been young. Back then, they had come for the Chinese. Every night now—fresh off the latest reports of ransacked villages, of people charred or beaten to pulp as if, nationwide, life had taken a turn to the cheap—the images of decades past flared again in her sleep-starved mind. Two families, she'd say, right here, just down the road. In the heart of a metropolis, returned in 2013 to the promise of cosmopolitan centrality, the mobs had set them aflame, for no offense greater than the accident of their origin.

Now they were coming for the Muslims.

Daily they were closing in. The trail of bodies, and the twisted, fuming rubble of their mosques and shops and houses, mapped the trajectory of bloodlust from western Rakhine state, where it had begun in June 2012, to Oakkan, a little town not fifty miles north of the city.

Minus had no notion of when his family had first arrived in Burma; generations before, probably. They belonged nowhere else. The question was as pointedly far-fetched as the idea that his struggle—the long struggle for democracy, for rights and justice and freedom—had somehow been restricted to the country's Buddhists.

No one would come to the rescue. Not the police, not anyone in uniform. Nor either the Americans or the countries of ASEAN. Even Aung San Suu Kyi was failing them. A member of government now, she had become a part of the establishment, and her criticism, if it came at all, was muted, relentlessly holding to a neutral, if unwittingly insipid line about the need for the "rule of law."

An atmosphere of siege, of the dead calm before the storm, hovered with the grime and the fumes from traffic that clogged the streets with four times as many cars, perhaps five, since the import market had been blasted open. Down the block, between the mosques and Hindu temples of the old multiethnic district of Mingalar Thaung Nyunt, people had started neighborhood watches—"interfaith" gatherings of Buddhist, Muslim, and Hindu elders, perched at the ready with strong flasks of tea and bats, holding forth through the night in case of renewed riots. Even the Buddhists had packed their emergency kits. At Nobelle's, they doubled as pillows.

A week earlier, Minus had taken a three-day bus trip to scout for a refuge. He found it just over the northern frontier with China: a ragged border town, built by people eking out livelihoods between cultures and countries. It was not the future. It didn't promise the prosperity of even his new little business in Dala, the ratty riverside slum whose proximity to Rangoon had meant its value had in recent months shot up to forty times its worth per square footage—higher than Bangkok, as high as San Francisco—on speculation of its demolition to make room for conference centers, golf clubs, and swanky condominiums for some chimeric middle class to come.

Back in Rangoon, insomniac enough without the added excuse of his mother's nightmares, he wandered after midnight down Sule Pagoda Road, alighting for the mud-thick teas of his cousin's mobile teashop that squatted in patches of alleyway around 35th Street, or Merchant Street, or Maha Bandoola, or wherever it could avoid the roving teashop police.

They were carting them away now—you'd see the little chairs and tables, legs upturned, on the backs of police vans, off to teashop prison. Licenses, or some of them, were being enforced. The land was too precious, the sight of anarchic sidewalk life a wart too many for the wealthy visitors to Rangoon that the new government was courting. Minus, a few old friends, and Nway, too, if they were lucky, gathered by night in the midst of it, watching it all and brainstorming about the likely consequences.

All of them were going to be priced out anyway, pushed to some nebulous nether-zone of newfound joblessness and beggary. The betel nut sellers and market hawkers and street-side noodle vendors—the life of Rangoon's street—had become endangered species. Already the cranes were going up. In lacquered lobbies or under the decaying eaves of the old colonial buildings, real estate speculators, fresh-landed from fancier foreign capitals, huddled over maps, carving out sections of the city and its surroundings as part of a plot for the great Rangoon raze.

But to head over the border, bound for exile as refugees, Minus and his family might at least be spared the menace of their neighbors turning overnight into *génocidaires*.

⤛⤜

BY MAY 2013, BURMA HAD SWAPPED out one fear for another—and the new version was darker and spreading like a black stain, because it was coming from the people, a voluntary mass of farmhands and shopkeepers and housewives whipped up by the pathological Buddhist ultranationalism of a movement called "969" and the demagoguery of its spiritual leader, a monk called Ashin Wirathu.

If outside menace there was—if global businesses and tourists were pouring in and the danger was a potential loss to national idiosyncrasy—the anxieties unleashed at home were both less profound and bleaker on account of it. There was nothing new about hatred, fomented by bigots, however much it came robed in a Saffron toga and enthroned in a crumbling Mandalay monastery.

There was nothing exotic about targeting Muslims—and with murderous intent. This was an old racism, masquerading under new crimes. Muslims had long been easy prey for premeditated scapegoating, at strategic inflection points when the junta had reason to deflect the inflamed energies of wider society from more pressing injustices. Now, freed of the Press Scrutiny Board, allowed a measure of open conversation of a kind never previously permitted, society was turning on itself. The only novelty was in its spread, and in the intimacy of the brutality—each discrete instance, metastasizing across the country, of a citizen picking up a maul and ramming it into another's home, or smashing in a skull, or watching it all happen and standing by, laughing. By May 2013, the violence was epidemic. Without a concerted effort from high authorities, there was no end in sight.

Wirathu, coltish and slinky, held court for a stream of press inquiries in his room at the venerable Masoyein monastery, beside a wall plastered in self-portraits and blown-up photos—four times as many as images of the Buddha. An agent each from Military Intelligence and Special Branch took notes on either side of him; whether they were there to protect or to intimidate him, the effect was immaterial. Delivering sermons in town after town, he had become, without government sanction, the most articulate spokesman for a newly shaped idea, in which Burma, and Burmese consciousness, were threatened not by a constitution that still preserved all power for the military; nor either by the systemic material corruption; the destabilizing influx of Western money; the ongoing civil war and wipe-'em-out counter-insurgency campaigns against the embattled Kachin and the Shan and other border peoples; nor even by the unabated land grabs of businesses still jointly owned by former or current military officers; an economy that remained opaque; the non-existent infrastructure; the broken education and health care systems; or the lapsed capacity for critical thought that came of generations of citizens being denied the right to it.

Wirathu's speeches instead drew new chauvinism from an oft-used well, a hodgepodge of catchphrases about Muslims raping the Buddhist women, or manipulating them into the slavery of their marriages. The country's Muslims, he said—a population that few could measure but that the last census in 1983 estimated at four percent—posed the greatest threat to the country, by which he meant to a Buddhist country, belonging to the Buddhist Burmans.

The violence had begun in northeastern Rakhine state against the Rohingya, a widely reviled Muslim minority of about 800,000 or, possibly, 1.3 million. No one could say for sure because they had never been considered one of the 135 ethnic "nationalities," and what ancient rights they had to citizenship had been stripped from them in the 1982 Citizenship Law. To the administration of President Thein Sein, the Rohingya were "Bengalis"—implying a false narrative of recent migration from Bangladesh, when most had been in Burma for generations. To the mainstream, they didn't even merit their ethnic label; as part of the social fabric they simply didn't exist.

A report had circulated of the rape and killing on May 28, 2012, of a Rakhine Buddhist woman, allegedly by three Muslim men. On June 3, a group of Rakhine villagers stopped a bus and killed ten Muslims aboard. Five days later, Rohingya rioted by the thousands in a town far to the north, ransacking Rakhine properties. In successive attacks thereafter by Rakhine Buddhist mobs, hundreds of Rohingya had been killed. At least 140,000 others were displaced and pushed into camps where they were denied medical care and aid, and kept under conditions so severe that outside watchdogs were calling it ethnic cleansing, with complicity from local security forces. For a while it had been possible to treat the violence as the isolated vitriol of one marginalized minority against another. To extend a stereotype almost as blind as those they themselves perpetrated about the Rohingya, the Rakhine were prideful and protective of their history. They had a long history of resentment against the Rohingya, who shared the same scrubby land. The Rohingya had received aid from international nonprofits that they withheld from the Rakhine, who were also destitute but a hair less visibly oppressed. This had happened before, in these lands, between these peoples.

But then the violence had moved to the mainland and expanded to Muslims writ large, people who had lived among Buddhists for an age. Since a massacre on March 20 to 22, 2012, in Meiktila, a central city whose prior claim to renown had been a limpid lake that featured in a lullaby, the violence had burned a southward line that hewed mysteriously to the highway, encroaching on Rangoon.

Always the incidents turned on the report of an inciting quarrel: a Muslim man or woman somehow insulting a Buddhist. In Meiktila there had been a dispute over a gold clip in a Muslim-owned gold shop. In Oakkan, a Muslim woman on a motorcycle had, accidentally or not, collided with a Buddhist monk and refused to apologize for the resultant smashing of his alms bowl.

Within hours, houses were savaged and restaurants turned upside down, the tarpaulin tenting torn and shredded, the contents of huts ransacked and tipped into the mud. Always they blasted the Muslim-owned properties, and with a targeted precision suggesting that someone had plotted ahead and marked them with red flags.

Weeks later, Meiktila was still black with the ash of whole neighborhoods, a carpet-bombed configuration of twisted metal and rubble, and smashed jewelry shop-fronts. Far from the blank Buddhist stares, in a makeshift camp in a hangar on the outskirts of town, Muslim runaways from it all lived now in stinking, tattered misery. There they walled out little squares of earth with their salvaged luggage. They were denied visits and the right to circulate beyond. No one could enter or exit without express permission. Segregation was the order of the day.

Satellite imagery from Meiktila told of a path of destruction as indiscriminate as Cyclone Nargis—828 houses burned to the ground, 35 partially destroyed. Forty people had been killed, and sixty-one wounded. On the banks of the lake, a crowd had watched and jeered on the thugs. U Win Htein, Aung San Suu Kyi's old personal aide and a former army captain elected in 2012 as the NLD's Meiktila representative in parliament, had watched them watching. The sight appalled. He'd managed, in the absence of helpful security forces, to fend off a second wave of murderous thugs.

Every day he was swallowing pills to assuage the half-dozen ailments that twenty years and two months in prison had hammered into him; his last return to prison had come within hours of his release from a previous twelve-year stint; his former jailor, and fellow graduate of the Defense Services Academy, had publicly shaken his hand with an unironic smile at a recent opening session of parliament. But this took the cake. The police had been impotent. And Meiktila was a barracks town. Army officers should have been deployed within minutes, should have known how and where to quash.

Whether they stood by passively through incompetence or tacit assent, it raised people's hackles that the same security forces that could or would do nothing about murderous Buddhist-on-Muslim violence had been without qualms about smashing down on civilians in times past. Even recently, up north, police had violently dispersed protesters who had been agitating to shut down a Chinese-owned copper mine whose development threatened to wreck the site of a sacred Buddhist shrine.

At dawn in Oakkan, the planks of wood and chalky remnants of the foundations of two farm sheds were still smoldering around the corner as an elderly man crawled out of hiding. Long of beard and bloodshot in the eyes, he craned his neck through a gate down a goat path from the back edge of his madrassa. Seeing nobody, no hint of the mobs that had torn through the previous afternoon, he blinked at the daylight and the sight of the madrassa. It looked as if a band of giants had blitzed through. How could they have accessed the second floor? With what pitchforks and farmer's implements could they possibly have wrenched down boulder-sized pieces from the upper reaches of the building's concrete edifice?

Near the madrassa's entrance, beside the remains of two thin huts, a child's bright green tricycle lay capsized in the dirt. It poked up from a mound of plastic hangers, strewn *longyis* and shirts, smashed plates; a cooking pot, a jar of detergent, and pages and pages torn from a Koràn.

The influence of 969, and the sermons of Wirathu and his associates, were easy enough to prove. Stickers bearing the number, framed in a chakra wheel, had appeared on shop fronts and in taxis, on flags and CDs. They sold on the street or circulated for free, dispersed at the packed appearances that Wirathu and his peers were making in towns around the country. They urged a boycott of Muslim businesses, shops, and stalls: best instead that people visit those stamped with 969. Buddhist employers felt pressure to let go of longtime Muslim employees. To face the ire of people's growing disapproval, keeping Muslims on staff simply wasn't worth the trouble.

Within hours or days of a visit, just down the road: a pogrom.

The numeracy of 969's name was intentionally symbolic. It was drawn from the three Buddhist jewels, the sacred *tiratana*: the nine special attributes of the Lord Buddha, the six core Buddhist teachings, and the nine attributes of monkhood. The resonances were sufficiently mystical, and nebulous, to be just appealing enough to the average Buddhist. To take a 969 sticker down was to risk legal accusations of defacing the good name of the Buddha.

The ideological origins of 969 were traceable to the paperwork of a member of the ministry of religious affairs in the 1990s. Wirathu had known the man, had advocated the same screed, and served in prison for inciting an explosion of anti-Muslim violence in Kyaukse town in 2003.

But 969 was an invention intended mainly as an explicit antidote to the alleged threat of 786, a sign that Muslims often posted on storefronts as a numerical translation of the Koranic phrase, "in the name of Allah, the Most Gracious, the Ever Merciful." According to 969 doctrine, Islam was to be vanquished because 786 pointed to a conspiracy to achieve world domination in the twenty-first century, because 7 plus 8 plus 6 added up to the number 21.

To Minus, it was absurd. Muslims posted the number 786 on restaurants or shops to indicate that their servings were *halal*. The ideas had infiltrated the chatter of the marketplace, and what the numbers meant and whom they were intended for was enough to make him feel like a stranger in his own land.

Not everyone fell for it. But not everyone had learned to shout down a demagogue. The moderate majority, as usual, chose silent disapprobation. There was no textual source in Buddhism that Wirathu and his ilk could claim. There was nothing Buddhist, even, in his rhetoric.

More troubling for most, there were suspicions of complicity from within the military, a nest of spoilers who had everything to gain from tripping up the reforms of President Thein Sein's government and the opening to the world that threatened their old monopoly on power.

The links were tenuous. But whenever else had proof been necessary? Paper decayed in the tropics. It wouldn't take more than five thousand *kyat* per day per thug, twenty-five hundred *kyat*, even, at the old rates. People talked of a training camp for paramilitaries in Thaung Tha, the same scorched-earth town where the Swann Arr Shin supposedly had a base.

The violence fit a growing pattern. From the crowds, locals spotted the faces from out of town—toughs with bats and sledgehammers, trucked in on pickups. There was talk of bogus monks—real bogus monks—draping their robes wrong and failing to use the vocabulary of address that genuine monks would never fumble. It was not hard to shave a head; the shops in Rangoon were said to have been cleaned out of Buddhist robes.

Then again, the clear-out came within days of the New Year's festival. Tradition demanded a popular retreat to the monasteries and, with it, offerings of the same robes to their abbots.

People blamed the old spymaster, Khin Nyunt, fresh out of house arrest and "reforming" in a monastery. Likewise they fingered the nephew of a general connected to a Chinese pipeline project. Most suspect of all was the minister of industry, who had headed the USDA before it had become the majority party. Thaung Tha was his home, and there he had allegedly overseen the Swann Arr Shin—the hooligans-for-hire responsible for the junta's dirty work. They had been credited with the attack at Depayin on Auntie's convoy in 2003 that had left at least seventy people dead, and likewise with smashing apart the protests of September 2007.

And so the rumors churned.

To Nway, it was all of a piece. He had not expected heaven. He had not fallen prey to the conviction that a toxic tyranny—the junta—had been the root of all evil, though inevitably that public position had been his most abiding preoccupation.

How much easier to attribute the societal meltdown to a dark hand, to the nebulous meddling of powers on high? If only it were so simple.

The problem was that the spoilers had a vast ocean from which to draw their virulent armies. Hearts were cracked and fragmenting, retrenching into ethnic labels in ways that hinted at some amorphous disillusion, some terrible sense that they had been waiting for something, for redemption. But how it would take form, and what it was exactly, would never be. There were no easy answers. There was no sense of arrival.

The unresolved question of what Burma was, and what it was to be, hovered now as an urgent provocation. The old bugbear of national identity had never been resolved, not since the Panglong conference in 1947. For decades it had hung at the center of the civil war. Now it had returned to the foreground of debate, and with the right to debate, the question had unleashed a furor of mixed sentiment. By venturing a forceful answer, even Ko Ko Gyi, the beloved Big Brother strategist, had courted bitter controversy. The answers were bound up, partly, with anxieties less about the end of an era than the birth of another, less defined, entirely uncertain.

Modernity's arrival threatened, in oblique ways, the wearing of the *longyi*, the spirit of Buddhist devotion, and the respect and pride for an age-old culture that had held at bay the perceived moral degeneracy of the world beyond, beginning with neighboring Thailand. Aung San Suu Kyi had made it to Naypyidaw, and she was now able to travel abroad. An air of openness, of open conversation reigned in the cities. But the poverty was as deep, the hunger as gnawing. Without even the focus of the old fear—the arbitrary oppression of a merciless junta—came a sudden loss of center, or the sudden sense of a loss, and who was left to blame? President Thein Sein himself had been hailed even at home as a reformer.

The laws, as they changed, were growing more insidious. Under new regulations on protests, friends from the old underground networks, from Generation Wave, from Kachin development organizations, were marching by the dozens: for peace with the ethnic minorities, for an end to exploitation of the national heritage sites, for whatever right they could find to protest now. Then they were slammed with legal charges: eighteen per person for crossing a like number of jurisdictions without advance permission. They had applied for permission, didn't get it, and went anyway. They held standing-room-only press conferences to denounce the allegations, then sidled across town to one or other little wooden cabinet of a local courtroom for their sixty-third hearing in seven months. Irreverent, battle-hardened revolutionaries all, they slouched, sent text messages, updated their Facebook pages on new smart phones, as a pinch-faced judge in a pink silk Shan cap questioned an alleged witness who had no clue why he had been pulled off the street, out of his day, and into court.

At the center of their protests, and of Nway's abiding malaise, was this:

The country was not free. Not yet.

And yet, to the excuse of dust and poverty, to the travails inflicted on a people who were victim still to economic inequality and unreformed injustice, the greatest scourge of all was ignorance. In a land of deepest appreciation for the freedoms of unfettered consciousness, among a people who apprehended the quality of expansion that could be arrived at by insight meditation and the truest ideals of Theravada Buddhism, the paradox pressed. One tug at the social fabric—at the thousands of young men in the slums with too much loose testosterone and nothing to burn but their nihilism—and years of half-finished efforts to penetrate the countryside with ideas on universal rights, on what democracy meant, would come to nil. Then everything would blow.

The thugs for hire stared out from every street corner. Nway had grown up among them. Without politics, without a moral anchor, he might have become one of them—he of the near turn in his teens to a dark world of drugs and anarchic gang violence. Of all his friends in that tight core of ten NLD youth members, he was the only one left. They had drifted away, one after the next, sucked back into the constraints of a society that offered them no other goals, no consolation from the despair of unemployment, of poverty, except drugs, exile, so many avenues to erring. Better than most, better than the fresh-eyed idealists and the enthusiasts landing daily from the West, opening businesses, scouting for opportunities, Nway sensed how easily it could all rip apart.

They had fought for these mindsets. He had fought for these mindsets. They had a little perch in parliament to show for it. It had been a start—that, and the constant multi-fronted assertiveness of a web of activists—but to end it there, to smile and say it was over, was to fall dupe to potentially the military's greatest victory to date.

The junta had dismantled itself on its own terms. Analysts were calling it a top-down managed "transition." The generals had done well. They had only to make a few selective gestures and—lo!—the world, the West had eased sanctions. Invitations from afar had flowed.

What if, instead, it was nothing more than a great pulling of the wool over the world's eyes? No one had been held to account; no one of significance. Not a single general had been felled for the sins of the past.

Of late, no activist had called for it, because they couldn't, because any effort to appeal for justice—for accountability or truth telling that might narrow the circle of permissible lies or begin to address years of torture and incarcerations and disappearances, the responsibility for destroying a society—would derail all.

It was enough for now to push however they might.

What few reforms there had been were mere "corrective measures." The work of rebuilding the nation had not even begun. So said "DNA," former joint leader of the jungle-based All Burma Students' Democratic Front, from Mae Sot, where he and a hardened trove of professional revolutionaries had kept their outposts, to keep their independence. They'd come back, one by one, on invitations from the state, to fanfare paralleled in a local press that could newly mention their names. But the mood that greeted them was not that of warm welcome for returning heroes.

Invitations from the government to the most prominent among them landed in due course. But, as they traveled round the country for the first time in years, agents monitored their every move. It made them less susceptible to potential government cooption. And when they saw the lie of the system, or the lie against them, they called it.

DNA returned to newly cooked-up allegations that he had been responsible for executions of students in the 1990s in Kachin state, although he had been nowhere near at the time. No problem, DNA replied. Let there be justice— so long as it was impartial, and applied to all parties. Bo Kyi, who had spent more than eight years in prison before he became the founder of the Assistance Association for Political Prisoners (Burma) in Mae Sot, Thailand, had joined a government commission to advocate for the release of the remaining political prisoners. When it quickly turned into a talking shop, he thundered and advocated and went public. He had opened an AAPPB chapter in Rangoon, and his associates had started a unit to address the matter of former inmates' trauma, and the potential, along with it, of countrywide brain damage.

It was the fate of the exiles, the leaders who had dared to hold to their convictions abroad, and fight in creative new ways, willing to take onboard with it the false idea that they had sold out. Aung Zaw, the founder of the mighty *Irrawaddy* magazine, kept his newsroom in Chiang Mai. Best, he said, to keep one foot out of the country, watching from afar with the critical strategic detachment that was their only lasting luxury, and their wiliest weapon.

Their funds had dried up. Few donors would justify funneling help to the margins, to the border areas, when the center seemed, suddenly, so accommodating. They couldn't come home permanently. They no longer belonged even if they belonged nowhere else. Burma was home, but Burma had become an idea. Exile was a state of mind. It was its own imprisonment. All they had ever done was dedicate their lives to their country. But what was that to a population who only saw in most of them a single, irreversible decision to cut and run?

They were not the only misfits. There were other activists who had willingly sacrificed their reputations on the altar of a larger cause.

Months after the ugly final meeting of Togetherness in 2011, Nway had kept alive the rump of his little network, which he had managed to turn into a research institute. Coordinating with some of those exiles, turning to them for their evident know-how, he had ambitions to build it up as succor to the NLD's ongoing material deficiencies ahead of its biggest test yet, the national elections scheduled for late 2015.

The reigning USDP, and the government of Thein Sein, had all the benefits of worldwide attention. They had resources, and contacts in every country. The biases of the international system meant it would always favor the ruling administration, not its scrappy opposition. The NLD had only its myth, and its shining symbol of leadership in Aung San Suu Kyi. But that would never be enough. Not anymore.

At its first ever national party congress in March 2013, the NLD had held internal elections at last. From the ground up, with a vast restructuring, it had flung open its doors wide to democracy. Candidates had stumped and campaigned, and held to the lofty values that the NLD had always represented, but there had been no way to filter out intolerance. Into the party's midst too had walked the bigots and the uneducated. The rule of the majority aligned with the rule of the mob.

There was work to be done.

Forsaken up north, far from the eyes of the tourists and the businessmen come to explore the country's virgin markets, in a land of jade and teak on the long border with China, the war with the Christian-majority Kachin raged.

Stripped naked and forced to prostrate themselves on the cold stone of a Buddhist monastery as on a crucifix, in mocking tribute to Jesus and the God they worshipped; forced to commit sexual acts upon each other; hung upside down for five days; smashed in the face beyond recognition, with grenades periodically stuffed into mouths: the local round-ups and detentions of Kachin men had yet to stall.

Negotiations were stuttering. Even China, concerned with "border instability" had played broker, breaking with a longtime policy of nonintervention.

Meantime, the helicopter gunships and fighter jets and intermittent crossfire had sent more than a hundred thousand fleeing since the breakdown of the 1994 ceasefire in June 2011.

In the camps for internally displaced persons, the reality of endless war had created stories of atrocity so prevalent that they registered as mundane. People middle-aged now had been fleeing burning villages since childhood. Husbands of fighting age were largely absent. The risk of leaving an IDP camp for a livelihood, to sell water buffalo by the side of the road, say, was arrest and detention—until a confession that one's purpose had been to fill the ranks of the Kachin Independence Army.

The only possible option for the Tatmadaw had been to assume that the entire population was complicit. Every local supported the Kachin Independence Organization and its army, so every passing civilian was fodder for its recruitment.

It wasn't meant to be happening, not now, not as praise for President Thein Sein's reforms were being sung across the world's capitals.

Not as the financiers of the Davos World Economic Forum descended on Naypyidaw. Already Coca-Cola had taken out billboards in Rangoon's Mingaladon Airport. Visa and Mastercard had set up the first automated teller machines. The tourists had begun to rush in, hundreds of thousands more than in previous years, encouraged by glossies that billed the country as the most glamorous destination of the year, and still authentic! The burgeoning hotel industry scrambled to play catch up. Prices rocketed in the most derelict little guesthouses because there were simply not enough rooms in the country to accommodate.

Up north, in Myitkina, Kachin state, it was old Burma still. The airport spat its sporadic passengers onto a frayed little field, and a customs official recorded passport numbers in a thick ledger with a ruler and Bic pen. Buses departed every other day, and the train took twenty hours to Mandalay, stifling, reeking of urine, rocking southward through a landscape still unremittingly dark, at the speed of the urchins who sprinted beside the tracks and hopped aboard with baskets of mangoes.

In Kachin state, the billboards threatened death to drug users, the Internet café was slammed by power outages, and the churches were crammed with pilgrims, overflowing beyond back entrances. A lone HIV/AIDS clinic, run by an Irish nun, catered alike to Burman and Kachin, soldier and rebel, young mothers and lost men—and what they shared were secret tales of contracting their disease from dirty needles, from the heroin and opium cultivated on the poppy-rich hills and passed around as a weapon of war with the inevitable consequence of indiscriminate addiction.

It wasn't, in the end, the Chinese whom the Burmese had to fear. The ethnic minorities of the borderlands were too weak to invade, and too caught in the mire of their own unresolved conflicts. In the Burmese mainland, society had only to face itself.

There were problems enough for a lifetime.

Nigel, irredeemably maverick, eternally broke, could not get back in time to Naypyidaw for the new session of parliament after the annual shutdown of the 2013 Water Festival. Waylaid in Rangoon, all he needed was forty thousand *kyat*, or about forty dollars, for the bus fare.

The second youngest Member of Parliament, he had been the first to interrupt the staid procedure of its sessions by standing up in the middle of a full assembly with—a question. Ever since the parliamentary sessions had grown a little more boisterous, a smidgen less dull. Now everyone was interrupting.

Lately he had been demoted as the party's deputy whip. There wasn't much explanation for it. He suspected he was too renegade. He didn't follow orders. Even Auntie was getting frustrated.

The way he saw it, he had more pressing problems. The state salary had been a boon, but it wasn't enough to cover the material needs of his constituents: village upon village lacked water, which meant he was digging wells; and schools were nonexistent, which meant he was building huts, then finding paper and pens and teachers.

Within days of the April 1, 2012, victory, concerned to begin on his campaign pledges, he had paid his respects to a famous matinee idol turned purveyor of free funerals to the poorest. Nigel had requested a modest amount, about the price of three SIM cards. The matinee idol, taken by the young man's honesty and the promise of the NLD triumph in the by-elections, chuckled an instant and handed him ten times the sum, a fat check that Thant, Nigel's by-election wingman, had helped him record in a budgeting book that fattened with dozens of new donations from rich donors with every passing month.

He was filling another album with evidence of his constituents' new wells and schools. It wasn't enough. It would never be enough. The needs were cavernous. The terrible anti-Muslim violence, the situation with the Kachin: these were issues to study and raise in the next parliamentary sessions. Meantime, his people faced the more immediate thorniness of land grabs and a deprivation so deep that children were growing up, in his district, down his road, illiterate. Men, without livelihood, were still going mad.

To supplement his income, he had spent his off-season from parliament back in Rangoon, teaching a month's worth of classes to a family of rich merchants. Now it was time for the merchants to settle up. They had reached a moment of mutual, and mutually befuddling, *anade*. The merchants could not bring themselves to insult a parliamentarian with something as undignified and meager as a salary; the parliamentarian could not, in turn, find it in himself to ask a hard-working citizen for a wage.

At least he had another night to spend with his son, and Khine Sandar Win, who lived most of the week in Dawbon since she had been elected to the local NLD chapter. At last she had returned to politics, in a way they would never have imagined but exactly as they might have dreamed.

The conundrum of Nigel's lack of bus fare gave him time, as well, to track down Nway. The occasions were rare enough. Nigel was always in Naypyidaw, and even when he was back in town, it was ever more difficult to pin Nway down. The man never stopped. He zigzagged between the Uncles, his network, and the exiles, and now, too, foreign visits. Invitations had been landing through the NLD office—from the US State Department, from the European Union, from a British human-rights activist—for the young man who seemed its most active and competent backdoor strategist.

That night, over whiskey, Nway unpacked his latest situation. An offer had arrived for a week in the Philippines. He didn't want to go. There was so much to do. Every day mattered. But the contacts might prove useful. In much that way, he had finally secured funding from an outside organization for Togetherness—a legitimate source for a legitimate organization trying for legitimate change.

But Nway could not bring himself to tell Nigel about the most troubling turn of previous days. A text message had landed from an old friend, a young woman he would have trusted with his life. To the news that she could henceforth have a salary, she had returned that she was cutting off all contact with Nway. Rather than take his money, she would find a job with Special Branch.

Nway had stewed in it. He had no solution. How could it be that an offer of salary was so offensive that his friend, or anyone, would actively threaten to turn to the dark side? How could they hope to rebuild their country when the effort to change, to adapt and improve, one bamboo stick at a time, was tripped up even by their own ideals?

Another blow that he could or would not indulge in the telling, even to Nigel:

At last, he had fallen in love. She was beautiful, and an activist. She was kind and creative and brilliant and brave. Ten years his junior, she was wiser than him in a dozen ways. They laughed as he had never laughed. With her, he had discovered joy. In her, in a life with her, he had everything he could have dreamed possible.

On the promise of it, she had tried to sabotage an arranged betrothal to a rich young shipman.

But her parents disapproved—Nway had no money, no prospect of a stable paying job. And his brothers, and all of Twantay, disapproved—he owed his hand to one of his near-adoptive sisters. In the rural morality of the village that had rescued him, he had tainted them with his intimate friendship, however fraternal. It didn't matter that neither Paw Paw, nor Acca, nor Snow had the faintest desire, in turn, for him.

So Nway could not marry his sweetheart. And so it went.

Grandpa would have dismissed the issue in simple terms. They had too much to do. Better, in any case, to cultivate a solo existence.

Whatever Nway was, whatever he might yet be, he let it be a mystery attuned to the unfolding uncertainty of his country. It was a time of reform, a time of revolutionaries learning to be politicians.

Nway, long since given to a different kind of service, would glide on, adapting as Burma needed to its shape-shifting trajectory.

ACKNOWLEDGMENTS

This book could never have been written without the hundreds of Burmese citizens who shared with me their personal stories and ideas, most often at risk to their security. For that reason, some still would prefer that I didn't name them, but they know who they are and I hope, as an expression of my gratitude, that they may recognize in these pages how or where they informed my knowledge of and abiding love and respect for their country and society. Any insights belong to them. All errors are my own.

I was immensely lucky that my first friend in Burma was the brilliant, hilarious, and devious Dr. Myint "Miracle" Oo. Others also quickly became invaluable mentors and teachers who steered me fast and right, and with great patience endured my repeated questions, even if they saw no discernible evidence of progress. To the always-insightful and brave Dr. Khin Zaw Win, I owe a particular debt of thanks, and likewise to the young man who exited fourteen years of prison, blind in one eye, turned around and smuggled me back into Insein Prison. My thanks also to Gerhard Baumgard, Bertil Lintner, Thiha Saw, Dr. Naing Aung, "Thadin Ninja," San San Tin, Ko Ko Aung, Ko Ko Gyi, Andrew Kirkwood, Ma "Aye Aye," Benedict Rogers, Kelley Currie, Bill Berkeley, John Dale, Daw Kyi May Aung, David Scott Mathieson, Minka Nijhuis, Liz Tydeman, Alix Clarke, Michele Bohana, Thant Myint-U, Priscilla Clapp, Gabrielle Paluch, Ruth Bradley-Jones, Lex Rieffel, David E. Steinberg, Bo Kyi, U Han Thar Myint, "Pyint," "Pyone," "Nobelle," "Paw Paw," "Acca," "Snow," "Minus," "Arthur," "Kay Thee Oo," "Glimmer," Moethway, Min Yan Naing, Swe Win, and, of course, Naing Ngan Lin and "Nway"—my friends, my brothers.

Thanks to my editors on the Foreign Desk at the *Washington Post*, the best of the best—John Burgess, Keith Richburg, Tony Reid, Scott Wilson, Kevin Sullivan, and especially the great David E. Hoffman, who took a chance on a rookie in a newsroom full of Titans—for their early encouragement, and for everything I ever heard and learned from them and dozens of others in that greatest of universities and rarest den of uncompromising excellence.

The East-West Center in Washington under Satu Limaye gave me a Southeast Asian Fellowship and an incredible platform of thinkers and resources with which to conduct a leg of my research and writing. For another leg, John Schidlovsky of the International Reporting Project gave me a home at SAIS Johns Hopkins, projecting, as always, the warmth of an extended family. My gratitude also for the support, singular civility, and creativity of the editors, past and present, at the *Virginia Quarterly Review*—Jon Peede, Ralph E. Eubanks, Paul Reyes, Allison Wright, Donovon Webster, and Ted Genoways—the best place to call home for a long-form writer. Thanks also to my colleagues at DECA Stories, talented dynamos all, who have succeeded in launching a globally minded journalist's dream, and patiently endured my absence as I worked on this. And for a perch in the jungle, or at least in Bangkok, there was always, thankfully, the Atlanta Hotel.

Don Fehr dared to take me on as a client when few imagined that my story could sell. Carl Bromley believed as no one else did in this story, and his early enthusiasm as editor was immeasurably helpful; I wish that he and I could have seen this through together to the end. Thanks also to Luba Ostashevsky for her thoughtfulness and invaluable advice steering me through rewrite to production, and to Clive Priddle, Dan LoPreto, Melissa Raymond, Alessandra Bastagli, and the team at Nation Books, with extra gratitude for the careful eye and hard work of Sandra Beris and Karl Yambert.

To great friends who received my doubts, rough drafts, ongoing panics, and unhinged monologues, and who variously returned counsel, insight, inspiration, wit, liquor, love, or dreams: Nancy Youssef, Kelly Johnson, Anna Mulrine, Laura Engelbrecht, Mary Kostovny, Christina Davidson, Sabaa Tahir, Catherine Wiesner, Vanessa Gezari, and Sir "Ian Fortescue Smythe."

Special thanks to Doug Ollivant, whose friendship never wavered, and whose wise and serene support on matters great and microscopic, at any time of day and night, and from any patch of the planet, accompanied this book from its incipient idea to the end, proving to me that he is indeed a commander to have followed into the jaws of Hell. Benedict Rogers has proven the most generous of colleagues, and a wonderful companion for tag-teaming in interviews or traveling with in a vehicle when it explodes into flame. Chris Bartlett and I were teamed on a story for VQR, and along with a great photographer, I found a creative partner for many a project to come. And to Dexter Filkins, for setting my imagination on fire and for a very long and beautiful conversation that left its traces all over this manuscript.

To my extraordinary parents, Leonard and Patrizia, who struggled with my choices and loved me anyway—and who in the end became the greatest of supporters and the best of friends. I owe them everything.

Thanks, above all, to the glorious Mark Chimiak, and the rare and true genius of Teresa Chimiak: most triantic of thinkers, wisest and most compassionate of friends, and force of nature. Hours and hours Teresa dedicated to my manuscript, helping me crack problems about the placing of this paragraph, the choice of that word, the sensitivity to know—and at the speed of light—just when to take a pair of scissors or where instead to expand. This book is better for it. And we should all be so lucky to discover such a friend.

A NOTE ON BURMESE NAMES

In Burmese society, it is exceptional to use someone's name without an accompanying prefix, relative to rank and age. Aside from professional titles such as doctor, teacher, or captain, standard prefixes for men are *U*, for elders, derived from "uncle"; *Ko*, from "brother"; or *Maung*, for boys. Comparable terms of address for women are *Daw*, from the word for "aunt," and *Ma*, for younger women, from "sister." There are no family names in Burma.

NOTES ON SOURCES

This book draws primarily from my own reporting and observations in seven trips to Burma between May 2008 and May 2013, each weeks or months long, and from ongoing conversations with activists, exiles, scholars, and others in Mae Sot, Chiang Mai, and Bangkok, Thailand, in Washington, DC, and elsewhere. From my second trip onwards, I switched on a pocket digital recorder nearly everywhere I went. The result is many hundreds of hours of recorded conversations or of life unfolding, and those recordings, together with accompanying notes, and my observations from visits to almost every place I have described in detail, have provided my chief source material. Had I legally been able to take up residence in the country, I would have done so, but staggering my trips—in part precipitated by the Burmese Embassy's unwillingness, between June 2010 and May 2011, to issue me a new visa—gave me a different advantage, which was to gauge changes in people's lives and broader developments across the arc of time.

I supplemented and checked what I observed or heard with relevant reports, news clippings, diplomatic cables, books, or the insights shared by others. Though the nature of acquiring information in Burma has presented extreme challenges for scholars in previous decades, there is nonetheless an excellent and extensive literature on the country. A select bibliography of books and major articles is offered below, and elaborations or suggestions for further reading are inserted into the reference notes.

For a country or specific issues in which official data were often wholly unreliable, if they existed at all, I have relied on the extensive documentation and fact-finding authority of the Assistance Association for Political Prisoners (Burma) (AAPPB); Human Rights Watch; ALTSEAN-Burma, the Alternative Association of Southeast Asian Nations; the United Nations; the Network for Democracy and Development; EarthRights International; the OpenNet Initiative; the International Crisis Group; and the East-West Center in Washington, DC. For historical reconstructions, or for scenes in which other reporters or researchers were on the scene when I was not, or for more holistic overviews, I have likewise checked my versions against the Associated

Press, Reuters, Agence France-Presse, and other credible news sources, and sometimes quoted them for added detail. Burmese exile news sites, such as the *Irrawaddy*, *Mizzima*, the website of the Democratic Voice of Burma, and the news section on Burmanet.org, the website kept by the Open Society's Burma division, were also of particular help.

I am likewise indebted to individuals who gave me access to material for background that is not publicly available and not intended for circulation. I have notes on them, or copies of the originals on file, and at a future point where these documents no longer have the potential to harm organizations' activities or individual human beings, I will willingly list or release them.

Where I was able to access official documents, I have made use of them, such as a transcript of a closed trial in the Insein Prison court, which lent invaluable detail to accounts from Win Tin and other inmates about the Insein "Joint Action Committee" as related in Chapter 4. In other instances, such as to reveal the state's motives for the manhunt for Nway, or the government version of Nigel's arrest and detention as related in Chapter 2, police reports were unavailable to me. For every story of organizational rigor and sinister exactitude, I heard another of remarkable gaps in intelligence, such as the fact that Nigel's interrogators never suggested to him any knowledge of his parents' prior arrests. Likewise, names commonly overlap in Burma, such that a young man who had the misfortune to be called "Ko Ko Aung" found himself swept up and locked up in a cell with fifteen more "Ko Ko Aungs." More broadly, during the time period in which I conducted my research, there was no procedure comparable to US Freedom of Information Act requests, and no means to seek official documentation without in some way casting suspicion on the people who would have asked on my behalf or disclosing my purposes to Burmese officialdom with potential due consequences to my sources. Where this book is lacking, as such, it reflects inevitable limitations of researching dissent under an authoritarian system.

Where I present people's thoughts, this is most often from asking them or hearing it directly, at the time or in later interviews and conversations. Paw Paw's thoughts, for instance, as she shuts the door and swallows back tears as described at the beginning of Chapter 7, were conveyed to me then and there, because I was sitting right beside her and simply asked. Often I borrow words and phrasing directly, without quotes. For instance, Minus's sentiment that heaven was on its way, and in a matter of days (Epilogue); U Khin Maung Swe's feeling that they had all been dreaming for so long (Chapter 6); Nigel's thoughts on being a dead man as he was being questioned (Chapter 2); U Han Thar Myint on the nature of power (Chapter 6); or Nway on how the democracy movement is like a car (Chapter 5)—these were their exact words. I simply removed the quotation marks and wrote in the third person.

My intention in this book was always to dig into motivations and, though I profess no psychological training, repeat interviews about particular incidents and deepening acquaintance both with individuals and the culture and context in which they operated allowed me greater insight into the deeper reasons behind their choices and actions.

The people I depict here are real, and their lives are still playing out. This is nonfiction. But there is inevitably an aspect of portraiture in the selection and emphasis of details that another might have chosen and written very differently. Not everyone, for instance, will have drawn a connection between Nigel's sense of dying at the moment of his arrest in Chapter 2 and his attempts to quell his emotions to the deeper cultural lessons of meditation. Nor might another writer have employed the framing device of Nway's motorcycle escape in Chapter 5 to connect his personal perspective on revolutionary strategy to the broader history of the movement. This may in certain instances lend me open to charges of over-interpretation. But one of my chief endeavors was to understand ideas as they saw them, such as freedom and democracy or the sense of *anade*, working to understand their behavior and actions through the less visible prism of history and culture. I felt part of my job was dig into ideas that I might take at face value, or with my inherent ethnocentric biases, and so potentially discover subtle differences.

I studied Burmese in Chiang Mai, Thailand, with the great Professor John Okell, but not nearly long enough to be able to conduct conversations that untangled interlocutors' more sophisticated thoughts. I found it was often better to forgo a more polished translator and so talk directly to my interlocutors, even if they spoke English badly, in part because of the shyness of people who weren't always happy to speak honestly in the presence of another Burmese they trusted less.

The narrative is a combination of reconstructions and contemporary scenes or events that I witnessed in whole or in part, including most of Chapters 6, 7, 8, and the Epilogue. For reconstructions of scenes or events that I didn't see, or couldn't reconstruct based on immediate re-reporting, such as Nigel's arrest and detention, Win Tin's experiences in Insein Prison, or the Burma leg of Nway and Nigel's journey to Mae Sot in Chapter 3 (although I retraced their footsteps in Mae Sot and as far as I could in Myawaddy in 2010), I also relied on repeat interviews, working to reconcile facts that might have slightly altered in different tellings.

My reporting was greatly aided by the relative opening of the country since 2012. This meant I could walk in and out of the NLD headquarters, talk to dozens of newly freed activists and—crucially—cross-verify nearly every incident by checking them against other people's accounts in a spirit of much greater openness. I could also meet more freely with the relatives and friends of the main protagonists in their homes in the slums of North Okkla, Hlaing Thayar, Twantay, and elsewhere. Until that point, a foreigner snooping around in their vicinity would have invited upon them the worst kind of attention from block police or informers, although I did and could visit as a passing tourist.

To the best of my ability, I also retraced routes and visited all the places that I describe in detail, with the exception of the Aung Tha Pyay detention center—impossible for a foreigner at the time of my reporting. Two former prison inmates succeeded, however, in smuggling me into the Insein Prison compound in April 2013, disguised in traditional Burmese dress. For an afternoon I was able to tour around and talk to a prison guard in the privacy of his hut. Alas, we were discovered in the final lineup into the red gate and the inner circle when a prison warden took one look at my face—which is too white—and decided I was a foreigner. We were quietly asked to leave. (It could have been worse. Friends the night before—"Nway" among them—joked that if they never heard from me again, they'd be sure to bring me food and care packages through the prison gate.)

ADDITIONAL NOTES AND
REFERENCES

PREFACE

xv **On August 8, 1988, at least two million people poured into the streets:** The definitive, primary-sourced account of 1988 remains the very first: Bertil Lintner's *Outrage: Burma's Struggle for Democracy* (Hong Kong: Review Publishing, 1989).

xvi **"Some people have been saying . . . that I know nothing of Burmese politics":** from "Speech to a Mass Rally at Shwedagon Pagoda," in Aung San Suu Kyi, *Freedom from Fear and Other Writings* (London: Penguin Books, 1991), pp. 192–198.

xvii **In 1997, in a bid to join ASEAN:** Bertil Lintner, then a correspondent for the *Far Eastern Economic Review*, was among the first to expose the SLORC's payments to Jackson Bain and Jefferson Waterman International, two Washington-based public relations firms hired to clean up its image. See also R. Jeffrey Smith, "Burma's Image Problem is a Money Maker," *Washington Post*, February 24, 1998.

xx **On the night of the storm, 660 people of a former population of 943 had disappeared:** These numbers, and my associated reporting, first appeared as: "'To Be Busy Helps Them Forget'; Burma's Storm Survivors Cobble Together a Meager Future," *Washington Post*, July 5, 2008.

CHAPTER 1: NWAY

Details of the story that forms the backbone of Chapters 1 and 5 appeared first in an article I wrote in the *Washington Post* on August 9, 2009, "In Burma, Carefully Sowing the Seeds of Resistance: Fragile Opposition Wary of Confrontation." Nway's escape is partly reconstructed, partly based on my presence at the scene at its tail end. I retraced Nway's footsteps to Twantay in 2010, and again, with him, in April 2013. I met with Nway just before the incidents of this chapter, immediately after, wrangled other details in repeat interviews, and separately interviewed his brothers, mother, the "poet" and "tycoon" of Chapter 5, and two of the individuals who joined in the beer den in Dala. Interviews and encounters with dozens of other individuals who know Nway also indirectly informed many of the details of these and other chapters.

As elsewhere in the narrative, my reporting and ability to cross-verify Nway's account was greatly aided by the relative opening of the country since 2012. Alas, it remained impossible to find or talk with the beer den manager, or any of the agents who were tracking Nway. The descriptions of Dala, Twantay, the road between, the journey from Office to jetty, and from jetty to Dala, the ferry and skiff crossing, and the view of Rangoon from Dala are all from my personal observations.

The dialogue is reconstructed verbatim from Nway's recollections, including the sometime awkwardness of the English, which reflects the fact that he was translating from Burmese.

> 13 **Observers read into the soupçon of novelty an intentional olive branch intended for the NLD:** See, for instance, "Myanmar Rulers Wave Olive Branch on Army Day," *Reuters*, March 27, 1998. Six years later, the deal which Aung San Sun Kyi almost struck involved NLD participation in the constitution-drafting convention, and her release from house arrest, together with Tin Oo.

CHAPTER 2. NIGEL

The reconstruction of Nigel's detention and arrest, including the dialogue and the descriptions of Aung Tha Pyay detention center, are based on Nigel's account in multiple interviews and conversations between 2010 and 2013, supplemented with interviews with his wife, parents, brothers, and sisters, several of Nigel's students from the time, Kyaw Kyaw's brother, and the circle of other activists around Nigel and Nway.

The date of his arrest checked out in three very limited public references I found: the first on the US State Department's 2009 Human Rights Report for Burma, available at http://www.state.gov/j/drl/rls/hrrpt/2009/eap/135987. html, although my account has Nigel released three months earlier. A second reference refers to a "friend" arrested from an Internet café along with the DVB reporter who appears in the chapter as Nigel and Nway's friend, "Kyaw Kyaw."

See: www.freeburmavj.org/DVB-journalists-in-jail/ngwe-soe-lin. A third is in
the AAPPB's "Monthly Trend Analysis" for the month of August 2009.

My descriptions of Aung Tha Pyay rely on Nigel's and his wife's separate
observations, and Google Map imagery. Despite its location in the heart of Rangoon, references to Aung Tha Pyay detention center remain opaque. In interviews with former inmates in Burma's prisons, I found that very few could offer
me a firsthand description. Where I refer to it as Special Branch headquarters,
this is derived from an AAPPB report that listed all the centers and prisons along
with their chief wardens.

32 **What happened next was formulaic, a variation on a theme of four days:**
    For more detail on the contortions that detainees were forced to adopt,
    see, amongst other reports, "The Darkness We See: Torture in Burma's
    Interrogation Centers and Prisons," Assistance Association for Politi-
    cal Prisoners (Burma), December 2005, available at http://aappb.org
    /category/books/.

33 **There were so many ways:** Internet surveillance, as described, derives
    from news articles, people's observations, conversations with Internet
    café managers, and Burmese computer engineers. The OpenNet Ini-
    tiative's 2011–2012 report on Burma provides a good overview of a
    shifting situation, accessible at: http://access.opennet.net/wp-content
    /uploads/2011/12/accesscontested-burma.pdf.

    Dozens of articles on the incremental changes to Internet policing
    include: "Slow Internet Speed Cripples Rangoon Businesses," *Mizzima*,
    February 18, 2010; "Internet Policing in Burma Stepped Up," *Mizzima
    News*, January 10, 2007; and Clive Parker, "Bagan Cybertech An-
    nounces Further Internet Restrictions," *Irrawaddy*, June 7, 2005.

    Also instructive was my visit to Yadarnabon "Cyber-City" in May
    2009, then still under construction in the hills near Pyin Oo Lwin, and
    an interview in Mandalay with one of its early private-sector propo-
    nents before it became a wholly government-run initiative.

37 **In previous months alone, three of Khine Sandar Win's friends had died:**
    Khine Sandar Win's account aligns with separate reports of deaths in
    custody at the race horse stadium. See, for instance, "Bullets in the
    Alms Bowl," *Human Rights Documentation Unit*, National Coalition
    Government of the Union of Burma; March 2008, at pp. 134–135.

52 **It was the last Nigel heard of him:** "Kyaw Kyaw," aka "Ngwe Soe Lin,"
    had been a DVB journalist since 2008. At the time of his arrest, he had
    been working on video footage that contributed to a "Channel 4" docu-
    mentary called "Orphans of Burma's Cyclone." Taken to Insein Prison
    after a few weeks in Aung Tha Pyay detention center, he was tried on
    January 27, 2010, in a special military court and sentenced to thirteen years
    on charges related to the Electronics and Immigration Acts. On February
    18 he was sent to Lashio prison. His work on the documentary earned
    him the 2009 Rory Peck Award, awarded while he was in detention. See:
    www.freeburmavj.org/DVB-journalists-in-jail/ngwe-soe-lin.

55 **With their lives, they wanted and sought that definition of freedom:** Isa-
    iah Berlin, the Russo-British philosopher and historian of ideas, fa-
    mously made a distinction between "positive" and "negative liberty"
    in his 1958 essay, "Two Concepts of Liberty." For the notion of a more
    expansive meaning of freedom, and the role of "mental freedom" in
    the Burmese democracy movement, an anthropological account can
    be found in Gustaaf Houtman's definitive text on the subject, *Mental
    Culture in Burmese Crisis Politics: Aung San Suu Kyi and the National
    League for Democracy*, (Tokyo: Tokyo University of Foreign Studies,
    Institute for the Study of Languages and Cultures of Asia and Africa,
    Monograph Series No. 33, 1999).

60 **Never hiding, never denying his own name:** The laws used to suppress
    dissent were many, deliberately vague, and designed to be whimsical,
    for application at a judge's discretion. In interviews with three work-
    ing Burmese judges I learned that political or politically sensitive cases,
    though never officially recognized as such, came with orders from on-
    high to convict. The most a judge could do was fiddle with the length of
    sentencing within the prescribed minimum and maximum for each law.
    From the patterns with which prison sentences have applied to activists
    in the past, this bullet-point listing is my best interpretation of the likely
    consequences from the contents of Nigel's bag.

CHAPTER 3. CITY OF EXILES

This chapter reconstructs Nway and Nigel's clandestine journey to Mae Sot
from their recollections combined with my reporting on the economy among
migrants and exiles in Mae Sot and Myawaddy in May–June 2010.

The research on the borderland economy is extensive, as indeed is the literature on the conflicts with the border peoples. See, for example, Martin Smith, *Burma: Insurgency and the Politics of Ethnicity* (London: Zed Books, 1999) or Ashley South, "Burma's Longest War, Anatomy of the Karen Conflict," *Transnational Institute Burma Center Netherlands* (Amsterdam: March 2011). For more on the economy, see Sean Turnell, *Fiery Dragons: Banks, Moneylenders and Microfinance in Burma* (Copenhagen: Nordic Institute of Asian Studies Press, 2009).

65 **"dotted with palms and every now and then"**: Aung San Suu Kyi, *Letters from Burma* (London: Penguin Books, first issue 1997, reissued 2010), p. 3.

65 **"the tender green of the graceful paddy plants"**: Ibid., p. 4.

65 **"a straggled out place with a slightly battered air"**: Ibid., p. 7.

66 **"As we approached Thamanya"**: Ibid., p. 8.

67 **Complete with controlled itineraries:** The International Confederation of Free Trade Unions estimated that one million inhabitants were expelled from their homes to make way for developments such as the Myanmar Golf Club. See, for instance, Peggy Teo, T. C. Chang, and K. C. Ho, *Interconnected Worlds, Tourism in Southeast Asia* (Oxford, Elsevier Science Ltd., 2001), pp. 22–23.

93 **The great theorists of strategic nonviolent action:** Phone interviews with Gene Sharp and Bob Helvey in February 2010. I am grateful to Professor Sharp for an unpublished survey of the SLORC's condemnations from February to July 1995. In her *Letters from Burma*, Aung San Suu Kyi had some funny words to say about the ways in which the writings of Gene Sharp, sounding in Burmese much like "jeans shirts," had been "exercising the authorities in Burma considerably," but that actually "political defiance is no more synonymous with Gene Sharp than with denim shirts. It can be defined simply as the natural response of anybody who disagrees with the opinions of the government in power." *Letters from Burma*, pp.163–164.

CHAPTER 4. GRANDPA

The profile of Win Tin is based on four interviews with him that I conducted between 2009 and 2012, multiple articles, and accounts of him that I heard from others. I also drew extensively from his autobiography as it appeared in Win Tin and Malibeaux, Sophie, *Une Vie de Dissident* (Neuilly-sur-Seine: Michel Lafon, 2009).

For descriptions of life inside prison, I relied on the reports and monthly chronologies of the AAPPB, personal accounts that appeared in blogs and on Burmese news sites, and, mainly, my detailed interviews between 2008 and 2013 45 former prisoners and detainees, many of whom had spent months or years in Insein Prison. Some of those interviews followed up on reporting that I originally published as "Burma's Prisons a Caldron of Protest Fury," in the *Washington Post*, August 2, 2008. This included access to prisoners' thoughts, such as the prison "diaries" kept by one inmate on thirteen plastic bags, which he smuggled out of Myitkina prison on July 6, 2005. For reconstructions of the activities of the "Joint Action Committee," I made good use of "Pleading Not Guilty in Insein," a report of the summary trial of twenty-two political prisoners, translated by Naing Luu Aung and published under the auspices of the All Burma Students' Democratic Front. I separately interviewed five of those key prisoners subsequent to their release, including Win Tin, and heard accounts from others who participated in the JAC's activities, if only by signing a plastic-bag petition or in other fragmentary ways.

Win Tin is a treasured national figure, and what I have written here will and should be measured against the trail of words that he left behind. I wish very much that I might have checked my facts with him before publication, but he passed away, to great general sorrow, on April 21, 2014. Still, I felt it was fair tribute to describe him from within his mind and, as truthfully and faithfully as possible, attempt to reveal not just a series of biographical moments, but his essence and his drive.

> **95** **"Today is March 12, 2010. Today I reached the age of 80":** I owe this fragment, and other translations from Win Tin's memoirs, *What's That? A Human Hell*, (Mae Sot: Assistance Association of Political Prisoners, Burma, March 2010), to Daw Kyi May Kaung.
>
> **96** **he had never exactly shikoed in abasement:** See George Orwell, *Burmese Days* (Orlando: Harcourt, 1934), p. 8, for usage that Orwell possibly adapted from the Burmese word *sikho*, for the traditional posture of bending in respect, or kneeling to the ground and pressing hands and head to the floor.

100 **Truth was truth to the end of reckoning:** Shakespeare, *Measure for Measure*, Act 5, Scene 1, as "truth is truth . . ."

107 **There had been a time when editions went to press:** For a pioneering description of censorship, with the effects on short stories that managed nonetheless to convey political messages, see Anna J. Allott, *Inked Over, Ripped Out; Burmese Storytellers and the Censors* (Chiang Mai: Silk Worm Books, 1994). For its evolution since, interviews with Burmese journalists and writers in Rangoon and U Tint Swe, then head of the Press Scrutiny Board, on March 21, 2012, were instructive.

108 **The NLD party spokesman, U Nyan Win, had been duly summoned:** The details of this derive from a diplomatic cable from the US Embassy Rangoon on January 17, 2008 (made public through Wikileaks, along with 1,863 other US Embassy Rangoon cables sent between 1992 and 2010).

109 **And Mandalay!:** Descriptions of the city are supplemented by my repeat visits to Mandalay, including interviews conducted in the Ludu publishing house in May 2009 and April 2010.

110 **"Why am I speaking with so many people?":** This and following quotes are from "Doing What Needs to Be Done," *Irrawaddy*, September 26, 2008.

111 **Again and again, he stressed "unity" and "dynamism":** Assorted interviews in *Mizzima*, *Irrawaddy*, and DVB.

111 **the biggest prisoner amnesties tended to coincide with visits from foreign dignitaries:** Win Tin's September 23, 2008, amnesty defied this trend. It happened as world leaders were gathering for the annual UN General Assembly in New York, and the US ambassador to the UN had already made clear that the United States had plans to call for increased global pressure on Burma. The regime's state mouthpiece, *The New Light of Myanmar*, instead said it had released the 9,002 prisoners that day "to enable them to serve the interest of the regions and their own and the fair election to be held in 2010 together with the people after realizing the government's loving kindness and goodwill."

118 **a still unaccounted-for sum derived from opium, heroin, and methamphetamine:** Although there is little direct evidence of top-level junta members involved in drug-related activities, a number of reports have found a link between Burmese military officials at various levels and earnings from the narcotics trade. See, for instance, Liana Sun Wyler,

"Burma and Transnational Crime," *Congressional Research Service*, (Washington: August 21, 2008), Bertil Lintner and Michael Black, *Merchants of Madness; The Methamphetamine Explosion in the Golden Triangle* (Chiang Mai: Silk Worm Books, 2009), and "Bouncing Back; Relapse in the Golden Triangle," *Transnational Institute* (Amsterdam, June 2014).

CHAPTER 5. CITY OF WRAITHS

125 **Yellowing, Nway's father had gone mad:** Consequences of advanced liver disease include confusion and other neuropsychiatric problems, or hepatic encephalopathy, the deterioration of brain function because of the buildup of toxic substances. See, for instance, Robert S. Porter (ed.), *The Merck Manual of Diagnosis and Therapy* (Whitehouse Station, NJ: Merck Sharp and Dohme, nineteenth edition, 2011), p. 219.

My reconstruction of Nway's father's thoughts during torture and his descent into madness are based on piecemeal information and insights derived from interviews with his contemporaries in Insein Prison, interviews with acquaintances and family in Twantay, and details I combined from his legacy of ideas to his family and friends. This includes his appreciation for Rudyard Kipling and strands of world philosophy, which surfaced in conversations with Nway, who otherwise avoided the subject directly. That Nway found it particularly difficult to talk about his father was my first indication that something about his demise was ugly. Nway, indeed, asked me not to ask his mother for details. But inevitably the details surfaced whether I inquired or not, the more time I spent in the company of friends and family, probing about Nway's childhood and personal history.

125 *The mind as its own place that in itself can make a Heav'n of Hell, a Hell of Heav'n*: "Where joy forever dwells: hail horrors, hail / Infernal world, and thou profoundest Hell / Receive thy new possessor: one who brings / A mind not to be changed by place or time. / The mind is its own place and in itself can make a Heav'n of Hell, a Hell of Heav'n."—John Milton, *Paradise Lost*, Book 1, lines 250–255.

126 *twisted by knaves and made a trap for fools . . . unforgiving minute:* Rudyard Kipling, "If."

126 **But a man of influence, of *awza*, could not and would not hide in that way:** For rich discussions on *awza*, see Houtman, *Mental Culture in Burmese Crisis Politics*, and David I. Steinberg, *Burma: The State in Myanmar* (Washington, DC: Georgetown University Press, 2001).

128 **the most secure lock-up of their empire:** Cited in Emma Larkin, *Finding Orwell in Burma* (London: Penguin Press, 2004).

128 **To scrawny little visitors who squatted all day in that gate's shadow:** I was able to align Nway's recollections about his childhood visits to Insein with my own observations from inside the prison compound.

132 **To the left, in a passing black blur:** This historical reconstruction is based primarily on a retelling by "Arthur," one of its protagonists, supplemented by daily news archives from wire services and newspapers.

142 **They knew just where on a street corner to position themselves:** The monks were the most visible protestors in September, and their demands not at first deemed overtly political, but the protests had begun in August and continued afterward in civilian, and overtly political, society. In the end, between August and October, reports tallied 227 distinct protests from both monks and civilians, with various demands against military rule in sixty-six towns and cities in each of the country's seven states and divisions. See, for instance, "Bullets in the Alms Bowl," National Coalition Government for the Union of Burma.

157 **Case after case, year after year:** "The Power of the Powerless," in Vaclav Havel, *Open Letters: Selected Writings 1965–1990* (New York: Vintage, 1992), paraphrasing and quotes from pages 146, 147, and 150.

CHAPTER 6. THE STAKEHOLDERS

I accompanied Nway and Nigel in the scene that opens the chapter, and spent time with them throughout March–April 2010. I was made privy to the contents of the damaging email and talked with its author, but for his or her sake, I thought it more ethical to keep his or her identifying details out of the book.

The profiles of Dr. Zaw Myint Maung and Khin Maung Swe are grounded in the details of the interviews with them on the days I describe, in Amarapura and Rangoon, respectively, and in follow-up interviews since, combined with case information about their respective arrests and release from outside watchdogs and accounts about their lives from other acquaintances and prison inmates with whom they shared cells. For Khin Maung Swe, I also relied on his private thoughts as related to diplomats in US Embassy cables and his public expressions in news articles. I met with Nway and Nobleyan immediately after they were chased from Win Tin's home (and was the recipient of Nway's text messages as he ran away) and retraced their steps and reported the details in that and in subsequent interviews.

Interviews with U Han Thar Myint, Win Tin, Nyan Win, and others at the scene underpinned the final section, for whose details I also relied on accounts from news articles.

173 **Normally it belonged to the Lady of the Emerald Palace:** See Donald M. Stadtner, *Sacred Sites of Burma: Myth and Folklore in an Evolving Spiritual Realm* (Bangkok: River Books, 2011), pp. 119–121. Contemporary rumors about the shackling appeared, among other places, on the *Irrawaddy* news site.

CHAPTER 7. CITY OF KINGS

The scenes described in this chapter and individuals' stories derive in the majority from my presence to witness them. I had also spent time with Nway in the 2010 flashback scenes in which he was homeless, roaming between the street and Arthur's apartment. I rely on Nway and Nigel's accounts of what passed with Auntie when she offered them their scholarship. I was not at the scene of intelligence officers threatening Nigel's family school with closure, but I visited North Okklappa and re-reported the events shortly afterward.

225 **Official results emerged two weeks later:** For an excellent analysis of the vote results, see Richard Horsey, "Outcome of the Myanmar Elections;" *Conflict Prevention and Peace Forum*, Social Science Research Council, Brooklyn, November 17, 2010.

227 **"We climbed a slippery pole, knowing it's slippery":** My account of what might have led to Nay Win Maung's alleged heartbreak is based on four interviews with him conducted between June 2008 and September 2011, other open-source reporting, and reporting among the students and teachers of his organization, Egress. I borrowed this quote in translation from David Scott Mathieson, "Burma's Elections: Towards Realistic Hope," OpenDemocracy.net, November 10, 2010.

240 **Even Auntie had faced as poisonous a test:** There are excellent biographies of Aung San Suu Kyi. For the details of this, I am grateful to Justin Wintle, *Perfect Hostage: Aung San Suu Kyi. Burma and the Generals* (London: Arrow Books, 2007).

CHAPTER 8. THE ROAD TO NAYPYIDAW

The contents of this chapter first appeared in modified form as Delphine Schrank, "Dissident Thunder; How an Insurgent Movement of Pro-Democracy Activists—from Underground, in Exile or in Prison—Returned to Take Burma's Military Junta by Political Storm," *Virginia Quarterly Review*, Summer 2012.

All the scenes I described derive from my firsthand reporting, with the exception of the early scenes of euphoria in Rangoon on April 1, 2012, which I was late to see because I was still making my way south by bus from Naypyidaw. For additional detail, I was grateful to the photos and accounts from multiple witnesses, including Chris Bartlett and his portfolio of portraits. The final scene depended mainly on accounts from Nway and other NLD Uncles, confirmed by news clippings.

EPILOGUE

Scenes in the Epilogue derive from my firsthand observations and reporting in Rangoon, Myitkina, Kachin state, Meiktila, Mandalay, and Oakkan in March to May, 2013. I interviewed Ashin Wirathu in Masoyein Monastery on April 8, 2013, and toured Meiktila two weeks after the violence of March 20–22 with help from a local NLD representative who also negotiated a way into a no-go Muslim IDP camp, a de facto refuge on the outskirts in Meiktila. The camp authorities quietly kicked us out, without further fanfare, but we had about twenty minutes to talk with individuals and snap photos.

The list of abuses against Kachin detainees derive from separate interviews with a recently released detainee and the wives of three current Kachin political prisoners on April 5, 2013, in an IDP camp on the outskirts of Myitkina. I also conducted interviews with dozens of IDPs in two camps in Wai Maw, on the outskirts of the Kachin capital, Myitkina, respectively run by the Roman Catholic Church and the Kachin Baptist Convention, on April 5, 2013. Those accounts corresponded without inconsistency to the abuses compiled in the case reports of a Kachin human rights lawyer, whom I met with on April 6 and who conveyed details of local detainees' case reports.

For my reporting among IDPs in Kachin state, I was fortunate to join Benedict Rogers, East Asia Team Leader at the Christian Solidarity Network, and my notes can be checked against his more detailed report, and the full testimony of several IDPs, as a "Burma fact-finding briefing" for Christian Solidarity Network in April 2013.

For an overview of the higher-altitude vicissitudes of the Kachin conflict at the time, see "A Tentative Peace in Myanmar's Kachin Conflict," *International Crisis Group*, Asia Briefing No. 140, Yangon/Jakarta/Brussels, June 12, 2013.

The scene of activists slouching in local district court I witnessed on April 24, 2013. It was a rare indication of times changing—that a foreigner could unobtrusively stand outside the room and listen in.

My trip to Oakkan township took place on May 1, the morning after anti-Muslim clashes.

The satellite imagery and analysis of the destruction in Meiktila derives from analysis at Human Rights Watch, and is available at http://www.hrw.org/sites/default/files/related_material/HRW_Meiktila_Damages_Presser_2013.03_1.pdf.

> **279 narrow the circle of permissible lies:** Or more accurately, to "narrow the range of permissible lies." This phrase belongs to Michael Ignatieff, quoted in Priscilla B. Hayner, *Unspeakable Truths; Facing the Challenge of Truth Commissions* (New York: Routledge, 2002), p. 25.

GLOSSARY

anade. A feeling peculiar to Burmese culture of guilt and shame in anticipation of causing discomfort.

awẓa. Personal influence such as clout, stature, or reputation, contrasted sometimes with *ana*, or authority.

bogyoke. General (military rank); usually a term of deference; often carries beyond military designation. (See the Note on Burmese Names, p. 289.)

dukkha. From Pali and Sanskrit; concept central to Buddhist tradition, commonly translated as "suffering" or "dissatisfaction"; one of the three marks of existence, alongside *anica*, impermanence; and *anatta*, non-self.

hti. The ornament that tops pagodas in Burma; a figurative term meaning "the best."

kalar. Pejorative term often used to refer to foreigners; most often for darker-skinned persons of South Asian origin, especially Muslims. The term is rooted in historic distrust of South Asians, and its mercantile *chettiar* classes, who were often under the employ of the British colonial administration in Burma as landowners and creditors.

kyat. Burmese currency; longtime major disparities existed between the official rate, fixed at one US dollar to 6 *kyat*, versus the fluctuating, and more accurate, street rate of one US dollar to anywhere between 750 and 1,335 *kyat*. On April 2, 2012, the government central bank floated the *kyat* with an initial rate of one US dollar equaling 818 *kyat*.

longyi. Burmese cloth wrap: *paso* for a man; *htamein*, for a woman.

metta. The Buddhist notion of loving-kindness toward all sentient beings.

nat. A spirit distinctive to Burma, worshipped in conjunction with Buddhism or other local religions. The 37 *nats* of the official pantheon were real human beings who met violent deaths. Devotees also build shrines to the many lesser *nats* that inhabit the trees or rivers or other elements of nature.

pinni. A Burmese jacket of salmon or ochre-colored cloth, usually worn with a white collarless shirt by democracy activists, in tribute to the anticolonial nationalists who encouraged the wearing of homespun cloths as part of a boycott campaign against British goods.

pwe. All-night, outdoor performances, traditionally held by mobile acting troupes, and often including puppet shows, dancing, and comedy routines.

sangha. Monkhood.

saya. Teacher (male), or saya-ma, for female.

Tatmadaw. The Burmese Armed Forces.

thanaka. Yellow sandalwood paste smeared on faces as sunblock and cosmetic.

SELECTED BIBLIOGRAPHY

Alagappa, Muthiah, ed., *Civil Society and Political Change in Asia: Expanding and Contracting Democratic Space* (Stanford, CA: Stanford University Press, 2004).

Allott, Anna J., *Inked Over, Ripped Out; Burmese Storytellers and the Censors* (Chiang Mai: Silk Worm Books, 1994).

Aung San Suu Kyi, *Freedom from Fear and Other Writings* (London: Penguin Books, 1991).

———. *Letters from Burma* (London: Penguin Books, first issue 1997, reissued 2010).

———. *The Voice of Hope; Aung San Suu Kyi, Conversations with Alan Clements* (New York: Seven Stories Press, 1997, 2008).

———. "Liberty," Reith Lectures, 2011, BBC Radio, June 28, 2011.

———. "Dissent," Reith Lectures, 2011, BBC Radio, July 5, 2011.

Berlin, Isaiah, "Two Concepts of Liberty," *The Proper Study of Mankind: An Anthology of Essays* (London: Chatto and Windus, 1997), pp. 191–243.

———. "Nationalism: Past Neglect and Present Power," Ibid., pp. 581–605.

Callahan, Mary P., *Making Enemies: War and State Building in Burma* (Ithaca, NY: Cornell University Press, 2003).

———. "Myanmar's Perpetual Junta; Solving the Riddle of the Tatmadaw's Long Reign," *New Left Review 60*, November–December 2009, pp. 27–63.

Charney, Michael W., *A History of Modern Burma* (Cambridge: Cambridge University Press, 2009).

Dale, John G., *Free Burma: Transnational Legal Action and Corporate Accountability* (Minneapolis: University of Minnesota Press, 2011).

———. "Burma's Boomerang: Human Rights, Social Movements and Transnational Legal Mechanisms 'From Below'," *International Journal of Contemporary Sociology*, Vol. 45., No. 1, April 2008, pp. 152–184.

Fink, Christina, *Living Silence in Burma; Surviving Under Military Rule* (London: Zed Books, 2001; revised edition, Chiang Mai: Silk Worm, 2009).

Gunaratana, Henepola, *Mindfulness in Plain English* (Somerville, MA: Wisdom Publications, 2011).

Havel, Vaclav, *Open Letter: Selected Writings 1965–1990* (New York: Vintage, 1992).

Houtman, Gustaaf, *Mental Culture in Burmese Crisis Politics: Aung San Suu Kyi and the National League for Democracy* (Tokyo: Tokyo University of Foreign Studies, Institute for the Study of Languages and Cultures of Asia and Africa, Monograph Series No. 33, 1999).

Jordt, Ingrid, *Burma's Mass Lay Meditation Movement: Buddhism and the Cultural Construction of Power* (Athens: Ohio University Press, 1997).

Kyaw Yin Hlaing, "The State of the Pro-Democracy Movement in Authoritarian Burma," (Washington, DC: East-West Center Washington, Working Papers No. 11, December 1997).

———, "Challenging the Authoritarian State: Buddhist Monks and Peaceful Protests in Burma," *Fletcher Forum of World Affairs*, Vol. 32:1, Winter 2009.

Larkin, Emma, *Finding Orwell in Burma* (London: Penguin Press, 2004).

Lintner, Bertil, *Burma in Revolt; Opium and Insurgency since 1948* (Boulder: Westview Press, 1994).

———. *Outrage: Burma's Struggle for Democracy* (Hong Kong: Review Publishing, 1989).

———. *The Rise and Fall of the Communist Party of Burma* (Ithaca, NY: Cornell Southeast Asia Program Series, 1991).

———. *Aung San Suu Kyi and Burma's Struggle for Democracy* (Gyeonggi-do: Prunsoop Publishing Co., Ltd., 2007).

Ma Thanegi (transl.), *Selected Myanmar Short Stories* (Rangoon: Unity Publishing House, 2009).

Maung Htin Aung, *Burmese Folk-Tales* (Calcutta: Inland Printing Works, re-printed 1954).

O'Donnell, Guillermo, and Philippe C. Schmitter (eds.), *Transitions from Authoritarian Rule: Tentative Conclusions* (Baltimore, MD: Johns Hopkins University Press, 1986).

Pandita Bivamsa, U, *In This Very Life: The Liberation Teachings of the Buddha* (Somerville, MA: Wisdom Publications, 1992).

Pascal Khoo Thwe, *From the Land of Green Ghosts; A Burmese Odyssey* (New York: Harper Perennial, 2002).

Pe Maung Tin and G. H. Luce (transl.), *The Glass Palace Chronicle of the Kings of Myanmar* (Rangoon: Unity Publishing House, ed. 2008).

Popham, Peter, *The Lady and the Peacock: The Life of Aung San Suu Kyi* (London: Rider Books, 2011).

Rieffel, Lex, ed. *Myanmar/Burma; Inside Challenges, Outside Interests* (Washington, DC: Brookings Institute, 2010).

Roberts, Adam, and Timothy Garton Ash, *Civil Resistance and Power Politics; The Experience of Non-Violent Action from Gandhi to the Present* (Oxford: Oxford University Press, 2009 and 2011).

Rogers, Benedict, *Burma: A Nation at the Crossroads* (London: Rider, 2012).

———. *Than Shwe: Unmasking Burma's Tyrant* (Chiang Mai: Silkworm Books, 2010).

Scott, James C., *The Art of Not Being Governed: An Anarchist History of Upland Southeast Asia* (New Haven: Yale University Press, 2009).

Seekins, Donald M., *Historical Dictionary of Burma (Myanmar)* (Lanham: Scarecrow Press, 2006).

Selth, Andrew, *Burma's Armed Forces; Power Without Glory* (Norwalk: EastBridge, 2001).

Sharp, Gene, *Waging Nonviolent Struggle; 20th Century Practice and 21st Century Potential* (Boston, MA: Extending Horizons Books, 2005).

———. *From Dictatorship to Democracy; A Conceptual Framework for Liberation*, (Boston: Albert Einstein Institution, 1st edition, May 2002; 3rd US edition, 2008).

Shway Yoe, *The Burman: His Life and Notions* (New York: Norton, 1963).

Silverstein, Josef (ed.), *The Political Legacy of Aung San*, (Ithaca, NY: Cornell Southeast Asian Program Series No. 11, Revised Edition, 1993).

Skidmore, Monique, *Karaoke Fascism: Burma and the Politics of Fear* (Philadelphia: University of Pennsylvania Press, 2004).

———(ed.), *Burma at the Turn of the 21st Century*, (Honolulu: University of Hawaii Press, 2005).

South, Ashley, *Civil Society in Burma: The Development of Democracy amidst Conflict* (East-West Center, Institute of Southeast Asian Studies, Policy Studies 51).

———. "Burma's Longest War, Anatomy of the Karen Conflict," *Transnational Institute Burma Center Netherlands* (Amsterdam: March 2011).

Spiro, Melford E., *Burmese Supernaturalism: A Study in the Explanation and Reduction of Suffering* (Englewood Cliffs, NJ: Prentice-Hall Inc., 1967).

Stadtner, Donald M., *Sacred Sites of Burma: Myth and Folklore in an Evolving Spiritual Realm* (Bangkok: River Books, 2011).

Steinberg, David I., *Burma: The State in Myanmar* (Washington, DC: Georgetown University Press, 2001).

————. *Burma/Myanmar: What Everyone Needs to Know* (Oxford: Oxford University Press, 2010).

Taylor, Robert H., *The State in Myanmar* (Singapore: NUS Press, 2009).

Thant Myint-U, *The River of Lost Footsteps; A Personal History of Burma* (New York: Farrar, Straus and Giroux, 2006).

Turnell, Sean. *Fiery Dragons: Banks, Moneylenders and Microfinance in Burma* (Copenhagen: Nordic Institute of Asian Studies Press, 2009).

Wakeman, Carol, and San San Tin, *No Time for Dreams; Living in Burma Under Military Rule* (Plymouth, UK: Rowman and Littlefield, 2009).

Win Tin and Sophie Malibeaux, *Une Vie de Dissident* (Neuilly-sur-Seine: Michel Lafon, 2009).

Wintle, Justin, *Perfect Hostage: Aung San Suu Kyi, Burma and the Generals* (London: Arrow Books, 2007).

PHOTO BY CHRIS BARTLETT

DELPHINE SCHRANK is an award-winning reporter, a contributing editor to the *Virginia Quarterly Review*, and a co-founding member of DECA Stories, a pioneering writers' cooperative for deeply reported, global journalism. She was the Burma correspondent for the *Washington Post*, where she was an editor and staff writer.

The Nation Institute
The Nation.

Founded in 2000, **Nation Books** has become a leading voice in American independent publishing. The inspiration for the imprint came from the *Nation* magazine, the oldest independent and continuously published weekly magazine of politics and culture in the United States.

The imprint's mission is to produce authoritative books that break new ground and shed light on current social and political issues. We publish established authors who are leaders in their area of expertise, and endeavor to cultivate a new generation of emerging and talented writers. With each of our books we aim to positively affect cultural and political discourse.

Nation Books is a project of The Nation Institute, a nonprofit media center established to extend the reach of democratic ideals and strengthen the independent press. The Nation Institute is home to a dynamic range of programs: our award-winning Investigative Fund, which supports ground-breaking investigative journalism; the widely read and syndicated website TomDispatch; our internship program in conjunction with the *Nation* magazine; and Journalism Fellowships that fund up to 20 high-profile reporters every year.

For more information on Nation Books, the *Nation* magazine, and The Nation Institute, please visit:

www.nationbooks.org
www.nationinstitute.org
www.thenation.com
www.facebook.com/nationbooks.ny
Twitter: @nationbooks